Mama Mputu

Mama Mputu

The Missionary Reflections of Buena Rose Stober
(1897–1972)

BUENA ROSE STOBER

Edited by
SCOTT D. SEAY

WIPF & STOCK · Eugene, Oregon

MAMA MPUTU
The Missionary Reflections of Buena Rose Stober (1897–1972)

Wipf & Stock
An Imprint of Wipf and Stock Publishers
199 W. 8th Ave., Suite 3
Eugene, OR 97401

www.wipfandstock.com

PAPERBACK ISBN: 978-1-5326-9259-8
HARDCOVER ISBN: 978-1-5326-9260-4
EBOOK ISBN: 978-1-5326-9261-1

VERSION NUMBER 042726

All Scripture quotations, unless otherwise noted, are from the King James Version, which is in the public domain.

The editor would like to thank Disciples of Christ Historical Society (Bethany, West Virginia) and Christian Theological Seminary (Indianapolis, Indiana) for permission to use the photographs in this book as credited.

Contents

Timeline of the Life of Buena Rose Stober

1897 Born in Bluff City, Kansas, to Henry Ceward and Ellen Jane (Badley) Stober (July 27).

1909 Mother died of tuberculosis at the age of 45 (March 18).

1911 Baptized by Rev. D. L. Ammons at First Christian Church (Disciples of Christ), Newkirk, Oklahoma (September).

1917 Entered Phillips University, Enid, Oklahoma (September); became active in the student volunteer movement and University Place Christian Church (Disciples of Christ), committing herself to foreign mission work.

1918–21 Trained as a registered nurse at University Hospital Nurses' Training School in Enid, Oklahoma.

1921 Applied for missionary service with the United Christian Missionary Society of the Christian Churches (Disciples of Christ) (March 9).

1921–23 Completed course work at Butler University and the College of Missions in Indianapolis, Indiana; developed close relationships in the women's missionary societies at Tabernacle Christian Church (Disciples of Christ), Franklin, Indiana.

1923 Ordained at the College of Missions and commissioned for missionary service in the Belgian Congo (June 5); sailed from New York (September 19); arrived in Brussels (late-September) and spent two months preparing for entering the Congo.

1923 Began first term of service in the Belgian Congo (December 2), supported by the United Christian Missionary Society of the Christian Churches (Disciples of Christ). Additional support came from the Women's Christian Missionary Society of Tabernacle Christian Church (Disciples of Christ), Franklin, Indiana.

1924–26 Itinerated between Lotumbe, Monieka, and Bolenge stations; learned some French and Lonkundo, and apprenticed with medical doctors of the Disciples of Christ Congo Mission, especially Dr. J. P. G. Barger.

1926–27 Furloughed in the United States (began December 6).

1927 Completed course work at Phillips University, Enid, Oklahoma; began second term of service (June 18), studying French language with a private tutor in Brussels (July–October) and tropical medicine at École de médecine tropicale (began in October).

1928 Completed the course work in tropical medicine, graduating second in her class (February 11); returned to the Congo, stationed at Lotumbe (early April); awarded the AB degree from Phillips University, Enid, Oklahoma (May 22).

1931 Began serving at Mondombe (September), her home station for the remainder of her service in the Congo.

1933–34 Furloughed in the United States (began June 20). Undertook additional course work in chemistry at Phillips University.

1934 Began third term of service in the Congo, stationed initially at Bolenge (November 2); her father passed away at the age of 76 (November 4).

1935 Following brief visits to Bolenge, Monieka, and Boende (spring), stationed temporarily at Wema to relieve fellow missionary Goldie Alumbaugh while she was on furlough (June).

1936 Resumed work at Mondombe (September).

1937 Transferred to Lotumbe (November) to replace Dr. William Davis and Newell (Trimble) Davis who were on furlough. Because of the Great Depression, there had not been medical staff at Lotumbe for six months.

1938–39 Furloughed in the United States (began July 31); studied dentistry with Dr. Lloyd E. Warder of Enid, Oklahoma.

1939 Began fourth term of service in the Congo (April 17), arriving at Mondombe (June 14). Began three projects that would be the core of her work at Mondombe for the next twenty years: (1) basic dental care; (2) a leper colony at Lomina; and (3) prenatal care, an infant feeding program, and weekly baby wellness clinics.

1942 Assigned to First Christian Church (Disciples of Christ), Charleroi, Pennsylvania, as a Service Link missionary.

1944 Furloughed in South Africa because of travel restrictions during World War II (began in March); undertook further study at the University of Witwatersrand School of Dentistry; began fifth term of service in the Congo, returning to Mondombe (September).

1946 Furloughed in the United States (began May 1).

1947 Visited the American Leprosy Mission in Carville, Louisiana, and secured its support for the Lomina leper colony in the Congo (June). Returned to Mondombe to begin sixth term of service (July 16).

1951 Furloughed in the United States (began July 16).

1952 Returned to Mondombe (July 26) to begin her seventh term of service in the Congo.

1953 Assigned to First Christian Church, Nash, Oklahoma, and Central Christian Church, Magnum, Oklahoma, as a shared Service Link missionary.

1955 Furloughed in the United States (began April 19).

1956 Began her eighth and final term of service in the Congo, returning to Mondombe (April 7).

1960 Evacuated from the Congo amidst the growing political unrest (July 15).

1961 Retired from missionary service with the United Christian Missionary Society (June 30); settled in a mobile home on her brother Jim's property in Harrah, Oklahoma.

1960s Compiled her letters and diary entries into a memoir of her missionary service in the Congo. An active member of the Nicoma Park Christian Church (Disciples of Christ), she continued speaking occasionally about her experiences as a missionary in the Congo.

1971 Robert Nelson, Africa Area Executive for the Division of Overseas Ministries of the Christian Church (Disciples of Christ) reluctantly agreed to produce limited copies of her memoir (November), but they were never made.

1972 Died at the age of 74 (March 25).

Preface

In December 2017, while shifting boxes in the archives and special collections at Christian Theological Seminary (CTS), I quite literally stumbled over a corrugated cardboard box labeled simply, "Stober." Inside was an unexpected treasure—a substantial cache of letters written by Buena Rose Stober (1897–1972), a career missionary with the Disciples of Christ Congo Mission (DCCM). Curious, I turned immediately to Edith Eberle Yocum's indispensable biographical compendium of Disciples missionaries, where I met Stober for the first time.[1] That brief introduction was enough. I was instantly captivated, and over the next ten years—intermittently but persistently—I immersed myself in her life and work as she described them in these letters.

Stober's correspondence did more than illuminate a single missionary career. It deepened and expanded my long-standing interest in the history of the DCCM, in Protestant missions in the Congo, and in the cultural and spiritual worlds of the Congolese people themselves. Through her words, the past took on texture and immediacy, revealing both the ambitions and the ambiguities of missionary life in central Africa.

How Stober's letters came to CTS can only be surmised. Most likely, the box arrived after the 1996 relocation of the international headquarters of the Christian Church (Disciples of Christ), known among Disciples as the "Missions Building." During that move, an extensive body of missionary manuscripts, scrapbooks, photographs, and assorted realia was transferred to the seminary's archives, where much of it sat largely undisturbed for more than two decades. Whatever their precise provenance, Stober's letters now constitute the heart of the Buena Rose Stober Collection within CTS's substantial archive documenting the history of the Christian Church (Disciples of Christ) and its affiliated ministries.

1. Yocum, *They Went to Africa*, 52–53.

I am deeply grateful to CTS for granting me a year-long research leave in 2018–19, during which I worked primarily on this book. Much of that year was devoted to selecting, transcribing, editing, and annotating the letters presented here. Two subsequent research trips to the Disciples of Christ Historical Society (DCHS) in Bethany, West Virginia, further enriched the project, uncovering an even more extensive record of Stober's life and work in the Congo, along with a significant trove of additional correspondence. I owe particular thanks to Shelley Jacobs, then archivist at DCHS, whose generosity allowed me nearly unrestricted access, even to unprocessed materials. I am grateful as well to both CTS and DCHS for permission to publish the photographs included in this volume. Finally, I thank Philippa Rossman, Archives and Special Collections Librarian at Phillips Theological Seminary in Tulsa, Oklahoma, who provided digital access to key archival materials that shed light on Stober's involvement with the Newkirk congregation and her education at Phillips University.

Stober herself clearly believed her letters mattered. In retirement, she selected a portion of her correspondence, which a staff member at the Division of Overseas Ministries of the Christian Church (Disciples of Christ) transcribed and arranged into a manuscript intended for publication. Internal memoranda reveal, however, that Robert Nelson (1917–1988), then president of the division, regarded the project largely as an indulgence. In an era when the Disciples were rethinking the theology and practice of foreign missions, he feared that Stober's letters—if mistaken for a serious missiological study—might have a negative effect. Stober died in November 1972 before even the limited number of copies promised to her were printed. The sole manuscript apparently remained at the division until 1983, when it was transferred to storage at DCHS, where it lay dormant until Shelley Jacobs and I unearthed it nearly fifty years later.[2]

By that point, I had already transcribed most of the letters included in this book. Many overlapped with Stober's own manuscript, though I have also included letters she did not select. Discovering her manuscript—and learning of her earnest desire to see her words in print—only strengthened my resolve to complete this project. In recent years, progress has been interrupted more often than I liked by teaching and administrative responsibilities at CTS. Still, it is with a deep sense of honor that I now present Stober's own account of her life and work, preserved in her letters, in published form at last.

Scott D. Seay
Indianapolis, Indiana

2. DCHS, Manuscript Collection 83-32, Buena Stober.

Introduction

A Life Well Lived

On the afternoon of June 10, 1960, celebration filled the brick and tin-roofed church in Mondombe, a small village in the heart of the Belgian Congo. The pastor, lay leaders, and congregants gathered to honor Buena Rose Stober (1897–1972)—known and beloved as Mama Mputu—who was retiring after nearly thirty-seven years of missionary service with the Disciples of Christ Congo Mission (DCCM). The air pulsed with joy. Dancers of every generation, dressed in bright colors, moved to the beat of *ngoma* drums. Hymns rose with the unmistakable energy of Congolese worship. Though fellow missionaries were present, this was above all a celebration of Congolese Christians for their Mama Mputu.

At the heart of the ceremony, Mondombe's pastor and Stober's long-time colleague, Ntange Timothy, presented her with gifts from the community and a *diplôme du bonne vie*—a "Certificate of a Life Well Lived." Written in Belgian French, the certificate named three defining characteristics of her ministry: as a missionary nurse, she had devoted herself to bringing new life into the world and caring for the sick, especially those suffering from leprosy; as a witness to Christ, she had shaped new converts and nurtured Congolese children in the Christian faith; and as a mentor to women, she had committed herself to their development, teaching and modeling the practices of a productive domestic life. When Stober later returned home, the United Christian Missionary Society of the Christian Churches (Disciples of Christ) also honored her with a certificate and gifts. Yet it is easy to imagine that none meant more to her than those placed in her hands by the people of Mondombe.[1]

1. Both certificates are preserved in DCHS, Manuscript Collection 2001-068, Buena Rose Stober Papers.

Throughout her long service with the DCCM, Stober wrote letters—a lot of letters. Some she typed on thin onion-skin paper suitable for airmail; others she hastily scrawled on whatever scraps of paper were available to her; she composed others carefully in her own hand on heavy, elegant bond stationery. Many functioned as mission newsletters, reporting the daily progress and frequent frustrations of her work. Others were intimate and personal, written to family and friends and sometimes she enclosed pressed insects, flowers, leaves, or other small tokens of life in the Congo. She even wrote letters meant for no one but herself, reflective pieces that read like diary entries. Spanning her entire missionary career from 1923 to 1960, more than five hundred of these letters survive—an average of fourteen or fifteen each year.

This book presents an edited and annotated transcription of 148 of those letters. Read together, they offer a rich, textured portrait of a life devoted to ministry among the Congolese people. At the most basic level, the letters provide invaluable information about the work of DCCM, particularly at remote stations far from the mission headquarters. They also open a window onto the lives of Congolese communities in the backcountry, describing beliefs and practices with attention that is sometimes almost ethnographic. Stober's correspondence chronicles both the promises and the limits of her medical work, recounting moments of success alongside the frustrations of practicing nursing without a physician, adequate supplies, or reliable medications. In short, the letters illuminate the intertwined stories of a missionary nurse, the organizations and partners that supported her, and the Congolese people with whom she lived and worked.

To help readers navigate this collection of letters, this introduction provides essential context for understanding Stober's life and ministry. It begins with a concise history of Belgian colonial rule in the Congo, from European contact in the late 1870s through independence in 1960, a period that encompasses Stober's service. It then recounts the history of DCCM itself, with some attention to the larger context of Christian missions in the Congo from colonialism to independence. It then offers a biographical sketch of Stober, from her birth in a Kansas frontier town and her training as a nurse and missionary, through her thirty-seven years in the Belgian Congo, and finally to her retirement in suburban Oklahoma City. The introduction concludes by suggesting some of the ways in which Stober's correspondence is significant for those interested in the history of modern Christianity, mission studies, and cultural anthropology.

Ultimately, however, the heart of this book is Stober's own words. Readers who spend time with her letters will discover quickly why her reflections on ministry—her testimony to a life well lived—are best heard in her own voice.

Belgian Colonialism in the Congo

When Welsh explorer and newspaper editor Henry Morton Stanley (1841–1904) returned to England in 1878 after a long and perilous journey through the Congo River Basin, he captivated the public imagination with his reports. He spoke of vast, untapped wealth and boundless opportunities for commerce and Christian missions alike. No reader was more enthusiastic than Belgium's King Leopold II (1835–1909), who saw in the Congo the promise of immense personal fortune, national economic expansion, and the institutional growth of the Roman Catholic Church. By late 1879, Stanley was back in central Africa, not as an explorer, but as Leopold's royal agent. In this role, he coerced more than 450 local tribal chiefs to enter unequal treaties that transferred ownership of land and sovereignty over people directly to the Belgian king for very little in exchange. Backed by the *Force publique*—a heavily armed colonial police force composed of Belgian officers and Congolese soldiers—Stanley imposed forced labor on the population under conditions no different from chattel slavery. When he returned to Europe in 1885, the machinery of empire was firmly in place in what Leopold ironically named the Congo Free State. His personal colony spanned nearly 905,000 square miles, a territory that was home to an estimated thirty million people.[2]

Leopold's gamble soon proved enormously profitable. In 1888, Scottish engineer John Boyd Dunlop (1840–1921) invented the pneumatic rubber tire, igniting a global rubber boom as industrial economies expanded in Europe and the US. The Congo River Basin, one of the few regions in the world where rubber grows wild, instantly became the focus of Leopold's economic ambitions. Acting under the king's direct authority, colonial administrators and the *Force publique* spent the next two decades forcing Congolese people to harvest rubber, demanding impossible quotas. Inevitable failure was met with terror: workers were flogged with the *chicote*—a whip of rhinoceros hide—mutilated through the amputation of hands or feet, or summarily executed. When Leopold died in 1909, his personal

2. Nzongola-Ntalaja, *From Leopold to Kabila*, 14–25; Van Reybrouck, *Epic History*, 29–56. By way of comparison, in 1885 Belgium was just under twelve thousand square miles, with a total population estimated to be 5.8 million. Thus, the Congo Free State geographically was seventy-two times the size of Belgium, with a population more than five times larger.

wealth from the Congo Free State was estimated in 2026 dollars to be $2.8 billion. The human cost was even more staggering. Although estimates vary, roughly ten million Congolese—perhaps a third of the population—died from exhaustion, disease, and punishment in what many historians rightly describe as an African Holocaust.[3]

Many world leaders knew about these atrocities but they were slow to act. In 1899, British novelist Joseph Conrad (1857–1924) wrote a series of articles that would become the novella *Heart of Darkness* (1902). His searing account exposed the greed, racism, and brutality of Leopold's colonial regime. Around the same time, Edmund Morel (1873–1924), a shipping clerk in Liverpool, noticed a disturbing pattern in cargo manifests: ships bound for the Congo carried large quantities of ammunition, while those returning to Europe were laden with rubber, ivory, and other valuable resources. Convinced that these trade imbalances could only be explained by corruption of some kind, Morel launched a public campaign through newspapers and lecture tours across Britain. His efforts prompted the British Parliament to order an official inquiry in 1903, led by diplomat Roger Casement (1864–1916). A 1904 report confirmed widespread abuses and sparked international outrage. In response, British and American intellectuals formed the Congo Reform Association, which successfully pressured Belgium to end Leopold's personal rule.[4]

In 1908, the Belgian Parliament formally annexed the Congo Free State, transforming it into the *Congo Belge*—the Belgian Congo—and placing it under state control for the next fifty-two years. Governance was defined by the Colonial Charter of 1908, which established a rigid centralized authority. Executive power rested with the Belgian Minister of Colonial Affairs in Brussels, assisted by a colonial council. In the colony itself, a governor general and several vice-governor generals administered expansive provinces, while 130–150 territorial administrators enforced colonial policy at the local level. These officials maintained order, supervised labor, inspected production, and reported upward through the colonial hierarchy. All administrators were Belgian politicians; neither Congolese people nor European or American settlers had any political voice, and all political

3. Nzongola-Ntalaja, *From Leopold to Kabila*, 26–60; Van Reybrouck, *Epic History*, 57–100.

4. Hawkins, "Joseph Conrad"; Hawkins, "Mark Twain's Involvement." Casement's original report and the diary he kept during the inquiry recently has been republished as Casement et al., *Eyes of Another Race*. See also Pavlakis, *British Humanitarianism*. Recently Vincent Viaene has raised important questions about the precise relationship between Leopold's imperialism and the motivations of international concern. See his "Internationalism, Religion."

activity was strictly prohibited. This form of governance, known as "direct rule," was experienced by Congolese communities as absolute and crushing power, captured in the Kikongo phrase *bula matari*: "rock-breaker."[5]

As under Leopold II, economic extraction remained the overriding priority of the Belgian colonial state. After World War I, global demand for Congolese rubber fell sharply, prompting the Belgian government to encourage private investment from Europe and the US. Mining soon became the most lucrative enterprise in the Belgian Congo, particularly of copper, diamonds, and gold, followed by industries dependent on palm oil, resins, and other agricultural products. The colonial administration also imposed a system of "mandatory cultivation," forcing Congolese farmers to grow export crops such as cotton, coffee, and cocoa. Both the state and private corporations profited enormously from the colony's natural resources on the backs of poorly paid Congolese labor. With the exception of a sharp downturn during the Great Depression, these exploitative economic structures remained largely intact until the late 1950s, on the eve of Congolese independence.[6]

White Europeans and Americans never made up more than 0.8 percent of the population of the Belgian Congo, yet colonial society—especially in the cities—was rigidly segregated by race. Belgian officials justified this system through a deeply paternalistic ideology captured in a phrase repeated for decades: *dominer pour server*, "dominate in order to serve."[7] In their own telling, the Belgians had created a model colony: orderly, productive, and prosperous, governed by benevolent imperial authority for the good of the Congolese people. This self-image left little room for Congolese voices or aspirations.[8]

Yet colonial domination never went entirely uncontested. Armed resistance occurred, though it was rare and usually confined to specific regions. More commonly, resistance took other forms. By the 1930s, labor strikes among Congolese workers in mines and ports had become frequent and often escalated into violent confrontations with company officials, colonial administrators, and the *Force publique*. These periodic waves of labor unrest

5. Lemarchand, *Political Awakening*, 55–75; Dembour, *Recalling the Belgian Congo*, 17–44.

6. Buelens, *Congo, 1885–1960*.

7. A recent helpful treatment of Belgian colonial ideology is Stanard, *Leopard, Lion, and Cock*, esp. ch. 1.

8. Nzongola-Ntalaja, *From Leopold to Kabila*, 26–60; Van Reybrouck, *Epic History*, 101–226. The ideology of "dominate in order to serve" was popularized by Pierre Ryckmans (1891–1959), who served as Governor General of the Belgian Congo from 1934 to 1946. Vanderlinden, *Pierre Ryckmans*.

foreshadowed the rise of nationalist movements that gathered force in the late 1940s and 1950s, ultimately carrying the Congo to independence.

Even more widespread—and more difficult for the authorities to suppress—were African-initiated Christian movements that blended African traditional religious practices with Christian theology and a growing desire for political freedom. The most influential of these movements emerged around Simon Kimbangu (1887–1951), a catechist associated with the British Baptist Missionary Society. By 1921, Kimbangu and his followers proclaimed that he was the incarnation of the Holy Spirit, endowed with powers of healing and resurrection. Alarmed by his popularity, Belgian authorities imprisoned Kimbangu, where he remained until his death in 1951. His movement nevertheless endured and expanded. Central to Kimbanguist teaching was the conviction that the end times would bring liberation to all Africans living under European colonial rule—a powerful spiritual challenge to imperial authority.[9]

The question of Congolese independence began to take concrete shape in the early 1950s, as African nationalist movements matured across the continent. Leadership emerged most clearly among the *évolués*, an educated Congolese elite. These men and (rarely) women had completed secondary education, spoke French and often English, worked in white-collar professions, and adopted some aspects of European and American culture. Ironically, they often received an education in mission schools and were employed by the very private enterprises benefitting from colonialism. By the mid-1950s, they had organized themselves into several technically illegal political parties, each offering distinct and sometimes competing critiques of Belgian colonial rule. Drawing inspiration from the Universal Declaration of Human Rights, issued by the United Nations in 1948, they demanded dignity, freedom, and equality. Their confidence was bolstered by successful independence movements elsewhere in Africa in the 1950s, including Sudan, Morocco, Tunisia, and Ghana.[10]

Mounting political pressure from these Congolese nationalist leaders forced the Belgian administration to introduce reforms. In 1955, Antoine van Bilsen (1913–1996), professor of colonial and international studies at the University of Leuven, proposed a thirty-year plan for the gradual

9. Young, *Politics in Congo*, 273–306; MacGaffey, *Kimbanguism*; Gampiot, *Kimbanguism*.

10. Nzongola-Ntalaja, "Bourgeoisie and Revolution," 511–30. Using Marxist political analysis, Nzongola-Ntalaja describes the role of the *évolués*—which he calls the *bourgeoisie*—as "intermediaries" between the colonial powers and the masses of impoverished Congolese. See also Young, *Politics in Congo*, 73–161; Nzongola-Ntalaja, *From Leopold to Kabila*, 61–93; Van Reybrouck, *Epic History*, 227–66.

emancipation of the Belgian Congo.[11] Though controversial and opposed by many in the Belgian government and most Congolese nationalists, some elements of his plan were implemented. Municipal elections held in 1957 allowed black Congolese men, for the first time, to vote and run for office in major cities. Educational opportunities expanded with the growth of the University of Lovanium, which graduated its first class of Congolese students in 1958. Colonial authorities also eased curfews and travel restrictions, enabling Congolese leaders to travel abroad and engage the international community with unprecedented freedom.[12]

For many Congolese activists, however, these reforms fell far short of their expectations. In early 1959, mass demonstrations led by the *évolués* erupted across the colony. Fearing a prolonged and violent war like the one France had just fought in Algeria, King Baudouin of Belgium announced that independence would be granted "without delay, but also without irresponsible rashness." His plan envisioned a five-year transition and continued Belgian economic involvement. Events on the ground quickly overtook these cautious intentions. By the time King Baudouin (1930–1993) visited the Congo in December 1959, the momentum for immediate independence was irresistible. Nationalists demanded, above all, the release of Patrice Lumumba (1925–1961), who had been imprisoned for leading a major independence protest in Stanleyville just a few months earlier.[13]

In February 1960, Congolese nationalist leaders met with Belgian officials and business representatives in Brussels at the Belgo-Congolese Roundtable Conference. Contrary to the expectations of the Belgians, the result was immediate Congolese independence. National elections followed in May, and voters overwhelmingly supported Lumumba, electing him prime minister of the newly formed Republic of the Congo. On June 30, 1960, dignitaries from Belgium and journalists from around the world gathered in Léopoldville for the transfer of power. King Baudouin's speech portrayed independence as the culmination of a civilizing mission begun by King Leopold II. Lumumba's response sharply contradicted this narrative. He spoke instead of exploitation, suffering, and humiliation, insisting

11. Van Bilsen, *Un plan de trente ans*; van Bilsen, *Congo 1945–1965*. McStallworth, "Congolese and Self-Determination" lists van Bilsen's plan as one of five major political documents issued in the 1950s that inspired increasing longing among the Congolese for independence.

12. Nzongola-Ntalaja, *From Leopold to Kabila*, 61–93; Van Reybrouck, *Epic History*, 227–66.

13. Nzongola-Ntalaja, *From Leopold to Kabila*, 61–93; Van Reybrouck, *Epic History*, 227–66. For a sympathetic biography of Lumumba, see Kanza, *Rise and Fall.*

that independence was won through struggle by the Congolese people, not granted through Belgian benevolence.[14]

The weeks following independence were chaotic. Most of the remaining eighty thousand white Europeans and Americans fled the country, while the fragile coalition of Congolese leaders fractured into rival factions. Conflict centered especially in the mineral-rich provinces of Katanga and Kasai.[15] With the backing of Belgian and American interests, Katangan leader Moïse Tshombe led a successful coup against Lumumba's government. In January 1961, Lumumba was executed, his body dismembered and dissolved in a drum of acid.[16]

Lumumba's death plunged the Congo into years of violence and instability. The central government in Léopoldville changed hands repeatedly, Katanga remained in rebellion, and eastern regions became strongholds of rebel groups loyal to Lumumba. Known as the Congo Crisis (1960–1965), the series of scattered rebellions and military coups soon became entangled in Cold War rivalries, as both the US and the Soviet Union sought influence in the resource-rich nation. By 1965, Joseph Mobutu emerged as the dominant military figure, promising order and unity. Instead, he established a brutal dictatorship—sometimes called a "kleptocracy" because it was a government dominated by thieves exploiting the nation's natural resources—that would dominate Congolese political life for more than three decades.[17]

Disciples of Christ Congo Mission

Modern Christian missions in the Congo took shape in the closing decades of the nineteenth century alongside the machinery of empire. The British Baptist Missionary Society (BMS) opened the first Protestant mission station in 1878 in Matadi, a centuries-old trading port near the mouth of the Congo River. From this strategic base, missionaries pushed upriver, establishing at least four additional stations along its banks.[18] That same year, the

14. Nzongola-Ntalaja, *From Leopold to Kabila*, 94–120; Van Reybrouck, *Epic History*, 267–80. See also van Bilsen, "Some Aspects," 41–51; Van Lierde, *La pensée politique*.

15. Young, *Politics in Congo*, 307–57.

16. Belgium universally condemned the secession of the Katanga Province. Lemarchand, "Limits of Self-Determination," 404–16; Crowley, "Politics and Tribalism," 68–78. For the most recent treatment of the execution of Patrice Lumumba, see Gerard and Kucklick, *Death in the Congo*.

17. Nzongola-Ntalaja, *From Leopold to Kabila*, 121–40; Van Reybrouck, *Epic History*, 281–330.

18. W'ehusha, "Christianity," 531. For contemporary accounts of the BMS work, see Myers, *Congo for Christ* and Bentley, *Pioneering on the Congo*.

interdenominational Livingstone Inland Mission (LIM) was founded with a more ambitious vision: expanding even further upriver and into the interior along the tributaries of the Congo River. By 1884, it had established roughly ten stations but soon transferred ownership to the American Baptist Missionary Union (ABMU).[19] The Congo–Balolo Mission, established in 1889, also committed to mission work to the interior. These early missions laid the foundations of a sustained Protestant presence throughout the Congo River Basin, including permanent stations, basic schools, rudimentary medical work, and fragile, missionary-led churches.[20]

Africanized expressions of Roman Catholicism had been deeply embedded in some communities of Congolese people since the late fifteenth century, a byproduct of early diplomatic efforts by the monarchs of the powerful Kongo Kingdom in their relationship with the Portuguese.[21] In the modern era, the papacy and leaders of the Roman Catholic Church in Belgium eagerly aligned themselves with Leopold's colonial ambitions. They were drawn by the Congo's vast missionary promise, the alarming presence of Protestant missions, and a potent mix of religious conviction and Belgian nationalism.[22] By 1888 the Congregation of the Immaculate Heart of Mary (the Scheut Fathers) and the White Fathers had established missions in the Congo Free State, followed by the Jesuits in 1894, all concentrating their efforts along the Kasai River near the Angolan border.[23] Leopold rewarded these missions with generous land grants, government subsidies, and the protection of the *Force publique*. Yet the sheer scale of the colony soon made clear that Roman Catholic missions alone could not sustain his ambitions, prompting the king to extend similar privileges to Protestant missions as well. Until the outbreak of the First World War, Catholic missionaries typically gathered converts into segregated Christian villages, echoing the *reducciones* long employed in South American missions. Separation from

19. W'ehusha, "Christianity," 531; Guinness, *First Christian Mission*. On the sale of the LIM mission stations to the AMBU, see Merriam, *Congo Mission*.

20. Armstrong offers a retrospective account of the early work of the Congo-Balolo Mission in his *Sunrise on the Congo*. See also Guinness, *First Thirty Years*.

21. W'ehusha, "Christianity"; Hastings, *Church in Africa*, 71–129; Isichei, *History of Christianity*, 63–67. See also Thornton, "Development,"147–67; Thornton, "Afro-Christian Syncretism," 53–77. Perhaps the best example of Africanized Roman Catholicism in the precolonial Congo is the Antonian Movement, established by Kongolese prophetess Kimpa Vita (1685–1706). See Thornton, *Kongolese Saint Anthony*; Pemot, *Kimpa Vita*. Both biographies stress her role in leading a resistance movement against the European slave trade in the Congo.

22. Pereira, "Catholic Church," 82–104.

23. Isichei, *History of Christianity*, 193.

traditional Congolese society, they believed, was essential for nurturing a disciplined and untainted Catholic faith.[24]

By 1900, Roman Catholic missionaries—about 150 in all—were spread across seventeen stations, while their Protestant counterparts were even more numerous, with some 230 missionaries working from forty stations.[25] Together, these missionary efforts formed the complex religious landscape in which the Disciples of Christ eventually established their own mission in the Congo.

The Foreign Christian Missionary Society (FCMS) of the Disciples of Christ first turned its attention to the Congo in 1884. After consulting with more experienced Protestant missionaries, however, the FCMS reluctantly set its plans aside. The vision was ambitious, and the estimated $25,000 required to launch the work lay beyond its financial reach. A decade later, in 1895, the FCMS made a second attempt. This time it commissioned Ellsworth E. Faris (1874–1953) and a young physician, Harry Biddle (1872–1898), to establish a mission in the Congo Free State. The two men arrived in early 1897 and spent more than a year searching for a viable site. Protestant missionaries had begun to speak openly about human rights abuses in the region, and colonial officials, wary of further scrutiny, were increasingly reluctant to grant permission for new mission work. During this period Biddle became gravely ill and died while returning to the US. Faris remained behind, eventually negotiating the purchase of an existing mission station at Bolenge.[26]

Bolenge lay some seven hundred miles inland from the mouth of the Congo River. Established in 1883 by the LIM and later supported by the ABMU, the station was once a promising upriver outpost. By the time Faris arrived in 1899, however, the ABMU had decided to sell of its upriver stations and concentrate its efforts in the Lower Congo. The Baptists offered Bolenge to the FCMS for $2,500—about half of their original investment—and assisted Faris in getting established. The station itself was modest: two thatched-roof houses totaling less than ten thousand square feet. From this unassuming base, the DCCM began its work.[27]

Soon after the purchase of the Bolenge station, Dr. Royal Dye (1874–1966) and his wife, Eva Nichols Dye (1877–1951), joined the mission. They immediately opened a small clinic and began a boarding school. Alongside

24. Isichei, *History of Christianity*, 195–96.

25. Isichei, *History of Christianity*, 193.

26. Warren, *Survey of Service*, 494–95; Smith, *Fifty Years in Congo*, 3; United, *They Went to Africa*, 14.

27. Gates et al., "Report," 302; Smith, *Fifty Years in Congo*, 16.

Faris, the Dyes immersed themselves in the Lonkundo language and undertook the formidable tasks of translating the New Testament, writing doctrinal tracts, and producing educational materials. Three Congolese Christians—Ikoko, a skilled carpenter, his wife, Bokama, and Josefa, a disabled fisherman—proved indispensable to these efforts. Josefa, in particular, emerged as a gifted evangelist and, in 1902, played a central role in the mission's first baptisms.[28] From the earliest days, DCCM missionaries depended on the knowledge, skills, and companionship of local people, who served as guides through unfamiliar terrain, interpreters, and indispensable partners in the work of the mission.

From the outset, the DCCM envisioned an indigenous church that would "transform the whole Congo social order through the vital application of the principles and life of Jesus."[29] In early 1903, the mission organized its first congregation with twenty-four members. Leadership was shared between missionaries and Congolese Christians, though initially no Congolese were ordained as elders. One of the earliest and most difficult issues the church confronted was the widespread practice of polygamy. After years of discussion, Congolese leaders agreed with the missionaries that abandoning polygamy would be required for church membership. Determined to foster self-support, the missionaries also emphasized stewardship education. Tithing was established as a minimum expectation, and "thank-offerings" at Christmas and Easter encouraged sacrificial giving beyond the tithe. The church adopted the Lonkundo word *iboko*—meaning a grouping or following of a particular way—to describe itself, signaling a meaningful degree of indigenization from the beginning.[30]

Among the earliest and most influential Congolese leaders was Njoji Mark. Born into a prominent family, his father belonged to the chiefly aristocracy, and his brother was a renowned *sangoma*, or healer-shaman. Around 1900, he began attending the mission school at Bolenge, quickly distinguishing himself as a natural leader. He was among the first baptized in 1902 and became a charter member of the Bolenge congregation the following year. For several years he served as an evangelist in surrounding villages and helped establish additional mission stations. Between 1907 and 1909, he accompanied the Dyes to the US during their furlough, studying at Eureka College and later at a sanitarium in Battle Creek, Michigan. In 1914, DCCM leaders selected him to be the mission's first Congolese

28. Dye, *In His Glad Service*, 13–71.

29. Warren, *Survey of Service*, 495.

30. For a detailed analysis of polygamy in the early DCCM, see Efefe, "Doctrine biblique"; Smith, *Fifty Years in Congo*, 22–24.

pastor. He served the Bolenge church faithfully for many years, and on July 4, 1920, a large crowd gathered to witness his ordination. Beyond his local congregation, he became the principal spokesperson for Congolese Disciples throughout the region, a role he held until declining health forced his retirement in the late 1950s.[31]

DCCM personnel could not ignore the brutal system of exploitation in the Congo Free State and had been aware of these abuses from the beginning. Because establishing the mission required a degree of cooperation with colonial authorities, early criticism was largely confined to private journals, correspondence, and reports to the FCMS. Between 1904 and 1908, however, DCCM missionaries spoke out more forcefully, publishing sharp critiques in Disciples periodicals. Most notably, in 1904 a small group of Protestant leaders—including FCMS president Archibald McLean (1850–1920) and DCCM missionaries Edward A. Layton (1880–1938) and Robert Ray Eldred (1872–1913)—unsuccessfully urged the US government to intervene. Although their protests were fueled by deep moral outrage, DCCM missionaries consistently distinguished between the political responsibilities of the state and the spiritual mission of the church. After 1908, they largely withdrew from political engagement and returned their focus to evangelism and education.[32]

Within five years of establishing the mission, some DCCM workers believed they had mastered Lonkundo sufficiently to begin creating a written form of the language. Eva Nichols Dye relied heavily on her "word hunters," students who consulted respected elders and helped her grasp Lonkundo vocabulary and structure. Using the English alphabet, she developed a written form between 1905 and 1907. Years later, she candidly acknowledged their early limitations, recalling that "ludicrous mistakes were made because of the differences in the meanings of words by intonation and accent."[33] Despite these challenges, the mission's small, foot-powered press produced hymnals, tracts, and educational materials in Lonkundo. In 1917, DCCM missionaries joined colleagues from the Congo-Balolo Mission and Congolese Christian leaders to begin translating the Bible into Lomongo-Lonkundo. After more than four years of work, the *Bonkanda wa Nzakomba*—the "Book of God"—was published in 1921, making the Bible

31. Dye, *Bolenge*, 133–39; Ross, "Ordination of Mark Njoji," 30; United, *Njoji Mark*; Merrill, "Bolenge," 22–23.

32. Williams, "Disciples and Red Rubber," 3–18.

33. Dye, "Bonkanda wa Nzakomba," 34.

accessible to an estimated one million Lomongo-Lonkundo speakers across central Africa.[34]

Disciple churches in the Pacific Northwest rallied behind DCCM with remarkable generosity, raising more than $15,000 to purchase a steamship. At the Pittsburgh Centennial Convention in 1909, the newly acquired vessel—the SS *Oregon*—was formally dedicated to mission service. A year later, it made its maiden voyage up the Congo River, inaugurating a new era in the mission's work. For the next four decades, the *Oregon* became the backbone of DCCM transportation, carrying missionaries, evangelists, medical personnel, and supplies deep into the interior. For most of those years, the ship was captained by Congolese Christian Inkema Jean, whose leadership left a lasting imprint on both vessel and mission. Following his example, Congolese Christians and missionaries alike called the ship *Nsango Ea Ndoce*—"Good News" in Lonkundo. Preaching from its deck in 1938, Inkema Jean declared, "She is a gospel boat, so that our people may know the God of love, our heavenly Father . . . that they may be released from the dreadful fear of the spirits, the strong bonds of ignorance, of superstition, of sin; that they may receive instruction which will lift them up to better living."[35] Eventually, rising maintenance costs and improved transportation systems throughout the Congo made the ship obsolete, and in 1949 DCCM leaders reluctantly retired the *Oregon* from service.[36]

The impact of the *Oregon* on the mission's growth was profound. By the 1920s, improved river transportation enabled DCCM to expand steadily along the Congo River and its tributaries, establishing six additional mission stations: Longa (1908), Lotumbe (1910), Monieka (1912), Mondombe (1920), Wema (1925), and Coquilhatville (1925). At each station, missionaries replicated the basic pattern of work first developed at Bolenge. Churches were organized, boarding schools for boys and girls were established, hospitals offered basic medical care, and large numbers of Congolese evangelists were trained and sent out to itinerate among surrounding villages. Each station oversaw a vast territory, often covering as much as ten thousand square miles and serving populations estimated at a hundred thousand people each. The central station functioned as a training hub, especially for Congolese evangelists who traveled for months at a time before returning for *ekitelo*—gatherings for worship, fellowship, and the baptism of new converts. Whenever possible, missionaries themselves joined in this

34. Dye, "Bonkanda wa Nzakomba," 34–35; Hobgood, "Lomongo-Lonkundo New Testaments," 36–37.

35. Yocum, "*Oregon*—A Gospel Boat," 44.

36. Sly, "Farewell to the *Oregon*," 22–23.

itinerant work, offering counsel and encouragement to emerging Christian communities.[37]

As the mission expanded geographically, it also grew in personnel. Between the founding of DCCM and 1929, eighty-four missionaries served in the Congo, each contributing in significant ways. Among them, however, the work of two early missionary couples stands out. Andrew F. Hensey (1880–1951), a gifted linguist, arrived in 1905 and immediately began collaborating with Eva Nichols Dye to develop a written form of the Lonkundo language. Though not trained as a printer, Hensey ran the Bolenge mission press for nearly twenty-five years, overseeing publications that were crucial to the mission's educational and evangelistic efforts. One such publication was *Ekim'ea Nsango* ("News Messenger"), a quarterly Lonkundo-language journal launched in 1913. Hensey's cultural fluency and diplomatic skill also led to his appointment to the Belgian government's Royal Commission for the Protection of Natives. After leaving the Congo in 1931, he continued shaping missionary education as a professor at the College of Missions in Indianapolis and the Kennedy School of Missions in Hartford. Hensey's wife, Alice (1885–1950), arrived in the Congo in 1907 and contributed her own considerable talents to the mission. A gifted musician and poet, she translated hymns into Lonkundo and taught them to Congolese congregations. Widely known as the "official hostess of Bolenge," she welcomed visiting government officials, denominational leaders, and representatives from other Protestant missions, helping to build goodwill and cooperation across institutional lines.[38]

Another pivotal couple, Herbert Smith (1880–1954) and Mary Hopkins Smith (1881–1952), arrived in 1909 and devoted the next thirty-seven years of their lives to the Congo mission. They were instrumental in opening the Lotumbe station in 1910 and served there as its only missionaries for several years. In 1928, they spearheaded the establishment of a central training school for Congolese evangelists at Bolenge, later known as the Congo Christian Institute. Both taught there until their retirement in 1946. In recognition of the mission's fiftieth anniversary, the Herbert Smith authored *Fifty Years in Congo: Disciples of Christ at the Equator*, a landmark account of the mission's history.[39]

Though medical work had been a feature of DCCM work from the beginning, it also expanded after 1908. By the 1920s, at least six missionary physicians were serving in the Congo. Dr. Louis Jaggard (1877–1951),

37. Holder, "Church in Congo," 15–17.

38. United, *They Went to Africa*, 24–25.

39. United, *They Went to Africa*, 34–36.

who arrived in 1908, devoted thirty-six years to medical service. He was joined by Dr. W. A. Frymire (1883–1954) in 1913, followed by Dr. Gervase Barger (1882–1966) and Dr. Ernest B. Pearson (1886–1976) in 1915 and 1917, respectively. Although Bolenge, Lotumbe, and Monieka served as their primary medical centers, these physicians regularly itinerated to outlying stations and villages. Particularly notable was their success in using the newly developed antibiotic Salvarsan to treat children suffering from yaws, a chronic and debilitating bacterial infection. Medical care often opened doors for evangelization, building trust and goodwill within local communities.[40]

From its inception, the Congo mission was marked by a strong ecumenical spirit. DCCM missionaries participated actively in the General Conference of Protestant Missionaries, a gathering held every five years that brought together Protestant workers from across the Congo for worship, fellowship, and shared problem solving. In 1911, DCCM hosted the conference at Bolenge. Two significant initiatives emerged from that meeting: the mission press began publishing *Congo Mission News*, an interdenominational quarterly for Protestant missionaries, and participants organized the Congo Continuation Committee, modeled after recommendations from the World Missionary Conference in Edinburgh (1910). This committee served as an advisory body for Protestant missions and often represented their interests to the Belgian colonial government. DCCM further demonstrated its commitment to cooperation by joining five other Protestant missions in establishing the Union Mission House in Kinshasa in 1922, which became a vital center for training and collaboration.[41]

By the 1910s, education had emerged as the cornerstone of DCCM's mission strategy. When FCMS secretary Stephen J. Corey (1873–1962) visited the Congo in 1912 to assess the mission's progress, he was most impressed by its schools. He became convinced that education was essential not only for building strong churches but also for cultivating indigenous leadership capable of shaping both church and society. This assessment was echoed in 1921 when the Phelps-Stokes Commission evaluated DCCM schools and praised them as exemplary. The commission commended the mission's cooperative approach, the quality of its curriculum—modeled on

40. United, *They Went to Africa*, 30–31, 45–46, 48–51; Pearson, "Healing of Africa," 22–24; Barger, "Fighting Yaws," 31–34. Sokhieng Au argues that the type of medical care offered by Protestant missionaries from Britain and the US often brought them into conflict with colonial authorities because it different markedly from the medical care offered by Roman Catholic missionaries from Belgium. See his "Medical Orders," 62–82.

41. Smith, *Fifty Years in Congo*, 43–44; Ross, "Union Mission House," 29.

American industrial education with a strong general education component—and its emphasis on moral and religious formation.[42]

The numerical growth of the mission during its early decades was striking. In 1903, Bolenge stood alone as DCCM's sole station, with a church membership of just sixty-four and one school enrolling 110 students. No Congolese workers were yet employed. A decade later, by 1913, the mission had expanded to three stations, employed 209 Congolese evangelists and teachers, organized 124 churches and worship centers, and enrolled more than thirteen hundred students in thirty-five schools. By 1923, DCCM operated six fully functioning stations, employed 689 Congolese workers serving nearly 350 outstations, and oversaw 549 churches and regular worship sites. Church membership had risen to 8,679, and 275 schools served more than 4,400 students.[43] In just over twenty-five years, DCCM arguably had become the largest and most successful foreign mission of the Disciples.

This rapid growth underscored a pressing need for advanced leadership training. Early attempts in the 1920s to establish a cooperative school with neighboring missions faltered due to limited resources. After United Christian Missionary Society (UCMS) executive Cyrus Yocum (1883–1958) visited the Congo in 1924, however, North American Disciples recognized the urgency of the situation. In 1928, the *Institut chrétien congolais*—known in English as the Congo Christian Institute—opened with thirty-four students enrolled: eighteen men and sixteen women. The three-year curriculum combined academic subjects with practical training, aiming to prepare not only pastors but also teachers, medical workers, agriculturalists, and ethical business leaders. Students paid their tuition by cultivating and selling cash crops.[44] Graduates of the institute—such as Iso Timothy, Bokomboji Pierre, Bongolembe Natanaele and Bombongo Bofale Sarah became among the earliest and most influential Congolese Christian leaders.[45]

By the late 1920s, DCCM leaders also grew increasingly concerned about the spread of Islam in areas surrounding their stations, particularly near Mondombe. While many Muslims arrived as traders, missionaries feared that Islam's accommodation of polygamy would make it appealing to Congolese Christians. In 1926, Royal Dye warned supporters in North America that Christianity in equatorial Africa faced a challenge similar to that of North Africa in late antiquity, where a complacent church had been

42. Smith, *Fifty Years in Congo*, 44–45; Ross, "Phelps-Stokes," 21–23. See especially Berman, "American Influence," 132–45.

43. Fey, "Through the Years," 38–39.

44. Smith, "How Shall," 19–20; Smith, "Training Leaders," 14; and Smith, *Fifty Years in Congo*, 72–74, 83–84.

45. United, *Our Workers in Africa*.

overtaken by Islam. Unless Protestant missions were better equipped, he cautioned, history might repeat itself. Echoing this concern, E. R. Moon (1879–1962) urged greater commitment to the Congo mission: "May we hasten to occupy the remaining portions of our territory," he warned, "so that Mohammed shall find on his arrival a well-established church of Christ."[46]

Like all missions around the world, DCCM was hit hard by the Great Depression. By 1934, the mission's budget had been slashed to half of what it had been just four years earlier. Salaries were cut, furloughs cancelled, and supplies grew scarce, even for hospitals and schools. Yet at great personal cost, missionaries and Congolese leaders refused to abandon the work. Every station remained open. Remarkably, these years of material deprivation became a season of spiritual and institutional growth. Between 1929 and 1939, DCCM membership increased by nearly 40 percent, reaching 48,019 Congolese Christians.[47] The depression years also deepened the mission's commitment to cooperation. DCCM strengthened ties with neighboring missions and embraced new forms of "union" work. In 1933, missionary Emory Ross (1887–1973) began editing *L'Évangile en Afrique*, the first interdenominational newspaper for Congolese Christians. Two years later, DCCM joined other missions to open *La librairie évangélique au Congo* in Léopoldville, a union bookstore that served Christians across denominational lines.[48] Although missionaries and Congolese leaders had embraced an ecumenical spirit from the beginning, the hardships of the Depression sharpened their resolve to work together.

Certainly, the growth of the DCCM was impressive, but it unfolded alongside—and kept pace with—a much broader expansion of Christian missions across the Congo. Throughout the mid-century, the number and diversity of Protestant missions increased dramatically. In 1936, 725 full-time Protestant missionaries were at work in the colony; by 1958, that figure had more than doubled to 1,652. The expansion of Roman Catholic missions was even more striking. Although Catholic missionaries were scattered throughout the Congo and concentrated especially in the southern provinces, their numbers grew rapidly as well—from 2,475 missionaries in 1936 to 5,904 by 1958. Together, these figures underscore the scale and intensity of Christian missionary expansion in colonial Congo.[49]

46. Moon, "Breaking the Wilderness," 14. See also Dye, "Crescent Conquest," 8–10.

47. *Year Book* (1930), 56; *Year Book* (1940), 22.

48. Smith, *Fifty Years in Congo*, 76, 110.

49. Isichei, *History of Christianity*, 193. For a helpful compendium of Protestant missions that eventually joined to form the *Église du Christ au Congo*, see Irvine, *Church of Christ in Zaire*. The relationship between Protestant and Roman Catholic

The most consequential development of the era—for DCCM and for Protestantism in the Belgian Congo more broadly—was the formation of the *Église du Christ au Congo*. Since 1902, missionaries had coordinated their work through a representative body that became the Congo Protestant Council in 1924. As Congolese leadership matured, the council was reorganized in 1934 and renamed the Church of Christ in Congo. This change marked a decisive shift: Protestantism in the Congo was no longer merely a missionary enterprise but an indigenous church in which missionaries and Congolese believers belonged together. Over the following decades, authority steadily passed to Congolese leaders, culminating in 1969 when a new constitution transferred full responsibility for the church to them.[50]

Developments at the Congo Christian Institute reflected this same process of indigenization. When the school opened in 1928, missionaries alone served as trustees and faculty. By 1940, however, Congolese leaders were teaching alongside missionaries, and the board of trustees was nearly evenly balanced. Explaining the philosophy behind these changes, H. Gray Russell (1890–1978) wrote in 1941, "We feel that the control of all policies should pass gradually into the hand of those most affected."[51]

Congolese Christians also demonstrated growing financial responsibility during these difficult years. By the early 1940s, churches across the mission were collecting a monthly *mpoji e'isei*, or "gifts of mercy." First introduced at Bolenge, the offering initially helped sustain DCCM during the Depression, but it soon expanded to support neighboring missions whose funding had been disrupted by World War II. Missionary Herbert Smith later reflected that the *mpoji e'isei* aided "orphaned" missions across the Congo, provided milk through the Red Cross to infants in Belgium and Greece, supported Bible societies, encouraged soldiers and prisoners of war, built churches, and even purchased gifts for a DCCM missionary held as a prisoner of war. Long known for careful stewardship, Congolese Christians emerged from the Depression and war years with a broader vision of the church's global mission.[52]

missions was not always cordial. They sometimes clashed over competing imperial, evangelistic, and humanitarian goals. In addition, all European and Christian missions disregarded as superstition African traditional religions, even in "Christianized" forms. See Kenny and Wenger, "Church, State," 156–85. Christian missions were complicated further by the competing interest of private enterprises that operated in the Congo, such as the Lever Brothers, a British soap and consumer good company. See Loffman and Henriet, "We Are Left," 71–100.

50. Smith, *Fifty Years in Congo*, 90.

51. Russell, "Christian School," 12.

52. Smith, *Fifty Years in Congo*, 104, 106.

In the immediate aftermath of World War II, UCMS executive Virgil Sly (1901–1978) spent three and a half months touring the Congo. He visited DCCM stations throughout the region, observing their evangelistic, educational, and medical ministries. Deeply encouraged, Sly urged the UCMS to commit more than $190,000 from the Crusade for a Christian World to fund major building projects. He also called for the recruitment of additional, better-equipped missionaries, noting that only twenty-eight missionaries were serving nearly sixty thousand Christians.[53] His appeal bore fruit. By 1950, eighteen new missionaries had arrived, and two new stations—Bosobele (1945) and Ifumo (1947)—were opened. DCCM even captured international attention when *Life* magazine devoted a nine-page photographic essay to the work at Monieka in its June 2, 1947 issue, highlighting the medical ministry of Dr. Alfred G. Henderson (1912–1986) at Lockwood-Kinnear Memorial Hospital.[54]

DCCM marked its fiftieth anniversary in 1949 with a Golden Jubilee celebration at Bolenge. Planned jointly by missionary H. C. Hobgood (1886–1979) and Congolese pastor Mbowina Mattieu, the celebration included an address by the mission's first missionary, Ellsworth Faris (1874–1953), graduation exercises at the Congo Christian Institute, and numerous social events. The Jubilee carried deep symbolic meaning. As Virgil Sly observed, it was "not a conference of missionaries, but of churches," represented by Congolese delegates from all nine stations and many outlying areas. In his words, it marked "the beginning of the adult life of these churches."[55]

The 1950s ushered in a new era of cooperation and expansion. DCCM joined five other missionary societies in establishing the *Institut médical evangélique* at Kimpese. Each society contributed $20,000 toward construction, with additional support from the Belgian government. When the institute opened in 1953, it included classrooms, a clinic, and housing for students and instructors.[56] Another significant partnership emerged in 1959 with the founding of the Protestant Theological Faculty at Elizabethville. Political upheaval and educational reforms repeatedly disrupted its work, and later state secularization policies nearly forced it to close. The *Église du Christ au Congo* intervened, assuming full responsibility for the institution as a private enterprise.[57]

53. Sly, *Report*; Baker, "Personnel Needs in Congo," 26–27; *Year Book* (1948), 52.

54. Burke and Farbman, "Photographic Essay," 105–14.

55. Sly, "Congo Golden Jubilee," 12.

56. Johnson, *Congo Centennial*, 37.

57. *Institut médical evangélique, Kimpese.* After settling permanently in Kinshasa in 1979, the faculty eventually became the *Université protestante au Congo* in 1994, offering programs in theology, law, medicine, business, and economics.

Meanwhile, DCCM dramatically expanded its own ministries. With $2.8 million raised through the denomination's Capital for Kingdom Building program, the mission completed nearly four hundred projects across the Congo. The number of missionaries peaked at eighty-eight in the late 1950s, a new station opened at Boende in 1957, and pastoral training schools were established at three stations. Radios were installed at all mission sites, and extensive construction projects produced new churches, schools, and medical facilities, including the Dye Memorial Church at Bolenge. By 1959, DCCM reported more than nine hundred places of worship serving over 107,000 members, 308 schools educating 14,400 students, and medical facilities delivering more than half a million treatments each year.[58]

As Congolese nationalism intensified in the late 1950s, DCCM leaders moved decisively to transfer authority to Congolese Christians. In 1957, decision-making bodies composed of both missionaries and Congolese leaders were introduced at the station level. The following year, the first Congress of the DCCM convened at Bolenge, bringing together all missionaries and three Congolese delegates from each of the mission's ten stations. Between biennial sessions, a Central Committee with equal missionary and Congolese representation governed mission-wide affairs. Although missionaries still outnumbered Congolese delegates in the Congress, momentum toward local control was unmistakable. In 1959, the creation of a central fund administered by Congolese leaders further signaled the shift. For the first time, the UCMS no longer controlled the financial resources, marking a decisive step toward an autonomous Congolese church.[59]

Within weeks of Congolese independence on June 30, 1960, the situation had deteriorated so severely that the UCMS evacuated all but seven missionaries from the Congo. When missionaries cautiously returned later in 1960, they found their work fundamentally transformed. Their first task was no longer evangelization or institution-building, but working alongside Congolese leaders to draft a new constitution for the DCCM. Those leaders moved swiftly to establish a fully autonomous church, transferring all mission property into Congolese hands.[60] Missionaries were often startled by the clarity and urgency of these demands. "We are children no longer, and we do not want to be treated as children," Congolese leaders insisted. "We need you as older brothers in the faith, and we welcome you—but many of

58. Johnson, *Congo Centennial*, 52–54; Dade, "Capital for the Congo," 19–20; Buckner, "To a Changing Continent," 9.

59. Johnson, *Congo Centennial*, 47; *Year Book* (1958), 239; *Year Book* (1960), 272; Buckner, "Congolese Churches," 5.

60. *Year Book* (1961), 269–71; *Year Book* (1962), 268–69; Hobgood, "Returning Missionaries See Changes," 36.

you will have to change your attitude toward us if you want to work with us."[61] Lessons learned in the Congo soon would reverberate throughout the UCMS, contributing directly to significant revision to the theology and practice of missionary work by the Disciples.[62]

Biography of Buena Rose Stober

Buena Rose Stober was born on July 27, 1897, the third daughter of Henry Ceward Stober (1857–1934) and Ellen Jane (Badley) Stober (1863–1909), into a family shaped by the restlessness and optimism of the American frontier. Her parents were part of the "Boomer Movement," a loose coalition of poor families, soldiers, and railroad entrepreneurs who spent years pressuring the US government to open the Unassigned Lands of the Oklahoma Territory to white settlement. When the government finally agreed on April 22, 1889, the result was a series of frenetic land runs. Over the next six years, nearly two hundred thousand settlers poured into the territory, transforming it almost overnight and pushing it toward statehood.[63] This mass migration provoked bitter conflict with the Native Americans to whom the land had been promised, and with African Americans who had settled there to escape the racism and violence of the Jim Crow South.

The Stobers were among those settlers. Married just two weeks earlier in a makeshift camp of hopeful homesteaders in Arkansas City, they joined the First Land Run, racing south from Kansas to stake a claim of up to 160 acres on which to build their future. The terms were daunting: if they could make the land habitable and productive within five years, the government would grant them legal title.[64] They claimed a parcel in rural Logan County, outside the newly established town of Mulhall, and set about the hard work of survival.[65]

For Ellen Jane, subsistence living was familiar territory because she came from a formidable frontier family. Her father, the Rev. John Nelson Badley (1837–1908), was both a circuit-riding Methodist preacher and a US Cavalry scout who had participated successfully in multiple land runs in

61. Crane, "Congolese Leader Agrees," 38.

62. See United, *Strategy for World Mission*. For a discussion of the *Strategy for World Mission* in the context of the history of Disciples missiology, see Pittman and Williams, "Mission and Evangelism," 206–47.

63. Baird and Goble, *Oklahoma*, 141–52; Hoig, "Boomer Movement."

64. Hightower, *1889*.

65. Unless otherwise referenced, the narrative of the Badley and Stober families has been crafted from available genealogical evidence on ancestry.com.

Nebraska and Texas in the years following the Civil War. Her mother, Mary Ann (Wells) Badley (1844–1923), managed a household that included Ellen Jane and fifteen siblings, raising them on successive family farms. Henry, by contrast, had less experience with homesteading. His parents, Urias Stober (1831–1872) and Ann Maria (Benbow) Stober (1832–1893), had operated a stable farm near Hagerstown, Indiana, since the early 1850s. Their son appears to have left Indiana around the age of thirty to seek opportunity farther west. Despite the hardy, homesteading spirit that inspired their families, however, the newlywed Stobers failed at their first attempt at land ownership for reasons that are not entirely clear.

By the mid-1890s, the Stober family—now including two daughters, Anna Mary (1890–1972) and Florence (1894–1972)—had moved into a small, rented house in Bluff City, Kansas, a village of fewer than two hundred residents just north of the Oklahoma border. Henry likely found work there with the Kansas Southeastern Railway, while Ellen Jane kept house and raised the children. It was here, in this modest home, that their third daughter, Buena Rose, was born. As the pace of the land runs slowed down and the family's finances stabilized, the Stobers were finally able to purchase a modest forty-acre farm in 1900 or 1901, just outside of Newkirk, Oklahoma.

A town eight miles south of the Kansas border in the Cherokee Strip, Newkirk was founded during the Fourth Land Run of 1893. The town had sprung up rapidly around the bustling Topeka–Santa Fe Railroad depot, fueled by growing oil and livestock industries. A devastating fire in 1901 destroyed a full block of wooden buildings along Main Street, but the town rebuilt quickly, replacing them with buildings of limestone quarried locally.[66] By 1910, the town's population had reached almost two thousand residents. The Stobers contributed to that population growth in 1904 with the birth of their fourth child, a son, James Otwine (1904–1984).

The family's stability was shattered on March 18, 1909, when Ellen Jane died unexpectedly of tuberculosis at the age of forty-five. In the aftermath, the two older girls remained in Newkirk with their father, working as housekeepers in town. Twelve-year-old Buena Rose and her five-year-old brother James were sent to live with their maternal grandparents in Beaver, a small town in the Oklahoma panhandle. The arrangement proved temporary. By the fall of 1910, the children returned to Newkirk so they could attend its superior public schools. The school building in Newkirk made a striking impression: a two-story limestone structure with an arched

66. Dye, *Newkirk*, 1–6.

entrance and a bell-crowned cupola.[67] In a region and era where permanence was rare, the building's architecture signaled stability, ambition, and confidence in the future.

Uniquely suited at the time to the American frontier, the Disciples also took root in the area through vigorous evangelism and church planting. By the time statehood was granted in 1907, the Disciples had established 491 congregations in Oklahoma, almost all of them among white settlers who arrived during the land runs.[68] One of the earliest was First Christian Church of Newkirk, founded in 1895 at Ninth and Walnut Streets. After returning from Beaver, Buena Rose and James began attending First Christian without their parents. At that time, David Leroy Ammons (1852–1925) served as pastor to the surprisingly large congregation.[69] At a revival meeting in September 1911, both children were baptized. Stober left no indication that she sensed a missionary calling at such a young age, though the possibility cannot be dismissed. More likely, her vocation crystallized during her years as a college student.[70]

In the fall of 1917, following her graduation from high school, Stober enrolled in the College of Liberal Arts at Phillips University in Enid, Oklahoma. Founded by the Disciples in 1907 as Oklahoma Christian University and soon renamed in honor of benefactor Thomas W. Phillips (1835–1912), the institution quickly had become a regional center for higher education. In the 1910s, Phillips sustained an enrollment of nearly four hundred students on a sprawling 267-acre campus in the heart of Oklahoma wheat country. Its offerings included a preparatory high school, undergraduate colleges of liberal arts and education, and a graduate seminary known as the College of the Bible.[71] From its earliest years, Phillips University explicitly aimed to "inculcate the missionary spirit" in its students. It sponsored an active chapter of the Student Volunteer Movement, offered numerous courses in foreign missions, and maintained a missions library and museum. Furloughed missionaries regularly visited campus as guest lecturers, a tradition in which Stober probably participated later in life.[72] More than

67. Oklahoma Historical Society, "Photograph of High School." This photograph also is featured on the front cover of Dye, *Newkirk*.

68. England, *Oklahoma Christians*, 102.

69. "First Christian Church"; *Year Book* (1912), 114. At the time, the congregation reported a membership of 128.

70. "Who's Who Among Our Missionaries," DCHS, Buena Rose Stober Biography File.

71. Marshall, *Phillips University's First*, 1:115–35.

72. Phillips University, "Mission Studies," 142.

any single individual, Dean Frank Hamilton Marshall (1868–1956) shaped the university's strong emphasis on foreign missions.[73]

Even while working part-time as a saleswoman in a department store, Stober completed a year of coursework at Phillips and finished the required examinations successfully. Beyond the classroom, she joined the Student Volunteer Movement at a time when it was nearing the height of its influence in recruiting college students for overseas service.[74] She also became deeply involved in University Place Christian Church in Enid, a congregation known for its wholehearted support of Disciples missions, partly because of its proximity to and relationship with the University.[75] Recognizing the practical value of medical training, Stober transferred to the Nurses Training School in Enid, a tuition-free cooperative program between the College of Liberal Arts and the university hospital. After two and a half years of study and apprenticeship, she graduated in May 1921 and soon afterward passed the state examination to become a registered nurse.[76]

Even before completing her nurses training, Stober resolved to serve as a foreign missionary, even thinking about how to fund her work. In a later letter to Cyrus Yocum, she reported that while still at Phillips, she approached a friend, a Presbyterian and a teacher, who had investments in oil and might support her missionary work or even visit wherever she served.[77] In her March 1921 application for appointment as a missionary for the UCMS, she cited the writings of several prominent Protestant missionary leaders as formative influences on her vocation.[78] Her first hope was to join the renowned Disciples missionary Dr. Albert Shelton (1875–1922) in Tibet, and she wrote to him to inquire. Shelton responded kindly but firmly, explaining in a brief letter that, although he had requested another nurse,

73. Myers, *This One Thing I Do*.

74. "Who's Who Among Our Missionaries," DCHS, Buena Rose Stober Biography File. On the Student Volunteer Movement, see Parker, *Kingdom of Character*, esp. 105–31.

75. "50th Anniversary: University Place Christian Church."

76. "Who's Who Among Our Missionaries," DCHS, Buena Rose Stober Biography File.; Phillips University, "Hospital and Training School," 124–26. Stober's nursing license is preserved in DCHS, Manuscript Collection 2001-068, Buena Rose Stober Papers.

77. Buena Rose Stober to Cyrus Yocum, January 29, 1926, DCHS, Division of Overseas Ministries, Africa, Box 7.

78. "Application for Appointment as a Missionary," DCHS, Buena Rose Stober Biography File. Stober mentions three books that influenced her decision to apply for appointment: Brown, *Foreign Missionary*; Corey, *Among Asia's Needy Millions*; Cory, *Trail to the Hearts*.

"the time has not come as yet for single ladies in Tibet."[79] Less than a year later, Shelton's work was tragically cut short when he was shot and killed by highway robbers outside the mission headquarters in Batang.[80]

Undeterred, Stober sought another path into missionary service. In the fall of 1921, she enrolled in the College of Missions in Indianapolis, Indiana. Over the next two years, she undertook an intensive program that included biblical studies, church history—especially the history of Protestant missions and the Disciples—preaching, apologetics, and foreign languages. She may also have studied international law, colonial administration, world religions, and sociology.[81] During this time, she became active at Downey Avenue Christian Church, one of the leading congregations of the Disciples in Indianapolis and widely respected for its leadership in foreign mission support.[82] Inspired by the work of veteran missionaries Andrew F. Hensey (1880–1951) and his wife, Alice (1885–1950), Stober eventually set her sights on the Belgian Congo.[83] On June 5, 1923, she graduated from the College of Missions and the faculty ordained her to Christian ministry as a missionary nurse, formally launching a vocation that would shape the rest of her life.[84] Sadly, she received little encouragement from her family; she noted that none of them were committed to the church and were largely "indifferent" to her decision to become a missionary.[85]

On September 19, 1923, Stober departed New York City aboard the RMS *Majestic*, beginning a long journey that would carry her across the Atlantic and deep into the Congo interior. She travelled with four newly appointed DCCM missionaries: Newell Trimble (1899–1981) and Myrtle Whaley (1893–1979), both also single women and classmates from the

79. Albert L. Shelton to Buena Rose Stober, May 4, 1921. This letter is preserved in DCHS, Manuscript Collection 2001-068, Buena Rose Stober Papers.

80. The most recent treatment of Shelton's work in Tibet is Wissing, *Pioneer in Tibet*.

81. Founded in 1909 by the Christian Woman's Board of Missions of the Disciples of Christ, the College of Missions trained more than four hundred missionaries until it merged with the Kennedy School of Missions in Hartford, Connecticut, in 1928. The college was located on the campus of Butler University and, although a separate institution, shared administrative, faculty, and library resources with the university. Shaw, *Hoosier Disciples*, 309–10 and 343–45; Williams, "College of Missions," 226–27.

82. Owen, *Century of Witness*.

83. By the time Stober determined to go to the Congo, Andrew Hensey had published two gripping accounts of the missionary work of DCCM: *Opals from Africa* and *Master Builder*.

84. Warren, "Appointed to Serve," 34. Stober's ordination certificate is preserved in DCHS, Manuscript Collection 2001-068, Buena Rose Stober Papers.

85. "Application for Appointment as a Missionary," DCHS, Buena Rose Stober Biography File.

College of Missions; and a missionary couple, Willard Learned (1897–1995) and his wife, Grace (1896–1999). The group stayed briefly in London and then continued on to Brussels where they spent nearly two months in a boarding house, studying French and meeting with veteran missionaries from the Congo. On November 30, the group departed from Antwerp, landing on December 2 at the bustling port of Matadi in the Belgian Congo. A grueling three-week train journey followed, bringing them at last to the DCCM headquarters in Bolenge just before Christmas.[86] From departure to arrival, Stober's passage from the US to the Congo lasted a little more than three months.

During her first term of service, from December 1923 to December 1926, Stober moved among the mission stations at Bolenge, Lotumbe, and Monieka, gaining experience wherever she was sent. At each post she was apprenticed to a seasoned DCCM physician, forming an especially close professional bond with Dr. Gervase Barger, the longtime director of the Bolenge mission hospital. Her letters from these early years convey a vivid sense of discovery: her fascination with the wide range of illnesses treated in the hospitals, her growing admiration for Congolese evangelist Njoji Mark, and her excitement over a high-profile humanitarian visit to DCCM from the Belgian Prince Leopold (1901–1981). Even in this early period, Stober's correspondence reveals a deepening concern for Congolese mothers and their newborn children, an interest that soon would crystallize into a defining focus of her missionary vocation. Just before she completed her first term, Cyrus Yocum wrote in glowing terms to her father, "Miss Stober has given a mighty good account of herself this first period of service in Africa, and we are proud of her."[87]

Stober returned to the US just before Christmas 1926 and spent six months reconnecting with family and rallying support for DCCM among Disciples congregations, especially her "living link," Tabernacle Christian Church in Franklin, Indiana.[88] But she cut short her time at home, boarded the SS *Arabic*, and eagerly returned to Brussels in June 1927 to gain more fluency in French and to complete a certificate at the *École de médecine tropicale*. She trained with leading authorities in tropical medicine, including

86. Unless otherwise referenced, the details of Stober's work come from her letters.

87. Cyrus Yocum to H. C. Stober, November 4, 1926, DCHS, Division of Overseas Ministries, Africa, Box 7.

88. The term *living link* refers to a Disciples congregation that directly supported an individual missionary or missionary couple. The support of living link congregations was a crucial supplement to that given by the UCMS. Tabernacle served as Stober's living link throughout her service as a missionary. See CTS, Tabernacle Christian Church, Franklin, IN, Congregational Files.

Jérôme Rodhain (1876–1956), the foremost Belgian physician and parasitologist of his day. Her studies were wide ranging and demanding: anatomy and physiology, pharmacology and minor surgery, as well as hematology, bacteriology, and pathology in both humans and domestic animals.[89] Back in the US, Phillips University accepted credit for this work and awarded Stober a Bachelor of Arts degree in absentia in May 1928. More importantly, she regarded the training as essential for the work that lay ahead: "My tropical medicine course looks as if it will be just what I need to help me in my work in Africa," she wrote to Cyrus Yocum. "In fact, I feel that I could hardly face the responsibility of the work without it."[90]

By April 1928, Stober was back in the Congo, assigned to the remote upriver station at Lotumbe at a moment of acute need. With no doctor on site and assisted only occasionally by another missionary nurse, she found herself running the hospital almost single-handedly. She delivered more than two hundred treatments each month and cared for an average of six inpatients at a time. The work was relentless and often heartbreaking. She took in an orphaned infant, Bokune Jean, and struggled to nurse her back to health. Her sudden, unexpected death scarred Stober deeply. From that moment, the care of new mothers and infants became a consuming priority of her missionary calling. Amid these demands, she also taught Sunday School to younger girls and boys and traveled through the surrounding countryside, offering medical care at rural dispensaries to those who could not reach Lotumbe.

During this second term, Stober's confidence as a missionary grew significantly, and she emerged as a forthright advocate of Disciples foreign missions, especially DCCM. That confidence sharpened her willingness to speak out. When the February 1929 issue of *World Call* portrayed DCCM stations as generously staffed and equipped with modern hospitals, all the missionary nurses bristled at what they saw as a serious misrepresentation.[91] On their behalf, Stober fired off an indignant letter to the editors to set the record straight. She challenged anyone to compare the mission's mud-brick, thatched-roof buildings—without running water or sewers—to a modern hospital in the US. Even more sharply, she rejected the claim that the stations were adequately staffed. Drawing on hard experience, she fumed, "In the four years I've been on the field, I've never had the privilege of being on

89. Stober's certificate awarded by the *École de médecine tropicale* is preserved in DCHS, Manuscript Collection 2001-068, Buena Rose Stober Papers.

90. Buena Rose Stober to Cyrus Yocum, October 29, 1927, DCHS, Division of Overseas Ministries, Africa, Box 7.

91. Warren, "New Way," 42.

the station with a doctor except for short periods of a week, a month, or six weeks when a doctor happened to be passing through or visiting our station. This is not my idea of a modern hospital!" While she was at it, Stober also challenged the patriarchal assumptions among UCMS leadership for their reluctance to send women doctors to the Congo: "Please don't ever let any of us hear again that there is doubt as to whether it is wise to send out women doctors." She wanted, above all, to be heard; but she also expected someone to act.[92]

"Your letter," Cyrus Yocum, one of the executive staff of UCMS, wrote in his cordial reply, "indicates that the temperature in *Congo Belge* at about the time that you wrote was somewhat above normal." He acknowledged Stober's concerns and agreed that the article regrettably had misrepresented conditions on the ground and promised to raise the matter with the editors of *World Call*. On the question of women doctors, he explained that most of the reservations among the UCMS leaders stemmed from the situation in India, where cultural and social conventions limited the work that women physicians could perform. He conceded that the Congo might present some comparable challenges, but insisted that no serious objections had been raised about sending women doctors to the Congo.[93] Surely Stober was gratified later that year when DCCM's first woman physician, Dr. Myrtle Lee Smith (1901–1954), arrived at Lotumbe, where they worked together for more than two years.[94]

In September 1931, Stober began serving at the station that would become her home base for the rest of her missionary career. Mondombe is located almost a thousand miles from Bolenge when travelling by the winding Tshuapa River. A trip to this far-flung station deep in the rainforest to the DCCM headquarters would take the better part of a week, even on the steamship *Oregon*. The same trip would take almost a month by *pirogue*, a flat-bottom, dugout canoe.

As a mission station, Mondombe originated from the efforts of Congolese Christians. As early as 1918, DCCM sent Congolese evangelists Olenga Stephen and Is'Oyela Cornelius as itinerant preachers in Mondombe and the surrounding villages. Their work laid the spiritual foundation for the

92. Buena Rose Stober to the editors of *World Call*, May 19, 1929. Her letter is included on pp. 71–72[XREF].

93. Cyrus Yocum to Buena Rose Stober, July 17, 1929. His letter is included on p. 73[XREF].

94. United, *They Went to Africa*, 68. Serious repeated illness prevented Dr. Smith from serving for more than one term, and she returned to the US in 1931. Another woman physician would not be appointed to DCCM until after the Great Depression—namely, Dr. Marjorie Horner (1912–1974), first appointed in 1940.

mission, even as it met with resistance from local tribal chiefs who were wary of a permanent Christian presence in the area. After almost a year of their work, the DCCM took steps to establish a formal mission station. Under the leadership of Boseke Paul, land was cleared and the first mud-and-pole houses were constructed, marking the physical beginning of the mission station. Fifty Christian families from other DCCM mission stations voluntarily relocated to Mondombe, providing a stable Christian witness during the station's earliest years. The first DCCM missionaries, E. R. Moon (1879–1962) and his wife, Bessie (1887–1985), along with Goldie Ruth Wells (1893–1979), arrived at Mondombe in May 1920, joining an effort already shaped by Congolese initiative and leadership.[95] For the next decade, medical care was limited; missionary doctors and nurses from other stations visited Mondombe only periodically to provide treatment as needed. And at such a distant outpost the need was great.

Medical work took on new significance when Dr. Donald Baker (1897–1986) and his wife, Lelia (1903–1979), joined Stober at Mondombe near the end of 1931. While Lelia Baker helped stabilize and develop the station's educational program, Dr. Baker worked closely with Stober to build a comprehensive medical ministry that extended well beyond the mission station itself. Together they oversaw the operation of Shotwell Memorial Hospital, which by the late 1940s had grown into a thirty-eight-bed facility. They also established a network of ten rural dispensaries and trained a large corps of Congolese nurses equipped to treat minor ailments and dispense medications in outlying communities. Emphasizing preventive medicine, they developed programs that addressed public health concerns rather than merely responding to acute illnesses and injuries. The effectiveness of this work earned repeated recognition from the Belgian colonial government.[96]

From the beginning, the professional respect and personal admiration shared between Stober and Dr. Baker was evident; in her correspondence she frequently praised his abilities, particularly his surgical skill. Writing for *World Call*, for example, she recalled a Belgian colonial administrator who remarked, "Well, after seeing him do an operation I wouldn't mind having an appendicitis out here."[97] Except for periods of furlough or temporary

95. Ntange Timothy, "Life in the Mondombe Church," a Lonkundo-language manuscript typed and translated by Hattie Mitchell in DCHS, Manuscript Collection 818, Hattie Mitchell Personal Papers. See also Warren, "New Advance in Africa," 50–51; Pearson, "Mondombe Moons," 36.

96. United, *They Went to Africa*, 70; Stober, "Report from Mondombe," 39. The Baker's daughter offers an account of her parents' long missionary service in Wente, *And We Ate*.

97. Stober, "New Missionaries Keep Busy," 40.

assignment elsewhere, Stober and Baker worked together at Mondombe for nearly twenty-nine years, finally realizing her long-held vision of a station staffed by both a doctor and a nurse.

Stober's second furlough, which began in June 1933, coincided with the bleakest years of the Great Depression and revealed both her practical resolve and her deep loyalty to DCCM. As mission funds dwindled, she volunteered to go off salary to support herself as a private nurse in the US until the UCMS financial situation improved. Her main goal, it seems, was to make sure that doctors were in the field. "Selfishly speaking, I want to get back to work in Africa," she wrote to Cyrus Yocum, "but it would not be right . . . to push myself in when two MDs are waiting sailing orders."[98] During this period she also strengthened her own medical skills, completing additional coursework at University Hospital, her alma mater, even as she traveled extensively to raise awareness and financial support for the mission. When she finally returned to the Congo in November 1934, she did not go empty-handed: she took with her fourteen thousand pounds of baby clothes, surgical dressings, and other essential supplies, tangible evidence of her determination to sustain the medical work at Mondombe despite the economic hardships that threatened it.[99]

During Stober's third term of service, extending through July 1938, she itinerated among six DCCM stations, largely to cover the furloughs of other exhausted missionaries and to compensate for persistent staff shortages caused by the lingering effects of the Great Depression. Just two days after landing at Bolenge, she received word that her father died at the age of 77 from influenza, complicated by his chronic asthma. While her relationship with her father long had been strained, she continued to worry about him and at times wondered whether she should return home permanently to care for him. Missing his funeral because of long delays in communication, she carried this loss throughout the three-and-a-half-year term. Her letters from this period frequently reveal her exhaustion, frustration, and emotional strain.[100] Of course, there also were many bright spots. Grounded in years of close, practical work in the field with Congolese mothers, she

98. Buena Rose Stober to Cyrus Yocum, August 2, 1934, DCHS, Division of Overseas Ministries, Africa, Box 7.

99. Rains, "Station UCMS Broadcasting," 40.

100. In her pre-furlough medical exam in February 1938, a DCCM missionary doctor notes the excessive toll that this term of service had taken on Stober. See Louis Jaggard, "Medical Certificate for Buena Rose Stober," DCHS, Division of Overseas Ministries, Africa, Box 7.

published a hands-on manual in Lonkundo and French in 1936, offering guidance on pregnancy, infant care, and maternal health.[101]

For several years, Stober had been aware of the pressing need for dental care among the Congolese people, fellow missionaries, and Belgian colonial officials in the field.[102] After crossing the Atlantic aboard the SS *Brittanic* and beginning a furlough in July 1938, she apprenticed herself to Dr. Lloyd E. Warder, a dentist in Enid, Oklahoma. She was well ahead of her time, because in the late 1930s, dental care still was widely regarded as a luxury available primarily to the wealthy. Nonetheless, at considerable personal expense, Stober also purchased and shipped a used pneumatic dental chair, a slow-speed drill, and other essential dental supplies from Enid to Mondombe. When she returned to the field in April 1939, she set up a makeshift dental practice, the only one for more than a thousand miles in any direction. In addition to her apprenticeship with Dr. Warder, she completed course work in the school of medicine at University Hospital and worked closely with former DCCM colleague, Dr. Myrtle Lee Smith, then in private practice in Tennessee.[103] In addition to these professional development opportunities, she also kept a busy schedule of speaking engagements, including the 1938 International Convention of the Disciples of Christ in Denver, Colorado.[104]

From April 1939 until her evacuation from the Congo in July 1960—five more terms of service, averaging three-and-a-half years apiece—Mondombe was not merely Stober's assigned station but her beloved home. In addition to assisting Dr. Baker at Shotwell Memorial Hospital, she poured herself into three major projects that expanded the station's reach and impact. Of course, there was her much-appreciated dental practice. She also assumed from Dr. Baker full responsibility for the leper colony at nearby Lomina, where an average of 160 patients lived. The 1940s and 1950s composed a period of profound transition in the treatment of leprosy and she worked very hard to remain up-to-date. She appeared to be most passionate about her work with new mothers and their infant children. She developed a comprehensive program for them, including prenatal care, an

101. Stober, *Mbatela bana ba tosisi*.

102. Stober was especially concerned about the practice among Congolese people of filing their teeth to a sharp point as a rite of passage, an aesthetic enhancement, and a marker of tribal identity. See Stober, "Dental Problems in Congo," 43.

103. Buckner, "Station UCMS Broadcasting," 34.

104. Buckner, "Station UCMS Broadcasting," 30. Sadly, no records of her speaking engagements have survived, including records of what she said. It is reasonable to assume that the content of her addresses included some of the stories included in chapter 5 of this collection.

infant feeding initiative, and weekly wellness clinics. By the mid-1940s, this program served on average about a hundred new mothers and their infants. Over time, the steady rhythm of her work at Mondombe took on the character of a spiritual practice, punctuated only by periodic furloughs, which she used both for rest and further professional development. In a report for *World Call* commemorating the twentieth anniversary of Mondombe as a mission station in 1940, she already could write with the authority and commitment of an eyewitness who had lived and worked through much of its history.[105]

The disruption of World War II prevented her from taking a regular furlough in 1943–44, prompting her, along with several other DCCM missionaries, to travel instead to South Africa. There she completed courses in dentistry at the University of the Witwatersrand in Johannesburg and studied at a state-administered leprosarium. During a later furlough in 1947, she visited the American Leprosy Mission in Carville, Louisiana, where she studied with medical staff and secured ongoing financial support for her work at Lomina.[106] While on furlough, she also strengthened and expanded her network of living link congregations, including First Christian Church in Charleroi, Pennsylvania, and two Oklahoma churches—First Christian Church in Nash and Central Christian Church in Mangum. Stober promoted the work of the DCCM among all four of her living link churches, which frequently responded with much-needed financial support, supplies, and even occasional luxuries.[107] Tabernacle Christian Church in Franklin, Indiana, for example, established an "Ice Box Fund" and eventually shipped to her a modern refrigerator. Characteristically, she redirected the gift from personal use to Shotwell Memorial Hospital, where she and Dr. Baker used it to store temperature-sensitive medications. Travel to and from furloughs became markedly more efficient in the 1940s and 1950s with the advent of commercial airline travel, a luxury she thoroughly enjoyed.

105. Stober, "Mondombe," 26.

106. Founded by seven pastors in New York City in 1906, the American Leprosy Mission opened a national leprosarium in Carville, Louisiana, in 1917. There, specialized medical personnel pioneered innovative treatments for leprosy with great success. Throughout the middle of the twentieth century, the mission funded leprosy treatment centers across the globe. Known since 2025 as Hope Rises International, the organization has expanded its focus to include other diseases that impact public health, especially in developing nations. See Hope Rises International, "History of Hope."

107. Recent scholarship has stressed the role of returning missionaries in humanizing foreign peoples to Americans back home, and in advocating for tolerance and inclusion. Sometimes they did so by assuming policy-making roles in government. See Robert, "Influence," 59–89; Hollinger, *Protestants Abroad*; Hollinger, *Christianity's American Fate*, 45–67.

Even in her later years of missionary work at DCCM, Stober continued to worry about her family in the US, especially her youngest brother, Jim. As his health declined, it became increasingly difficult for him to find steady work and support himself. She frequently asked the UCMS to divert a portion of her meager monthly salary to him as a form of assistance. Her letters reveal the emotional strain that this situation caused her. "Sometimes I've even wondered if I should stay home and help him," she confessed in one heartfelt letter to Cyrus Yocum. "He is such a good man and has tried so hard and was so loyal to dad. He deserves more than I am able to give him at present."[108]

In her last decade with DCCM especially, Stober settled comfortably into the role of veteran missionary, one that brought her immense joy. She delighted in welcoming new personnel to the field, especially in passing on hard-won wisdom learned during her decades of service. In 1956, she added to her legacy by publishing a second book in Lonkundo and French, a practical three-volume guide to hygiene, etiquette, and social graces written especially for Congolese women and young mothers as they navigated family life in a rapidly changing world.[109] There was deep gratitude, too, in seeing her medical work bear new fruit. The wider availability of effective medications, especially antibiotics, made her work with those suffering from leprosy more effective than ever before; in fact, the population at Lomina slowly dwindled to zero just before she retired. These years were also enriched by long-standing friendships with fellow missionaries, especially Hattie Mitchell (1893–1980), Goldie Ruth Wells (1893–1979), and Gertrude Shoemaker (1899–1990), who with her shared the work at Mondombe for many years. They, too, were single women who had devoted their entire lives to missionary work with and to the Congolese people.[110]

Travel remained central to her ministry, made much easier by improved roads, access to automobiles, and even a mission airplane. She spent long stretches visiting backcountry dispensaries, working alongside a large and capable corps of Congolese nurses and medical assistants, many of whom she herself had trained. Her respect for Congolese church leadership deepened as well, particularly for Ntange Timothy, pastor of the Mondombe church, whom she came to regard as her own pastor. This growing esteem found expression in her letters, which frequently included aphorisms and wisdom sayings in Lonkundo. She rejoiced in early efforts to form a

108. Buena Rose Stober to Cyrus Yocum, April 4, 1940, DCHS, Division of Overseas Ministries, Africa, Box 7.

109. Stober, *Bonnes manières*.

110. Wells, *Sila, Son of Congo*.

colony-wide, united Protestant church, the *Église du Christ au Congo,* and welcomed the expanding cooperation among missions, especially in medical work.[111] In these final years, her ministry bore the marks not only of perseverance but of humility, partnership, and hope for a church, schools, and medical facilities increasingly placed in Congolese hands.

At the same time, the growing momentum toward Congolese independence left Stober bewildered. Concentrated mostly in the cities, restive nationalism felt distant from the rhythms of life in the backcountry stations where she spent most of her time. Yet beneath that bewilderment there was anxiety: she feared for the future of the Congolese people—especially the churches—and wondered whether they would be able to withstand the upheaval she believed independence inevitably would bring. These were the mingled hopes and fears that she carried with her into retirement.

Stober left the Congo for the final time in mid-July 1960, just as the violence accompanying independence began to engulf the country. She remained on the UCMS payroll for another year, formally retiring on June 30, 1961. Upon her retirement, UCMS executive Virgil Sly (1901–1978) remarked, "Miss Stober will long be remembered in Congo for her devoted service among the leprosy patients and in maternity work." Noting the versatility of her work, he continued, "She had many outside interests; she was an avid reader and letter writer, as well as a gardener and a naturalist."[112] She soon settled into a tiny home built on the property of her brother Jim in Harrah, Oklahoma. There she gradually reacclimated to life in the US, received occasional visitors, and exchanged letters with friends in the Congo and at home for nearly twelve years. Stober died on March 25, 1972, and a memorial service was held at Nicoma Park Christian Church in Oklahoma City, where she was a member. Her modest, ground-level grave marker reads simply, "Buena Rose Stober, 1897–1972, Missionary to the Congo, 1923–1960," a spare inscription that conceals far more than it reveals about a life deeply given—and, by any measure—a life well lived.

Contribution to the Historiography of Christian Missions

To read Stober's letters is to enter a world at once intimate and unsettling, characterized by devotion, endurance, affection, and contradiction. Written over thirty-seven years of service in the Congo, her correspondence offers far more than a record of missionary activity. It opens a window onto the

111. Buckner, "Health for Congo," 34.

112. Sly, "Seven Missionaries Retire," 29–30.

everyday realities of colonial-era mission life and invites readers to reckon honestly with the moral and cultural complexities of that world.

Even when her letters were intended to be official reports, they were written with intimacy to family, friends, and supporters, often in moments of fatigue or delight, frustration or wonder. Precisely for that reason, they capture the texture of daily life with unusual clarity: the rhythms of teaching and worship, the strains of illness and isolation, the challenges of travel, the slow work of learning local languages and customs, and the deep bonds formed with Congolese colleagues, students, and neighbors. As the letters unfold, the mission stations where Stober served emerge, not as abstract outposts of denominational work, but as lived spaces shaped by relationships, improvisation, and constant negotiation.

Stober's perspective as a woman is central to the value of this collection. Women missionaries frequently bore much of the mission's educational, medical, and pastoral labor, yet their voices were often sidelined in institutional histories. Her letters reveal how gender shaped both opportunity and constraint: how authority was exercised informally, how emotional labor sustained communities, and how women navigated mission hierarchies that rarely granted them formal power. In doing so, they restore a voice long underrepresented in the historical record.[113]

At the same time, Stober's letters reflect the assumptions of the colonial world in which they were written. Subtle racism and cultural chauvinism appear at moments in her descriptions of Congolese people, and their beliefs and practices. Such passages may trouble modern readers, but they are essential to understanding the moral landscape of twentieth-century missions. They show how genuine affection and deep commitment could coexist with unexamined hierarchies of race and culture, and how paternalism often operated alongside sincere love. To publish these letters is not to excuse these attitudes, but to make them visible, open to scrutiny, and subject to historical and ethical judgment.

Read carefully, Stober's correspondence also reveals a long arc of change. During her time of service, the Congo itself was transformed, and so, too, were the missionary assumptions brought from Europe and the US. The letters trace shifts in church life, education, and leadership, as Congolese Christians increasingly assumed responsibility for their own institutions. They also hint—sometimes clearly, sometimes ambiguously—at changes in Stober's own understanding, as experience challenged inherited certainties and colonial rule moved toward its end.

113. The life work of Dana Robert, in particular, has accomplished much in reclaiming the rightful place of women in the historiography of modern Christian missions. See especially her classic *American Women in Mission*.

For historians, theologians, anthropologists, and students of mission and empire, Stober's letters are invaluable primary sources. They offer an external yet intimate view of Congolese communities during the late colonial period, preserving observations that might otherwise be lost. When read alongside Congolese voices, they contribute to a fuller and more balanced account of the past. For churches and mission-sending bodies, they offer an opportunity for moral self-examination, prompting reflection on how faith, power, culture, and good intentions have been entangled—and continue to be so.[114]

Above all, this collection resists simplification. It neither canonizes Stober nor condemns her outright; she is neither the heroic missionary sent to save the Congolese people nor the heartless conspirator with imperial power. Instead, the collection presents her as a human being shaped by her time: devoted, but limited; compassionate but flawed. In preserving that complexity, these letters help us confront the difficult truth that history is rarely tidy, and that love itself, when filtered through unequal structures, can carry unintended harm. To read them is to be invited into an honest encounter with the past, one that challenges, instructs, and still speaks to the present.

114. Scholars are beginning to return with renewed interest to archival sources like Stober's letters as a way of recalibrating mission historiography. See, for example, Wild-Wood, "Interpretations, Problems, and Possibilities," 92–112.

1

1923 to 1929

Buena Rose Stober to Friends, September 7, 1961—Oklahoma City, Oklahoma[1]

Just for looking back thirty-eight years, I'm going to write here of my first trip to Congo, as I just reread it from my diary and carbon copies of letters I've written home. There were six of us to leave from New York, all new missionaries: Mr. and Mrs. Don McGavran and Margaret Conkright for India; for Congo were two school teachers, Miss Newell Trimble and Miss Myrtle Whaley. Miss Conkright and I were nurses.

We sailed for London on September 19, 1923. In New York we had the business of getting our visas for London and Belgium for we three, India for the other three. The McGavrans had their tiny baby along, so we were really seven. After we got our visas and business settled and still had a little time before our boat sailed, we did some sightseeing and took in some movies and plays. None of us had been in New York before, except Don, who was born in India where his parents were missionaries, and also another member of the family before them.

We were a gay bunch of young people bubbling over with energy and anxious to try out our hands as missionaries. Don surprised us with several bits of wisdom that helped us out, but after one play we saw, we were

1. Stober wrote this letter after her retirement while living in Oklahoma City. However, because she describes retrospectively her travel to the Congo in the fall of 1923, her letter has been included here.

coming out of the theater when he saw that the man ahead of us was the general of the play we have just seen. The first thing we knew he had darted out through the crowd to catch up with him and stop him, telling him that there was a bunch of missionaries who wanted to speak to him. He was going on the same subway as we were, and we visited all the way. He was just "chammed," and our trip home took on an English accent. He didn't know there were any young people save those wrapped up in the "almighty dollar" and then [said], "Well I am dashed." He was very much surprised when he asked Myrtle what made her choose missionary work and she replied, "In order to do some good." When we asked why he was an actor, he replied he had been an actor for about fifteen years and if he had another means of making a living he would retire.

Foolish as it was of a bunch of greenhorns, we almost missed our sailing. When we finally got our fifteen suitcases in the taxi and the baby basket pushed in our laps, we were off at 12:00 p.m. to sail at 1:00 p.m. We had to wait for the ferry, and then the driver got lost in Hoboken; but we got there in time for them to put the gangplank back down for us while several stewards grabbed our baggage. The band was playing "The Star-Spangled Banner," and we went through the formalities in a hurry.

We had the usual fog horn, seasickness, happy times on deck, movies every night, etc., and spending our last night on board all four singles piled into an upper berth that had two portholes. But even that was a little skimpy for four single ladies to view arriving in the Thames and going into London about 3:00 a.m. The McGavrans were a little more dignified, and after we pulled in there was nothing to do but go back to our own berth and go to sleep since we could not get off until 7:30 a.m.

In London we saw as much as we could, and in Belgium we studied French and waited for Mr. and Mrs. Learned to go with us to Congo. Our Indian friends went on to India from London.

Our boarding house in Belgium didn't serve much food so we were always hungry and decided to buy some cakes and have tea. When the Learneds came, we usually went to their room for tea, and what a happy, noisy time we had. There was an old duchess boarding there and after hearing our afternoon celebrations said we must have had lots of wine or we couldn't have had that much fun.

December 2, 1923. Congo at last! The two years of Lonkundo we had studied under the Henseys fled as we disembarked and met the Congolese.

Buena Rose Stober to Her Diary, December 5–7, 1923—Matadi, Congo Belge

December 5, 1923. We took a hike up the railroad before breakfast. It was surely beautiful to see the Crystal Mountains in the distance and the deep gorge made by the mighty Congo as it cut its channel to the ocean, the whirlpool and rapids, and hills lighted up by the morning sun. The ocean steamers could not come that far; in fact, it was all they could do to get through the Devil's Cauldron just below the port, which is a great curve in the river. We could see it, too, downriver and the steamer at the port and little wooden hewn-out canoes crossing the river.

The railway, by the way, is narrow gauge, about two feet between rails and the tiny engines looked like toy affairs.

In all that beauty we were truly over-awed and inspired to say, "The heavens declare the glory of God and the firmament showeth his handiwork" (Ps 19:1).

Then we prepared our lunch for the two-day train trip. Bofale, a Bolenge school youth who had come downriver with the Byerlees as they started homeward and remained to take us back, had quite a time to find food; and, of course, Matadi was just as strange to him as it was to us. By that time, we were trying our Lonkundo on him, but not too successfully.

Then we took a very pleasant trip to have tea with Mr. Gordon, a Jamaican Negro, who had done a wonderful piece of missionary work with the natives there. Besides, he has experimented with gardening and animal husbandry until he is full of valuable information. We are to take four goats and twelve chickens from him upriver to our mission. His wife is home on furlough. It rained while we were having tea, a real tropical downpour, so it was nearly 5:30 p.m. before we started home. Since it was such a long walk to the American Baptist Mission where we were staying, Mr. Gordon put us on a big boat, one hewn from a tree. The glow of the sunset against the very steep hills that were the banks of the Congo was most gorgeous. I've never seen anything like it. The sky was a dark purple-gray down to the sunset on the west bank. At first the sunset glow was bright pink which changed to scarlet and then gold as we were rowed by five or six paddlers. Next to the bright sunset was the bright green hillside with a few palm trees scattered over its side and at the foot flowed the deep, deep river turned scarlet. Across the sky floated a few fleecy clouds. Another piece of his mighty handiwork.

December 7, 1923. Our train left at about 6:30 a.m. We were off for Kinshasa.[2]

2. Henry Morton Stanley (1840–1904) founded the city as a trading post in 1881

Buena Rose Stober to Her Diary, December 10, 1923—En Route to Kinshasa

The train from Matadi to Kinshasa was narrow gauge, but not as uncomfortable as we thought it might be; however, on the trip we seemed to go straight up into the Crystal Mountains for miles and miles. We actually broke down four engines. They have the sauciest little whistles, sounds like a child's toy. But to some of the earlier missionaries it must have felt like riding in state the way they had to walk all that way to Léopoldville. We were supposed to spend two days traveling on the train, and we had sent word to the halfway place for some rooms and two meals; but we spent the night on the train, struggling up on hills only to break down and wait for another engine. The train chairs were straight and narrow so that it was impossible to curl up or lie down in them, except Mrs. Learned, who is able to fit into a much smaller place than the rest.

As night came on it became cooler and cooler and even began to rain, so we had to hunt out some wraps. I had my cape, and we did Mrs. Learned up with it as she wasn't well. We used bath towels for shawls but there were not enough out, so I used an old nightie. Miss Trimble had her kimono on top of her clothes; Miss Whaley wore Mr. Learned's white coat; and he had on an extra shirt. The dust and dirt were impossible, so we were not white very long and then when the dark came so did the mosquitos. There were no lights on the train as we were supposed to be in Thysville but the Learneds had a flash and so did I, but of course the batteries did not last all night. We had only brought lunch for four meals and had to make it do for six.

The Africans kept warm because they were so crowded together; in an open car they were piled up three or four deep. Some were even sitting on top of the coach. Even our coach was so crowded with Belgians, Portuguese, French, and English traders, government officials, plantation owners or workers. A good time was had by all?

Each little station where we stopped for water or passengers was crowded with Africans in all stages of dress. Most of the men wore loin cloths, some had shirts, some even European vests, while some were quite up-to-date. The older ones had their tribal marks and we saw many of them with their front teeth filed on each side to make a point, an indicator of cannibalism and a desire to look fierce. Many were smoking cigarettes, copying white men.

---

and called it Léopoldville, its name throughout the colonial period. In her correspondence Stober most often uses the colonial names of places, but here she uses the traditional Congolese name. Kinshasa was recognized as the city's official name following independence in 1966.

We finally reached Kinshasa at 4:00 p.m. the second day and our poor goats and chickens were nearly dead from thirst locked up in the baggage car.

A Mr. Schlotter of the Union Mission Hotel met us with a car and conducted us to the hotel, a nearly finished building. We three singles were put in a room for five. The other beds were occupied by Swedish girls who only knew about as much French as we did.

Buena Rose Stober to Her Diary, December 17–23, 1923—Bolenge, Congo Belge

Monday, December 17. We sailed upriver, nearly missed our boat again trying to hurry a company truck up with our goats and chickens. We sailed on the old *Kigosa*, the largest and swiftest river steamer and said to be a sister steamer of our SS *Oregon*, of the same company. We reached Bolenge December 21 and enjoyed Christmas there.

December 21, 1923. The beach at Bolenge was crowded with a crowd of Christians to meet us, all singing Christian songs in Lonkundo. It was an inspiring and thrilling sight for five new missionaries who had been on the way or in Belgium since September 19. All the Bolenge missionaries were on the beach: the Rosses, Bargers, Boyers, Athertons of Monieka, Edwards, Ruth Musgrave of Lotumbe, and Mr. Watts, supervising building the church at Coquilhatville, I believe. We arrived at 12:15 p.m. and were taken to have lunch with different missionaries. I ate at the Bargers. Mr. Watts and Miss Musgrave were there too.

December 22, 1923. Saturday. We took in the station. Dr. Barger's new hospital is surely inviting. I was assigned to Bolenge but loaned to Lotumbe for a year. It almost made me want to stay. That evening we helped decorate the Christmas tree and lo, it was a shrub that didn't look much like Christmas. Mr. Watts likes jokes, so he was favored with a doll and some women's clothes. A package came that cost $4.00 duty and was only worn-out clothing for the boarding school. It even had a funny old muff and scarf for the tropics, believe it or not.

December 23, 1923. Sunday. A mighty interesting day for we green, new missionaries. The Sunday School had an attendance of around six hundred, and since there wasn't room in the church, the classes were scattered all over the lawn and in the school building and missionary homes. Every teacher vies with the others in talking the loudest and, as Newell said, "All of them won." Coming home from church we met the dearest old lady who had come the six miles across that big Congo River in a tiny canoe. They say she never misses a service, even if she is old and a bit feeble. Before she became a Christian, she was one of a harem; but in spite of temptation, poverty, sickness, and all she has been faithful. Mrs. Edwards had given her a man's old bathrobe several years ago and she wore it each Sunday on the cool trip across the river.

Buena Rose Stober to Her Diary, December 31, 1923—Lotumbe, Congo Belge

Today we started to work in earnest with an African teaching us Lonkundo. My class was from 6:00 a.m. to 7:30 a.m. We ate at the Hobgoods this week. After breakfast I put on my uniform and get to the hospital. Newell goes out in the village after breakfast and has a class of twenty-five or so in arithmetic. After lunch we rest and read until after 2:00 p.m. Newell has her class in Lonkundo while I study. About 5:00 p.m. Miss Alumbaugh and I go to see her patients in the village. We have a pneumonia case with a temperature around 103° or 104°. He won't drink water and they keep moving him from house to house to get away from the evil spirits. His pulse is going bad.

Buena Rose Stober to Her Diary, January 1924—Lotumbe, Congo Belge

January 5, 1924. Nothing special happened, but on January 5 the pneumonia case died. They made him walk to another house last Friday to flee from evil spirits. It was clear across town and he was not strong enough. His people were Christians, but the superstition is so great in their minds they can't get away from it. The wife is left with several children and to think he might have lived if they had believed us.

We had a trip into the forest and took our suppers. We saw the African graveyard and the grave of Ekotia Mboyo. Mrs. Hobgood is named after this Christian they wanted to remember.

By the way, we have received our African names. Newell is Mama Bakando and I am Mama Mputu. Miss Trimble is named after a downriver woman and I was finally named after an upriver woman after the church elders nearly came to blows settling it. The upriver folks said it was their turn and the downriver ones wanted to name me Balinga for one of theirs. I was very proud of the name Mputu because it was the name of a fine Christian woman. Her brother worked as a house helper for several white folks and is a very quiet, earnest Christian who tried to do everything for me. His wife, too, was sweet.

January 6, 1924. Today I am very proud that I gave nine needles right on the point. A new group of patients had just come in. Myrtle's Lonkundo name is Mama Mbela, Mr. Learned is Lofembe, and Mrs. Learned is Mama Niembo.

Buena Rose Stober to Friends and Family, May 3, 1924—Lotumbe, Congo Belge[3]

I have enjoyed your letters so much and I hope you won't forget to write often. Your letters help me keep up courage, a visit with a friend who is interested goes a long way to cheer one up.

I like Congo better all the time, and as far as health is concerned it is a regular health resort if one observes the tropical health rules. I was surprised to find it no hotter than at home. I love the sunsets at Bolenge especially, and as I think I told you the Congo River is about seven miles wide at Bolenge and is full of little islands that one hardly realizes when one reaches the other shore. The colors from the sunset reflect in the river in all its splendor and create my favorite picture. These sunsets, the lovely birds, their morning songs, the variety of flowers and the joy of the work make one forget the other side.

Last Thursday a much-loved woman died in the Inganda part of Bolenge. They wailed most all day long and in the evening Miss Whaley and I walked out to see them. There were about a dozen women in the group and all of them wailing as loudly as they could, which is terrible sound. When we passed, they were repeating over and over and over again, "Our mother is dead! Our mother is dead!" In the early morning, they had paraded the whole length of Bolenge and Inganda, wailing all the while, and the rest of the day they spent walking up and down in front of the dead woman's house. They believe that if they don't take part in these ceremonies the relatives and the dead person's spirit will think they are not sorry or even caused the death. When a woman who is a good gardener dies, all the women of the village will come with a plantain (a cooking banana) and a cutting of the cassava (or tapioca plant), and after they have paraded from one end of the village to the other they will plant these and other seeds in front of the dead woman's house so they will have good gardens as she had.

3. Though the return address on this letter is Lotumbe, in a later hand-written addition Stober notes that she actually wrote it "from Bolenge where I was trying to learn a bit with Dr. Barger. The Hurts were also there for the birthday of Virginia Ann."

We stopped at Nyang'ocinda's house that evening as we passed and tried to find out what she thought of all the above. She is one of our most consecrated Bible women and she said if they had been truly Christian, they would have gone with their sorrows and sat down quietly and talked with Jesus about until they felt comforted. They had been taught and taught, she said.

You should see the new tractor in its work. They have been needing a tractor at Bolenge for some time but did not have the money to buy one. At last, [the] Bolenge folks decided to pool their money from their own pockets. There is such a lot of work that must be done by manpower as we have no horses or cows or cars. They do not live here successfully in this sleeping sickness area, and for the cars no repair garage or decent roads. Men have had to carry trees from the forest on their backs for all our brick buildings, not to mention bricks to and from the kiln for all our buildings; at present Bolenge is in the process of building hospital wards, a guest house, and sawmill, and light plant buildings. Besides those loads, there is gardening that must be done by hoe, which won't dig deep enough for crops like corn. With a hoe, African food shortages will never be solved and Africans with hungry bodies are not very capable of thinking on greater things, neither are bodies straining under these heavy loads. They were disappointed when it couldn't carry all their loads when they gathered around. The next morning after it came one asked Njoji Mark if he had seen it and he replied, "No, but they tell me it doesn't succeed."

I suppose you have seen the picture of Njoji Mark in the *World Call*.[4] He is such a fine fellow and can tell the finer meaning of the words in the New Testament and the whole Bible in a way no white person can do because he knows how his people think and how they explain their thoughts. Miss Whaley and I passed their house, too, on an evening stroll. They have a four-room house of mud and pole walls with a palm-leaf (a certain kind of palm) roofing. It is neatly finished with whitewash and paint, and you feel like you are entering a nice home in the States. Amba, his wife, keeps it nice. The parlor is not elaborate, but it is neat and well arranged. Mark speaks English fairly well after his trip to the USA, but Amba only understands Lonkundo. Some time ago the *World Call* had an article about how Mark turned down the inheritance of his father's wives and property. His father had been a wealthy witch doctor and Njoji, being the eldest, he also gave up the chieftainship of a large district for our Master's work.

4. Published between 1919 and 1973, *World Call* was the monthly publication of the UCMS of the International Convention of the Christian Churches (Disciples of Christ). Stober is probably referring to the photograph of Njoji Mark and his family appearing on the inside cover of the March 1924 issue.

The Nyang'ocinda mentioned before is a faithful worker with the women. Nyango means "mother," and Bocinda is the name of a girl she raised. She spent hours and hours of her own time going up and down the river visiting in this house or that, talking to this woman or that or to groups. She has been a real soul winner and worked without pay for years. Recently she had been paid by the mission to talk with people who come to the hospital and to make visits in and around Bolenge.

One time, several years ago, a young woman died when her baby girl was born and the husband, being a heathen, followed the custom to bury the living infant with its mother since ordinarily there was no other source of milk or none that didn't have an evil spirit, so he thought. Nyang'ocinda heard about it and asked that she be given the infant to raise on canned milk. There was an argument, but she won and began buying milk for it.[5] As soon as she was large enough, the little girl entered the girls' dormitory, but she never forgets her foster mother. She is ten years old now. Her father comes back every so often to claim her, but they do not let her go and she does not want to go at all. He told the mission once that he would report them to the state, and they begged him to do it as they really considered reporting him themselves. So, he no longer pushes the matter. Perhaps someday he, too, will become a Christian, and will try to make her care for him as she does for Nyang'ocinda.

I wish you could know Captain Jean of the *Oregon* as he, too, is a character about whom you could really write a book. He had been captured as a child by a man on a steamer and was taken many miles from home. Later, he found his way into an English mission school and later came to work at Bolenge on the *Oregon*, our mission river steamer of three cabins. He became captain, and one day as the steamer pulled into Lotumbe a woman on the beach let up a cry of joy. She recognized the tribal marks of her son stolen so long ago. One day he came into the mission office with a very ashamed look on his face. He said, "I lied today." They asked him what about and he told this story. Some big company at Coquilhatville called him in unexpectedly and offered him three times as much as he received from the mission if he would be captain of their boat. He didn't want to give away the fact that the mission was giving him so little, so he lied to them. He could get work at most any big company, but he doesn't wish to leave the mission as he considers himself a minister to the workmen on the steamer and to

5. Stober later added the following hand-written note on her copy of this letter: "Coquilhatville was beginning to have a few things like that for sale but it was a really big task for an African woman who hasn't any husband or any means of making money other than her garden, but she succeeded with very little help from anyone. The father furnished the milk for only a short time."

the villagers wherever he stops. He has more truly a missionary spirit and a great desire to win his people to Christ than any African minister I have heard. He has a tremendous influence on Africans, and we white folks go to him for help in many problems and usually find a quiet, dignified, Christian solution. He never neglects his evening service for the villagers wherever he stops. He is considered one of the best, most capable captains on the river, as he can get the steamer through most any difficult situation.

Buena Rose Stober to Friends and Family, June 16, 1924—Lotumbe, Congo Belge

I hardly know where to begin this letter, but since influenza has arrived in Lotumbe it makes a good start for a doctorless hospital's news. All the white folks here and in Bolenge have been caught in its snares, but so far although they are pretty sick nothing serious has happened to either whites or Africans. Nevertheless, it has kept us busy; besides, there has been a chicken-pox epidemic and some small-pox cases.

The Africans are very afraid of small-pox and in the early morning no boats leave the beach until the fog is off the river as they think it carries small-pox. Captain Jean always ties up at whatever beach he finds himself with the *Oregon* until the fog lifts. It is so hard to make patients understand that the disease is contagious as long as there are open pox and when I insist on their staying in quarantine, they don't like it and run off scattering disease as they go. We lost one of our schoolboys two weeks ago.

Yesterday a young man came to the house carrying his infant son. I supposed the baby to be sick as he was crying. The father looked so desperate and said, "Oh Mama what will I do for my baby? My wife has the sickness now," then I knew he meant small-pox because it is a curse. I talked with him and arranged to give the infant bottles of milk until his mother recovered. We sent the mother to the pest house and the father comes after the bottles. The infant is husky and always gives me a smile for the bottle.

Tsa ifotekya loolo, an African proverb: "Heat can soften iron." The fire of the Christians of Congo can soften the hardness and darkness of the land.

We have had to close all public meetings; however, on Saturday night we had the baptismal service for all the converts brought in by the evangelists from their forest villages. There were ninety-seven. Because of the small-pox epidemic only part of the total came, they say, there would have been nearly two hundred. Beside the Hobgoods made a trip upriver and baptized quite a number. On our trip from Bolenge we stopped about a day below here on the river and baptized new converts, about sixty-five. This was my first experience helping baptize. It was very inspiring to see them so eagerly seeking truth. We held communion service afterward so that they could start back before they were exposed to small-pox. The communion service means so much to the Africans as it should to all of us.

Buena Rose Stober to Friends, January 24, 1925—Monieka, Congo Belge

If I get you all written to anytime soon, I guess it will be by carbon copies mostly, so please excuse me and perhaps I can do better next time.

In spite of my desire to get settled in Bolenge, I am having a good time here in Monieka. We are expecting Miss Williams back on the *Illinois* about Thursday, but it all depends upon her health condition. We are hoping for the best but do not want her to start to work again before she is strong enough, for the medical work here is very heavy.

I have been interested in the Monieka schools, which are noted as being the best on the mission. Today they finished their six weeks Bible institute for the backcountry evangelists and out station teachers. The teachers are also given instruction in teaching. During this time, they have only had regular school in the afternoon, so I have not tried to get the run of it but even at that they have about one hundred women and over one hundred men and children. The most interesting part of their schools is three nearby out-station schools, personally supervised by Miss Bateman. It gives you an idea of what all the out-station schools are like. There is one at Longa, three miles from here; one at Bongali, six miles; and one at Wenga, four miles.

Imagine yourself as a teacher of one of these places and remember you are only a fourth or fifth grader who attends school in the morning and then at high noon starts on foot to one of these villages, Longa. You have no more than gotten out of Monieka than you find yourself faced by a swamp that has to be waded, and because of the heavy traffic the water is not what you would call clean. Probably not an hour before, a yaws patient with hundreds of running sores on his legs or an advanced case of leprosy has forded the swamp which is stagnant and doesn't give you a very pleasant thought. Since you are pretending you were a brown boy of fifteen or sixteen years and have lived around such things all your life, you won't think much about it. After you have crossed over three of these muddy pools and walked over roots that coil up at you like great snakes, you come to the real swamp which is over-your-head deep and although it is running water it is still full of leaves and mud. But here the chieftain of Longa has had a pole and reed bridge built. It consists of a row or two of forked poles forced into the mud under the water; across these four poles are laid great slabs of trees bound together with reeds. Sometimes you will find your bridge covered with water and you have to wade after all. Now you are across and have forgotten that the bridge was not too substantial, because you are too busy getting over more roots and muddy places. The path itself is so much of the snake's trail that it keeps you busy even though you have been over that same path every day for school.

At last, you cross a clearing where a company used to be and then you pass another. Then some more roots and last enter Longa. The children began running to meet you saying, "The teacher has come," only shouting instead of just stating.

When Martha Bateman and I went to visit the school, we asked them could we get to Longa by bicycle and they said, "No," the road was too bad, and it was high water, but they always underestimate our ability to travel their paths, but we went by bikes and it took us and hour and a half. When we walked it later, we made it in forty-five minutes.

But to continue our visit: suppose you were teaching in Wenga, and traveled four miles over a fairly good road with pole-reed bridges to cross the swamps without wading and were anticipating a good school, but when you got there you found that most of your pupils were more interested in making money than in school and most of the children had gone to a rubber plantation to carry in the big bushels of white milky looking sap from the rubber trees at Busira, a nearby town. Or suppose you had gone six miles up and down hills to Bongala, over a well-worked path through a beautiful forest, passing through three little towns and inviting the children to come to school with you. At last, you walk up the clean street of real Bongala where the industrious young chief lives, who keeps the paths clean and furthermore is responsible for the good market brought by his villagers to Monieka for the out-of-town students and workmen to buy every Monday morning.

Then you reach the chief's house, across the street from which there is a long row of mud houses, one for each of his wives. In the middle of the street and under two big trees is your outdoor school. You do not have benches for your pupils to sit on but under one of the trees is a log on which pupils will sit while reciting to you. Your school numbers sixty children, besides a group of curious or interested relatives standing around as they have nothing to do at the moment. You call them together, have a song and prayer, and then start instruction. All the beginners, those learning A and O will stay while you explain them (nearly every day you will have one or more new pupils, so you always have that class). The MA and MO classes and the LA, LE, LO class will write until you are ready to examine their knowledge and give them more work. But you never can guess what they write on! Out under a shady, sandy spot and each boy or girl makes a dive for the place he likes best and with a stick marks off on the sand his slate and no one is supposed to trespass. He writes with his fingers in the sand his A's, O's, MO's, MA's, etc. Some of the advanced classes sit with a book or a slate, a real one, working arithmetic. You will remember that the only equipment for your school is a blackboard about a yard square; a chart showing syllables, letters, and words; two primers; a piece or so of chalk; five to seven slates and pencils. Now if you can keep sixty children busy for an hour you are a good out station teacher, provided that they have made progress by the time Miss Bateman visits again.

Buena Rose Stober to Her Diary, June 15, 1925—Bolenge, Congo Belge

A most interesting happening has come to Bolenge since I wrote last. Prince Leopold, crown prince of Belgium, made us a visit last Wednesday.[6] Mrs. Byerlee and Mrs. Hensey spent the last three weeks teaching the school and singers the National Anthem in French and the rest of us superintended the cleaning of the station, paths, and the beach for he was to come to us by boat.

The day was just cloudy enough to make it very pleasant. Nobody worked before 8:00 a.m. when he arrived, except the decorating force and the hospital boys who have to have things ready, such as fires, in order to show His Majesty their work in full swing. At 8:00 a.m. the whistle blew announcing the steamer's arrival, the church bell rang, and everyone hurried to the beach. I can't imagine a prettier sight in Congo than what the prince must have seen from the steamer deck as he watched them pull into the beach. There are the big newly painted white stones that announce to the seven-mile-across river passengers, whoever they are, that this is Bolenge. As his steamer drew in close, he could see the singers lined up along the green grass bordering the path up the beach, then the girls of the dormitory, twenty-six in number, dressed in their costumes of bright orange and black trim with a spray of flowers worked in the front. How proud they were of

6. Named after his infamous grandfather, Prince Leopold (1901–1983) was the twenty-four-year-old *Duc de Brabant* when he made this study trip to the Congo. An amateur anthropologist and photographer, he was keenly interested in the Congolese people and their customs. Reports of the visit circulated widely in Belgium and depicted the prince as passionately interested in the well-being of the Congolese. Prince Leopold ascended to the throne upon the death of his father, King Albert I (1875–1934), and reigned as King Leopold III until he abdicated the throne in 1951.

these dresses, and they really had a right to be as they looked like a lovely bouquet of orange-colored blossoms. Next in line came our eighty-three dormitory boys all dressed in khaki and trying their best to look like real soldiers. At the top of the hill stood the last two, each proudly holding the Belgian flag. Back of them stood a big arch decorated with palm fronds and Belgian flags. The missionaries stood back of this arch and behind us was all the workers of the mission and many people of Bolenge village. Across from two palm trees a great flag was suspended, and we all wished the upriver station folks could have been there.

As the steamer pulled in at last everyone sang, *Le Roi, le Loi, la Liberte*, "The King, the Law, the Freedom, etc." All the white men went down the hill to greet the prince as he disembarked. As His Highness reached the line-up of boys, two elders who had been old soldiers led the boys in a salute and shouted, *Vive le Roi, Vive le Prince Leopold, Vive le Congo Belge*, through which the prince walked quietly up the hill as if nothing had happened while the little boys who made the noise were so excited they could hardly yell.

When he reached the top of the hill, he was introduced to each of us and somehow you didn't feel like you were meeting a worldly prince but a princely man. He was very tall and slender and was crowned with a head of curly auburn hair instead of a diamond-studded crown as the missionaries thought surely he would wear. He was only given one hour at Bolenge so there was no time to tarry but was immediately conducted past a new house being built and also passed our house, to the printing press.

In the meantime, the hospital boys and I rushed out to have things going before he arrived. It was a good three blocks to the hospital, so we had time to calm our nerves. When he arrived, I was going to be backward and let Mr. Hensey do the talking but somehow I never had a chance as the prince walked beside me and asked so many questions that I simply forgot he was a prince and answered as I showed the different departments of a dispensary hospital without an MD. He spoke English much better than I spoke French, so we used English. He wondered if I didn't get lonely and if I wasn't rather young for such a job. He seemed pleased to see how we did the work which of course made us glad.

From the hospital he went to the girls' school and women's school and found them all working on new dresses. Then he visited boys' and men's school and saw our future Congo Belge on its way. Then a tour of the workmen's housing, boys' dorm, saw mill, and carpenter shop brought him back close to the Hensey's home where his father had tea some years before.[7] We

7. Prince Albert visited the Congo in early 1909, just a few months after the Belgian

served tea and coffee and presented him with an ivory tusk carved with *Congo Belge* on either side of the Belgian flag inlaid in the ivory in colored woods of Congo: red wood, ebony, and the yellow wood that makes such lovely furniture. The other side of the tusk was carved *Mission de Bolenge*. It was polished up beautifully and was unique enough that he seemed very proud of it, and later a company that is just below us on the river told that he took the whole Gillespie force on board the ship to show them his tusk from Bolenge.[8] Mr. Edwards had been teaching some Africans to carve beautiful articles from the ivory tusks.

Mrs. Smith, wife of the assistant manager of Gillespie Company, told us a lot of interesting things about the prince's visit there. They had not been notified that he would visit them so of course it was a surprise. Mr. Smith (they are Americans) walked ahead of the prince, showing him their store of copal (a resin from a Congo swamp tree sold for us in varnish). The aide-de-camp took the first chance possible to whisper that Mr. Smith should let royalty walk ahead. She said he told the aide he would do as he pleased; but to tell the facts he probably dropped meekly behind a few paces. Mr. Smith is a writer and his only interest in Africa is to get material while he works. Although their ideals are not as high as they might be, we like them very much and enjoy them being here. She invited the prince and his followers into her house to have a drink and when they started to seat themselves, Mr. Smith almost sat on the helmet of His Highness who reached quickly for the endangered article and considered it a good joke. She brought out a tin of cookies to serve with the drink and proceeded to open it in the parlor. But the prince would not allow the lady to open the tin herself and gallantly reached for it. She meekly surrendered the tiny knife to him, which the cookie company provided as an opener for cookies sealed for the tropics, and he opened her tin. I wonder how many funny things happened on the mission that we didn't see. Poor aide-de-camp must have been badly shocked a time or two.

Mr. Hensey provided several breaks to get folks to relax: at the hospital when we opened the storeroom for medicine, he swung the door open, exposing a full-sized skeleton Dr. Barger had ordered out from the States

---

Parliament had wrested control of the Congo Free State from his father, King Leopold II. Reportedly the aim of his visit was to investigate the claims of human rights violations in order to develop a program of reform. When King Leopold died later that year, the Prince ascended to the throne as King Albert I.

8. Established in Kinshasa in 1918, the New Jersey-based company L. C. Gillespie and Sons was an exporter of natural resources from Congo, especially copal and other tropical resins. Later the company served as the agents of the Ford Motor Company and the Bull Line, a US shipping company. Gillespie and Sons went bankrupt on the eve of the Great Depression.

for educational purposes. Mr. Hensey announced, "This is Miss Stober's friend." At the tea the coffee pot was empty, and Mrs. Hensey whispered out in typical Congo style, "Boy, Kawa." Of course, everybody laughed and enjoyed it even if Mrs. Hensey was embarrassed. They say at Léopoldville the prince slipped away from his aide-de-camp and had a lovely visit with the Africans in the village.

The prince has come and gone, and we are all enjoying things back to normal again. I can imagine that the upriver station folks would enjoy a few of the excitements that we have at Bolenge.

Buena Rose Stober to Her Diary, Late 1925—Bolenge, Congo Belge

There is little need of establishing the necessity of baby welfare work when we see the way infants have such poor care and the high infant mortality rate among them in their first year of life. Medical reports show infant mortality in this part of Congo from 50 to 75 percent.

When we watch naked infants fighting pneumonia, malaria, influenza, or all three diseases at once, when we see them die with untreated venereal diseases contracted from parents that do not understand, when they are kept underweight by poorly prepared, unclean foods, or their little bodies are covered with horrid suppurating sores all over, and the thousands of witchcraft devices practiced on them, one needs not to argue that something ought to and must be done to help them and teach the parents to save as many as possible. Then, too, the old saying that you can win your way into the heart of the parents through the child always holds true. If Christianity is to have a future in Africa, we must save the babies and teach the parents how to care for them.

We hope to reach the babies and mothers every week to have the infants weighed, examined, and treated if they are not up to standard, to give the mothers talks and practical demonstrations of how to give proper care and safeguard their little ones in health and sickness. We hope not only to reach them at the clinic, but to get out into their homes and study the conditions of their home life. It is also hoped that more work might be done in the way of teaching expectant mothers how to care for themselves and to prepare for the coming of their little ones. We would like to have someone on each station carry out this work . . .

Here in Bolenge in the middle of March one of the hospital boys and I made house-to-house calls on all the mothers who had little children in Bolenge, Inganda, and our workmen's houses and told them of our plans and got their promises to bring their children. Mrs. Davies of the mission at Kinshasa and Miss Williams gave us many plans and ideas that had worked elsewhere, and we fashioned our program with their help. This is our plan: each child has a health card, on which its health record is kept. The Inganda and workmen's children come on Tuesday at 2:00 p.m. and the Bolenge children on Friday. They are weighed, examined, measured, and treated. All treatments are given free, including neosalvarsan. The parents are given teachings.

The first day we called them, we had over one hundred children from one month to twelve years, but after it was explained that it was only the little ones at least under six years we wanted, the number decreased after a few weeks. I have not been able to keep up my visits to the homes but am still hoping to do so. By these weekly checkups and treatments, we have been able to avoid some serious illnesses. Some of the mothers have been very regular and the children think it is a great sport; but some mothers think it too much trouble and send their infants with older children. Some shirts Mrs. Davies recommended that I ask the church women in the USA to send me came, along with a bunch of little caps, so we gave every child who came six times a shirt or cap. The average is still only twenty a week but I'm sure it will grow as our results show its worth.

At Mrs. Hensey's suggestion and invitation, the Belgian state doctor and Dr. Rhodain, who is inspecting hospitals in Congo, came to visit the clinic and afterward sent a few supplies.[9] We are to report regularly to the society in Belgium and they will send us more supplies.

As to the problems of the work, we must first gain the interest of the parents who do not realize that they can save their infants from the thousands of ailments by proper care, and it may prove necessary to give material gifts such as clothes from time to time.

Buena Rose Stober to Unidentified, April 4, 1926—Bolenge, Congo Belge

Having just finished my regular morning tasks of tying bows of the belts of several of the dormitory girls I thought I would take this minute left before church to start your letter. One day the girls found that if they rushed up before Sunday School and asked, I would help them get their belts pretty.

9. Despite her misspelling of his name, Stober is referring to Dr. Jérôme Rodhain (1876–1956), the leading Belgian parasitologist and chief medical officer for the Belgian Congo in the 1920s.

Our kind of bows are difficult for them to learn, and they look so unkempt with ties stringing down every which way.

This is Easter morning and what a lovely sunny morning it is. There will be no new hats to cause jealousy and mar the day. Even if it rains it will only cool things off and be welcome. The cement and brick platform in the back of the church for the pulpit is finished. The whole church had a brick floor in it before and really resembled a barn, but it is much nicer and more like a church now. Africans and whites can't get over talking about how nice it looks. Of course, they see the big Catholic church at Coquilhatville and think it is so wonderful as it is so much larger than ours. It cost us around $1,000.00 and was a gift. We plan on fixing stained glass windows in the back of the pulpit, fixing the ceiling, and re-whitewashing it. That will help a lot but even then, we will have no new seats; the old ones are wooden and so was the pulpit furniture. But no wooden thing without paint or varnish lasts very long against dry rot, wood bores, and termites, and the only wood painted in the church are the pulpit furniture, and it hasn't much to its credit except age. Creosote is used for all wood in the beginning usually, but it loses its effect after a while. At any rate, we are happy for the improvement we have made and perhaps sometime something more can be done. Here I started to tell about the plans for Easter services and they have already happened.

The school girls decorated a large wooden cross with a dainty bluish green vining fern that is found all along the roads and used here and there in the [one word is illegible], a small white flower that resembles a lily of the valley a little and this was put in front of the church. There were several baskets of other flowers and Congo has a lot of them. The choir sang, "Christ is Risen," and Mr. Edwards preached a wonderful sermon. It was a beautiful and inspiring service. I wish you could have heard Mrs. Byerlee's fine choir of boys of twelve to twenty in age. She has a beautiful voice and knows how to get the most out of African voices . . .

We are having quite a siege of epidemic measles, whooping cough, mumps, and chicken pox. I have one little fellow about two years old with whooping cough as it is a killer of infants out here. Combine it with malaria and convulsions from high fever and you have something formidable to fight.

I had two men in smallpox quarantine and one of them had never tasted orange juice, so when I offered it to him, he refused it. The other fellow drank his and other liquid foods and of course was dismissed sooner. Then the old fellow decided he would take his orange juice and get out also. I couldn't imagine what had brought about the change, but one of the hospital boys told me the first man had been telling the old fellow that orange juice was not good for very sick patients. There are tricks in all trades it seems, and self-appointed medicine men do not help.

Later I went over to ask Mrs. Ross if I might go with her, and she chaperoned the boarding school girls to the afternoon church services in the village. There are twelve girls and instead of going with us she asked me to chaperone. So, with twelve noisy, giggling girls off to the services we went. Goodness how do matrons manage fifty girls! One surely has to keep one's eyes open, and even then, I'm sure one sees only a part of what goes on. They are a fine bunch of girls anyway even if I don't believe I would have the energy or brains enough to care for them.

Buena Rose Stober to Friends, June 5, 1926—Bolenge, Congo Belge

I have been trying for two weeks to get this letter started and now that I have started, I wonder if I'll ever get it done. There have been so many interesting things happening that I am peeved at myself for not getting it off.

Bolenge is so pretty and such a nice place to live. Miss Whaley and I enjoy our screened porch since the Boyers moved out of the other half to a house for themselves. We can see a wide, lovely stretch of the mighty Congo from our dining table on said porch. The Boyers used it before. It is about a mile and a half to the first island, which from the porch looks like the other shore; but it is only one of several swampy islands between this beach and the other shore. It is a changing scene with each morning sunrise or at evening with the parrots flying across to their island homes and other birds keeping up the beautiful chorus at all times. It is most terrible to be caught on the river in a storm; even sizable steamers like the *Oregon* have a very bad time and many people are lost in their canoes.

We have had a series of fashionable weddings in the church, a bit of civilization and pageantry they love. Njoji Mark's oldest daughter was married a few weeks ago to the young man who brought we five young new missionaries to Bolenge from Matadi. He got rid of all the harem his father willed to him. Somehow it came back to his first love, Sala Bomongo. His name is Bofale Anoke. They had a best man, bridesmaids, flower girls, rings and all the nice things that go with a nice wedding at home but of course not so elaborate and expensive.

One of my young nurses is soon to be married to one of the girls of the girls' school. He is so happy I can't get much out of him anymore. They are from up in the Ubangi and have no relatives here except for a few students from their tribe. He has been saving his money to buy her wedding clothes and things for their home, which is unusual for an African as they usually do not plan ahead. If they make as nice a married couple as they are individuals, they will be a good Christian example for the community . . .

Last Monday was a holiday and so we went on an all-day trip to the botanical gardens of Eala, about seven or eight miles from Bolenge to Coquilhatville to Eala and onto the Catholic mission at Bamania where there is a sister who does dental work and many of our older missionaries know her and love her. She doesn't know French so our only means of conversation with her is Lonkundo and does that ever seem queer to talk to a white person in Lonkundo. The Catholics have a big work at Coquilhatville and at Eala also.[10] It is about as far on the other side of Coquilhatville as Bolenge is on this side. We have work in Coquilhatville too. The population is around twenty-five thousand people in Coquilhatville alone, not counting all the little villages on both sides, up and down the river from Coquilhatville. Even with a big Catholic work in two places and our two places, it is hard to realize how many Africans within reach of Bolenge are still not changed. We have ten missionaries, and they have fourteen sisters and ten priests and brothers.

We also went through the soldiers' barracks and saw their housing and families. It makes one sick to see what civilization is bringing and how slow we are. There are three hundred whites in government and commercial positions and some of them are bringing more harm than good to Africa. Civilization simply must come from Christians who really believe in Jesus Christ and his command to "Go ye," instead of asking, "Am I my brother's keeper."

Buena Rose Stober to Her Diary, July 1926—Bolenge, Congo Belge

Mr. Edwards, Miss Whaley, and I made the trip from Bolenge upriver to Longa on the little steamer, *Missouri*. We waited at Longa the three days to watch Mr. Edwards care for an in-gathering of evangelists, Christians, and inquirers from the villages back of Longa. Inquirers were inquired to see if they were in earnest seeking Christ or another charm; they took offerings, paid the evangelists, and baptized sixty-five converts. We were able to

10. The Trappists began mission work in the Tshuapa region, headquartered at Bamania, in 1895. They focused primarily on conversion, catechesis, and church-building. However, in 1926 the Missionaries of the Sacred Heart took over the work. These zealous nuns, with the help of the Brothers of the Christian Schools, greatly expanded the medical and educational work of the mission.

help only in little ways. Most of those baptized were young people eager to understand Christ's message.

Longa is a very beautiful ex-station with staunch Christians who support their own work. It makes one feel sad to see the house where the Eldreds lived, but when you think of how well the Longa people are carrying on the work and how easy it is for Bolenge to look in on that work, it seems that we saved the money that would have been spent in upkeep as a permanent station and spent it on the fields that could not be reached so easily. Mr. Edwards was to go from Longa to care for the Mongo and Ngombe districts across the river, and we were to go back to Longa visiting churches until we arrived back at Bolenge field.

While we were at Longa our troubles began and never stopped until we reached Bolenge. The old teacher who had been assigned to go with us all the way had been fighting a cold for a week and unfortunately had not considered it bad enough to let me know, so he came down with pneumonia; and then one of the hospital boys who was to go with Mr. Edwards broke out with measles, so when Monday morning came we were not sure whether we were ever going to leave Longa. Finally, we decided to leave one hospital boy to care for the two sick folks, having asked the Longa evangelist to go with us on the trip, we were off.

We seemed more like an army with twenty carriers for books, medicines, kitchen utensils, bedding, and food; two girls for the dormitory in the future and two old ones to draw more, besides evangelists, wives, new converts, and Christians who had been at the in-gathering, the *ekitelo*, at Longa, and the medicine boys. Imagine, if you can, this procession taking two white women on foot, dressed in khaki. Because we wore skirts and walked, we were mistaken for Catholic fathers. We were greeted all along the way by good Catholics dropping on one knee and saying, "Bonjour Tata!," "Good day, Father!" In one part we were the only white women they had ever seen except Mrs. Boyer who went through last year, but we didn't even have nice long hair we could let down and show that we were white women.

Buena Rose Stober to Dr. G. J. P. Barger and Family, August 9, 1926—Bolenge, Congo Belge

This is a combination of gossipy letter and business, so please excuse me if I put it all together to save time and write the whole family.

Wenona, Ben, Urma, and Rex are so lonely without you here at Bolenge. We have only three white children on the station now, so you just hurry along out here to help out. We play like Happy our dog and Simple, the Hensey's cat, are children, but lots of times they do not act like nice children especially when they are fighting. You know Dora, my dog, died last fall and Happy is her son. He looks like Dora except that he isn't as large as most collies.

Betty and Roger and mother come to the hospital every week on Friday to be weighed but Rachel gets weighed at the mill on the other kind of scale.

We all feel so badly about Billy Learned's death we can hardly write about it. He was such a lively little fellow and it came so suddenly. The doctor at Coquilhatville pronounced it cerebrospinal meningitis from malaria.

Most of the white folks are keeping well now. Betty has a cold. Among the Africans there isn't so much sickness either but among the schoolboys there is almost an epidemic of tropical ulcers on legs, feet, and toes, but it is letting up a little.

A number of English missionaries, Mr. Wilkenson, Mr. and Mrs. Speed, and Miss Thompson, a nurse, stayed with Myrtle and me. They are having their steamer gone over at Wenji, and incidentally Miss Thompson had come with the bride-to-be and the Speeds were married in our church, Mr. Hensey conducting the service. Myrtle and I and Miss Thompson decorated the church. Incidentally, too, Mr. Hensey forgot when he read the vows and started out in Lonkundo. It didn't matter of course because their mission speaks Lomongo which is almost like Lonkundo. He corrected himself and went on in English.

The hospital force is nearly all grown into men now. Bongengu and Nkembo have both been married recently to very nice girls, who were in the dormitory for five or six months. Wanjola and Bongengu seem to be getting along fine except that she has been sick with malaria and refuses to take the quinine and then blames us for neglecting her. Friday she took a notion to get native medicine so slipped away in the night. Wanjola, the head nurse, was so blue when he found out for sure; but after consulting with Mrs. Ross, we decided he had better go after her as we were fairly sure it was malaria for fear her fever would go up again. She is about well now but so mad at us she will hardly speak. Mbula has a girl in the girls' dorm also, but she hasn't yet received baptism. He seems to be trying to live straight now. Yo and Myengen are still sweethearts but still quarreling as often as ever. Buketela has a new baby girl and has now gone home to settle the dowry and bring Mboyo and the baby back to Bolenge.

Wanjola is taking a course in French in Coquilhatville given for workmen, etc., after 5:00 p.m. He rides the nine kilometers if his bike is working and if not, he walks. He is mighty determined to read French in order to read the French books about medicine. We are treating all workmen at noon and Wanjola works at that time and then gets off in the afternoon at 2:00 p.m.; another nurse helps him. Bulamba is a faithful old soul and about as lonely as any African I ever saw. He has some intestinal parasites and an inguinal hernia. He spends most of his hours off from the hospital gardening and selling his produce to white folks at Coquilhatville.

Yendaola is making a good nurse and one of the best for the night work, willing to do anything. The other younger boys you left, Manjei and Nsambela, are making good too and we have taken on four other boys and an older woman, Iyombe, who belongs to Mboloko's harem but left him. She works in the fermentation department and with the women. She is a very quiet woman. All the older ones except Iyombe give intravenous injections and have had at least two months in the laboratory, except Balamba. As you might expect Bongongu is especially good at the microscope, and all the others found at least one or two trypanosomes of sleeping sickness.

Some time ago Longa asked about a medicine boy if they pay the bill. The station took it into consideration and decided you would approve such a move, so we left a half promise with them. Last month they sent down five hundred francs in a canoe, so we had to produce the boy. We had wanted to send Mbula, but since Loene's wife was there we could not very well send him; so Nkombo was the next in line, so we sent him. Yo doesn't have a wife and Bongongu just married.

In regard to available funds for the diathermy and other electrical equipment: most of all the stations have a large deficit now, especially Bolenge. Our appropriation for Bolenge medical was only $1,200.00, which barely includes the expenses, and this enclosed order. Bolenge has had to make so many raises in salaries that she is about to go broke. However, we ask for $2,000.00 on the survey and might get it later for electrical equipment. I hope that would include x-ray. Surely, we can get money from somewhere for treatments so helpful.

There was no pump sent from Kinshasa and the present pump is no good; however, Mr. Edwards took home some washers and was to try to find some new ones for this pump and that seems to be the main trouble. Even the tripod that was the big pest fell in one day; we were in desperate straits for water while they dug the well deeper and put up an angle-iron tripod.

I hope I'm breaking the news gently but there really isn't any gentle to it, only I hope you will feel that everyone has done the best they could under the circumstances. You probably will find lots of things I've done that will make you discouraged but I'm not making excuses. I'll confess I've thought "what is the use" several times.

There has been practically nothing done to the building since you left. The flue back of the fomentation tank is caving in but the masons have been too busy to fix it. The flue under the beds in that one ward is caving in also in two different places. We have used those two unfinished wards for cases needing constant treatment. The chimney in the fomentation room never did draw right although several white men have tried to fix it. We have used it all the time anyway. They finished putting the roof on the guest house. They are now screening the windows of the second story of the main building and putting in the stairway for the office. The fence is in fair condition; in fact, many of the posts have grown into trees. Mr. Byerlee put in angle-iron posts at the gate. The fence around Nsanza's quarters is about down. The flooring has been put in above the storeroom. We have a bunch of six or seven sickies who have no other income and are able to work and keep things up around the hospital. Mpete is in charge of them, and he also works fomentations.[11] He is about to get his wife's palaver settled . . .

The government just sent us a new microscope without oil immersion, but very good for other work. They also sent us a Bausch and Lomb hand centrifuge, have sent the regular supply of medicines and syringes but insist that we send a yearly report of our medical work. I will try to get this year's report as nearly ready as possible. We're planning on sailing November 2 and have the approval of the field but not from home as yet. I'll enclose a copy of the supplies received. We have two large tubs for baths and two smaller ones for sitz baths. The old tubs are practically gone. We have six new buckets, twelve pans, twelve cups, twelve spoons, and the like enough for some time. But you will need to get more forceps and surgical scissors. We have an oversupply of potassium iodide, but the quinine supply is nearly nil. We're supposed to have an every-three-months order of syringes, and needles, and neodiarsenol. All the doctors seem to recommend it instead of neosalvarsan and as far as I can see, which isn't far, it is just as good and probably better. Bolenge's every-three-months order for it is one hundred ampules of 0.3 grams, one hundred of 0.45 grams, one hundred of 0.90 grams, and twelve hundred of 0.60 grams. We are treating a hundred to a hundred fifty patients with it per week . . .

The baby clinic has been a fair success with fifteen to thirty infants coming each week for examination, weighing, and treatment if needed. The government medical has sent us for this work cotton, castor oil, santonine, sulfur, and a small quantity of rice for use for sick infants. I am hoping to

11. Stober added the following hand-written note to identify Mpete: "a man who lost his hands in the rubber war."

get in touch with the Society for the Protection of Congo Infants[12] and perhaps they can send us more supplies. Our main ailments have been malaria, whooping cough, intestinal worms, measles, colds, and unfortunately venereal disease, as you know.

Everyone is looking forward to your return in good health and your usual store of fine workable ideas. Hurry back.

Buena Rose Stober to Her Diary, Undated—Lotumbe, Congo Belge[13]

The same five, Mr. and Mrs. Learned, Miss Newell Trimble, Miss Myrtle Whaley, and I left Congo together, sad because of the death of Billy Learned from malignant malaria. We were all so tired we were listless and disheartened. When we reached Brussels more sadness waited us as Newell's mother had died.

In Brussels, Hattie Mitchell was going back for her second term, and a group of new young people were nearly ready to leave for Congo: Mr. and Mrs. Snipes, Georgia Bateman, the new nurse, Gertrude Shoemaker, educational worker, and Stanley Weaver, for the treasurer's office.

We had Thanksgiving dinner together in a restaurant where we asked if they knew how to make pumpkin pie. They assured the committee of missionaries they did. There were some twenty-five missionaries from or to the Congo in Brussels at the time and we all had watering mouths at the thought of a real pumpkin pie. The turkey and everything else were very nice but oh, that pie! It was just a sort of thickened, sweetened thickening with slices of pumpkin roasted on top. We tried not to show our disappointment but managed to eat a little of it for politeness's sake.

When I got to the States, I asked permission to continue work on my college degree and in six months to proceed to Belgium to study French and prepare for entrance into the course in tropical medicine for nurses and sanitary agents in Congo.

While I was home on furlough my sister lost her husband and was left to support her two little boys. It was hard to leave her, but she liked to be independent, too, so I went on to spend a very lonely time learning French. There were only a few Americans going through and were there only a

12. Stober is probably referring to the *Ligue pour la Protection de l'Enfance*, founded in 1912 by Belgian philanthropist Félicie Dubois Vandeneperre (1857–1928).

13. This diary entry was written later than late May 1928. It has been placed here because Stober describes events during her first furlough in the United States and Belgium.

short time. My companions were Belgian, French, or Swedish missionaries so I had to learn French. I never could stand not to talk. We received our diplomas on February 18, 1928, and by that time Dr. and Mrs. Davis, formerly Newell Trimble, were in Brussels. It was hard times at home and the Learneds and Miss Whaley never got back to the field. Miss Whaley married a Mr. Noah and settled in her own home.

Newell and Bill and I joined some other missionaries while we had to wait for a boat and made a very interesting tour of Belgium. A colorful Canadian who had been helping American missionaries through customs furnished the car and drove, a Mr. George Wilson, and his wife went along for the trip. About every farmhouse we passed she would pull his sleeve and remind him, *George, George, miliki, miliki!* She was Flemish and apparently they could get fresh milk to drink at nearly any good-looking farm. We visited Bruges, Ostend, Ypres, Mons, Dinant, Namur, Louvain, but didn't have enough time for Liege.

With the credits I received in Belgium I got my degree May 22, 1928, with the rest of the class at Phillips University but I couldn't be present.

Buena Rose Stober to Friends, April 21, 1928—Lotumbe, Congo Belge

I have been at work just two weeks and how good it is to be back. Lotumbe was out of medical help again so here I am filling in again. We had a nice enough trip out, but I was so anxious to get here . . .

I wish you could have seen the reception we got as our steamer pulled into the beach. We were scheduled to get in Thursday night but got in at 8:00 p.m. the night before. Even though we slipped in, the Africans were there in crowds and as we neared the beach they began singing a welcome of Christian songs. We were right proud of the stir caused among white passengers on the boat when they saw electric lights thanks to some good church people at home who sent the plant as a gift to Bolenge. They look so pretty beyond the night's blackness. These were the first electric lights seen since we left Kinshasa. The boats are afraid of snags and sand banks during the low water, and they consider Bolenge a hard beach to get into with a big boat so it seemed ages before we could get in. Our baggage and bags were all ready to be carried off quickly, so we spent very little time with goodbyes as the gangplank was put down. What a lot of joy in one evening as both black and white friends greeted us. My ex-hospital force and my little brown babies were in a lineup to greet us. They knew Mrs. Davis and heard that he was a doctor, so they received part of the enthusiasm even if they hadn't been on Bolenge staff.

My how the babies and children had grown! The next day I was showered with gifts of chickens and eggs from my namesakes. I didn't realize how many little Mputus there were until I gazed upon these tiny hopefuls.

There are five white families at Bolenge with fifteen children, Miss Shoemaker, and Mr. Weaver. The ones of the children old enough to have school with Mrs. Barger. They have a little club and play-publish a little magazine every so often.

Our trunks didn't get on the same boat as we did so we had to wait even though the *Oregon* was ready to take off right away. I had been assigned to Lotumbe and Davises to Wema, but they had to pack Newell's belongings at Lotumbe and this gave Bill a chance to see Dr. Frymire at work before he left for furlough. I had a chance to visit with my Bolenge friends while we waited and help Dr. Barger a wee bit and Dr. Bill could observe his methods too. We got part of his yearly report on the baby welfare done. They are having from forty to sixty infants a week in the clinic and the hospital boys are doing all the weighing and examining except for serious illnesses. They kept the records, too, and that is pretty good for fellows that have only been out of heathenism for six or seven years.

It was April 6 when we arrived at Lotumbe. I had brought along a little brown baby whose chance of living was pretty poor but wanted to see if I could continue the good work of Tessie Williams and get her up to normal weight. She was born the February of the year we went on furlough, and I had wanted to try then but didn't get to. The doctors all say she has a chance, so I should like to give it to her. Her father deserted her mother, and she expected the baby to die so did very little to help and was willing to give her over to our care. In these two weeks she has only gained four ounces but has gained in intelligence and is a much happier infant. Our Lotumbe baby fund is feeding five babies at present, besides Bokune, the infant I brought. One infant weighs only five pounds and its mother has tuberculosis. We use lime water, orange juice, rice gruel, and thinned milk. Lotumbe pays out $40.00 a month for the five . . .

I got quite a laugh at Dr. Davis one day when he was diagnosing and prescribing for my patients. He doesn't have much Lonkundo yet so after sitting, listening, and having me translate, an old man began describing his pains in joints. Dr. Bill is from Walla Walla, Washington and the old man said his pain walked around all over his body and describe it by saying, *asolanda walawala*. Bill pointed his finger and said in English, "Hey that is my home!" The old fellow was frightened out of his wits, so I had some explaining to do.

Buena Rose Stober to Friends, May 27, 1928—Lotumbe, Congo Belge

I haven't received much mail so far since I arrived. But I expect most of you do not know where I am. I didn't write very many letters in Belgium while I was so engrossed in schoolwork; still, I believe I answered every letter written to me so if you didn't get one it is probably because you didn't write.

This month I moved all to myself and I have all green school boys to help me while I'm at the hospital. Things have been going rather strangely: clothes get mildewed, get half ironed, and food is often burned or raw, but they are nice, willing, and learning when they're not in school or when I'm gone. Besides these inside utilities for food and clothing I have one ten-year-old who looks after chickens and gardens, and another who cuts wood and grass around the yard. Last term I paid my wash-lad who had training by another missionary 29 francs and this term both of these untrained schoolboys receive 45 francs a month, of course the schoolboys are not quite grown, though nearly so. The minimum wage for a man is 168 francs a month. The boys can earn enough to buy food and clothing while in school this way. They have very little help from relatives.

Mr. and Mrs. Hobgood and children are at Bolenge for the advisory committee at the moment, so I am looking after their livestock, which includes chickens, two cats, and a dog. One cat has succeeded in running off. It belongs to baby Kathryn and she treats it rather roughly so I guess it thinks this is a good time to make its escape. Every once in a while, someone's pigs get out and come into my yard. To be sure I don't get lonesome and the one and only horse in this part of the country (it belongs to the station and helps carry bricks, etc.) calls on me, too, when he thinks there is some chance of getting any ear of corn begged off of my chickens. Counting my chickens that makes quite a bit of livestock and add to that a few pesky goats from the villagers and that is enough.

The hospital work goes on pretty much as usual. We have our lessons every morning with the nurses and then some of them take their turn teaching in the school besides their work with patients. Two hundred forty-five patients treated this month. We have six inpatients in the wards and ten outpatients; we're feeding three infants, one only part time, besides my little Bokune. We are now having twelve to fifteen in the infant clinic.

I have acquired two other jobs permanently: Junior Endeavor and a girls' Sunday School class; the girls come one evening a week to my house where we play games, have health talks, and guard and helps.[14]

14. Junior Endeavor refers to the children's branch of the Young People's Society for

Bokune is demanding her milk so I must close.

Buena Rose Stober to Friends, July 17, 1928—Lotumbe, Congo Belge

I was so glad to hear from all of you and I hope you keep it up instead of dropping me as most second-term missionaries find their friends doing.

We got mail yesterday and I'm never any good when the mail comes; I get so excited over it I can't keep my mind on my work but thank goodness we were not very busy at the hospital yesterday.

I am beginning to cry the same old cry for a doctor. If I just had someone I could reach in an emergency. I lost a little two-month-old baby with double pneumonia and I think I'm going to lose a fight for a tuberculosis patient now. He was in a rather bad condition when they took him to the hospital but should have succeeded. We were giving him a tin of milk a day until our supply ran out and we couldn't get enough eggs to give him eggs. He was such a nice young evangelist from upriver, one of the brightest in the school and a very energetic evangelist. His poor little wife is so scared and worried, and I don't know anything else that will help him. It would surely be grand if we could have enough money to care for fellows like that, wouldn't it?

I'm having such a lot of fun watching my baby chicks hatch. I have eight so far out of eleven eggs, four of the eggs were European stock so I'll have some real chickens bigger than bantams started soon. The hens were so happy over the newcomers they laid four eggs yesterday and I usually get only one a day or one a week. It is getting harder to buy eggs these days so my little brown Bokune has to depend on these hens for breakfast.

You should see Bokune Jean now, she is getting as fat as a pig. She weighed nine pounds when I took her, and now she weighs fourteen pounds. She can sit alone a little now and can stand holding onto my fingers. She thinks she is so smart doing it she laughs about her abilities every time. She can be stubborn too; we ran out of the special powdered milk for babies and had to feed her condensed milk. It was sweetened and now we can't get her to take anything that isn't sweetened and I'm not sure so much sugar is a good idea.

Christian Endeavor. Formed in 1881 and reaching a peak membership in the 1910s, this nondenominational, evangelical educational program aimed at cultivating in children and adolescents a vital Christian faith and a commitment to compassionate service to others.

Buena Rose Stober to Friends, December 28, 1928—Lotumbe, Congo Belge

It seems good to have a minute to write to you about our happy Christmas here, most especially of the pageant of the nativity my girls gave. We have been working on it, especially the songs directed by Mrs. Clarke and the memorized Scripture over which I was in charge. We started in early October, only my twenty girls taking part except for some women for the wisemen's parts. The girls had so many giggles over the wisemen's beards it was nearly impossible.

When we began practicing, we thought Mary and Joseph would never get over their embarrassed giggles when they came to the platform. Joseph was the daughter of Bombo and Elima Salome, one of the most industrious and finest Christian women in town, in fact she is so very important no one ever thinks of saying the wife of Bombo as it is common, but one says instead Bombo the husband of Elima Salome. The girl, Mboyo Malia, is about fifteen and is engaged to a nice fellow somewhat older who cooks for the Hobgoods. Elima and Bombo wanted her to wait to get married until she is a little older.

Mary was a worse giggler than Joseph. Her name is Etuli Sala, and she is the daughter of the church janitor. These two have been chums for some years and are from a group of children that helped make the booklet of pictures of the life of Christ we sent home to the University Church Juniors in 1924.

Besides giggles, wiggles, and embarrassing beards, there was the problem of curious crowds watching them get dressed for the pageant. Mboyo got so interested or embarrassed she twirled her beard in a very authentic gesture that captivated everyone. We couldn't keep the windows and doors to the dressing room closed because of the ever-watchful audience sneaking in but we finally got the girls dressed and then we nearly had to shove them out in front of the lights. Mr. Hobgood had directed the carpenters in making an inn roof, a stable with a manger, and we had the front of the church decorated with palm fronds until it was very real looking with trees, straw, and before Mary reached the inn front there was even a pile of stones where Mary rested a bit.

There was no speaking, but the choir of girls sang the songs of the story and recited from Scripture the whole story by memory while it went on. There were twenty-three in the choir and fifteen in the pageant.

There was such a crowd that they filled the whole church and it took some force to get them back from the front far enough, so the performance could go on. We had no electric light, so we borrowed from all over town fourteen kerosene lanterns for the front and a carbide lantern to shine on Mary and Joseph and the manger.

I took this letter over to the Clarkes to have them read and censor it and Roger reminded me that so far I'd left his part out entirely. He had a terrible time with the star. First, he tried a kerosene bicycle lantern with the star of paper over in its face but the first practice it blew up during the performance, as it was let down from a window in the front of the church where the stable was placed. He kept working with other types of stars and finally got a very lovely one suspended from the window. This time he used the carbide bicycle lantern. Our Lotumbe crowds hadn't seen many pageants before, so they were really packed in and outside the church.

Buena Rose Stober to Her Diary, Undated—Lotumbe, Congo Belge

A Day with a Missionary Nurse

At 5:30 a.m. on waking from pleasant dreams with a sound of the Yokoke bird (the wag tail) and the church bell, then peeking out from under the covers to find the sun rays streaking the sky and the river's calm and color promising a bright day, it is a very pleasant thing. But on the other hand when the clouds make the sky gray and gloomy, or fog makes the river threat of smallpox, according to old tales, one wants to crawl back under the covers but one can't as the bell has rung and there is no chance of using the extra time gained from hospital work; because of a rain you feel cheated, especially if you'd been up with some sick person or were hoping to find time for letters, among them a translation of another chapter of my infant care, I had hoped to get off for our little quarterly magazine in Lonkundo.

But out of bed I come, hurriedly dress, and go to the kitchen to prepare formulas for the infants we are feeding. We are feeding three at present. We're teaching our cook to make up the milk from these formulas while I go to the hospital. Henri, a ten-month-old infant, commonly called "the elephant" to his back, is often fed meat and improperly prepared manioc bread, hard for him to digest, and so he is constantly plagued with high fevers, usually malaria, 102° and 103°, etc. When I try to teach the mother, she only answers, "When a baby wants a thing, don't you give it to them?" Sometimes she doesn't bother to explain but just lies to quiet me.

Nsombo is about eleven months old. No parent that can't read, which is most of them, ever knows the age of her child, and even some that can don't bother to keep track. When she came in from the back country ill, skin and bones, not enough milk, we managed to see him through several fevers, one of pneumonia. He has a cold now and his mother has finally learned to bring him in for care in the beginning.

Ilele is the third. He lived here with me the first three weeks of his life until he got past the dangerous stage and his mother almost died so of course had no milk for him, so he is partly mine, you see.

6:00 a.m. I am off for roll call of my hospital crowd followed by a prayer service of fifteen minutes.

6:25 a.m. finds me at the hospital helpers' class in French. Some are doing well in French but others after a whole year still can't conjugate *avoir* or *etre* just in the past indicative however that doesn't matter as I remember what a time I had learning what little I know.

7:30 a.m. Breakfast hour at our house. Miss Musgrave and I take a week about running our household, especially eats, but this is my week off. We laugh at each other and say that if you complain you have to do it yourself; so, if something isn't as tasty as it should be we just eat gayly on saying, "Oh, but I like it that way."

8:00 a.m. I have been having a Lonkundo teacher come at this time to help me in the translation of infant care; this morning I tried to finish it before the boat came but didn't succeed.

9:00 a.m. I ride out to the hospital on my bike to see new patients and perhaps improve or change the care of ones not doing so well. You see I'm not just doing a nurse's job, but we have no MD and at times I make a miserable failure. There is no doctor in miles of Lotumbe except downriver, and that takes half a day's travel or more by canoe, and twice that coming back. Upriver there isn't any MD at all. The farther upriver you go the wilder the people are.

This morning, I went to see my week-old baby. He has gotten along fine it is so white you would think he was a white person's child. His father is quite black, but his mother is a lighter hue, but both are pure Congolese. Most babies are pink or red like white folks' infants, but they gain color in a few days. This mother has four other children, but this is her first in the hospital or rather with the nurse's care instead of an old heathen grandmother or friend.

This morning, I spent the rest of my time helping the nurse's aides prescribe and the others to treat patients. There was a little of everything: coughs, colds, malaria, tropical ulcers, diarrhea, yaws, syphilis, gonorrhea, leprosy, etc. We have four leprosy patients now who come for treatment regularly; two boys about seven and ten, a girl about eight, and a mother of one of the babies we are feeding. Poor thing! It is so pitiful that she must not handle her baby if she wants to keep it free of her ailment. Another Christian woman cares for it.

An ulcer case came in with Bofunga, one of our nurses who is an evangelist in the back country but who had training under Dr. Frymire so takes medicines out with him. The ulcer covers the whole upper side of his foot and runs up onto his leg, a horrid deep thing, but it has been getting better under Bofunga's care. He put the patient to bed with his foot elevated and fed him cod liver oil. We have two other old ulcers beginning to heal. Another new one came in Saturday.

10:30 a.m. Bofunga and I went to count his money which he was paid for giving injections of neosalvarsan to treat yaws. You see we have what we call a "yaws revolving fund." The Africans are willing and able to pay for this drug so we put a price on the injections which will cover cost and the equipment and nurse's time, that is ten to fifteen francs. This also covers a bit for free doses to children and very poverty-stricken folks. So Bofunga has a nice extra sum of money some of which will be turned in to buy more drugs and equipment. While we were counting, they sent me word from the laboratory that they had found sleeping sickness microorganisms in a blood specimen of a fellow who had rheumatism. We had suspicioned the cause and when I went to confirm their diagnosis sure enough there was the proof. He is going to stay in the hospital for ten weeks of treatment.

11:30 a.m. finds me on my bike, hungry as a bear and rushing home for dinner.

12:55 p.m. finds me typing furiously on that day, late, an article on infant care. From 1:00 to 2:00 p.m. I nap when I can, or read, or prepare for women's school.

2:00 p.m. finds me typing again but it doesn't last long as I had to get out some corn to have pounded up for my cornmeal demonstration of making mush for little children and babies.

2:30 p.m. The first bell for school rang and I hurried to the hospital where I found twenty-three babies and their mothers or fathers waiting for us to weigh and examine the infants then give talks on feeding them. I gave my demonstration. They were fairly well this time; two had itch, four had colds, and two intestinal worms.

3:45 p.m. I was on my way back to women's school followed by the women with their infants. They come to school carrying their little ones on their hips and study industriously as if they didn't have to hold a wiggly infant and work.

There are 115 women in this school. Besides reading, writing, and arithmetic, they are taught hygiene by nurses (who are in morning school), music, and sewing. They have made by hand some quantity of shirts and children's dresses which we will sell to pay for the material of next year's work. They have also learned to patch. My class is the same girls I have in

Sunday School and the Thursday afternoon club. Their motto is 2 Timothy 2:15 and besides playing they have a short service and talk on how better to live up to their motto. They are a lively bunch and keep me busy. Of course, one of their chief amusements is my Victrola, and some stereoscope views.

Women's school lasts from 2:45 p.m. to 5:00 p.m. And by the time we are through we are all pretty cross and tired, so if possible, we like to create a new atmosphere by playing games, swimming, fishing, or just sitting on the porch and visiting. Only birthday parties or emergencies can entice me away at these times. Today we went to the tennis court and had a game of croquet including Mrs. Clarke, Miss Musgrave, Mr. Hobgood, and I. We got so interested we almost forgot to stop at dark; in fact, Mr. Clarke played a joke on us and sent the boy out yelling their kitchen was on fire. Nevertheless, we finished the game.

7:15 p.m. I meet my expectant parents' class. They are a happy group. At one time we had twelve, but now we only have five. The women sew baby garments and some of the men play the Victrola or look at the views, while others sew in spite of superstition. They have a belief that if you sew for an infant before it arrives you will bring about the possibility that an evil spirit will find out about it and will injure the infant. So, you see, it is quite a brave step forward but as they learn the care of infants in these meetings, they begin to be less afraid. Also, some of them have never held a needle in their hands let alone learned how to use it, but of the nineteen women we have had in the class no one has ever objected. I started this class last November and I have hardly missed a Tuesday since. I have two women helping that have had more or less training in caring for infants and their mothers. All of our first group have nice clean healthy babies and are so proud of the clothes and lessons they learned. One woman who helps me teach them is the wife of my head nurse, Bekai, and can read and write as she is the daughter of one of our early evangelists but her husband, although even a capable assistant in surgery when we have a surgeon, is not able to read and write. The other woman is older than Bekai and not so capable in school. Her name is Bolumbu. They only can work in the mornings at the hospital and for deliveries. My ambition is to train every nurse's wife as a midwife, which is quite an ambition.

9:00 p.m. They have gone, and I must grade some arithmetic papers.

10:00 p.m. Whoops I forgot I had an appointment to give Mrs. Hobgood a massage but completely forgot it. This day was a little busier perhaps than usual. Two evenings a week I have Lonkundo lesson with Mrs. Hobgood, one evening I have the girls, one the expectant parents, two I go to church services, and one I have free more or less and I usually am in bed by 9:30 p.m.

Buena Rose Stober to the Editors of World Call, *May 19, 1929—Lotumbe, Congo Belge*

Herewith I want to raise my voice in protest against a certain statement made in *World Call* of February 1929, page forty-two in the article "The New Way on the Congo." It says, "Every station has a modern hospital with a nurse and a doctor, excepting Wema, our newest station. Its hospital is in the process of construction and will soon be ready for work." Now I have never been to Wema, so I can't say whether this new hospital is actually soon to be ready for work, except that I have heard rumors that the doctor and nurse who have been on that station have been working in an open shed which had a palm-frond roof. As I understand, since they went home from the conference in April, 1929, one at small unit of their hospital has been finished and will soon be usable. Very few folks realize how long it takes to get a building up when all the work has to be done by hand instead of by machines. But that really isn't the crow I have to pick with you. It is the part that says each station has a modern hospital with a nurse and a doctor. It might be wise to visit a modern hospital in the States and then come and visit one of ours. Has the author of this article consulted Mr. Yocum, who visited our Congo stations recently, and asked him to compare our hospitals with modern hospitals at home? I don't think our modern hospitals at home would be willing to own us as even first cousins to them. Ask some of them what they would think of the modern hospital in which there was no sewage system. What would they think of having running cold water that would not run a hundred feet, and no plumbers to call in to mend the situation, or a steam sterilizing system that runs hot water instead of live steam. Oh yes, of course, the situation could be mended if we had someone that knew how, and if we had some money to buy equipment to do it. Besides, in dry season our wonderful system runs dry and last year we carried water from the river a distance of two or three city squares. It is true that our hospitals are much better equipped than they were five years ago when I first arrived out here, but please don't call them "modern" or any ways near to modern. And even if they were modern and wonderfully modern, I'll tell you another secret about them, there has never been in five years of my experience a time when any more than one of our five stations have had a doctor and a nurse on the same station working together; it has always been as it is now: Dr. Barger is working at Bolenge without a nurse; Dr. Davis is at Wema without a nurse; Dr. Pearson and Miss Williams are working together at Mondombe; Miss Bateman is alone at Monieka; and I am playing quack doctor-nurse at Lotumbe without even a suggestion of a doctor for miles. In fact, in the four years I've been on the field, I've never had the privilege of being on the station with a doctor except for short periods of a week, a month, or six weeks when a doctor happened to be passing through or visiting our station. This is not my idea of a modern hospital! It is yours! As far as educated native nurses, one of our head boys here cannot read or write, and although all the rest can, they wouldn't be passed the fifth grade and primary education although they are fine assistants in medical work in some ways.

It is rather discouraging to us who have been begging and pleading for doctors in the Congo to see the public lulled into peaceful dreams by reading about the happy condition of our stations in regard to medical work. We are told everything is being done to get doctors, but it seems strange that such a statement should get by if you actually studied the condition.

I do hope that this statement will be corrected before the public, and some definite propaganda put forth to get doctors and funds for the equipment their work, etc. If you could see some of us nurses agonizing over someone's sickness that we don't know how to diagnose or treat, and have a life slipping away from you when you feel sure that an MD would know what to do, you would know something of how a statement like that in *World Call* hurts. Just the last month a little baby died whose parents wanted and needed it so much, and if I had been a doctor would probably have realized that it was malignant malaria and given it the one chance it had, hypodermic injections of quinine. I did recognize it, but after it was too late.

I hope you will understand the hurt that makes me write a letter like this. Love and best wishes to you all and may you bless others in your Christian publications.

PS. Please don't ever let any of us hear again that there is doubt as to whether it is wise to send out women doctors. We out here know that there is no objections and anyway you'd better experiment in the real thing than in nurses who have to do an MD's work. I feel all radical and wrought up after rereading that article, but I've got to get it off my system and the sooner the better, but please don't let all my ravings fall on shallow ground if you can help it. We nurses at conference held an indignation meeting over this article and I think you all ought to know how we feel. These are my sentiments and I expect the other nurses have written as much or more.

Cyrus Yocum to Buena Rose Stober, July 17, 1929—Indianapolis, Indiana[15]

Your letter of May 19, addressed to the *World Call*, indicates that the temperature in Congo Belge at about the time that you wrote was somewhat above normal. Of course, I understand the circumstances which created the excessive heat. After reading your letter, I went at once to the *World Call* office and procured a copy of the February number and read the article to which you refer. I have not seen it previously. In some way or other I had hastily glanced over the pages of that number and had not read the particular article to which you take exception. While I was in the *World Call* office a few minutes ago, the editor was not present, hence I was not able to talk over the situation with her. I shall do so, however, at my very earliest convenience.

I do not know who is responsible for the article to which you refer. I think possibly someone either in the Missionary Education Department or more probably in the Missionary Organizations Department prepared the article. I regret that it was erroneous. I doubt, however, if it will do the missionary great harm. Nevertheless, it does give them this impression. I think your reaction to the article was quite normal.

I am not sure that I understand your postscript in which you refer to some doubt as to whether or not it is wise to send out women doctors. We have been sending women doctors to the field for many, many years, especially in the India field, and we have no doubt as to their usefulness there. So far as I know, no serious question has been raised by anyone in the office as to the advisability of sending a woman doctor to Africa. The question was raised a little while ago as to whether or not Miss Smith should go back to the India field on account of a very serious situation in which the India Mission finds itself just now. In India there are many things which a woman doctor simply cannot do. That is probably true in Africa to a certain extent but not to the extent which it is true in India, and we wondered for a time if we were able to secure a man doctor to be sent to Africa in the very near future if it might be wise to send Miss Smith to the India field. This was not done, however, and Miss Smith will soon be on her way to Africa.

Assuring you that we regret very much indeed any of these slips which creep into our literature from time to time, and anxious to make all of them right, trusting that your work at Lotumbe is moving along nicely and with kind personal regards I am, cordially yours.

15. At the time Stober received this letter from him, Cyrus Yocum (1883–1958) was the state-side Administrative Secretary of DCCM and one of the executive staff of the UCMS.

Buena Rose Stober to Friends, July 20, 1929—Lotumbe, Congo Belge

Miss Musgrave and I are going on an overland itineration for about twenty-four days starting Monday and I wanted to write to you before we left so you won't think I had deserted you all. That is, we are going if something does not happen between now and Monday. One day Mr. Clarke was kidding Virginia and commented, "Well you never can tell the evangelistic school isn't over yet and you might run off and leave us." It wasn't two days from that when baby Ben Hobgood was so sick, I thought we should get him to a doctor quickly and the nearest was about half a day downriver so off we sped.

The doctor was a Belgian, working for a big company palm-oil plantation, Lever Brothers.[16] He was very nice to us. Ben had a stubborn old case of malaria, so we had to stay a whole week in the most miserable excuse of a house. It was brick with brick floors and plenty of bugs and mosquitoes. There were two rooms so Mrs. Hobgood, baby Ben, and I took one room while Mr. Hobgood and the other three children had the other. There was an open space between these rooms where we ate, but the cooking had to be done on an open fire in the back. I proceeded to get a cold and enough mosquito bites to last me for a long time. So, did all the Hobgoods and I at least carried enough of our Lotumbe variety to add to the cold and produce a fever; and since I had only recently finished a course of quinine I thought it couldn't be malaria so I went to the MD and he proved by blood smear that I had malaria too. Anyway, he taught me a new method of staining the slide, so I got something good out of the trip besides seeing Ben get well. He was very kind about explaining each treatment and answering my unnursely questions, so I guess I could afford to carry away a lot more of his malaria.

The last six months of evangelistic work here around Lotumbe made everyone happy; there were in all Lotumbe field 716 baptisms and an

16. An English soap manufacturer, Lever Brothers was founded in 1885 by William Hasketh Lever (1851–1925) and James Darcy Lever (1854–1916). By the 1890s, the growing company was producing and marketing a new kind of soap using glycerin and vegetable oils. In 1911, with the assistance of the Belgian government, the company began acquiring large palm-oil plantations that employed thousands of Congolese. Throughout the colonial period, the company was widely suspected of forced labor, and of disciplinary measures that exceeded what was allowable by law including public whippings with the *chicote* (a heavy whip made of rhinoceros hide). Company administrators were also accused of maintaining sub-standard living conditions in the plantation work camps and failing to provide adequate medical care to Congolese workers. (Note Stober's complaint about their accommodations in this paragraph). At the time of its merger with a Dutch manufacturer in 1930, Lever Brothers was the largest and most profitable company in Britain, with subsidiaries all over the industrialized world.

offering from the Africans of forty-five thousand francs, about $1,285.00, enough to support a large part of the evangelists. It doesn't seem to go far to pay evangelists, but it is a fine expression of the African Christians' interest in evangelism.

Mr. Hobgood was able to look into our church roll while we were in Boteke, or Flandria as the Belgians call it. The Lever Brothers Company often use Protestant Europeans to run their work, but they are predominantly Catholic, and they wish to cater to the Belgian Congo government officials who are Catholic, so his efforts to get a place on the plantation for building a church was useless even though the director was Protestant. They had already given a plot to the Catholics and built their church. We have many Christians in the company, and they were already raising money to build our church, so it wasn't a question of money. Our teacher-evangelist is a fine young peppy fellow, and he was able to get a plot nearby that is perhaps better than on the plantation. He will have school besides his church work. There are some Africans there, English-speaking coast men who work for the plantation, and since some eight of them are very well educated and have their families with them they are a good influence. One wanted to go to school in America, but it was so far from Togoland he lost courage and is sorry now. They are well paid and live more as we do.

We lack English reading material for these people so do not throw your old Sunday School papers and pictures away. Send them as printed matter as they will not cost as much. Mrs. Clarke sent them some literature of that kind so remember we can use the literature that way and the pictures in all our schools and evangelistic work. Children's leaflets have such nice usable pictures on them and they are appreciated by all. Please send them as printed matter and there will not be customs charges.

Please! Some of you good busy folks send me some infant shirts made from two stocking tops, that is if there still exists such a thing as stocking tops so you could use old ones. My supply has run out and there are always naked babies. Old baby clothes folks have around will be serviceable too. Be sure to mark your package "used baby shirts value fifty cents" or thereabouts. The caps with the bright tops, too, are much in demand. New things should be sent in a separate package and marked and valued new.

We have had several exciting things besides the ones already mentioned. Mr. Clarke's hunter found two baby leopards in their lair and since the mother was absent, he brought them home and we tried to feed them on tinned milk. The first few days they brought them over to my house as I'm the official motherless baby feeder, but my wisdom didn't seem to extend to the wild animal family and they proceeded to starve to death, or nearly so; so, they had to kill them. One evening, as Mrs. Clarke and I were trying to feed them, a white company man walked up to our porch and received quite a surprise seeing two tiny leopards and several human babies each with about half a bottle of milk he was rapidly devouring. He thought it was funny but advised us to cut their tiny claws and house the leopards out of the house where if the mother came to find them in a trap she would get caught but she never accommodated us. She or some other leopard has been killing the goats in town and prowling all around. We're not the only station that has excitement as Wema folks killed two elephants and a hippo and Bill Davis was really able to present his Newell with a baby elephant as she asked, however, he hadn't intended to kill a female but in the jungle he couldn't see well enough. It drank a whole case of tinned milk almost at one meal and even then dwindled away until they had tried everything and had to kill him.

We are sending six young men down to the institute (Congo Christian) at Bolenge, our advanced school, recently started there. Three of them are married and three are single men. The wives have school too but are not far enough along to enter the institute classes.

It is fishing season now and everyone has simply gone nuts about fishing. They come to work only when they please, and don't believe in sickness or school at this time. The river is very low and at present the SW *Missouri* is grounded. They say it is no trouble to get it afloat again though. If we were not going on this itineration, I expect we would be going often to the sandbar for evening picnics. I will have my birthday party out on the road.

Buena Rose Stober to Friends, August 27, 1929—Lotumbe, Congo Belge

I must take time to write to you about our trip in the back country. We left Lotumbe by the SW *Missouri* on July 23 and got back August 12 from Boyela, about six miles upriver from Lotumbe and then leaving the steamer we plunged deeper and deeper overland into the jungle.

Wild in more than one way because the further you get upriver or overland the wilder the people are and the wilder the paths are; as there are fewer white officials the paths are not kept up. After we left Boyela, however, we traveled on our bikes the whole of the way, except three days when we had our bikes tied to a pole and carried by two men while we waded water or crossed on wiggly logs by the hour, through swamp and through thicket. One day I was so far behind the first group of carriers and too far ahead of the ones following that I couldn't hear any sounds of them, only the sounds of woods, wading out of one swamp into the next, climbing over logs and whole trees that had fallen in the way, and enjoying immensely the quietness of the forest as I stumbled along. You see, when we got near a village, two white women riding on bicycles caused such a commotion that we were deafened by the noise all the time and a quiet was very welcome. Miss Musgrave was behind in her *teepoi*, a chair tied between bamboo or other lightweight polls and carried by four men, but I was too stubborn to let them carry me over the swampy part. After all, an hour or two of the dead silence was quite a cure and I welcomed the first bunch of the carriers that I caught up with. Three of the carriers' wives and I stumbled along together then. We counted the holes we fell into and made a game of laughing at the other fellows when, in playing follow the leader, we follow the leader and fall into the hole. We came to love these women following along with us and even had a party for them when we got back home.

We baptized forty-two older people or cripples who were not able to come in to Lotumbe and so had missed the gathering in July. We also married seven couples, both of us, as all our missionaries are ordained. I developed into quite a preacher as I had to take my turn as Ruth did morning and evening. We also helped settle troubles in each church group as we went along. Another job was managing the carriers and another cooking. We solve them by taking turnabout for them too. We made a different town every day except on Sunday when everyone rested and had a real Sunday service. The nurses, two of them and I, treated about 500 cases, giving 189 intravenous injections of neodiarsenol to adults and 234 to children for yaws, a tropical disease with sores like buttons and a skin eruption. The children were treated free and a few of the adults, but most paid. There were two or three chieftains who had helped us in some way or the other and charity cases for free treatment. The whole trip reminded us of One Day conventions only it was harder work. Ruth looked after the schoolwork of each evangelist, so we were in each even busier than the One Day conventions. The Christians in each town were wonderful to us, bringing feasts for our carriers, eggs, chickens, and fruit to us, water and wood so that we were positively spoiled. Nearly all of our carriers were student preachers, so we gave them whatever tasks they could do for the churches and even helped where we stayed longer as the villagers were building a new church.

At Iyembe the preacher, Ilonga Daniel, was on the go all the time and his Christians and even some heathens copy after him. And what a fine congregation he had. They didn't seem to mind our staying within three days even if they did almost feed us. Our men were very worn out so their three feasts helped put them back on their jobs. We baptized eleven there and married two couples.

All the way we did not find it so flowery and lovely as that, in fact down in the Ekonda part we found them indifferent to the teaching, even though terribly curious about us. They would run after us as if they were following a circus and yell at the top of their voices. Some of our colleges at home could use these African dandies to help with their pep yells. One fellow would yell out something about us and they would all answer in chorus, in perfect unison, a perfect college yell. The women would crowd around us and the braver would touch us, perhaps would take our hands and fingers to see if they were flesh and blood and bone but some would shake hands with us and then run as if they'd seen a ghost. In one village it was us that saw the ghost. As we traveled over an old forsaken village path someone yelled, "Be careful! There is a man in the path!" We couldn't see him and passing a big tree we saw between its roots this skull of a man sticking up where the dirt had worn off the head. We didn't cycle over it but when around. You would have thought the Siamese twins had come to the town by the way people coming to see us crowded about. Young dames, old dames, and children by the dozens. Hair dresses took my fancy: there was an old pigtail style with the ends of the braids sticking out; another look like an old oil mop and consisted of hair wound up with threads and oiled with palm oil and straining here and there are all over their faces and necks; little braided pigtails radiating from the crown of the head; hair gayly bedecked with red palm-wood powder and oil until they are bright shiny red heads; old men often wear monkey skin caps with the tail skin hanging down their backs. These monkey skin of the tail often hangs clear to their knees. Red, grey, and black monkey skins are used for this. The women's more modern hair dress is accomplished by wrapping little portions of the hair with fine black thread then bringing all the little portions down over the ears and binding them together to make a puff over the ears. Many times, they wear silk scarves like we wear hats. One day among a crowd with hair dresses of these kinds I took off my helmet to cool my head and what a lot of fuss of ohs and ahs greeted me. Then some came near and wanted to touch my hair. "How soft is it?" and then everybody had to try it until Ruth came up to rescue me and offered to take her long hair down if they would stand back and not finger in it. She so outshined me that I was immediately relieved. Then they got curious about my wristwatch and had to listen to it.

In one town we got into a regular old-time fight between the pygmies and the other tribe. We had a very bad morning balancing on logs for miles until we were so hungry and dizzy we could hardly stand and we were arriving in a town where there were no Christians, except one lone little old man who hadn't heard we were coming. We couldn't get anyone to get us wood for quite a while, so we ate our lunch cold, after having the service under the trees. With only our carriers to sing we made some queer attempts and a man who knew Lonkundo translated for us. We rested a bit, but I was awakened by quarreling and since I was afraid some of our crowd were in it I went out. The noise didn't stop, and we soon found it was a real tribal fight. There were about a dozen fights going on at once. The pygmies were not satisfied with the judge's decision to put two of their number in jail. Ruth almost got whacked in the head trying to stop it and one of the nurses grabbed the woman's hand wielding a knife. We finally persuaded them to give up their knives and try to settle it some other way. They gave us twenty-nine knives which we gave to the chieftain the next morning before we left to be returned so when we dispatched a letter to a white official not far from there we thought it was over, but we had word later that they started to fight again as soon as we were out of hearing.

Buena Rose Stober to Friends, November 11, 1929—Lotumbe, Congo Belge

So many things here pass as everyday affairs that we pass them by as ordinary but come to think of it there is hardly ever a day at the hospital dispensary when there isn't something interesting or unusual to you who have modern hospitals and doctor's care regularly.

From 9:00 a.m. to 11:30 a.m. we care for all new cases and check up on old cases who come to the dispensary. In the open waiting room, most in the morning you will find some twenty or thirty waiting for us with a relative or someone in attendance. There are always a bunch of cases with topical ulcers on their legs, feet, or toes and once in a while elsewhere on the body; a few new yaws cases with a typical yellow-looking button like sores on their faces or other parts of the body; there will always be some with colds in various stages of seriousness; syphilis and gonorrhea; several folks sitting around with thermometers in their mouths, or babies fighting having their temperature taken with a Congolese nurse standing by hoping and trying to prevent their breaking the thermometer; malaria is the most common cause of fever here but of course they have ordinary causes too.

Around one window in the treatment part of the building is a crowd gathered with various laboratory specimens being handed to a nurse at the microscope. As American crowds they push and try to get in first for the examination.

At a desk inside, patients passed a desk where Bekaw Malia, wife of the head nurse and daughter of one of Lotumbe's oldest evangelists, was getting out records for old patients waiting and writing out records for new patients. To the African this is very unusual as very few women have learned to write let alone care for records, besides it is well known that her husband reads and writes very little, almost not at all, but is a very good assistant in surgery trained by Dr. Frymire.

At another desk is Mbambo, a very fine nurse who will be writing histories, questioning and examining in a little room nearby, then sending them on for treatment or calling me for special cases, then sending them on to various treatment rooms.

There is a room where Malia's husband, Ifake Jean, gives intravenous injections of neodiarsenol for yaws or other ailments treated with it. He is the cleverest on the force at getting in the vein for these treatments. He seems to be able to persuade them to come back regularly for these treatments. These patients wait out back until Ifake calls them to his office. Others go to a room where clean ulcers are treated and others for infectious cases; another group waited in a room near the back where they receive hot fomentation treatments for swellings, backaches, or chest ailments from colds or chronic affairs that can be speeded toward recovery by heat. What a busy crowded place this treatment and dispensary building is. I am usually doing special treatments or milling around to each room helping or seeing that treatments are carried out properly. The room where pills and various drugs are administered by mouth has a half door and pills are given out and taken at the door, so the nurse cannot be crowded into confusion. Usually, they are reasonably orderly.

In the back of the building is the big boiler heated by wood, and producing the steam for sterilizing, hot fomentations, and hot water or steam. It is quite a novelty to the Africans who have not traveled by steamers.

Each nurse takes a turn at teaching hygiene in the school and when he returns he is followed by a group of six to ten boys he has found with itch, jiggers, or any other ailments that need treatment. Just as boys in the USA usually hate washing their faces our boys out here hate to dig the jiggers out of their toes and feet. The jigger is a small flea that delights in human blood and the female, in order to have enough food to develop her egg sack and young, burrows under the skin and finds her store of food plentiful no matter how much our victim suffers, and he or she will suffer if he or she doesn't dig out each tiny black insect from under the skin. Once they get a start, they often cause infection, so they should be removed daily. It is just as important as washing your face. Dormitory girls and boys get a paddling each when jigger egg sacks are found by the nurses. The girls as a rule are more careful about their feet, but some village school boys have given us so much trouble with jigger feet spilling tiny jiggers over the cement school building floors we have paid them pennies for cleaned up jigger feet. Where we have ten boys with jigger feet, we will only have three girls. Boys will be boys.

Buena Rose Stober to Friends, December 1929—Lotumbe, Congo Belge

We are being the busiest of busy folks these days as the in-gathering of backcountry evangelists is in full swing again. We're meeting with them, listening mostly at present to their discussions about who will be sent where and how much pay you will receive. Part of it doesn't require a lot of attention but it is important to let them get whatever they feel off their chest and then later we can get down to the business. We have finished counting the offerings and as there was a slump in business here as well as in all the world the offerings are down only 12,106 francs for this downriver part of Lotumbe's work and the last count of baptisms for both up and downriver churches in Lotumbe field was 1,403, not counting the group of Lotumbe yet to be baptized.

I wish you could look out over this crowd of evangelists as I can. There are tall black fellows and short brown fellows and middle-sized ones. Some of them are wearing shirts, pants, shoes, and the regular apparel of civilized folks with average wages, but others have only a shirt and a wraparound skirt to do service as pants and no shoes. Here is a nice-looking brown fellow with a very nice beard, a dirty pair of trousers, and an old black overcoat some white man has cast away. Here is a cocky little bantam with a bright sweater of red and yellow stripes. Here is a big yellow fellow, not mulatto, but a light-colored pure Congolese who owns a nice moustache and a short kinky beard. There are a few wearing vests and wraparound skirts only of many gay colors. Over here is a good old honest-faced teacher who is just as interested in his evangelism as anyone could be, and nearby another but a lazy old pill half asleep with his feet up on the bench and his head lolling on his hand. And over here is another not interested in anything but a good sleep, nodding away peacefully. The head preacher and his assistants are seated in front with the missionaries facing the evangelists. Ruth Musgrave is making a speech about how ours are paid from their own villages where they preach.

The church here is very large but not too large for this congregation. It is about 100 by 160 feet. There is a room at each end in an upstairs, too, which are used for Sunday School. They have ordinary floors and windows, but the middle section is open with big brick arched pillars to hold up the roof but let the cool breezes come through if there are any breezes. When one gets bored during the sermon one can gaze out upon the Congo splendor of greenery. If a discussion gets too hot one watches the chickens in the yard of the girls' dorm next door or an occasional passerby on the front path.

The evangelists have been paid their market, but they are a noisy bunch. I'll be glad when the day comes when they will be wise enough and do not need special instruction every six months. When you get one hundred of them together besides all the wives and followers it increases our troubles considerably. But I hope it does some good. Some of them work hard in their villages but some haven't much spirit of evangelism. I suppose that this is true at home, too, and I have simply forgotten. This is of course the happier inspirational side of the in-gathering too.

Ilonga Daniel, the evangelist in our school in the village church of Iyembe, has such a working bunch of Christians and it is of course because he works hard as an example. He has encouraged them to plant fruit trees and says his avocados are already bearing and two of his orange trees were as tall as he is. Also, his papaya, pineapple, and other fruit are doing nicely too. He said he wanted to get some good sweet potatoes and wound up saying, "Mama the thing I lack most is flower seeds." I supplied both. The natives look down their noses at us for growing flowers and think we must be witch doctors to plant them, so it is a pleasant surprise to meet a fellow who wants seeds.

I must close now as I cared for the baby last night and she didn't let me have my full night's sleep. She is gaining but lots of work at that.

After graduating from the University Hospital Nurses Training School in Enid, Oklahoma, in 1921, Stober applied for missionary service with the United Christian Missionary Society. Photo courtesy of DCHS.

Stober (left) studied at the College of Missions with fellow missionary Newell Trimble. They are pictured here with two Congolese girls shortly after they arrived in Congo in 1923. Photo courtesy of DCHS.

Stober was apprenticed to Dr. Gervase Barger during her first term of service in Congo. He is pictured here about 1925, with fourteen Congolese nurses of the hospital in Bolenge. Photo courtesy of DCHS.

Much respected and admired by Stober, Njoji Mark was the first Congolese person to be ordained in DCCM. This photo of him, his wife Amba, and their five children appeared in *World Call* in 1924. Photo courtesy of CTS.

Belgian Prince Leopold III visited the Belgian Congo in 1925, including a stop at several stations of the DCCM. Here he is pictured with two Congolese. Photo courtesy of CTS.

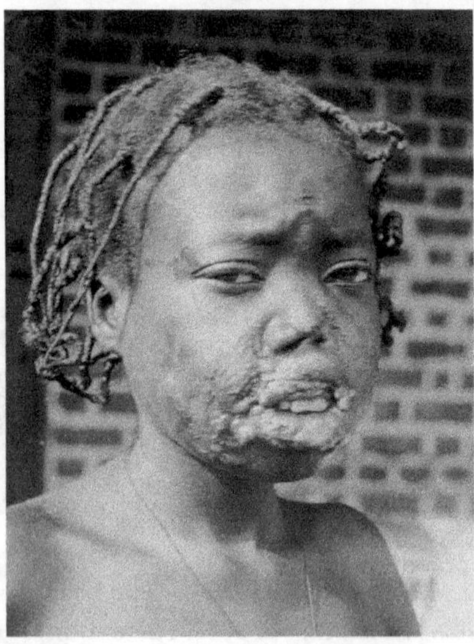

Prior to the development of sulfa antibiotics, Stober could offer only limited help in treating bacterial infections like this girl's case of tropical yaws in the late 1920s. Photo courtesy of DCHS.

While stationed at Lotumbe, Stober often itinerated in the backcountry with missionary colleague Ruth Musgrave. She is pictured here around 1925 with a leader in the Lotumbe church, Wetelo Tito. Photo courtesy of DCHS.

Stober's fellow missionary Getrude Shoemaker demonstrates the use of a push-push as a means of transportation in the late 1920s. Photo courtesy of CTS.

2

1930 to 1939

Buena Rose Stober to Friends, May 15, 1930—Lotumbe, Congo Belge

I have been wanting to write you what I know of one of our Congo veterans, Boyau Albert, even though my bed does look terribly inviting. I wish I was one of the older group of missionaries because I would be able to tell you more about him, how he came to work on the mission before even the steamship *Oregon* arrived in Congo in 1910 and was one of the evangelists who worked with Mr. Eldred. What a wonderful and large service he has rendered for his people. He had been a head evangelist in the part of Lotumbe field where Mr. Eldred was buried and has faithfully seen that the grave is properly tended.

He had a big church which he carefully tended even though the white missionaries could not make any itinerations back there. There was not a white missionary back there for over a year and a half when I saw him; and in spite of this fact, he has kept his church and other churches he supervised, giving substantial offerings and keeping up a good increase in membership each six months.

When Ruth and I got to the in-gathering at Wafania we heard that he was terribly sick and when they carried him in and told the story of his illness, I feared sleeping sickness or uremic poisoning; so, I insisted on his coming to Lotumbe as we returned. At first, in spite of his terrible headaches, he would hardly consent to the trip, leaving his work; but when his wife said they must go, he agreed. It was evident that whatever he had affected his mind as he was very apt to greet you several times and forget where he was. When he got to Lotumbe, Dr. Smith pronounced it uremic poisoning after examining his blood, then his glands for the trypanosomes of sleeping sickness with a negative result, except more indications of other trouble. After only four days in Lotumbe he started having convulsions and all the treatments were of no avail. Losing him is mighty hard on our work but we sent another evangelist, Efekya David, right away. Boyau's wife had been faithful and sweet through the years, and we hated having her go back alone to face her heathen relatives; so, we asked Efekya to look after her, then wrote a letter to the chief and asked him not to let the relatives sell her into a heathen harem and to see that her husband's property was divided with her and to allow her to live with the church community. Ordinarily they take all the husband's property and leave her nothing except disgrace that her husband died. But we hope the letter and Efekya can ward off the ravens.

Buena Rose Stober to Friends, June 3, 1931—Lotumbe, Congo Belge

You should come and see the community spirit we have stirred up in this big chief's village where we were having an in-gathering of nearby village evangelists. Last time when I was through these villages, I attempted to persuade the chieftains in each village to let the Christians or send them to build churches in each village. Sitting around doing nothing was easier than getting people to work, and in some places they were doing jobs that the chieftain wanted done, so were not allowed to work on the churches. In each village I am finding the framework done but nothing else. When I got in here Friday the big chief said he would send everyone for roofing and finish this week. This is Wednesday and here we sit out under some palm and some orange trees writing letters, signing evangelists' books of employment, and around there are some sixteen tying the *ndele* roofing, this is like a palm tree that grows in the water and the mats of *ndele* make a very fine roofing.

The chieftain, evangelists, and most of his men are out in the jungle hunting meat for us and themselves while we tie *ndele*. The women are cooking their manioc bread, also the leaves are used for delicious greens made up with palm-oil gravy. Everyone is laughing, telling stories, and having a good time in general. Here are a couple of young party fellows entertaining everyone with a ridiculous story of how hungry they are. Three evangelists are sick, and the nurses are giving them hot fomentations for their ailments. Two schoolteacher boys are copying some reading material for several village schools, and my helper Bokolombe is cooking a chicken in an open fire and baking bread in a hole dug in an anthill where he has a fire. He has put rice in the chicken, so I am to have something to eat it seems. Some evangelist's wife has presented me with a gift of *banganju*, manioc greens.

The evangelists from one part haven't gotten in but perhaps the government official is collecting tax there.

We are having an institute school from 6:00 a.m. to 8:30 a.m. of about twelve women and twenty-four men (evangelists mostly) and ten children. The two teachers' boys and the wife of one of them teach reading, writing, and arithmetic while I teach Bible and hygiene. The classes are going very well.

As little as some of the evangelists know of reading and writing it is surprising how many boys and young men in their churches have learned to read and write as there are no other schools in these villages besides theirs. There are two Catholic churches, but no schools. We are trying to raise the standard of the schools by getting better educated evangelists in the villages. We have three new young evangelists and their wives with us going into new Ekonda villages.

Buena Rose Stober to Friends, September 11, 1931—Mondombe, Congo Belge

Well, here I am at Mondombe. Getting my letters from Lotumbe makes all my mail a month late and they take six weeks to two months to come anyway. It is hard to answer a letter that is four months old, or at best three.

Mondombe is entirely different from Lotumbe. It is taking me some time to get over many surprises. For instance, the elders of the church here are nearly all young men and there are so few older people in the church that I miss them so. The villagers nearby are such rank heathens and covered with red calmwood powder and oil and dirt you should see my white uniform when I come in from the baby clinic in Lingomo, the nearest village. Soot, palm oil, red wood powder, and more dirt and itch than you can imagine on one tiny body, so frightened that they scream and fight to get off the scales. But with little presents of soap and cloth, this month some of them have begun to sit quietly on the scales. Oh, for another case of soap! There are twelve to eighteen every week but actually twenty-seven registered, I think probably some of their parents hide them out on clinic day, but I suppose they will get over it in time.

An old grandmother was especially funny when I stopped at her house and asked if I might weigh the infant and give it a piece of soap to clean it up. She rushed the baby into her low mud and thatch hut stooping to get in and every breath saying, *mpolang*, "I don't want to." When I followed her into the hut to ask her why, she told me a fib to get rid of me. She said the mother had gone for water, and when she came back I could ask her. When I returned from the other end of the village she and the baby were nowhere to be found. Next week as I stopped, the old grim and besmeared husband, complete with redwood powder and leopard teeth necklace, came out and informed me that they had twelve children and every one had died before they could walk, so they were not taking a chance with this one since it was beginning to walk. When I got the two women nurses who were with me to explain that I had come just for that reason to keep their infant strong and growing, he just picked up the child and walked off. To him I must have been an evil spirit ready to pounce on his child. Many mothers took pains to ask the two African nurses if there was any *elika*, or taboo, on weighing babies and were then informed that there was no reason to be afraid. Pour souls! They are frightened to death of breaking taboos.

Buena Rose Stober to Her Diary, February 9, 1932—Mondombe, Congo Belge

Gertrude and I made in-gatherings of evangelists in two counties where they are pretty heathen and although we have quite a few Christians we witnessed several marching demonstrations of the secret act of *botamba*. After playing the Victrola, having supper we were sitting in the moonlight when a man went tooting a bamboo flute. We had been hearing drums all day and dancing and general noise which they said was dancing for a wonderful medicine called *botamba* or "tree" in English. It appears that a man they call *nkumu-mpoke*, one who has at least three wives to give him enough honor and respect of villagers, is given the authority in the village who chooses him to give this *botamba*. He is generally buried alive, at least while barely breathing, because no one must ever see him die. However, the fear of being buried alive is great enough that Likumu, our little chicken lad of ten years, was very sick while he was still at home and heard his relatives wanted to give him *botamba* to make him live forever. But he was so frightened he ran off to one of our evangelists and was soon sent into the mission to school. He has been married a year and a half, but the fear is very real to him. He is a fine healthy little rascal and good in school. I asked the villagers what was in the gourd of *nkume mpoke*, and they replied that it was not strong enough to do even what tobacco does, and it was not always the same leaf. When you want to smoke *botamba* you go to the *nkume mpoke*, then he will ask you to pay him knives, spears, chickens, etc., or in money, Congo francs, then he will show you a certain leaf, even papaya sometimes or another leaf. You dry it like tobacco and bring it to him, then all your male relatives get together and make a joyful noise and cry, "Smoke it! Smoke it!" until you produce the desired amount of smoke, then all is well and live forever. If a man didn't blow smoke when he took *botamba* he would be accused of having a grudge or jealousy of someone. During the ceremonies everyone dances, sings, they have woven rattles that contains seed, the *basanga*, and wear a seed that looks like walnut seeds, rub themselves from head to foot with a bright red powder they make from a wood. The *nkombe*, the wooden portable dance drums, are always in evidence, only a man can wear these and no one can curse him and cause him to die if he wears them. However, women can take *botamba* too. At night if the *nkumu-mpoke* hears the *esukulu*, or night owl, crying, he will call some of his older boys to go out into of all paths tooting the bamboo flutes. The evil spirits are supposed to be out.

Buena Rose Stober to Friends, May 31, 1932—Mondombe, Congo Belge

I have been having what I call my furlough after the conference at Bolenge until the *Oregon* makes the second trip upriver in about three weeks. As you know I am supposedly on furlough but since the cablegram came telling of the cut in wages and requesting that we all stay over an extra year to help the low condition of travel and budget funds for the field from the society, I was due out of the country March 15, and as you see I have actually started my extra year. The joke is on me because in October, November, and December I had been running fevers and feeling quite no account. In January and February, I felt a little better and by the time the cablegram came it frightened any ailment out of me and I was feeling fine. Our doctors have examined all the missionaries and their children to see if they could take the extra year. They were all fine. The cut affects not only our salaries, but the number of helpers we can have in each field of service. In Africa we will carry on pretty much as before because some workers have been dismissed, and in most cases have been loyal and willing to take their cuts in pay and continue their work. There are, however, some evangelists who do not even receive enough to pay their yearly tax and it is hard for them to understand. Most of them will be able to sell some products and make up the amount of the tax.[1]

1. In the early years of Belgian colonialism, the taxation of the Congolese people

My three weeks waiting for the *Oregon* has meant a lot to me because Bolenge was my old home. I have been given the privilege of trying out some of my health projects in the schools here. I have been able to spend many times after work and school hours with Bolenge and Congo Christian Institute students. They are a fine bunch of men and women and are learning a great deal about how to be bigger and better men and women. Bolenge, too, has grown mentally and physically, and many of the quarrels that were formerly settled by violent fights and finally brought to the missionaries to settle, or at least to cure their wounds, are now settled in a much quieter way by the church elders. At least all the minor ones are settled in the village. The old brick church that was the first brick church in this part of the country was used also for the school, or at least some classes, but now the old industrial building, also brick, houses the school. There must be twenty-five classes of ten or more each. The institute, of course, is separate from Bolenge station and has its own brick buildings for classes. There are one hundred students, counting the women. This is our only advanced school for teachers, preachers, and nurses. It was always so hard for natives of different tribes to play games together and not get in fights, but they are actually learning teamwork and sportsmanship of the finest kind. Last Saturday I saw a soccer game, the European version of football. Now you can get the Africans to do a job because it is needed and when I was here before it was always pay, pay, pay. Their Christian enthusiasm is growing in leaps and bounds if only we can realize the challenge and seize the opportunity now . . .

It is hard to know that folks are having so bad a time at home; so many out of work and living on nothing, and we can do nothing much to help.

Buena Rose Stober to Her Diary, January–February 1933—Near Mondombe, Congo Belge

Gertrude Shoemaker and I on itineration into the Tofoke trip.

How interesting these people are, differing from the tribes next to them. The men are big and husky, and every woman is either pregnant or caring and nursing an infant and dozens of husky youngsters playing around their feet; while the Ladia people are scrawny, sooty, diseased babies

had been uneven and sporadic. During the period of exponential commercial growth in the Congo in the 1920s, however, taxation became much more systematic, mainly because the Belgians believed that the colony should be economically self-sufficient. Tax revenue usually was funneled into the developing urban commercial centers, where it rarely benefited the majority of Congolese people. During the Great Depression, the annual "head tax" became a tremendous burden for the average Congolese person.

or none at all. And while the Tofokes' backyards are full of nice bananas, plantains, and all kinds of food and are excellent hunters prowling plenty of good meat for their families, the Ladia often come in from their hunts with nothing or so small an animal to divide among so many. I got a lot of amusement peeking at a bunch of normal Tofoke boys at church poking each other as boys will and wiggling. The Ladia children are too quiet. There is no syphilis in the Tofoke tribe except those mixed with the Ladia.

A wrinkled old lady visited with us, telling us how they came from Lomami fighting their way through in what must have been a terrific succession of raids. A white man shot her husband, and he was thought dead, but lived, went to prison, and later turned out to be a friend of the white man. We have several fine Tofoke on the mission in school or evangelistic work and are training some nurses. The second group of Tofoke came from Lomami later but returned all but one man who has yaws. He is Bombande Lazare and was cared for by the first group, finally received neodiarsenol from the mission and was cured.

We had a funny incident the first night in the Tofoke village. They put us in a small house which we noticed needed the palm leaf roofing repaired and some of the Christians were up on the roof repairing it as there were clouds hinting at rain. It did. Our two cots were directly under the drip, so we thought we would put on our raincoats on top of the mosquito nets and be all right; unfortunately, it rained in torrents and as Gertrude raised up in bed later she bumped her head into the net thus tipping the accumulated rainwater into the middle of her bed so that everything was soaked. We finally put the two cots together fortunately my net and bedding were double-sized so we made out okay but laughed so hard over it we could hardly get back to sleep.

In the Ladia villages we were treating a twelve-year-old girl with injections for syphilis, and I was so exasperated to think parents had no more knowledge of their daughter's whereabouts when the nurse's wife spoke up and said, "Well, Mama don't be too sure that you wouldn't give in as she has. Once I would not accept a man my parents wanted for me, and I was tied to a tree covered with stinging ants until I agreed." I understood a lot more about several tribes when she got through telling her story.

Many Tofoke people do not understand Lonkundo so our Tofoke evangelist, Bikongo Nataniele, interpreted for her. They do not know much Lingala, either. The church is only partially roofed, no benches, no pulpit as they hope soon to move to a better location more centrally located. This used to be a church of two or three hundred but the depression was pretty hard on them so many went back to their Lomami relatives and thought that they could save them from all taxes and ills while the church could not. But what do numbers count when those left are so sincere and earnest?

The church in Bayenga, Ladia, had been nice with a *ndele* roofing or swamp palm leaf from the river. Here were neat benches made of arranging six stakes in the mud floor. These had their forked end up and poles arranged across them and a reed mat as the seat and back. Here were cupboards for books also made of poles and reeds, the pulpit was a tamped mud affair [seven lines are illegible].

Gertrude and Mrs. Hurt had spent hours recently teaching "Frère Jacques" to the evangelists so that they could in turn teach their schoolchildren. This song is "Are you Sleeping?" in English and can you imagine our surprise to be met with such a song after a hard morning's travel; we manage to keep our faces straight, but it wasn't easy. In all the villages where we had evangelists we were pleased to find them trying to put the health rules into practice: gardens made, trees and flowers planted, toilets dug, and springs properly dug, cleaned, and perhaps fence or cover to keep them clean.

January 31. We slept in the village where there was no evangelist there, only one Christian and he begged for an evangelist. Later Christians from nearby villages came over to join us about 6:00 p.m. One man brought us some little leopard babies to sell. They of course cried all the time. The mother had gone foraging, but the natives were so scared that the mother would follow the man's tracks into the village, and I of course was scared too; so, the man skinned and then buried or ate the meat, and he promised to bring the other baby that had been killed by a dog. I wanted the skins but not the care of the poor little things. They set a guard of five men with a big fire when we went to bed and Gertrude propped a gun against the bed and we were supposed to sleep. However, the light of the fire crackling and the five men's mumbling and playing an instrument all night long didn't leave much of a chance for sleep; besides, every noise frightened us into thinking the mother was there. One fellow had a terrible nightmare thinking the leopard was getting him but there had been no mother leopard when the morning came and later we learned the man had crossed quite a stream while carrying the babies, so we need not have worried.

February 1. We were awakened early as the men wanted to get out of there and our clothes were almost snatched and packed before we could get dressed, gulp some coffee, and eat an egg apiece. All the smooth riding on our bikes we had enjoyed so far was finished, and we were climbing or riding down rain-washed roads through steep hill country. The hills were so steep we had to have someone push our bikes and were barely able to make it climbing. We crossed many sandy- and pebbled-bottom streams, clear and lovely. What a contrast to the muddy coffee-colored streams of the swamp lands.

At 10:30 a.m. all loads were put down and we were directed into the forest to see the famous waterfalls of Bofelela. We could hear the roar long before we got near and the carrier said it sounded like a river steamer coming. Of course, the villagers were very afraid of it and had taken offerings of money and food to throw to its spirit. The fellows began giving the familiar steamer call we hear every time they hear a steamer approaching anywhere along the rivers. We joined again until we arrived here as a train plunging over a fifteen-foot-high ledge. It was about thirty feet across and when we came near, we could see the cave back under the falls. To the Congolese this is awesome. To us it was beautiful with its fern- and moss-covered rocks, some as big as a house. There were African violets all through the forest, a flower that resembles the maypole and the loveliest yellow begonia, a tiny thing and the leaves tinged on the border with a delicate pink. Everything was wet and beautiful with spray. It is the only waterfalls in this part of the country and only place for rocks of any size. We took off our shoes to wade but the water was so swift and had dug tremendous crevices between the rocks. In the cave under the falls were many old shells used in trading, many coins and bits of food thrown to the spirit. I snitched one small coin and one tiny shell. They said at one time when many tried for migrating from the north a group of Ladia men and women running from Mbelo warriors hid in this cave and a big piece of the overhanging shelf caved in on them. The village of Yayenga could not stand the noise of the falls so they moved further east. Other tribes found it and have tales about it during their migration. We waded over the top of the cave in a safe place and found there were no fish in the stream.

The next village we reached was Yongoli and at evening we visited with the evangelist and his family. Everyone had another Bofelela story and someone told of a Bokome native who lives on the main Tshuapa River and is said to rub his legs with a red body powder and walk across the deep river. We will see. The Sunday services were fine with a sermon by an evangelist, Ifalina, about having courage like Stephen did, in spite of danger.

February 2. The rising drum was beaten at 5:15 a.m. And I preached about our bodies as the houses of God. And Gertrude looked after the school while the nurse and I took care of sick folks. After breakfast we sent two men back to the station with the plants we had collected at the Bofelela. While we cared for more sick folks, Gertrude went off into the forest with some hunters and her gun. They got no meat. In the late afternoon a crowd of folks for neodiarsenol injections arrived and we had to finish by lamplight.

February 3. Soon we were back in a town that speaks Lonkundo and were escorted through the town by a group of children, old ladies, and even a chieftain; but after an hour or so it got tiresome and barely endurable, so we tried politely to send them back. Later we stopped to rest and read a story to each other. Gertrude killed the monkey for the carriers' food and all rejoiced. We met an old man burned from smoking tobacco in a bamboo water pipe; they get so much nicotine they faint and fall into the fire oftentimes. He had been at the hospital four or five months ago for treatment of similar burns. He fibbed about it and said his house caught on fire and in dragging out his child and to get his clothes, the house fell on him; however, everyone seemed to know he was lying.

The tax collector, a Congolese, came to call on us bringing a present of two chickens, fourteen eggs, *bieye*, something like asparagus, and a market for the carriers. He was having trouble with his eyes, so the government gave him a *teepoi* to ride in. He has collected tax here for five years and seems very nice and clean.

February 4. We have more trouble with Gertrude's bike, and since she is bigger than I am we decided that she had better ride mine and I took hers. The villagers had rushed out early to clean the path ahead of us that should have been done before, as word had been sent ahead, even if they have no pride to do it for themselves until they feared we might report this condition to the Belgian official. The two fellows that helped us get our bikes up the steep hills were good sports and in play put *ngoji*, a vine, around their necks so we did the same. An old heathen met us and asked who had put us in prison as the prisoners have chains or *ngoji* around their necks. We all had a good laugh. The brakes of the bike are not working so we cut the basket off and used the fiber on the brakes. I fell in the black-looking swamp water about halfway up my leg, so they said I looked like I was wearing only one boot. Gertrude tried for another monkey but failed this time.

When we arrived at the evangelist's village, Baenge greeted us but said his wife Bofili was fishing. It is such a nice clean place. The church has been rubbed with pretty pink clay wash and he has painted on it "*L'église de Dieu, mission protestante DCCM.*" There is a lovely big Boala tree with its foot-long pea-like pods hanging down and seeds bigger than silver dollars, a pretty, shiny brown under the tree. It provides a lovely shade for our impoverished dispensary and treatment with injections of neodiarsenol. Sometimes it is easy but at other times nearly impossible to get into the vein, so we have to give it into the muscles which is sometimes painful. A man arrives with yaws and also two infected children. Sometimes we give it free to children, but this man paid two knives a Congolese blacksmith made, but he was supposed to pay around thirty cents for his own, but it made him mad, so he took his knives and went off with his children untreated. He probably could afford it, according to information. The knives would have only been ten cents or thereabouts.

We are carrying a galvanized tub with our pots and pans in it, and you can imagine how good even a shallow bath feels after a hard day's travel and work. Some places have streams usable as baths, but many are too public or too dirty looking.

February 5. I slept through the early morning prayer service and only wakened when Gertrude returned from it and went back to bed. It was raining so we stayed until 8:00 a.m. How good it felt to have a time for diaries and letters. The big chief's son arrived in a *teepoi* and asked to be baptized. He wanted schoolbooks too.

We had eighty-nine at Sunday School. After church services, the nurse and I continued our injections for yaws and syphilis. The sous chef came in with an ulcer on his arm and the bone was eaten away until it hung useless and smelly, only hidden by his coat sleeve that he was careful to wear all the time. He had yaws, so we gave him an injection, then the chief's son had to have a worm medicine. What a life! I took a bath, then had to treat the evangelist's son with sulfur ointment, and my bike boy had to have itch medicine, too, so was instructed to bathe good and hard first and come back for more tomorrow. He will have to carry a load instead of helping with the bikes. In thirty minutes, he appeared after a good bath, completely covered with sulfur ointment. Later we had oodles of noodles and chicken for dinner. Bofili, the evangelist's wife, made us a present of palm-gravy and greens that were delicious. By the time we had finished the sun was going down as we were late with everything. We didn't need any supper. We all got fooled because there was no sun to show us the time of day. The chieftain said he would send some market, but it was already 4:00 p.m. or 5:00 p.m. we know now. Two of our crowd went to preach in a nearby village but it was dark before they got there. Another goes to see a relative and only gets half there when it is dark. We had thought it was noon at 4:00 p.m.

February 6. Off for Yansala. Some took a forest shortcut and often our path led us through sandy strips in which our bicycles revolted. Under and over fallen trees, tremendous roots, and ditches; but we took time to rest in a nice forest to read *Milestones* while the carriers went on past.

We were on our way to the village of Yansala and an old man passed with two antelope horns filled with witch medicine, a lot of leaves, and oil in them and no telling what else, but the old man assured us that they contain the spirit of his father. He wears them on the back of his neck and refused my offer of five francs if he would give them to me for my collection of Congolese medicine and charms. He said that although he could heal others with his father spirit, he cannot heal himself but would have to go to another medicine man for care.

Yansala has already built its mud-walled thatched church and is planning on other buildings. There is a nice group of Christians. The evangelist has planted young fruit trees. The school showed that the teacher had been trying, although he isn't very far in school himself.

February 7. There are so many old folks here that think it is their duty to beg money from us. We bought fifteen chickens and sent them to Mondombe, along with souvenirs such as knives, spears, and sent a letter telling our whereabouts.

Having finished the counties of Tofoke and Mpangu we were off to the beach at Bokone. We never failed to draw a crowd with their exclamations of, "What teeth! What legs! Look at her arms! She is laughing! She is mad Iyei! *Bekolo eki-nd-oya*, what legs!" We arrived at Yalikungu and stopped to see Monsieur Brebois, the sanitary agent who is examining all Mpangu. We drank coffee, ate cookies, and were very much impressed by his fine attitude for Congo's white and black. He does not know Lonkundo or Lingala but talks to his Kasai boys who translate for him. He has three helpers, and we were amazed to see how neat he keeps his medicine trunk, each bottle in a neat sack. Not all of the sanitary agents are so careful and interesting. My trunk of medicines doesn't look that good. He has already examined all the natives in the territory except Liondo, which is Dr. Baker's part, and very big. We will cross the river to Liondo next. On our way we almost passed the landmarks the carriers left for us to show the way; in fact, we rode right over these *mbune*, a twig that is broken to close the wrong way.

The Loile is a very swift stream and the reed and pole bridge swayed back and forth making one dizzy and unsure. We met up with two former Christians that Gertrude knew but they had both gone heathen because we didn't have a teacher at their village, so they said. It diverted our attention away from the rocking bridge and the tiresome miles of pole bridges over swamps, and some of the poles were rotten at that. It is about twice as far as we had understood. Even at the swaying bridge it was 2:00 p.m. Stumble on, on, on to the chieftain's where they told us he was not there and there was no place to spend the night and even though we are tired and hungry we must drag ourselves on to the Misasi's where there is supposed to be a guest house. On, on, on tired, mad, hungry, and hot until the Misasi's house comes into view but there is no Misasi guardian. However, he comes rushing up in a few minutes. He goes back to the chief who had been there all the time hiding as he was ashamed that he had no rest house. We found our carriers at the rest house and were able to rest off our tired, shaky legs. We begged for a market, but nothing happened, and our workmen were very tired and hungry too. The Misasi went on a rampage and finally produced food for the workmen to buy. After resting, we played the Victrola to a nice crowd and had evening services, then went to bed after a quick supper.

February 8. Out at 5:00 a.m. having a song and prayer, eating a little breakfast on the run and following the paddlers we were hiring, our carriers coming in the middle of the safari. My rubber sole to my shoe finished tearing off on the roots, so I tried tying the sole down, but it doesn't hold so it flops away until I finally go barefoot. Ugh! Through the swamps there was always the wet ooze between my toes even when you stubbed them on the hidden roots. When we reach the beach, the Tofoke carriers who were with us were afraid of the canoes and water and I never saw such stark fear registered on faces. While we were in the canoe, I opened the bag and found another pair of shoes, so I was comfortable again. We finished our breakfast on a lake leading to the main river. What a sameness of greenery there is on any water in Congo through the forest. We finally reached the Tshuapa River and were soon across where Madame Fausotte, a merchant's wife, met us and invited us to stay all night and we absorbed her wonderful hospitality. Monsieur Fausotte was at Coquilhatville for surgery and she was caring for things. She wore a long skirt of native material and looked like something from Paris. She has raised a chimpanzee and treats it like her own child. We had two white men from a steamer for breakfast the next morning and it seems that the chimp has learned to hunt the papaya we ate.

After breakfast we said our goodbyes and were off again, this time to a place called Yangili. In a place in the forest again we found the fork in the road but this time we stopped and read the sign the *lobuni* that our workmen had left for us to show us which road to take, and we soon caught up with them. We met two Christian boys who were very much surprised to see us; apparently, they had not received our message that we were coming. The two boys rushed back and soon a message about our imminent arrival was heard on the call drums. So, the evangelist will know. We stopped in a drum shed to rest and visited with a group of dirty and itchy and jiggery youngsters. A motherly little girl of seven is lugging a nine-month-old baby called Thomas who really bellows when I take him. The mother has gone to the woods to get food and wood. We pass so many drum sheds in every tiny village where there is the shed with its thatched roof of swamp-palm leaf made up like big shingles and tighter rafters that are again tied on the poles to protect the big drums sitting off the ground on four pegs. These drums are shaped different from any we have seen so far, that is, tapered off toward the top of the drum at each end. There are a few hills here, too, but it is mostly smooth riding. On the way, we pass another kind of shed for discussing palavers, and a man rushes out to sell us a small leopard skin but it is full of insects.

"How much is it?"

"$1.00."

"That is too much."

An old gray-bearded man appears and says, "Ten *mpata*," (which is equal to $1.00), "or you don't get it."

"Four *mpata* only will I pay."

He puts the skin on his head with the tail dangling down his back and begins a chant of "Ten *mpata* or you can't have it" and starts swaggering to his home. "Ten *mpata* or you can't have it."

"No, four *mpata* or I don't want it," and we get on our bikes and start off.

"White man, white man, would you pay five *mpata*?"

"Yes, bring it along to the evangelists."

When we arrive, sure enough they had not had our message and since the drum message had just been received there were no Christians to meet us.

Their houses are nice, and the church is big, but this time the roofing is another leaf from the forest but not quite as good as the *ndele* or swamp palm leaf roofing. It is tied into big shingles also. The church benches are big logs laid in rows. The platform and pulpit are tamped mud. The cupboard for supplies is made of the usual reeds.

The old man arrives with his leopard skin, but the evangelists and the man agree to accept four *mpata* and a half, or about two francs and fifty centimes. Later they come back for more money, so I give them the skin and take the money back. Our cots are here and made up, so we take a little rest. After rest Gertrude has school and I do my usual hygiene stunts but this time with posters and we sing the rules. It isn't a very big school.

The head man is a young fellow and very helpful to the teachers. He gets together a nice market for us to buy and then we have services with a nice crowd. We play the Victrola for them. Some of the crowd had never seen a flashlight and called it the light without heat, or the lightning.

February 9. We are out early to get the loads tied up, eat our breakfasts, have a brief service, and say goodbye after another session of school with them. We lectured the older folks on sending their children to school and wonder if any more will do it.

We were told that it wasn't far to the next evangelist. The streams are still, lovely little sand-bottomed, lovely and tempting to wade. They had evangelists who had come across river with us and four of his carriers went back across the river as we had doubled up empty boxes or other loads. The head evangelist of the Liondo field showed us the way from there on.

Boongo is an ex-evangelist of Lotumbe and the last one left from the first missionary work in Mondombe. Is'ea Simon, the Mpangu evangelist who just returned, is the last of the Monieka men sent to evangelize Mondombe. Both married upriver women. Is'ea Simon has several children, his wife is from Mpangu, but Boongo's wife is from way off in the same territory as the Tofoke, but she is of another tribe. He is much quieter than Is'ea Simon but a very good old soul. He hasn't been back to Lotumbe since the work was started in Mondombe. These two men and their wives are shining examples that marriages between different tribes can work but they usually are the exception. Is'ea Simon had superintended the buildings at Yangili so of course he was glad to visit there. Boongo's wife has been sick and has been off mentally, but she seems to be all right now. She came back from a visit to our home with a little boy about ten who has a harelip and it is doing her good to have someone to care for. She had a lot of fun comparing words with the Tofoke carriers. They found many words that were similar in their tribal languages.

We arrived at Yalofete about 10:00 a.m. at evangelist Boleko's. His wife is a lovely person and we are very fond of her. His Christian men work mostly at a big coffee and rubber plantation called Yalusaka in order to earn their tax money.

We try to find the arsenical soap we had packed to care for the leopard skins and ordered to treat them as Madame Fausotte had taught us; we found that one of the carriers had misunderstood washing the skins in the swamp water and using the soap on his own skin. At least no one could find the soap and his skin seemed to be well cured. After raving around a bit, I took the skins and washed them again and asked someone to show me the way to the swamp. One of the young Christians started downhill and it was very much downhill, when we met our wash lad just coming up with our clothes. I was pleased to find them so nice and clean but when I got downhill, I found he had been washing them in the spring of drinking water. I was pretty sore, but the teacher and some little boys following behind helped me open up a place in the side of this spring and let the dirty clothes suds run off. I suggested that we clean it while we were at it. When most of the worst had run out, we dipped out the rest, dug it deeper, and cleaned and closed the runoff place making a better dam so that I guess maybe Boleke forgave Bomanga for his nice clean clothes. I rinsed my furs in a pan outside of the spring.

School again after dinner, a rest, and clean-up.

February 10. Our last Sunday was to be at Nyangombula but we went through Yeleka and stopped for a while. We found a nice white folks' house, big gardens cleared, several new houses built by the Christians for their preacher and themselves. They were all very much disappointed that we were not to spend the night. We had services with them, then Gertrude had school while I sang songs, counted within in French, Lonkundo, and Lingala, and they did it in Ladia, their own language. Then we played games. Boonga and the headman's daughter helped me, then the girl and Boongo took them off to try reading and writing. I played with the little ones. It is interesting to me how quickly the most frightened heathen little ones will forget their fears and enter into games and songs. They had almost as much fun as I did. Even some of the old folks got so interested they could hardly keep out.

February 11. Sunday morning. At Yeleka, Liondo, we waited for church services and Sunday School until some other villagers could get in. After church I made a collection of native medicines, or rather charms, just strings and bits of fur we found on Christians' necks. Everybody wears them, and they were supposed to cure an itch, various ailments, make your wife or husband faithful, and prevent harm of various kinds. But somehow they do not seem to work at times. A group of drummers went by with several gayly painted, hollowed-out-of-a-piece-of-tree drums, the portable kind. They were wearing seeds around their waist, strung like beads, and various kinds of rattles. There being one Christian in the lot I managed to stop him and give them a piece of my mind for they were going to give some relatives the horrible medicine, or charm, called *botamba* that is supposed to make you live forever. I am not so sure the lecture took, but I was soon called to see a Christian who had a broken leg for about a month. A tree had fallen on him. I couldn't do much as it had been too long but showed him how to keep it bound up and how to wash the ulcer caused by a cut on the heel but also tried to persuade him to have them carry him in for Dr. Baker's care; but since he didn't come in the first place, he will probably not have courage enough to come now. Poor heathens, they are so terribly afraid of their *ndoke*, or evil spirits.

After dinner I had just fixed myself up on the cot very comfortably when the drums began beating that a certain woman was dying and some very much besmeared-with-ashes women, naked and wailing, came rushing up and saying that the woman's intestines had all come out. One of these women was a Christian and still had enough trust in our judgment to call me. The Congolese nurse's aide and I collected what we had that would probably serve us but of course we had no idea what we were getting into. Limame, the nurse, had his bike along, too, so off we went. It seems that it had happened the day before and they had just gotten up enough courage to call me. To my surprise the woman was able to talk, and although her pulse was faster and weaker than usual, she was not in shock as I half expected. She was lying in a drum shed on a bed of banana leaves and the supposed prolapse of the intestines was a uterine tumor that was so heavy it had pushed itself out and what they saw was a gangrenous tumor mass. She had one of them to take her to Dr. Baker the day before; and even at Christmas time they knew that she probably needed surgery, but the relatives would not agree to send her in. I was about decided that in spite of all the mourners I was going to be forced to hire some men to carry her to Mondombe. She said she was hungry, and they had given her nothing to eat since it happened; so, I had to rustle some food for her but not a soul had any food, so they said, and I got mad and went into the house and found a piece of manioc bread rolled in and steamed in a big leaf. The hostess couldn't well deny it was bread and so gave it to me. Everyone else said they had no food, which of course wasn't so, but an excuse to save energy by making some more for themselves. I took my little bundle back to my patient and the evangelist's wife who had arrived heated it for her. I finally threatened them that if they didn't get some men to carry her, I would write the state official and ask his help. Of course, they didn't want it reported, so they found two or three men willing to travel all night in the moonlight to and across the river to reach Mondombe. The story is that they arrived the next afternoon, that is, Monday, but when they came home, we found the doctor had already operated removing the gangrenous part without an anesthetic she was so weak. She is up and around now, and very gratefully came to our house to say thank you. She is happy as a lark and is reporting the fame of Dr. Baker abroad. We only hope she continues to improve. He is famous already of course because she is still living. Maybe even a fellow with a broken leg will come in now.

Up to now most of the surgery is last resort work for those who live a distance away and to some live close by also. They found out that we know what we are talking about concerning syphilis, yaws, sleeping sickness, hernias, elephantiasis, and other tumors, but they go to the heathen medicine man for all else whom they think can hocus-pocus them into health. It is evil spirits that cause disease, and it takes spirit medicine to fight them; so, the witch doctors fight us on every hand, as they must hold their means of gain. There are whole groups of them in nearby villages. We had a premature two months baby on its way to health but finally a medicine man told them not to give it its mother's milk and finally not to give it supplementary feedings, so of course it dwindled away. When I came back for my trip, Mrs. Hurt and Lois Marie who had been preparing the milk and taking it to them were just crushed to think they had lost it, but what they hadn't found out was that the baby had not had any milk. The Christians told us afterward the truth about it and how that many nights they secreted the infant out to do their hocus-pocus.

Against malaria, dirt, and ignorance we haven't even begun to win our fight, and of course they are saturated with fear, so that it will take many more hard years of work on the part of as many workers as our Christians at home can possibly send out before we win this battle in Africa. Of course, Mondombe is one of the most backward fields and one has to go downriver in order to get a little encouragement at times but even here there are those that are beginning to understand. We have some thirty families on the station who are actually doing a nice job of caring for their children's schooling, health, and Christian character, so although it looks hopeless at times it isn't when we really stop to count up.

February 12. When a horse starts home you know he always goes faster; so it was with us, for as we packed up, we decided that if we got a canoe we would visit the school at Yalikole and then come downriver and a canoe as Gertrude hadn't been feeling extra well since Yalifete and riding the bike made her feel worse. As we rode along, we gathered some lily bulbs to decorate Gertrude's side yard and I managed to get some blue sweet pea seeds and a few slips to see if I could get the wild sweet peas started on the station. We also found another pretty flower and gathered seeds to try it. Most of the houses along the way were pretty good but we passed through one miserable village of terribly dilapidated huts, only bark and leaves and too low to stand up in. A blind man came out of one of them and commenced grieving because the white mamas were passing, and he couldn't even see them. Poor thing! He will never know what he missed. One place we stopped early in the voyage we found all the loads put down and everyone seeking to buy food. It seems that one of the carriers had left his hat back where we slept so he had to go back and get it while the others waited. But they did not waste their time. We bought three pieces of bread for them, and they divided into such even pieces as only natives can. They surely were in good spirits. One fellow has been a perfect clown all the way in, so he amused us all by swinging from a palm branch and growling like a fierce wild animal. One day we asked Ilenge Thomas how he could be so gay and carry a load when he was no longer a young man but the father of a married daughter. He replied that he had to be funny as all the rest worked better if he kept them laughing and surely it was so. They tied a rattle on his leg and he sang and danced along like a sixteen-year-old while everyone got under their loads and sang and danced as they went in time to his monkey shines; as Gertrude says, it's a poor crowd that hasn't at least one clown.

Besides that, he never complained and was carrying his half of one of the heavier loads. His partner was a great big silent fellow whom everyone liked too. His daughter was unable to feed her baby and we are feeding it at our house although it lives with them.

We arrived at Yalikole about 10:30 a.m. Lokosa Paul is one of the new teachers, but he has a nice group of boys gathered around him and the administrator who is overseeing some work in Yangole closely has seen to it that they are building him a house. Lokake, his wife, has a new baby and was intending to go into the station for the arrival but she waited too long; however, they have taken fine care of the new one and it is a nice baby. I go over to see the administrator and his wife while Gertrude rests up. It is about half a mile away. There is a little stream on the way where Mr. Hendricks is overseeing the building of a bridge. I meet him at the bridge, and he goes with me up to see Madame. She is in pajamas endeavoring to keep cool. She is another fine Belgian woman, fair, freckles, and red hair, very interesting to talk to and a good sport. She travels around with him all over the country and that means on the road twenty days out of every month, living in native huts, eating tinned food and whatever fresh things one can pick up, which isn't much unless there are teachers of the mission at the villages. He has a motorbike with a sidecar and of course this is why he is interested in the roads. Motorbikes are an improvement over bikes, I assure you, although I'm afraid I'm not mechanical enough to run one. He is quite worried because I decline the offer of a little whiskey to rest me "or surely just a little for Miss Shoemaker since she said she isn't feeling so well." Instead, she insists on me taking her the whole custard she has made for dinner to my invalid. The administrator arranges for a canoe and then takes me back in a sidecar.

Buena Rose Stober to Dr. Myrtle Smith, March 2, 1933—Mondombe, Congo Belge

Well what news? Any nearer to sailing than you were when you last wrote?

After reading Ruth's letter, Gertrude and I thought it would be best for her to buy the bike from me and I'll pay the original six hundred francs asked for it by Bekombe. He probably needs the money worse than the bike, and Gertrude certainly needs a good one badly. She had trouble all the last trip and now it is deader than a doornail, so here with a check for $18.00 and I hope it will find you ready to start back to Congo.

I received Tessie's program and like it very much. I think it is just the sort we need for organized health work in our schools. As it is now, everyone works out his own ideas and the students all come down to the Congo Christian Institute with different standards of training, all good but not correlated. Again, with a health program a new missionary could teach health without so much confusion. I hope she will finish it soon and send it out for us to use as she knows what we need.

Thanks very much for the other path leads you sent as they will help me finish my baby welfare booklet in Lonkundo. I am still clinging to the hope of finishing it and getting it before the committee before I leave. We shall see.

I miss Bokolombe so even yet and hope I will get to see him before I leave. He writes such nice letters. His good cooking and antics or jokes put me in a good humor when I come home tired and hungry.

The Hurts are out on an itineration. Dr. and Mrs. Baker have just gotten back from making the medical census of the big *chefferie* across river from us, and Gertrude and I have only been home two weeks, so you see we have all been on the move in the back country.

I'm tired and ready to go home. Wish I could see you.

Buena Rose Stober to Her Diary, Undated

1933 to 1934 were my years of visit to the USA during the depression years when there was no money and church offerings were impossible. We lived on half salaries, and one time I remember receiving around $39.00 only. We all got by, and I even went to school and took some more chemistry. Jim sold his royalty for our place in Oklahoma City, and I kept mine, so I made enough from our interest in the oil to buy a little place in Arkansas. We moved dad out there the summer of 1934, but he died that fall, even though he enjoyed the place very much.

I use this poster message as a conclusion to my talks in conventions and churches here in the States and many Christians came to me and asked that I write Njoji Mark, Bokese Paul, and other workers in Africa that they would do their part. So, I wrote these messages to Mark on Christmas day, and this letter of his is the answer to it. Bokese Paul, head evangelist of the church at Mondombe, says that we must cooperate and have faith in each other, most of all in Christ. He says the missionaries and the Christians in the USA are like big logs that support the pot, and the little black sticks are the black evangelists. By their cooperation food is cooked by the fire of the teachings of Jesus, but if the big logs are taken out all the weight of the big pot will come down on the little sticks and soon put out the fire and the food will not be cooked, and the people of Africa will not be fed the teachings of Jesus Christ.

Njoji Mark to Buena Rose Stober, February 1934—Bolenge, Congo Belge

Your letter arrived here well, and I have written all the different stations, Lotumbe, Monieka, Mondombe, Wema, and Coquilhatville (to the native church leaders and elders) as you wished, and also the things you wrote. I rejoice with all the words that you wrote and think all the elders will rejoice too. And we have faith that the words which you wrote will come true, perhaps if they do not come true at once, they will later on.

Now we are in the midst of sending some very strong leaders into the Ubangi River district. The people of Ubangi called for someone from Bolenge to come strengthen them in doing the will of our Lord Jesus. The people of Ubangi want this, but the hard thing is the lack of funds. But in spite of lack, pray the Lord that this affair of the Lord will succeed greatly yonder on the river Ubangi.

Another thing of awe is how the white folks (missionaries) are all finished here by returning to America and I do not hear that others are coming back this year. How about this? We have scarcely no missionaries left here.

We had a very happy Christmas as usual, but the thing of sorrow is our lack for many things that we do at Christmas time, which could not be done because of lack of money, but those which we did have sufficed.

I thought you had forgotten the Nkundo of Congo altogether when, all of a sudden, I received your letter; thus, it was very good, Mputu. Abide in Christ and be strengthened greatly until you return to us in Congo because many people are looking forward to the return of Mputu if it be the will of the Lord himself. Greetings to the churches, remember them we do always, and may they continue to put their hearts here because the faith is there that Congo will succeed.

Receive many greetings for yourself and those of your own family. Greetings. The good news in Congo is succeeding in spite of the great lack of money, and the good news which you have heard, let it not stay there in one place at all.

Buena Rose Stober to Friends, January 27, 1935—Bolenge, Congo Belge

It is foolish of me to write each of you separately as I will be saying about the same thing, but while it is fresh on my mind I wanted to give you a summary of my first impressions after nearly two years' absence from my work. There have been both joys and sorrows, gains and losses, successes and failures, as of course you would expect during these hard depression years. Some of us returning to the field, although we saw the worst of the depression at home, are finding it exceedingly hard to adjust our old methods of working or even new ones dreamed up while on furlough to the present amount of money for the work. If I give a gloomy picture it is because I want you to see what I see and still keep faith with our fine Christians out here who have been able to hold their faith and work steadily on for the kingdom of God.

When I got to Bolenge my first impression was to find the SW *Oregon* tied up to the beach and all the crew dismissed except Captain Jean, and to hear that the four launches of Bolenge, Lotumbe, Monieka, and Mondombe were scarcely being used at all because there were no funds to buy gasoline or wood. Since they had to pay the student evangelists anyway, they were being used to paddle a canoe when missionaries or African pastors and evangelists went to visit back country village work. Sometimes there are Christians who volunteer for such transportation without pay; then the students need not be taken out of their schools. Traveling by canoe is not as comfortable sometimes and it takes lots of time; but money can be saved in this way. Even though time is lost it gives more money for evangelistic travel.

Although every six months a new eager group comes for baptism in all the districts there is unrest among those whose Christianity does not go very deeply, and actually some "go back heathen," as we call backsliding. The number of villages having evangelists has been drastically cut, not only because some evangelists refuse to work for such little salaries offered them; but even then, there wasn't enough left for what is considered a living wage out here. I was shocked to find out that some of our fine men graduates of our Congo Christian Institute are only receiving $1.00 to $1.50 a month. There are perhaps as many as ten of them receiving $5.00 a month but they are heads of some very special tasks, such as schools, where food is expensive and living on the smaller salaries is impossible. Do you wonder that two or three of these graduates have accepted fine jobs and salaries with companies and have left the evangelistic work to suffer? There are many of our less-educated evangelists receiving so much less than the amounts above that they have to spend months out in the forest hunting copal to sell and pay for their yearly head tax. Copal is still on the market and brings a smaller but fair price, as it is used for varnish. Hunting copal means being away from their little flocks or sometimes with them for months hunting in the jungle for the tree that drops its resin into the swamps or mud all around. Even with a low morale and unrest caused by this low wage scale, I believe that the real power of the life of Jesus Christ is gaining a progressive hold on these Africans or why would they stand by the work when they could live comfortably in their own home villages?

Of course, I haven't seen any farther than Bolenge and Coquilhatville, but one can get a great deal of information from the upriver missionaries and African letters. I will be going upriver to Monieka after I finish a stage at the Coquilhatville Government Hospital. After the arrival of the Watts baby, I will be stationed at Wema during the furlough of Goldie Alumbaugh. She leaves in June.

As to the school work it has grown in spite of the cuts. Bolenge alone has something over three hundred on the station in school, boys, girls, men, and women not counting the students of the Congo Christian Institute and their wives. Here again the small budget is preventing actual progress, where Miss Poole says she used to have over four hundred francs weekly for school materials and pay for her teachers she has now barely a hundred francs. Our schools are very poorly equipped in comparison with the Catholic schools financed by the government, where they have three or four white teachers we have only one, and the same applies to supplies. However, they do practically no school work in the back country villages away from their stations while each one of our evangelists is supposed to have a school each day. Some of the schools are fine while others not much to brag about that at least they are creating a hunger for learning.

In our boys' dormitory at Bolenge we used to have fifty to one hundred boys, but now we only can afford twenty-five. The girls' dormitory has only ten now and when I was stationed at Bolenge we used to have twenty to thirty girls. The standards of school have been raised on all the stations.

I appreciate the work of our Congo Christian Institute very much as they have not only put out finer, better prepared preacher-teachers, they have unified the work of our six stations and caused them to raise their standards so that their students will be accepted. This may seem of little importance to the casual reader, but it has a tremendous importance to the growth of the work as a whole.

If anything, our hospital and general medical work has gone backward or at least stood still, and this is a big disappointment to me. Because medical equipment, medicine, and medical workers are beyond our means at present, still the people suffer from a million ailments we might heal . . .

if! Of course, the number of patients coming to our dispensaries remains nearly the same and the few able to pay have made it possible to do something; still our crippled abilities have been hard for most of the Africans to understand, and I must admit it is hard for me to understand also. All children, our workmen, our evangelists and families are treated free so that the budget is mostly used up for them. Being liberal with free treatments in the past has made a medical work famous, but it has also made us look mighty stingy in this crisis. We have three MDs and three graduate nurse missionaries at present: Dr. Baker at Mondombe; Dr. Jaggard at Monieka; Dr. Davis at Lotumbe; Miss Alumbaugh at Wema; Miss Bateman at Bolenge; Mrs. Watts at Monieka who has two children and expecting another in April. Dr. Jaggard and Miss Alumbaugh will be leaving in June. I will take Miss Alumbaugh's place at Wema, but Mrs. Watts with three children will be holding on at Monieka. You can easily see why the medical work isn't growing.

There is practically no industrial or agricultural work being done at present because there are no funds, but of course gardening must go on to provide food. Many missionaries seemed weary and depressed after their long terms without rest and little encouragement from home. Some of them should have been home for health reasons but hid the facts, so that money used getting them home could be used to get the folks on furlough back to the field. In spite of all this, each one seems optimistic about the future of his or her work. This happy hope keeps the Christians' power ever growing.

The church here at Bolenge is full every Sunday. Although Njoji Mark and some other older Christians are showing their age, younger ones with better training and finer hopes and ideals are ready to take over. The work has been kept intact in spite of all the cuts and restlessness, and there is a deepening and broadening of the African Christian. But you folks at home must not relax your efforts, for if you do there is no limit to the damage you may cause!

I was happy over the growth of the women's work here in Bolenge. While it used to be hard to get 20 or 30 women out to their meetings, they are now having 60 to 120 each week, and each seems to enjoy her part of the program.

Njoji Mark preached a good sermon on January 6 and I believe you would enjoy the outline of it herewith. His texts were Ephesians 6:10–20 and Mark 9:28–29. (1) The demons would come out by prayer only. (2) A child has communion with his parents through visiting. (3) Our wooden call drum is our means of communion with our neighboring villages. (4) The telegraph and wireless are the white man's means of communion with their homeland. (5) Why were the disciples of Christ not able to cast out the demon? Because they lacked communion with God. (6) Just as white man's method of communion with his homeland exceeds ours, his method of communion with God also exceeds our method. (7) If we are to cast out the demons of Congo we must commune with God. (8) In spite of all the wisdom we are learning we know that we are nothing. (9) Let us use our new wireless of communion with God to cast out the demons of Congo.

Buena Rose Stober to Friends, April 1, 1935—Monieka, Congo Belge

This is a good way to spend April Fool's Day: breakfast, care of Mrs. Watts and ten-day-old W. Oliver Watts. He weighed ten pounds and one half but lost the half last week. He is getting along fine now.

The night before Oliver came, Mrs. Watts supervised making pots in women's school and I had to have a lesson or so, as I have taken it over since she has been down. I have molded three flower pots and am as proud as can be. The riverine people are the pot makers and the inland people do weaving so that each group lorded it over the other when they were doing their kind of work and teased the other group. We will do baskets after we have burned this group of pottery. I have enjoyed demonstrating infant care to these women.

We had a man brought into the hospital last Tuesday night after I had finished baby clinic who had been attacked by several hippopotamuses. Dr. Jaggard tried to sew him up, but he was torn and gouged in so many places he died before we hardly started.

Here is the interesting medical report from Goldie Alumbaugh for 1934 at Wema, where I'll be taking over in a few weeks: Sleeping sickness patients treated, 115 cases; trypanosome of sleeping sickness found in 67 cases; cases returned for third series of ten injections, 9; cases returned for a second series, 26; cases eyes affected by treatment, 6; deaths, 9; mental ailments, 3; cases under treatment at the close of the year, 33; leprosy patients treated, 86; treated throughout the year, 26; in treatment at the close of the year, 51; spots, etc., still present but patients very much improved. Total number of treatments given to all patients, 20,619; total number of new patients treated, 549.

I hope you know this peek into my future job is awesome, to say the least. The mission is so understaffed it is hard to know which station needs them most. The sudden death of Roger Clarke we do not know how to face.[2] So few folks are headed this way at present.

2. Along with his wife, Virginia (1902–1972), Roger Clarke (1899–1935) had been

Buena Rose Stober to Friends, June 10, 1935—Wema, Congo Belge

It has been some days since I stole a few minutes to write; what a lot has happened since! I scratched the first draft of this notebook as I was being rushed along the jungle path out into the back country of Wema to see a sick white woman, a state official's wife. I had arrived in Wema even if it had taken me a long time to get here. Everyone was well and glad to see a new white face as usual. Miss Alumbaugh had been kept very busy trying to keep a couple attempts at murder from finishing off their big wounds by dying, but otherwise everyone seemed gay and well enough. I had just finished one week here both packing and unpacking going on in the house, which made it quite interesting to keep one's own things where they were supposed to be. But suddenly Goldie came down with a big fever and her packing was put off another week when we got a letter SOS to come and help this white woman, way off at Itoko on a small river. They sent a *teepoi*, the chair to carry me, with eight husky men to take turns, four about, to whisk me across country. Since of course Goldie was in no condition to go, off I was carried by those speedy travelers.

It was a bright sunny morning and it seemed so strange to be rushed through the jungle again. I had never traveled this way any distance before and although it is pretty rough riding, one is shaken up so much, it still was the quickest and safest way to travel. My old helper Bokolombe went with me following along on my bike. The *teepoi* was a chair tied between bamboo poles with a carrying pole in the middle, in front and back. There was a mat and canvas roofing and it had an auto cushion in the seat. It was of course Madame Burhin's, the sick woman's own *teepoi*, in which she traveled from village to village with her husband twenty days out of every month. I travel with the usual bedding, pots and pans, and medicines for any sick folks as there is nothing but jungle villages between Itoko and Wema. Miss Alumbaugh said I would find many sick folks. Speaking of courage and bravery these little state women that follow their husbands around really have it.

The trip took two very hard days' travel, and it is a very lonely place. She has a six-year-old boy and a tiny two-months-old infant. They are on

---

a missionary with DCCM since 1927, primarily at Bolenge. During a trip to Léopoldville for a meeting of the Protestant Missionary Council in 1935, he fell severely ill with an acute case of malaria. On the return trip by steamer, he fell, striking his head and causing a concussion. Though treated at the hospital in Coquilhatville, he died several weeks later on March 14, 1935, from complications of malaria and head trauma. His death was a severe blow to a missionary force already depleted by the Great Depression.

a branch of the Tshuapa River called the Lomela, and the Africans around here are about as wild as they come.

Uphill and down we went with banks of green vines and ferns on either side of the path. Many times, the foliage shut out the sunshine except for occasional flecks of it. As we went through villages, the carriers sang my name good and loud, making up amusing choruses to it so that everyone would know who they were taking to Itoko. The people would rush out and comment on my ability to smile, or my feet, or my teeth, and that only two years before as the administrator went through these villages the people would all hide out in the forest. The path was in fine shape for one that crossed several large swamps. When the Rowes made that same trip five years ago they crossed those same swamps on poles and fallen trees while I rode across on pole bridges tied together by reeds. The carriers didn't even have to wade much. The men didn't want to sleep at the chief's village that night and Goldie had told me that he was the fellow where they had celebrated a cannibal feast two or three years ago, so we slept at one of our evangelist's houses further on.

About half the carriers wore the head dress of the Wema secret societies, hair stacked with all the combings for years high on the head like our old-fashioned turbans, but more so, with a nice shiny row of white buttons down the center of it. Then they wore an oily, sooty black cloth over it to keep their hair in order. It is often a bright shiny red made by smearing redwood powder and palm oil over it and their bodies as well. It rubbed off on the *teepoi* and everything else they touched. The state has authorized any police to capture a native traveling on the main path with a lance, knife, spear, or weapon of any kind, but they say that two years ago even the carriers carried spears always no matter what their load. For once Bokolumbe was willing to stay close by without being asked, even though the path was good enough that he could speed ahead. He is a good cyclist and hates poking along with those on foot, but he was never out of sight these days.

We traveled through several places where the elephants had been through the night before and cut up the path pretty badly. The Africans have real teamwork to carrying a *teepoi* or paddling a canoe or anything of the kind where they need to work together. It is a wonderful rhythm they get into their songs of the *teepoi* or canoe. Once as we were crossing a very bad place the old cannibal chief should have fixed, they sang out in perfect rhythm without losing a beat or stumbling, "You of Bofanya, we told you to fix this path we were bringing a white woman over it and you didn't do it. So now you'll be sent away to the militia, downriver, and you will die. Bad people! You do not work your paths," and all that as if they were singing an ordinary song. When they get tired, they sooner or later got to singing an old favorite. The leader would sing out, "We carry a load from morning to night with only hunger," then everyone would join and chant, "With only hunger!" and when they were singing their feet were literally flying down the path to the rhythm of the song, sometimes they would sing the same one over and over again for an hour or so.

When we got to Itoko it was pouring down rain and the things in my suitcase were soaked. The carriers' bodies were shiny and drippy with rain and they slipped around terribly until I asked them to stop in some shack, but they wanted to arrive at the chief's. So, on we went until we came to the white folks' houses and by that time the rain was over. I found Madame in a better condition than I feared, but she needed help and could not get to a doctor, so I was glad to help and was also able to help the evangelist we had in the village and we treated some 125 patients.

On the way back to Wema, we took more time but at night we had a letter from Goldie saying that Mrs. Boyer was running very high fevers, so I rushed back from there on. When I got to Wema, I found Goldie and Mr. Boyer frantically packing ready to catch the boat downriver the next day as Mrs. Boyer had a terrible infection in her leg. It was red and angry-looking from her ankle to her knee and red streaks going beyond her knee. That night she was delirious and so you know we were glad to have them get on their way to a doctor. We have word back that she was a little better, but they traveled all night to get to Boende where there is a doctor. Goldie and the Boyers had planned a hike over land and go out by the way of the Nile but they will go out by the first boat now.

Wema is such a mixture of the most beautiful in Congo and the most sordid. The hospital is the most practically arranged of any on our stations, besides it has a hedge on either side of the path leading to the entrance of a lovely cape of jasmines and in front of the hospital lovely mauve bougainvillea drapes itself in great clusters all over the roof. Inside what motley looking faces and bodies tortured by disease, fear, and hate. We have had five very serious stabbing wounds since I came. Two of them were four or five inches long, to the bone, and bleeding all over everything. I am going to become a surgeon from necessity.

These were all "eye-for-an-eye" wounds. One fellow even came in while we were sewing up the wounds of his relative, took an invoice of her wounds, and in fifteen minutes the other side were in the hospital with his victim with almost identical wounds. Ugh! Next time I'll know better than to let someone take an inventory of a patient's wounds.

There is so much yaws here and now we have an epidemic of whooping cough, not to mention thirty sleeping sickness cases in all stages of the disease all coming for weekly injections. Off from the hospital in an open building thirty or forty leprosy patients are treated twice a week or more often if they have ulcers. They are so happy because they are actually being helped by their treatments.

Wema has twenty evangelists in the back country and they say it is growing. Six weeks in Wema doesn't give me long to judge but it looks good. They have a school on the station of 250 boys, girls, and women. [Three lines are illegible]. I also teach hygiene in the afternoon school.

We have a children's clinic of around forty infants weekly and fifty preschool children to be weighed. We are feeding [four lines are illegible]. They lean their walking sticks against the wall and prop themselves in various comfortable positions and listen quietly through the service as if they understood every word. Some of them are too deaf and others too old to understand much. Some of them are only rice Christians,[3] but after all most of them have found kindness and love enough that they want the life of Christ and find the rest not worthwhile.

Buena Rose Stober to Friends, October 29, 1935—Wema, Congo Belge

I have been thinking of you all and when I bid you goodbye and the promises we made to each other about letters, etc.; so, I thought I had better get busy and try my hand at the mimeograph again. I think I will just outline some of the most important things that have happened since a year ago November 2 when I sailed from New York.

I arrived in Congo at Matadi December 6 and at Bolenge December 14, in 1934, spending a very happy Christmas and New Year at Bolenge. January 2 to February 2 I spent at the Coquilhatville State Hospital trying to increase my wisdom and getting authority from the government to practice as a sanitary agent at Wema.[4]

3. The phrase "rice Christians" is a pejorative reference to native people who pretend to convert to Christianity only to receive material benefits offered by the missionaries, such as food, medical care, and education. Originating in the late seventeenth century, the phrase was used commonly among missionaries in Asia in the nineteenth century and later among missionaries in other parts of the world.

4. Beginning in the 1930s, parastatal health organizations began developing and providing medical care in the Belgian Congo. Funded cooperatively by the government, private enterprise, and Christian missions, these organizations employed "sanitary agents" as the public health experts for specific regions. These agents were the frontline workers in the colonial government's developing program of preventative medicine.

On February 15, I caught the first most inexpensive boat up to Monieka where I was to help Monieka out until Miss Alumbaugh's furlough was due and little Oliver Watts arrived in the world.

These are the most important bits of news while I was there: I taught the four white children's school from 8:30 a.m. until 11:30 a.m.; taught hygiene in all the native schools (for men and boys the subject was "Our Parasites," for women and girls it was "Baby Care"). Mrs. Watts taught some pot making and I learned a great deal more about it so that I supervise it in women's school now if I have help. Twins were born in the native village and instead of dancing all night with the naked little fellows the mother and father experimented with white men's ways and both babies are still living and thriving. I helped Mrs. Watts with the baby clinic and sewing class and then took them over while little Oliver was getting used to the world and his mother recovering. While I was there, we had the sad news of Mr. Clark's death and Mr. Weaver's and Mr. Snipe's terrible sicknesses. It was all so hard on the Bolenge, Coquilhatville, and Congo Christian Institute work. Three mainstays of the work dropping out all at once. We had also just heard of little Elizabeth Rowe's serious illness and operation in America and we were depending on the Rowes to fill up some of the gaps.

Little Oliver was born on the last of March and I had to wait almost a month before I could get a boat up to Wema. I finally had to take the mail boat and it was more expensive. The magistrate from Coquilhatville was the only white man on board and he wasn't very sociable as he was accompanied by his native wife and was ashamed. After we got into Boende, the district capital, I fared better. At Boende I made several trips out to our church and visited with the evangelist and his family and Christians. They can't understand why we don't put a white person at Boende as we have so many Christians there and such a big field to draw from, but with present funds we can do nothing but supervise Njeku Paul's work from Wema. He is a fine evangelist, but he needs more help than the young school teacher and his wife who are with him. Mr. Johnston made a trip there this October and baptized eight or ten converts.

Monsieur and Madame and Freddie Membeck of the coffee and rubber plantation here at Wema were on board. She has undergone an operation for appendicitis in Boende. Monsieur and Madame Lucky were also on board. They had a new baby girl to keep their five-year-old boy company. Mark was born at Mondombe with Dr. Pearson and when he was a little older I had him in my care. He is pretty lively in spite of us. Mr. Lucky is a state official. Everyone at Wema were well when we arrived.

My first week in Wema Goldie Alumbaugh had a fever and three cases came to the hospital with terrible, angry-looking wounds to be sewed up.

Two of them were in exactly the same part of the anatomy. In fact, one was cut to avenge the other. The other was an accident.

One week from that time a letter came from the state post two days' hard traveling overland saying that Madame Burhin was very ill and had no way of getting to a doctor, would a nurse please come. Monsieur Burhin is another state official. They have a seven-year-old son and a baby girl about the age of the Lucky's baby, so of course I went. When I got back almost a week later, I found Goldie packing frantically and Mrs. Boyer with a serious looking infection in her leg and a fever over 105°, and the quickest boat whistled in our beach soon after I arrived by my *teepoi*. It was a Catholic boat and the father in charge was very kind to make her as comfortable as possible. Mrs. Boyer has since written that her leg was not entirely well until after she "waded in the Sea of Galilee" on her way home.

It took me a long time to find what Goldie had left and where she left them, but I seemed to have managed. Janet Johnson, twenty-three years old and much bigger than I, was a real help to me in finding out all about things. She helped me reorganize the child welfare clinic. We had in attendance between ninety and a hundred babies and preschool-age children to weigh and examine each week. I ran the women's school before breakfast every morning, and together Janet and I organized a kindergarten. I taught hygiene in the advanced school, but Mrs. Johnston supervised the village schools of about a hundred boys and girls and the advanced school of about a hundred men and boys. Mr. Johnston helped with Bible and some other classes.

Then in June, I managed to crowd in between my regular work fifty mimeographed letters to send home and some thirty or forty bills since the first year for treatment and natives sent in by white people. Most of them had to be done in triple copy and an accompanying letter and all such red tape that takes so much time; but it gives us a little extra cash if they pay their bills and most of them have already. Even in June we began meeting all the boats as we were expecting Myrle Ward, but we were always disappointed until at last we had word asking us to forgive them at Bolenge as they were using her to help on the treasurer's books. And were they in a mess! You see Mrs. Weaver was at death's door for three months before Mrs. Rowe, our other treasurer, arrived to take things over, so after all we were glad that Miss Ward could help, although I was beginning to wonder if Mr. and Mrs. Johnston were going to hold up under the strain of extra work. Mrs. is fifty years old and Mr. is fifty-six, and as you might guess, years of malaria haven't made them any stronger to stand day after day teaching with a cement floor underfoot. Fortunately, dry season came along, and the natives begged time off for fishing, so we got by until she came, and we opened school the first of August. In July, I had another fellow to sew up. He was wounded in eight places and the guilty party said of course he meant to kill the fellow. We had a nice Fourth of July wiener roast and the Membecks came in to celebrate with us. Another fellow came in with his leg mashed and cut terribly on either side, but he couldn't get there soon enough for sewing to do much good.

August and September found school at Wema in full swing. October is a regular vacation time and so I took time out to visit Mondombe and catch up on other work. Mr. Johnston made a trip to visit some of the backcountry work during vacation, and Mrs. sewed for Janet. Miss Ward served as Wema member of the mission committee meeting at Mondombe. Now we are all back ready for our students to get here for school. We treated around seventy-five patients at the hospital this morning, even though there were only two nurses and me back to do it. We found two new patients with sleeping sickness parasites and gave ten old ones treatment Tuesday.

We were all so delighted over the SS *Oregon's* new dress: lovely paneled walls from all Congo woods and at last Captain Jean has a cabin on top with a little privacy. Captain Jean, Njoji Mark, Bokese Paul, and Wema's Ifunza Phillip all are working faithfully at their jobs of evangelizing Congo and there are many others not so well known to you that are always faithfully at work. Our Ibela Jean of Lotumbe has become chief for a large territory and is doing us proud as a Christian chief. Bokese Paul has also been called as big chief but Mondombe has needed him too badly for him to leave; but I understand that he will go to Monieka in February. Many of our Congo Christian Institute fellows are out in isolated places strengthening the work, and we are proud of them. We have been disappointed with two of them here who left the station, forged the name of a state official in the tax books, giving them permission to go hunt work elsewhere. They could have gotten permission honestly, so no one can understand why they should have done it. The state has a penalty from six months to five years for forgery. Mondombe has been disappointed in one of their men too. He recently deserted his fine wife and has gone off with another woman. They were wanting Yoka to take the pastorate when Bokese Paul left, so I am not sure what they will do. I suppose it is human nature that some of them will fail, but how it hurts!

We had the finest sermon Sunday by Mpeku Mark, Bolenge's assistant pastor and their native committee member to Mondombe. The *Oregon* stayed over Sunday at Wema, so we had the benefit of Mpeku's cheerful and inspiring sermon. His text was 1 Corinthians 3:10–15 with emphasis on the eleventh verse and Jesus Christ as the foundation. He introduced the subject by picking up a stick and saying, "If I want to build a house what will I use as a measure?" And then he called Captain Jean and two others to the platform to show him how long they thought a meter stick was and they measured it on the stick he had; of course, each one was different than the other. "The measure for our lives is Jesus Christ and it is the only exact measure we have. Any other measure is only *wanya w'aiso*, or 'the wisdom of the eyes' and it exceeds in being wrong as their measure of the meter stick was. The foundation Jesus has laid is first of all love. Not even heathens lack of love all together, but their love fails many times. Jesus' love never fails. Our love exceeds fear and shame. Secondly, Jesus never praised himself. What is your meter? Yourself or Jesus? Repent from your sins and follow Jesus. There is no other foundation. Is the wisdom you are teaching yours or Jesus'? Why are you sitting down to rest when people are all about you who have not heard of Jesus? The mission lacks teachers to send to these people, why do you sit idle? You have the words of life. Jesus didn't have a bicycle to go from village to village. Stop using excuses such as that but go! Teach others!" It was the most inspiring sermon I ever heard in Congo and if it doesn't set some of our Christians to working, I will miss my guess.

Buena Rose Stober to Friends and Family, September 11, 1936—Mondombe, Congo Belge

I'll try to get this off to you on the Tuesday mail boat. Here we are at Bolenge having conference and you can imagine what a lot of fun it is to be with a group of your very best friends and be thoroughly engrossed in the conference program which is an excellent place to talk over our joys, successes, sorrows, failures, petty troubles, and find how many fine ideas our neighbors, missionary and African, really have.

Coming down to the boat at Mondombe, I decided to write this and scribbled down a few notes to tell you, but with Wema, Monieka, and Lotumbe getting on board the *Oregon*, it was too exciting to keep at the job. So, I have been here a whole week and haven't yet typed up these notes. It is twenty-five minutes until 9:00 a.m. Breakfast is over, and seven or so single ladies are rushing around me trying to get ready for the opening devotional and beginning discussions. This morning the topic is Congo Christian church services. I had charge of the devotions yesterday, my topic being encouragement and optimism. I feel relieved that I finished it. We are discussing and trying to make new workable programs for all phases of the work. The Africans, too, are battling with some fine ideas and how to work them. There is a fine spirit prevailing.

As we were going up the Momboyo River to get the Lotumbe folks, and we were headed back halfway to Coquilhatville, we watched an African handling the tiny canoe hewn from a tree and now at the hands of one of our evangelists, who had hitchhiked a towing job, deftly taking his tiny craft through the waves of the big steamer. We had arrived at the parting place and he untied the rear of his canoe, helped his wife get her baskets and baggage arranged in the canoe; then directing her to the front of the canoe, he untied the front of his canoe and adroitly swung away from the paddle wheel. He called back, "Throw my wooden stool into the river; we've forgotten it." The stool went floating downriver bobbing along toward them. Scarcely stopping his strokes of the paddle, he reached for it and tossed it into the canoe without even tipping it, though the waves were so big it looked like they would surely capsize. Then the steady strokes of the paddles sent them speeding away downriver and up a small branch of it to the jungle village where he and his new wife were teaching the story of Jesus and his patience and love. As I stood on the deck and watched the canoe disappear upstream, I thought of the boy he had been as I was stationed at Bolenge. How little artisanship of any kind he had to show in those days except his happy smile that was always ready. Nsambela Daniele was no different from his comrades. When he was about fifteen, Dr. Barger took him into the hospital to train as a nurse. Along with four others in 1927 he was caught diluting intravenous injections of neosalvarsan and making himself an outside source of gain above his salary. I had thought of all four of them as my children and had been very proud of their progress and the hospital and yet they had been getting by with such a cheat to our patients all the time. After it was found out, Nsambela said for several years he had not been interested in Christianity at all and had drifted very far away. Later a friend met him and persuaded him to come back and finish school and help in the teaching. He did come back and made good.

Sometimes we get discouraged when we look too close for results of our efforts and feel that we have accomplished nothing in their characters; then we see children like Nsambela face from their indifference and living the Christian life and live the abundant happy life that is meant for them.

Buena Rose Stober to Friends, November 8, 1936—Mondombe, Congo Belge

My mail is still going to Wema and it isn't so nice to have the mail boat whistle in every two or three weeks and all the mail goes to Hattie. Mine will get here eventually, but it will be the next boat. Hattie Mitchell and I are running Mondombe by ourselves but keeping well and mighty busy, nothing more serious happening save runaway wives, so I believe we will make it all right until the Hurts come. I will have to admit it is mighty lonesome sometimes and it must be rather hard on Hattie to see no other face but mine that is white. I have seen the state official and his wife (Belgians) three times as I pass their place about six miles from here on my way to see our out-station dispensaries, but she hasn't been off the station and the official is too busy to visit. They are not very well either, both have had dysentery and I am a little worried about him; he looks so pale and is carrying two men's jobs. They will be starting for a Belgian furlough of six months December 8, so maybe he will make it if he takes his medicine. This is rainy season and it is always a bad time for sicknesses. Yesterday they called me to see one of their soldiers whom they thought was poisoned but I know very little about the working of native poisons; he had a fever the day before and probably died of malignant malaria.

We are scattering fruit trees throughout the back country. Dr. Baker had a nice nursery of palm trees planted. I have many seedlings of oranges, breadfruit, sour sape, rose apples, etc. We are putting out eighty orange trees, seventy-five breadfruit, twenty-five rose apples, and twenty sour sape and a few other trees on the station and in nearby villages where school boys and girls can plant and care for them. All this to be celebrated Armistice Day as it is the ideal season for planting. At the hospital we are putting out some fifty of the doctor's special palm trees.

We had a good sermon today from a fellow who has just finished our advanced school at Bolenge. He preached from Joshua 24 about keeping our promises. As the Israelites kept their promises, he says we ought to keep our promises with God and we will be rewarded by happiness that cannot be spoiled by things. When we forget we are bound to see bad results of our carelessness. He finished by telling one of the fables of a man who wanted to have a successful hunt, so he closed in a lane with fences of reeds and vines compelling the animals to go toward his trap. Then he went to the witch doctor seeking medicine (charms) to kill animals. He took a lot of brass anklets to pay for them, but the witch doctor wouldn't agree until he agreed to neither hunt nor go beyond his fences. He promised but the next day when he was angry and didn't find anything in his traps, he disregarded his promise and picked some mushrooms on the other side of the fence. Later in the day after the mushrooms were cooked a friend went by hunting for his goat. He called him to eat with him. As he opened the leaves covering the pot to dish up the food, behold, it was pieces of goat meat and in his basket were hairs of his friend's goat. The friend became very angry of course and called witnesses to prove that it was his goat. The evidence was there so he had to pay a big fine and then he remembered his promises too late.

Buena Rose Stober to Her Diary, Late 1937—Mondombe, Congo Belge

The game Ikoke and Her Children.

This game is an African version of London Bridge and in different forms it is known to all of our natives. This is Mondombe's version. The two players who form the arch decide secretly which one will be an article such as a gourd and the other will be palm nuts or perhaps corn and tapioca root. As Ikoke and her long line of children file under the arch, someone is caught on the two sides by choosing one of the articles named. Then they are put in a prison camp marked off by nearby belongings to the side they have chosen. Ikoke steps along holding the hand of the first child and each child holds the one next to her or him. Ikoke leads the children through the arch with many tricks to keep from getting her children caught, dodging away just when the two of the arch think she's going under. When they finally trap a child by suddenly letting down their arms, the child must choose its side. The game is repeated many times until all are caught, but each time Ikoke begins to wail and everyone joins in "All of Ikoke's children are being finished," then all let out a wail "OOO Oh!" After all are caught a tug-of-war takes place between the two sides, each child holding the one in front around the waist. But the two of the arch are at the center of the tug-of-war and the children are holding on around their waists.

Buena Rose Stober to Friends, July 30, 1937—Mondombe, Congo Belge

How does it feel to be forty and just beginning life? Well, I started and two weeks before my birthday, Virginia Ann Hurt was desperately ill, then a plantation owner came in with his daughter dying with blackwater fever, my birthday was the day after the funeral. I am dreading for tomorrow to come as my Saturdays seem hoodooed. Next Sunday I will be starting on a three-week trip to the dispensaries and checking on our Christians in that part of the country. Pastor Ntange is going with me, so I will take a lot of the responsibility and then I will have the regular carriers for Pastor Ntange's and my camping, medicines, books, school supplies, church rolls, for of course there is no other way to have these things along except to take them. No hotels, no restaurants, no grocery stores. The fellow that helps me get my bike uphill is to be boss of the workmen, and my cook, bike mender, and general helper will be right on the job.

This morning, I spent time instructing the nurses and parents of four infants how to prepare formula, gruel, fruits, etc., for these little ones. After breakfast I managed the supplies for eight dormitory girls who were not on vacation, with food, salt, and a little money. After that I packed my boxes for the trip while the above-mentioned helper patched the hole in my mosquito net. At 10:00 a.m. The nurses were ready for me to examine the new patients and prescribe for them. Then I signed some fifty cards of dismissal from treatment for patients who will have finished their treatment before I get back and may go home. Incidentally the head nurse and I gave two pet dogs worm medicine. How is that for treating the natives? There was also a slide of malaria parasites under the microscope waiting for my confirmation as the laboratory nurse isn't really sure of himself in that examination. After lunch I see that my three dogs have food. I am keeping Virginia's dog, too, while they are at the doctor's at Monieka, also I have the Belgian lady's dog until she is home on furlough. Virginia left her two monkeys also in my care. All in this menagerie are lots of company, anyway. Beginning life at forty?

Buena Rose Stober to Friends and Family, July 1937—Mondombe, Congo Belge

If you could have been here just now as I got ready to write this letter you would decide that I am not the meek all-enduring book-type of missionary. I had been to the hospital, finished all my job, stood around waiting for a man they had to have an examination to enter the militia, but he didn't come. So, I came home and fixed the sheets and the machine, and just then my helper handed me a letter from the state official the man had reappeared for his examination. Yesterday he appeared twice but instead of waiting his turn he went off to see relatives and couldn't be found. This being the third time, I thought surely he would understand and in the little while it took me to type a *Certificat Medical* he was gone before I got to the hospital, but our call finally got him. He did not have a clear health record, so maybe he won't be sent; but at least the certificate records that and is signed and gone. He didn't seem extra enthused about going anyway. I lost my missionary temper but managed to take it out in a rather positive statement. We have to sign the certificates for companies hunting workmen. There is a mining company of Katanga hunting workmen in our territory, and Mrs. Hurt writes that a big fat white man is coming down from Ikela. He is after one thousand workmen and will have to have certificates for any takers. Hope they don't all come at once. No danger though since no one is especially enthusiastic about young men going so far from home. The natives, missionaries, and Belgian officials are all afraid of it. Of course, they are free to go if they pass their physical, but none of us will urge them. They are paid well enough, but the Katanga missionaries tell us the conditions at the mines are terrible, and food is hard to get even when the companies do try to improve conditions.[5]

The last white man from there was a terrible drunkard. Around here they all tease me about him because he said that I am the very image of his wife, most beloved one at that. She stayed in Belgium, however. After the first encounter I managed to stay out of sight. We all had a good laugh, but I couldn't return his enthusiasm.

Mr. and Mrs. Hurt are having the in-gathering of evangelists in Ikela, and we will be down on the mail boat Monday. Hattie and I have had another in-gathering of two fields nearby this week. The dinner bell is ringing so I will finish these personal letters to go with my news later.

We are having chicken, sweet potatoes, greens, and cookies for dessert. A little special today as Hattie and Virginia are having another siege of malaria and both are much better now. Meats and fish have been terribly hard to get for our diets these last days as our mission-paid hunter is no good, and the Africans are having a bad time too. The river is very high for this time of year. July is usually dry and there is an abundance of fishing out big lakes and more fish than needed.

Buena Rose Stober to Friends, August 20, 1937—Mondombe, Congo Belge

My letters must be awfully dull, being just a series of accounts of my trips into the backcountry but they seem to be interesting days in my life out here. This time I left the mission August 2 and returned August 14, and I not only visited my three rural dispensaries as usual but spent some time with seven different village groups where we have Christians in one territory and three in another territory, checking their church rolls and trying to help settle their palavers. The pastor of the Mondombe church was with me and

5. At the time Stober wrote this letter, the private mining companies operating in the Katanga Province had a long history of mistreatment of its Congolese workers. During the direct rule of King Leopold II, the companies regularly used forced labor under conditions no better than chattel slavery. Working conditions improved only slightly under Belgian rule. Because the Luba people often resisted exploitation, these companies often employed contract mercenaries to subdue them and protect their commercial interests. Unrest and violence in the Katanga Province remained almost constant throughout the colonial period.

in one place where thirteen Christians had taken a certain witch doctor's medicine called *botamba*, reputed to give you power to kill off your enemies, we were able to get six of them to bring up their bottles of *botamba*. Those who had the bracelets of it brought them, too, so that by the time the bottles were properly broken, and a service held in front of their new mud church, they had a much truer Christian spirit. It took courage to step out from the crowd and get your bottle, bring it, and put it in front of everyone and say that you were through with it, especially when a lot of your heathen friends were making fun of you. The preacher had already gotten several of the thirteen to give it up and it seems there was just one left who wouldn't even come out to services that day. In nearly every village of the one territory there were some Christians who had taken *botamba*, so we felt we did a little good in getting some of the backsliders started right again. In some places we found nice mud churches with nice mat cover benches and one has whitewash walls. One Saturday we did not travel but our carriers helped the Christians build their new church. In some villages, though, inactivity was due to the failure of the preacher to do his job, and in some places the indifference was due to the strong-headed, sometimes even weak-headed Christians. This *botamba* costs them a lot of money, too, so of course the witch doctor will fight us when he can. At one village there were five inquirers who couldn't get into Mondombe last month when their friends were baptized, so we baptized them. One was a chief, one a policeman and one a wife who couldn't leave their work, and the other two were an old man of about sixty years and an old lady of about fifty years.

Buena Rose Stober to Friends, November 2, 1937—Lotumbe, Congo Belge

It is terribly unhandy having my typewriter out of use. It has been a faithful old friend, even helping me to remember better spelling, so I shouldn't complain. Perhaps I will have it mended by the time I do my next letter. You see I have changed stations again and have been rather snowed under the process of getting settled. I am living in the house the Davises left last April and the termites have moved in, so there is plenty to do. I liked their fence around the yard so much I put my dimes together and had it rebuilt. The schoolboys rebuilt it and their pay has been Bibles, French books, hygiene, notebooks, pencils, geography, etc., and of course I bought the books they wanted for their pay. The Davises had built a lovely corner for picnics with a fireplace and rustic tables, benches, and chairs. It is surrounded by bougainvillea, acacia, cape jasmine, cannas, honeysuckle, and hibiscus. It had to be lovely with all that. Ruth and I have been taking our Sunday afternoon glass of milk out there and drinking it in peace and quiet and coolness. My garden fence is done, too, and it includes several vegetables that will grow here: lettuce, tomatoes, beans, peanuts, and other flowers, too, such as xenia, Japanese sunflowers, balsams, marigolds, and salvia. The schoolboys got their books and then I have the satisfaction of a pretty yard all outside the regular routine of sick folks, hospital cleaning, rearranging, and bossing my three nurses and hospital sentry.

Six months of a hospital out here without a doctor or a nurse in charge is something to discover, I'll admit, and the meager budget has to be made to fit the patient; so, we are busy. The three African nurses are old friends of mine, and the sentry too. Besides, one of the head school teachers who used to be a nurse helps me Saturday morning to keep the records in order. He graduated from the Congo Christian Institute and has kept a colony of backcountry schoolboys going for a year or so. We have the infant clinic going again and are trying now to get all the school folks examined and treated if they have ailments. We had about a hundred patients today (106, I believe). My second week here we helped twins into the world and a big boy this week. So, you see I am at my old jobs. I won't have any backcountry dispensaries to keep me making trips.

I have inherited the school for the kindergartners with two fine women to help me. The children are cunning and enjoy the benches and many of the games made for them by several classes at the school, hoping to be school teachers someday. They used only Congo material and it has been interesting to see what can be done without buying material.

Buena Rose Stober to Friends, November 20, 1938—Newkirk, Oklahoma

When I am not speaking in conventions, I think of so many things I want to tell you. I am in Oklahoma now for a while. I think I will have spoken of Congo in something like fifty churches by the time you get this letter, with an average of two talks in each church, so you see I have not been idle; but I have also gained weight, strength, and have even rested a great deal between trips. I almost froze seeing my first snow the other morning in Enid when I woke up to a white world, but it soon melted in the bright sunlight.

I am so happy that Mr. and Mrs. Hixon and their two children have actually sailed for Congo to take the place of the Watts family who had to resign on account of health. We are still needing badly and asking for eight new couples, so don't forget us in your prayers and teachings.

In a recent letter from Mrs. Hurt telling of a trip in the backcountry in Africa, she says they will have around a thousand baptisms to report for the first six months of the year and a fine spirit among the Christians.

Inkema Jean, captain of our mission steamer *Oregon*, once preached a fine sermon to some elders and deacons of the church at Lotumbe where they had a disagreement. It has meant a lot to me and I am going to pass it on to you. His text was about the "Cup of Water" and he interpreted it as "Our Cup of Love." He said that when the cup is full of pure water or love there is no room for anything else, but that when we let dirt or selfishness, prejudices, pettiness, jealousies, and indifference enter in, it will crowd out some of the love. He held up a cup of water before the crowd and reached down and picked up a handful of dirt; as he dropped it into the cup, of course some of the water splashed out.

I received a letter from Ifumo, Africa, written by Bokenge Daniele who is in charge of the evangelistic work where Miss McCune gave her last ounce of strength for Congo.[6] It was dated July 27, 1938 and he said they had just had a very happy in-gathering of the evangelists, 163 of them, with three weeks of school, and that even though the market price of copal, their chief commercial product, the resin from which we make our varnish, has fallen so low that their offerings were very short and as a result the salaries of all of them were cut severely. But in spite of this each evangelist went back to his village glad to be able to serve another six months. He finished his letter by saying, "Remember us that you return to Lotumbe to tell the good news. Get strong and well. We will pray always that you come back."

On the beach as I bid Bolenge goodbye in April this year he said to me, "Mama Mputu, tell the Christians in America to send us more missionaries that will love us as Vesta McCune did."

Buena Rose Stober to Friends and Family, July 1, 1939—Mondombe, Congo Belge

I am at work again in Mondombe, and with an MD! Think of it! I arrived June 14 about 3:00 p.m. with shouts from the shores of "Hello Stobie!" and "Mama Mputu, you have come! Are you well?" only the second part was not in English: *Mama Mputu, oya, Ole o boloci?* Evangelists, nurses, children, sick folks whom I had treated or worked with. My mistakes didn't come

6. Vesta Marie McCune (1897–1938) was a pioneer during the first effort of DCCM to open a mission station at Ifumo. She contracted blackwater fever, a severe and often fatal form of malaria, and died February 3, 1938. Temporarily halting efforts, DCCM finally opened a mission station at Ifumo in 1947.

to haunt me that first day. They were nearly as glad to see Cappy and the Bokolombes as to see me. The three Baker girls were so excited and out of breath trying to shout to me that they were going swimming at the sandbar. Everyone tried to talk and wanted me included, and when I got off there was a long lineup of handshaking and volunteers to carry my baggage off the boat. Mr. Hermans, the plantation man, and his German shepherd dog must have thought the jungle had turned loose. He came off to visit Dr. Baker while I unloaded.

Besides Gertrude Shoemaker and the Bakers, there was a white patient of the doctor's at the beach, a Mr. Hirahall, who was just recovering from wounds made by a big leopard which jumped in his open, screenless window, knocked him out of the bed, and tried to chew up his face while he was trying to extricate himself from the fallen mosquito net. He is minus several teeth and his face is pretty scarred up, but he is lucky to be alive. The mosquito net evidently frightened the leopard off but the next day they hunted down and killed it. Moral: Close your windows and screens so that a leopard can't get in without waking you. A screen would ordinarily scare a leopard out of a strange place, or of course this man would be dead.

I did not do much but unpack a few things and visit. My house, the upstairs of the station office and storerooms, needed new paint. The station had ordered white paint for the first coat and left choosing the colors for the rooms to me. The next few days I had a gay time teaching two natives who knew less than I did about painting walls. It is going to be like a new house, but you should see the drops of paint all over everything in spite of the canvases they had to protect things. It has taken them a whole week to scrape off what they'd slopped around and neglected to wipe off right away. Oh well, such is Congo. Mr. Birchall put up my new stove. He says American stoves are a great deal more complicated than Belgian ones. He knows English and has lived in England long enough that he is used to it. He gets so bored sitting around and he begged the doctor for a job he could do for us.

My dental equipment was all in good shape. In fact, I've already cleaned six people's teeth. My first filling was for Mrs. Baker and I nearly fainted when I found it in an upper incisor—more than one, in fact—and they were getting so much worse with time we didn't dare risk waiting. We were able to save the teeth. The Dell foot engine is working fine even though it is Dr. Warder's old machine with which he went to practice in 1901, I believe.

Besides getting my garden and flowers started, I have arranged for a new path to my front door as the old one served to direct a near river of rainwater into the basement to ruin anything like school blankets stored there. I have taught two classes to the evangelists and wives, supervised the hospital while Doctor was visiting his rural dispensaries last week, fixed gruel and milk night and morning for an infant, soups of milk for sick folks, one of them has been my helper, Bokolombe. He has run a fever of 102° to 104° every day since we got here and has been a very sick man. Doctor thinks it is parathyroid. James, the little son, is helping me around the house. My two big cases of baby clothes, etc., that left Newkirk the day I did came yesterday. I was really so surprised as freight is usually so very slow. Doctor is delighted over the surgical gowns, sheets, aprons, and towels that so many of you sent. They arrived in fine shape and Lelia and I are delighted over the infant clothing.

Buena Rose Stober to Friends, August 4, 1939—Mondombe, Congo Belge

Another three months have rolled by since I wrote. It took me so long to get from the coast of Congo May 10 until June 14 to Mondombe. Each stage of the trip took another steamer except for the twelve-hour train trip from Matadi to Léopoldville, and each steamer was a little smaller than the last.

After taking my share of the school for the in-gathering of evangelists at Mondombe, Doctor pleased everyone by having his little motor out and showing movies of Mickey Mouse, Lindberg's transatlantic flight, and two short scenes he had taken at Mondombe in color and one a very good fishing scene. You could even see the fish soar into the air in a supreme effort to avoid the nets, spears, and traps in a fishing-out of a drying lake where two or three hundred people were after them, driving them into the reed fence where they had to go into the traps or escape some way. It is quite exciting.

While the doctor was visiting his rural dispensaries, I of course had charge of medical, unpacked my cases, and cleaned some teeth. Since I arrived, I've cleaned some thirty-five patients' teeth, usually two patients a morning and then in the afternoon a filling or so. I also had a class with the nurses three days a week.

Miss Shoemaker, Litele Samuel, our Sunday School worker for the whole mission, and Pastor Ntange carry on three other in-gatherings at central villages in the backcountry. With 115 here, there were over 900 baptisms. All those baptized had been in daily Bible class instruction with their local evangelist. Taking care of them and helping them to develop into real Christians is the big task now, of course. Miss Shoemaker said the really gratifying thing was that most of them were mothers, fathers, sisters, and friends of other Christians.

Buena Rose Stober to Friends, September 4, 1939—Mondombe, Congo Belge

A lot has happened in these three months: Hattie Mitchell and our new family, the Roberts, have arrived. Dr. Baker has made another round of his rural dispensaries. I have been feeding four infants and they are all gaining weight as they should on good milk. The painting of the inside walls of my house is finished and it is so pretty and restful. I will admit that there are a number of places in the walls and screens that leak mosquitoes and other pests, but my bedroom is fairly well-protected against them now. We have not heard of raids of the leopard recently on the station, but the village east of us has lost several goats to him, not that I would grieve the loss of a goat!

Our patients come and go, a constant stream of sickness, death, and restored health. Mrs. Baker and daughter Margaret, the second daughter, both have had fevers but are feeling fine now. There has been lots of malaria in the Africans, so much that we gave the fifty dormitory boys and twenty dormitory girls a full week's course of prophylactic quinine in hopes we can save them from sickness. I have had one malarial fever since I arrived in Mondombe, but I'm feeling grand now.

The teeth cleaning and repairing goes on week by week. Sometimes I have gotten into conditions far beyond my knowledge, but I am so glad to be able to put the children's teeth in good condition. One little girl whose mother had neglected her had a baby tooth so covered with tartar that it was three times the normal size, in fact it could not come out without help and was displacing her permanent tooth, which was already part way in; besides that, she had about four cavities that were filled. Her brother, who is older and has all his permanent teeth and was in the boys' dormitory, had teeth as badly in need of care as hers. His upper incisors were all filed to a point and two of his bicuspids were only shells. After cleaning, extracting, and filling as necessary, I can only teach them how to keep their teeth cleaned and eat proper food! Those two being in the dormitory will be supplied with fruits and vegetables. We have insisted that every child appear at school with a toothbrush, made of a brush on the end of the softwood made by cutting slits or chewing it into a brush. I have tried them, and they will get the job done. They usually get plenty of greens and yellow palm gravy so that helps. This filing of teeth is an idea that your teeth make you good looking, fierce, courageous, or whatever they like about it, enough to endure the procedure but it complicates what might be good sets of teeth.

Here are some of the common types of mutilation: (1) all the incisors filed to a point; (2) upper incisors only filed; (3) the two upper central incisors filed diagonally toward the center; and (4) upper and lower central incisors knocked out. Lucky is the twelve-year-old girl or boy who has not had his teeth filed.

Buena Rose Stober to Friends, December 28, 1939—Mondombe, Congo Belge

Dear Miss Henderson, Dr. Warder, and Friend who made my dental equipment possible:

Different natives have asked me to write their thanks for the dental help. I am enclosing three letters from the evangelists' children expressing their thanks. I cleaned all the evangelists' children's teeth while they were on the station these last two weeks. There were forty-four of them big enough to sit up and have it done without being frightened to death. Most of them had nice clean teeth which speaks well for their parents teaching. Only one or two were frightened and most of them thought it was great fun. One little ten-year-old followed me around to the hospital for days until I finally got to him, then went around bragging about how I praised his clean teeth.

There was a darling two- or three-year-old who came following me with her mother to the hospital one day, and, if you please, she wanted her teeth cleaned. Three of the little ones' teeth were already badly decayed and Doctor advised me to pull out the broken bits and fill the cavities with cement that were possible to fill. Another five-year-old had five fillings and he never so much as cried. In fact, I think they enjoyed the novelty.

Since I came back, I have cleaned teeth for 142 patients, most of them were children, except for thirteen nurses. I had to fill 57 cavities from these groups, most of which were amalgam filling, a few temporary teeth among them. Laurette and Grace Baker called the pumice "my sand" and saliva "spitness." One time before Grace had any cavity, she cried after I had finished as I wasn't spending as much time with her as with her sisters, Margaret and Lauretta, and when I asked why she sobbed out, "I haven't any cavities!"

Here are the translation of the letters:

"To Dr. Warder and the women of a foreign country (Oklahoma was too much for them to write and any country not their own is *Mpoto*). Greetings. We are in the sixth class (about the third grade). We and our teacher have great joy in our class. Thank you because you gave Mama Mputu (my native name) the things for cleaning our teeth. We of Mondombe are well. We have only joy. Mondombe are trying to find the good things. We are in Lomboli Kaala's class, our woman teacher. (She is a girl of the dormitory who was far enough along in school to teach them). I am Elumbu Paul."

"To the doctor and the women: I haven't any news. All the people of Yeleke (where his father teaches and preaches) are in the forest hunting the resin copal, used by *mpoto* in making varnish. We have great joy in our class. Lomboli Kaala is our teacher. I am Bokomboji Joseph."

"To Dr. Warder and the women of *Mpoto*: many thanks because our teeth were very dirty and now you have healed them. We saw that you gave Mama Mputu a machine for cleaning our teeth. We of the sixth class are very well and we have a woman teacher and are doing well. She is Lomboli Kaala. I am Lokonga Pierre."

It is something very special to have a woman teacher as women are usually not allowed to get that far in school.

The steamer SW *Oregon* plied the Congo River and her tributaries bringing personnel, supplies, and mail to the stations of DCCM. Here she is docked at Mondombe beach about 1935. Photo courtesy of DCHS.

Stober was particularly critical of the practice of polygamy among Congo's tribal chiefs. Pictured here in 1937 is a chief of one of the villages near Mondombe with eight of his sons from multiple wives. Photo courtesy of CTS.

Despite strong opposition, Stober and her fellow missionaries encouraged Congolese girls to attend school. Pictured in 1938, some girls from Mondombe pose with their head scarves, given as rewards for perfect attendance in school. Photo courtesy of DCHS.

Stober lived on the second floor of this building for most of her time at Mondombe. It also housed the station treasury and main office. Photo courtesy of CTS.

Pictured here in 1937, Stober developed a passion for infant care very early in her missionary career. Eventually she published *Mbatela bana ba tosisi* for Congolese mothers, a manual on infant care. Photo courtesy of DCHS.

Taken in early 1939 near the end of her furlough in the United States, this photo shows Stober healthy and well-rested, ready to return to her work. Photo courtesy of DCHS.

The church building at Mondombe, pictured here in the 1930s, had brick walls, a tin roof, and ample windows to allow air to circulate freely. Photo courtesy of CTS.

3

1940 to 1949

Buena Rose Stober to Friends, February 7, 1940—Mondombe, Congo Belge

This is Mondombe's twentieth birthday year and I thought you would be interested in some of the sidelights of her growth. We are having the big celebration in May, and we hope you will all be thinking of us, rejoicing, and praying for us.

Miss Mitchell has just made a trip through our Mpangu field which is growing by leaps and bounds with hundreds of new Christians. They are asking for more evangelists. One of the first baptized from the village, Yalokele in 1920, is at present one of our strong young evangelists in another field. The number of Christians in the village Yayenga has grown until they have built four separate chapels. The first Christians, four in number and still active, were baptized in 1921.

In 1925 Miss Mitchell and Miss Wells made their first trip through Mpangu by bicycle and *teepoi*, the first white women that people had seen, and they were frightened because the bicycle left its tire prints in the path. They said, "Your machine leaves a path for evil spirits to walk right into our village." The pitiful part of it was that they had a lot of sickness in the village that year and blamed it on the bike. Now bicycle travelers, both white and black, are common sights in Mpangu. Miss Mitchell made the trip out there this time on her motor bicycle and she had an accident on one of the bad roads and broke her arm. Dr. Baker went out on his motorcycle to bring her in. She is fortunately getting along all right.

Even those Christians who fall back and take harems cling close to the church in other respects. But along with a faith in Christ are a lot of heathen customs, and if we are not on the job they do not understand his teachings. One little group of Christians was choosing an official leader, as they had no evangelist near; but the man they chose was a "Christian" that had two wives and was trying to dispose of the child wife. It is a long, tedious task, but we are gaining ground.

Before the first missionaries arrived here, all the three older stations had sent native missionaries to Mondombe. In 1919 Bolenge had eight men here; Monieka, ten; and Lotumbe, two. As a result of their work and the missionaries', Mondombe's own Christians have gradually taken these places, until now there is only one downriver evangelist among fifty-five trained men in various parts of Mondombe region, besides forty-five only partially trained men. By 1920 the work of these downriver men had produced eleven Mondombe evangelists, two of whom are still preaching: Ntange Timoteo, pastor of Mondombe church, and Boloma Jean, the head evangelist in our Bosondongo field. Dozens of villages are calling for preachers, school teachers, and nurses much faster than our school can prepare them, and we are pleased with the increasing number of little mud and leaf chapels springing up in the villages.

Along with the serious there is usually a bit of the ridiculous. Our evangelists are anxious to have these chapels look as nice as possible and Bible pictures are much in demand. One new chapel where there was no trained evangelist had a big whiskey ad on the wall, and when Miss Mitchell protested, the leader was quite unconcerned and said that he would come after a Bible picture when the evangelists came in. So, remember: your discarded Bible pictures or brand new ones are very welcome. Don't declare any value for the package and mark it "old pictures, printed matter, *imprime*, no commercial value," and we will not have to pay customs or at least very little.

In 1931 the church here was shocked at the news of the death of an evangelist, Botuli Simon, whose wife had just died. He was reported to have been killed by a leopard in broad daylight in his own house. But the Christians did not believe the story as he had defied the local witch doctor and eaten taboo food. They were taking him out to bury him when they met a group of hunters wanting some bait for their hunt, and it was agreed that they might as well pay for and use the available meat. But when the hunters opened the mat there was the body of their own relative, Botuli, who had been preaching at Yampete. A horrid story! Yes! But there are hundreds of scarcely touched villages where that could happen in Mondombe field now, so we must help these native Christians so that they will find trained men to go into these villages and preach Christ's love.

Buena Rose Stober to A. W. Curtis, February 19, 1940—Mondombe, Congo Belge[1]

I appreciate greatly your interest in our work, and although our work here in Mondombe is only in its beginnings, we have enjoyed a few interesting successes as well as many discouragements.

In the first place we are faced with providing a milk supply for undernourished babies where there are no cattle and only a few goats owned by more prosperous Africans who do not use the milk, but the goats are used for feasts and for buying wives. In fact, you can hardly get them to use goat's milk when it is available because of their belief in and fear of spirits, which has some connection in their thinking with goat's milk. The tinned milk is expensive for the mission purse and natives. Our only other alternatives are peanut milk or soybean milk. The peanuts do grow well and the soybeans sparingly. Even with peanuts, our natives have trouble getting enough to feed a baby; however, it is in the realm of possibility for them even though they are not far enough to carry out any elaborate method of preparation. We have worked in the hope that some industrious parents might be able to understand and follow instructions under our care.

We follow as nearly as possible the ideas given in the article (included here from the *Congo Mission News*, except that we have neither a peanut nor oil press. We use the native wooden mortar and pestle for pounding up the peanuts and skim the oil off the peanuts after the meal has set awhile in water). The Wembo Nyama missionaries used formerly, as we understand, one part peanut meal to five parts water; this is what we have done, although the scientific formula is our aim as soon as we have the equipment and can get some of our nurses, at least, trained to measure more accurately.[2]

1. Dr. Austin W. Curtis (1911–2003) received his PhD in chemistry from Cornell University and taught on the faculty at North Carolina Agricultural and Technical College. Between 1935 and 1943, he worked with Dr. George Washington Carver (1864–1943) at Tuskegee Institute researching peanut products and sweet potato starch. Following Carver's death, Curtis founded the Detroit-based Curtis Laboratories, which developed more than sixty health and beauty products from all natural, organic sources. Curtis retired from his work in 1999.

2. Stober is probably referring to the mission of the Methodist Episcopal Church, South in Wembo Nyama in the Kasai-Orientale province. Under the leadership of head nurse Dora Jane Armstrong (1898–1963), between 1925 and 1942, the Wembo Nyama

There are many complications to feeding babies who have no source of breast milk by this method as you will know; but of course, there are complications for any artificial feeding. We find it difficult to get all the oil out and although I have never seen any definite harm from what is left in, it is decidedly too much. Our doctor feels that they need more animal protein so we have had to use some tinned milk in the first few months for small babies. Banana, egg, gruels of manioc, corn meal, or rice, greens, orange juice, etc., have been added as per the printed instructions enclosed. We have not used plantain water as it is more difficult to obtain here although we hope our own will be bearing soon.

The following is an account of the babies we have cared for with peanut milk.

The twins: Born December 1936; mother anemic; had lost several pregnancies; still births; no history of syphilis but received ten injections of neosalvarsan and four of bismuth on suspicion before babies came. Babies did not gain on mother's milk, but peanut milk was substituted gradually until they received only breast milk and peanut milk by the fifth month. They developed normally and in December 1937 went home with their parents who had learned how to prepare the milk after the year's practice under our supervision.

Bolongo: He came to us in April 1937 at three months old when his mother died of pneumonia. His nearest relative was the caretaker of our girls' dormitory, so when he was put almost immediately on peanut milk the girls took turns about helping me and preparing his milk. He received this milk with other foods until he was one-and-a-half years old. He is a healthy, happy child.

Basanga: He came to us in May 1937 after the death of his mother. Both parents had syphilis although his mother died of pneumonia. He did not do well on either peanut milk or powdered milk and died later when his father ran off into their backcountry home. According to reports he died of a diarrhea. He had received peanut milk for about three months.

Nkasi: She was born in January 1939. Mother did not have enough milk. Family of five to care for, and all undernourished. She weighed seven pounds one ounce at six months when she began receiving peanut milk, gruel, mashed banana, greens, and egg to supplement her mother's milk. At one year of age, she was walking and had three teeth. We expect to continue with her until she is a year-and-a-half old. She weighs fifteen pounds eight ounces now.

---

mission developed an expansive infant care clinic. In particular, Armstrong pioneered the use of peanuts as a source of protein for feeding undernourished infants.

Nkasi Samuel: He was born in September 1939. Mother died at birth. An aunt attempted to nurse him along with her own year-and-half-old child. The baby had apparently lost some of his birth weight. The older child had also lost weight. He began making a slow gain with the addition of peanut milk. By the beginning of 1940, his aunt left for the village where her husband is minister and all began receiving all peanut milk and in addition are now receiving egg, gruel, orange juice, and banana. He is making splendid gains nearly every week. Our aim is to feed him until he is at least a year-and-a-half old.

Bitoko: She is the own child of the aunt of Samuel and received peanut milk, gruel, egg, and banana while her mother was here. She gained back her lost weight, had several teeth, and began to walk while she was here a little over a month. Her mother had some lessons in the preparation of peanut milk, and we hope she will continue them in her backcountry village.

Bononga: He came to us at one-and-a-half months. Mother very anemic and very little milk. He was put on powdered milk and gradually on peanut milk. At two months mother's milk was increasing and with the addition of peanut milk he was making good gains. Because of our general conference he was left for eight weeks in the care of the native nurses and was apparently all right when suddenly he had a fever or something. Instead of taking him to the nurses they rushed him home to a witch doctor and he died.

Sala: She came to us in July 1939 weighing less than her birth weight of April according to their story. Her mother told us that the baby had been very sick and then she herself developed an abscess in one of her breasts. We started Sala on peanut milk, gruel, egg, and banana with what little mother's milk she could get from her mother's good breast and in the meantime treated the other breast and fed her to increase her milk supply. In September Sala went home nursing from both breasts which were returned to health. Her mother had also learned to prepare the peanut milk.

Is'ea L'ona: He was born in 1938 but came to us in July 1939, when he was about nine months old. He weighed fourteen pounds nine ounces and the fontanels were still wide open along with other signs of malnutrition. We fed him peanut milk, banana, egg, gruel, etc., to supplement his mother's milk. He now has ten teeth, the fontanels are partially closed, he is walking, and is in fairly good condition, although his mother is not very cooperative and ran off with him in January to attend a relative's funeral. After two weeks' absence we did not call him back as it was a matter of forcing her to bring him. He has not gained since he stopped receiving peanut milk.

Two other babies were started on powdered milk and peanut milk, but one was a premature baby and only lived a week or two. It had some mother's milk and nursed willingly but was not strong enough to make the grade. The other one's father is a cook for a coffee plantation director and the father has plenty of powdered milk at his disposal, so we did not care for him long after his mother's death.

Pierre: He was three weeks old when he came to us about the last week of February. His mother's milk supply was lacking a bit as she had malaria and was anemic. He is receiving two bottles of peanut milk each day and is gaining and happy. His mother is taking her quinine and we are feeding her, too, in hopes of getting her milk supply increased to care for Pierre.

We should probably be following the scientific formula especially for the motherless small babies, but it hasn't been possible up to the present; however, we hope to work for a better system. The babies are kept by the relatives or parents in each case and a native nurse prepares the milk under supervision.

Our natives are fond of peanuts and we are trying to encourage their growth in use in as many ways as possible since their animal protein supply is very low. We should be glad for any suggestions or literature on the subject you could give us. We need a simpler method for making peanut meal and extracting the oil so that our measures will be more accurate. Also, any suggestions for cooking peanuts for adult use. Our natives have simple wooden mortars and pestles which they use to pound out their foods.

If you have any information or suggestions for the cultivation of soybeans, we should be very happy to have them. Avocado, pears, papaya, sweet potato, bananas, plantains, and pineapple are all available as well as oranges and several good kinds of greens. Could we use a sweet potato for making gruels? At present we use manioc flour, rice, and corn meal for gruels.

I have for some years been reading about Dr. Carver's wonderful work and have wished that more information on his splendid results, especially with peanuts and sweet potatoes, might be made available for us; and so I am doubly thankful for your letter and hope that what I've written of our efforts may prove interesting to you even though it is primitive and not very accurate work.

Buena Rose Stober to Her Diary, June 4, 1940—Mondombe, Congo Belge

Sometimes I think I'll organize a club for better parents, so many Africans want children and have so little of what it takes of faithfulness, patience, and perseverance to raise a healthy happy baby, let alone a sick or undernourished one, and there are plenty of the latter in Congo.

On a trip I had just made into our Mbelo field I found two little eight-year-old girls with syphilitic lesions and their parents are not willing to bring them to Mondombe for treatment. One mother had deserted her child entirely after contaminating her. We will have to report both cases to the state, and they will make them bring them in. But can you imagine a parent not wanting a child treated? It's all free, too!

One poor little mother, who was one of the 153 baptized on our trip, brought her one-week-old baby girl to me saying that it wasn't a bit well. I watched it an hour or so and couldn't see anything wrong except a dozen or so little strings tied around its little pinkish brown arms, ankles, and neck. The mother, too, was wearing several strings. When I questioned her she said the one around her chest across her breast [a line is illegible] and when I asked who said so, she replied that the witch doctor had told her so, and not to nurse it at the right breast as the milk was bad. Then I began to know what was the matter: too much witch doctor and only half enough milk. I insisted that she take off all the strings and come morning and evening to nurse the baby where I could see her. She was so afraid the first day she came that she trembled and giggled with embarrassment most of the time she was there. She stopped coming for two days and I insisted that she wasn't eligible for baptism as she was so afraid of the witch doctors, so she had better prove a little more sincerity, etc. She managed after that to come and all the strings disappeared. The baby was doing fine when she was baptized, Sunday, June 23.

Buena Rose Stober to Friends, October 1, 1940— Mondombe, Congo Belge

The calendar I planned for you this year cannot be done as our printer is on his way home and the Bolenge work is left with only two single women to carry on. Miss Poole and Miss Bateman are now doing, or at least are responsible for, what they and the two families, the Hixons and the Byerlees, were scarcely able to keep up. Both couples were advised to leave immediately for health reasons and the Edwards have not yet returned.

We have had two hard weeks that ended suddenly yesterday. Our administrator's wife had an attack of blackwater fever and with all our fighting it with known treatments of serums, glucose, transfusions, etc., we lost her and buried her yesterday morning. Poor Mr. Hendrick is going to pass some terribly lonely days in the future, they have been so constantly together. He had a sidecar to his motorbike in which she rode as they made all his backcountry visits. They were travelling most of the time.

Come and have Monday recreation with me! About 4:00 p.m. we found ourselves at the hospital finishing a filling in a tooth which I had filled last year, but since he couldn't keep his mouth open, I didn't do a very good job of it and had to do it over this year. I think I made a better job of it this time, but he chewed my fingers while I worked, and I "chewed the rag." Whee! I am ready for recreation but first I must finish the eight blood smears left from this morning, so that I'll know how much quinine will be needed for malaria. Two only? Well! That is better than five of seven on Saturday, not to mention a tuberculosis positive slide.

Now for my bike on the porch of the surgery building. I ring my bell to call my dogs who often find their way down the main path and wait there for me since they are not allowed in the hospital. No response! I will have a speedy spin home (about three city squares) and see what my gardener accomplished. Not too bad! I have eight ripe mulberries. Guess I will take them over to Gertrude's and Hattie's for supper. I have started ten new mulberry bushes and next year I am going to have mulberry pie. For Congo my garden isn't so bad: soybeans sparingly, green celery, broccoli, a few cabbages, onions, watercress, a bit of parsley, lettuce, eggplant in bloom, four kinds of greens, a little sweet corn but my seeds stopped coming from the USA, the company didn't want to take war risks, and I am sore!

Now I am going for a real spin, found the dogs, Cappy and Tippy, and we have a lively race down Mondombe's palm avenue that Gertrude's fifty dormitory boys have just trimmed up in fine shape. How the dogs love the race, and how lovely and graceful are the palms in the bright sunlight, not to mention the moonlight we have tonight.

My cook's little girl was sick yesterday, and we stopped there to begin their three-room mud house. No one home? Yes, they are back in the mud kitchen in the rear. Both youngsters came bouncing out at me followed by their mother. Mputu is better and as lively a little six-year-old sprite as you ever saw. Her brother, James, my own brother's namesake, comes frisking around the yard riding his dad's bike. I wonder if he has his dad's consent. Bokolombe, the father, is in second-degree school at this hour. James is nine and goes to morning school. Nku, the mother, takes me to the backyard to show off her lovely manioc, plantain, and banana garden. The storm blew down some of her tallest plantains. She tells me that she is getting all the greens she needs from her own garden and has already dug and eaten some of her sweet manioc. I moved from station to station so much she never could get much out of her gardens, as manioc, bananas, and plantains take over a year to mature. We have had a year and three months here this time.

Now we race back, detouring to another path that leads to the girls' dormitory to have a chat with my twenty girls. A dozen little fires with pots steaming on them are scattered along the kitchen porch. The little girl I had switched this morning because she wouldn't come up to the house and take out the jiggers from her feet (a jigger is a tiny flea that bores under the skin to develop its eggs) is gay and forgiving and caught me in a little game we play trying to get the other fellow to answer, "O" ("Yes") when one calls him. I catch another girl with the same trick just as we are leaving, cutting across to Gertrude's and Hattie's. We pass the girls' peanut garden and a pineapple patch just in time to meet Mrs. Roberts out walking with little Paul and Ned Owen who immediately clamor to ride on my bike basket while we walk along the palm avenue. We take another cross path toward the swamp, but decide that it is too far for two already hungry little boys, so we turn back a path that leads to the second-degree school building just now emptied at 5:00 p.m. This path takes us past another one of my prize jobs: the girls' soybean, plantain, and banana patch. We just put out one hundred new stalks and the soybeans and corn between rows are already up. Well, that is enough recreation for one afternoon. We all need supper!

Buena Rose Stober to Friends, January 21, 1941—Mondombe, Congo Belge

Herewith is one of my newsreels. I have just returned from a two-week trip into the backcountry with several high points to report: an increase for Mongandu *chefferie* (district) in offering; forty-two baptisms; several nice new mud-wall and thatched-roof churches to show for six months earnest Christian effort. Some of them are even calcimated white—the churches, I mean, not the Christians.

There were three new student-evangelists with wives and children ready to come to Mondombe for three years' concentrated Bible study and other school work; three other new fellows to step into their places with hopes of coming to school soon; two ex-evangelists who had lost their wives by death now taking up their tasks again with new wives to help them carry on; one new evangelist from the station ready for work in Mongandu. There are nineteen village churches in the *chefferie* and one coffee plantation where many of our Christians work. If not shepherded, they lay down their Christian principles. The saddest thing of this two-week itinerary was the discovery that the evangelist responsible for this plantation had done nothing. We were just sick over it and will have to find a better solution, although we couldn't do much at the time save scold and prod. He is a capable fellow, both as a teacher and preacher, but lazy.

Mrs. Baker was with me for the first five days. We were delighted with the converts of the one old preacher: a husband and wife with their ten children. This in itself is unusual in Mondombe region but still more remarkable is that all of them are Christians now. A widowed older daughter and a ten-year-old girl were baptized with their mother and father. The old preacher, whose three sons are evangelists and whose daughter is married to an evangelist, answered after we exclaimed over this family, "Well, this is the way we do things in Yalopoma."

Another preacher who has no closed offering box had taken a bamboo join with both ends intact, slit a hole in the side for inserting the money, and brought the piece of bamboo for us to open and count the offering.

As I started back, I came through another coffee plantation and met Miss Shoemaker who was caring for the work in that *chefferie*. That afternoon the inquirers of the plantation were questioned and the palavers settled. Sunday morning eight were baptized in the river just in front of the big coffee sheller and drying plant; afterward, we had church and then were invited to have dinner with the director of the plantation. Mrs. Roberts had joined us for the week and so we relaxed and laughed and discussed politics; had a ride in the big new truck, and then what a delightful surprise! He offered us horseback rides. I hadn't ridden a horse in twenty years, but I stayed on and liked it.

Miss Shoemaker reports good offerings, 120 baptisms and good work in Liondo. Miss Mitchell reports for Mpangu, 153 baptisms, also an increase in offerings. But for Moma, Bosongongo, and Makanza who came in to the station for their in-gathering, the offering was down for some reason. They had 16 baptisms, and from the school children and others on the station were 21. Mr. Roberts is leaving today to cover Yolombo, Ekuku, Monji, Mbelo, and Bolanda, a long trip. We are planning on 20 new student evangelists. There were 8 new preacher-teachers sent out to all the districts of Mondombe, one to a new *chefferie* that has asked for a long time.

Buena Rose Stober to Friends, February 17, 1942—Mondombe, Congo Belge

I was intending to get your letter finished for the last mail boat, but things happened so fast that I couldn't finish it. I ought to name this letter, "When a missionary needs a friend."

Billy Horner was born January 26, but the driver ants tried every day for a week before and after his arrival to toute [*sic*] us out of the house. The chimney caught fire and burned out all the woodwork around the cement which hung precariously midair until Mr. Johnston could get it fixed. We cooked on the burner oil stove and an open fire a day before and two days after the delivery. Then to clap the climax, I dislocated my left arm and was only "half nurse," the other half useless in a bandage. Billy and Dr. Marjorie got along beautifully even if Mondombe's contribution to their well-being was only half what it could be. It was very hot, too, and no one enjoyed the heat, least of all Billy. All of the Congo variety of itches get worse during the heat spells and my variety was terrible, almost like poison ivy. Mrs. Johnston had a fever, Myrle Ward, too, wasn't feeling very well, but through it all Dr. Howard kept a cool head and is one proud father.

I left Mondombe on December 29 and met with two groups of evangelists. The head evangelist was along. We baptized ninety-nine inquirers, I married six couples, the offering in one group was excellent, another good, and the third, poor. We had some knotty problems to solve and I'm afraid we didn't solve some of them properly; but as a whole the trip was a success and an inspiration. We went through about eight new villages that are begging for teacher-preachers. One big chief called on me in state and almost demanded a nurse for his people. They need one badly, too, but we haven't the nurse to send. We sent in to Mondombe evangelists' school seven new couples but could only promise work for two of the men; however, the others are willing to take their chances, selling firewood and doing odd jobs for a living while they study.

In one village they had been begging so hard for a teacher-preacher a policeman was standing watching me write a letter back to Mondombe. When I wrote the date he exclaimed, "That 1942 is the new year isn't it?" and of course I asked where he had learned to read as most of the village was wild, red-painted heathen. "I don't know how to read, Mama," he replied, "but I've watched those who write and have learned a few words." He was a big husky man in his blue uniform of shorts and jacket and a red fez, and he was so eager to learn he could think of nothing else but having a teacher.

We said goodbye to the Mondombe carriers and the evangelists at Ngwlewa where we met carriers sent from Wema to take me there. Cappy and Tippy and their two pups were with me. One pup for the head evangelist of Mbelo and one for Miss Ward's cook at Wema, the latter they named "Fatness Itself," Mafuta Mingi. He was more like a teddy bear. I intended going back after Billy's birth by bike, but my arm isn't equal to it so here I am halfway home on the state boat.

I have just opened the Mondombe mail sack and taken out my portion. What a lovely Christmas mail it is! A new dress, a pattern, pins, hankies, gum, a picture of my nephew, my gifts from Franklin and Newkirk, and enough letters to make anyone happy in spite of war. Thank you all so much and I will be writing you individual letters soon.

I wish for every one of you our slogan realized, "Keep growing in spite of war."

Buena Rose Stober to Friends, September 7, 1942—Mondombe, Congo Belge

Since I last wrote you a general letter, I have had a trip into the backcountry. We baptized 374 converts. After that school closed and my girls when home. Three graduated, one has acquired a husband since.

The doctor and family left for South Africa for a much-needed rest, eye examination, dental work, etc. We have had letters from them and they are having a happy time. Dr. Baker sent some seeds for some lovely purple flowering trees and they are already up. Miss Bateman and Miss Shoemaker brought back some gaillardia flower seeds and another flower so we are getting some lovely new plants from there.

Wednesday I transplanted two Japanese persimmon trees Doctor got in the colony before he left. Hope they are good.

After the Bakers left, we had a refresher class for our one hundred backcountry evangelists. I worked with the wives along with Mrs. Roberts and five native teachers. She taught the Bible women and outstanding Christians of other lands and times. One native taught Bible memory work and a course on kindness. A nurse taught food elements and values and care of teeth to both men and women. We had seeds for them of soya, navy beans, corn, cabbage, tomatoes, celery, arrow root, etc. A boy from the dormitory demonstrated making arrow root flour. Three others fed rice and fruit to all the evangelists' children and taught them games and songs, etc. I had sewing with them. Each one made a baby petticoat of scraps I had saved. Miss Mitchell and Mr. Roberts had classes for the men, looked after their offering and palaver along with native leaders of the church. At the hospital we checked them all for health, etc. The offering was good, and they were able to give each evangelist a little raise. They selected some twenty-two new married students to enter school here as future evangelists and eight from the third-year class here went out to new villages to preach and teach.

Since then, I have been busy getting my hospital records in order, supervising the beautifying of the church grounds, mending my clothes, and making two new uniforms and two new dresses. Now we are house cleaning, my helpers are mostly, but I've managed to make some new cushions and curtains, not to mention the hospital work: fifty to ninety ulcers per day, five babies receiving milk, four broken bones, and a few little things like that. Hattie and Ned have been on trips too.

The *Oregon* and mission advisory committee will be with us for the week of September 28.

My dog Tippy died and I miss him so much, but I will have my faithful Cappy, have had her since 1935; besides, I have a cat and the Baker's parrot that keeps us all laughing with its chatter. You see I am the proverbial old maid, except that I don't spin anything and I haven't any corkscrew curls.

I wonder what you all are doing these war-minded times. May God guide us each into a fuller, more efficient service and true happiness and life. Even if it is only September, school will start soon, and I won't have another chance to say Merry Christmas and Happy New Year.

Buena Rose Stober to Friends, June 2, 1943—Mondombe, Congo Belge

The boat may whistle in most any minute and I will have a grand scramble to get my baggage closed and on the boat, as I am off to Wema again to help them. This time we have all voted against driver ants, chimneys on fire, and dislocated arms. Here is just a glimpse into the activities I am leaving behind:

Women's school in girls' dormitory I am turning over to Mrs. Hurt, also my two classes of hygiene and French in the second-degree school and the feeding of two babies. Dr. and Mrs. Baker will care for my various garden projects and Miss Mitchell will supervise our rabbits.

This term in women's school we were proud to have thirty-two more-or-less perfect attendance as the women are so difficult to reach, since the proverbial clothes, husbands, and charms loom large in their thinking. They won tied-and-dyed head scarves as rewards. Besides reading, writing, hygiene, and Bible, we had an interesting project of hand work. They hunted two forest fibers and pineapple fiber, made thread, and I dyed it with forest dyes, and then learned to crochet and braid belts, purses, and three started tams, but they were not quite finished.

At the hospital, the doctor has been operating pretty steadily, and I have been mixing potions and making good, big supplies so that he wouldn't be tied up with any more of my work than necessary. How does this sound: ten quarts of 50 percent Epsom salts, ten quarts of sodium sulfate, ten kilograms of sulfur ointment, and three gallons of liquid quinine for babies. This week we had two healthy babies born but lost two little sick ones. I have only done a small amount of dental work these last two months. Last month

Margaret Baker was so desperately sick with complications of malaria, one of our good Belgian friends went on Doctor's motor to Bokungu, borrowed a car, and brought Dr. Horner from Wema to help us out. The two doctors fought for over a week with blood transfusions, etc., before there was much hope, and now she is up and around again, week and pale but gaining each day and her gay sweet self again.

One of the latest wonders is that I am learning to knit and like it. Virginia Ann Hurt is making soldiers' socks and took time out to teach me. How lovely it is to have the Hurts back again.

We had a feast for the four girls leaving the dormitory this year and our menu was manioc cakes, manioc greens, boiled rice, rabbit, and palm-gravy and bananas. Each girl had a rose, honeysuckle, or begonia for her hair. They seemed to enjoy it. Virginia and I did the serving.

So many of our supplies are entirely cut off or too expensive and difficult to get because of the war, but it is wonderful what we can get along without.

Buena Rose Stober to Friends, January 19, 1944—Muizenburg, South Africa

I expect you to wonder what has become of me since I last wrote you. I half-promised you a letter before Christmas but it never did develop and now the new year has passed its third Sunday.

We are having many useful and restful experiences here. I'm actually getting a little pink and tan in place of my former silly yellow. Some of the white people at the beach are so brown you would think they are half-castes. Looking at the sea rolling onto the beach here at Muizenburg at the Cape, it doesn't seem possible that all the terrible things are still happening on the ocean and on land. Just today we heard that one of the white chaplains for our Congo troops serving in the East had been killed. He left a wife and new baby in Congo.

At Brook House in Pretoria, a holiday home for ministers and missionaries, we were given wonderfully inspirational talks by our host, Mr. Gilchrist, a retired Scotch missionary from our part of Congo. He tells how Dr. Dye saved his life once and how he still follows some of Dr. Barger's treatments. He is truly a missionary to missionaries and ministers and saw to it that we had all the good home food that we could eat. I had never eaten so many peaches, nectarines, and plums in all my life! He gave us many flower seeds for Congo, all grown on the beautiful grounds of Brook House.

I did some useful reading, observing, and questioning in Witwatersrand University School of Dentistry and visited the dental infirmary where they examine and treat seventy thousand or more preschool children each year. It was a delight to see their well-kept teeth and their perfect confidence and lack of fear.

We were invited by the daughter of the bacteriologist to visit Medical Research. She also took us through the hothouse and gardens of a wonderful collection of South African wildflowers.

One of the other highlights of our stay in Pretoria and Johannesburg was out to visit to the leper colony where lepers are gathered together from Natal, Transvaal, Transkei, and Orange Free State. There are over a thousand of them—native, colored (Asiatic and mulatto), and around a hundred whites. It is a beautiful place and they have wonderful care, but even at the best it is sad beyond words. To see the sightless eyes, the mutilated bodies, the lumpy faces, and those gruesome fingerless hands reaching up to take three bits of candy or the comic strip our hostess had brought for them. How they loved and appreciated her visits! She has a church there and visits them two or three times a week. The hardest to see was the dozens of children with leprosy, but of course they stand some chance of health if treated early. It is said that many of them go out as arrested cases after a year. It is wonderful what they can do if they get the basics in the beginning. The nurses showed us two young girls who are ready to leave. Each patient must have ten or twelve negative microscopic examinations before they are permitted to leave. Their treatment is much the same as we use for our twenty lepers at Mondombe. Babies are taken away from leper parents at birth and cared for a year or two in a nursery where the parents can see them but not infect them. There were seventeen in the nursery with one white nurse and three native helpers. We met a white mother coming from having a look through the screen at her little baby. Afterward, these babies go out to relatives or in a home.

My! What a lot of work is being done and what a lot is left undone. There are many of my Congo duties I ought to be able to do better after having seen these folks at work in South Africa. We have found them a friendly, obliging people with a lot of Christian love in their hearts and works.

We will be going back to Congo in a couple of months, rested, seasunshine tanned, our lungs full of sea air, and ready for another try in our tropical harvest.

Buena Rose Stober to Friends, May 19, 1944—Mondombe, Congo Belge

I have been silent for a long time and now it is time to let you know that we will soon be at Mondombe and I will take up the old familiar round of tasks after my fine vacation: treatments of the sick, care of babies, girls' and women's work, hygiene, dental and general, simple dentistry, with a little school teaching and preaching. I have already been doing whatever dental work I could do for the missionaries and a few natives as we stopped at each station on our two-and-a-half weeks' trip on the *Oregon* on from Bolenge to Mondombe. They allowed me a day or so at each station for this work and I have my dental equipment set up in the lounge along with my bed and other baggage. My new flash headlight and the new spectacles make dental work much easier, not to mention the dental school's observation and studying I did in Johannesburg.

The Dr. Baker family will be leaving Mondombe on the *Oregon* along with Miss Shoemaker, so Mr. and Mrs. Hurt and I will be Mondombe's white staff until Miss Mitchell gets back.

We have some pretty fine native workers so we will do what we can, and the rest will be done by them or left undone but we always have the assurance that, "I know Him in whom I have believed and I'm persuaded that He is able to keep that which I have committed unto Him unto that day" (2 Tim 1:12).

Here is just a sketch about some of these native workers on whom we depend.

Ntange Timoteo and Bolei Mirium, pastor and head evangelist of Mondombe work. A graduate of our Congo Christian Institute and a fine, patient, progressive Christian. His wife helps with the women's work. They have no children.

Bowala Marc and Senga Yoana, Congo Christian Institute graduate, assistant pastor, caretaker of the forty or fifty dormitory boys, parents of nine children (one is married, two dead, and six at home). She helps with a prenatal care class and maternity work when her own do not keep her too busy.

Boombo Pierre and Boonda Malia, Congo Christian Institute graduate, church elder, head teacher in the boys' and men's school, and teaches in the advanced school. She does lovely crochet work and some knitting. They have no children.

Nkang'Itoko Timoteo and Ononga Yoana, church elder, head nurse of seven to ten other men nurses. He has been in the medical work since Dr.

Pearson's time in the 1920s. I met him as head nurse in 1931. They have five children.

Bononga Thomas, hunchback, single man with a happy smile for all, Congo Christian Institute graduate, in charge of women's and girls' school.

I could of course tell you pages about the eighty to one hundred evangelists in our backcountry work or of other fine nurses in five rural dispensaries, four coffee plantation dispensaries, and our little leper colony, or of our girls' dormitory and their caretaker, our student evangelists and their gardens and brick making, or of the carpenters or pages of their problems in these various tasks, but it is sufficient to say that we will carry on with our hands full of many tasks in a community that is trying hard to be a model Christian community in the midst of heathen poverty of body and spirit in this faraway bit of African jungle.

Buena Rose Stober to Friends, June 3, 1945—Mondombe, Congo Belge

Several of you have asked about the kind of home life that we as missionaries have, especially we single folks, who according to some can't possibly have a normal life and yet we do or at least we do and a very happy one. So here are some of the details of my home life.

You know from former letters of my dog Cappy, and Bonsela, Dr. Horner's dog, also about Tom Tigie and Purr, the Baker's cats, and the Baker's Polly with his chatter all day long of "Hello, Polly" spoken in each of the voices of the Baker family, also my voice and the voices of all the boys and men working around here. He calls the cats and they look bewildered; calls Bonsela and she rushes madly to the kitchen for her choice morsel and finds no one offering one; he calls Cappy but she can't be fooled even when I take my bike and start somewhere she loves to go. Polly's calling "Cappy" or whistling does not fool her; she waits for my call. The chickens and ducks are forever rushing around looking for the chicken lad with his basket of ground corn because Polly imitates him. The funniest times are when he fools me coughing and clearing his throat like Mr. Hurt. He sneezes like me and laughs like the cook, calls, "What's the matter?" "How are you, Polly?" "How's Polly?" and many other words.

Besides pets and gardeners, I have two men who were quite important to my well-being. Miss Mitchell's housekeeper, Elanga Timothy, and Banza Thomas, whom he is training to take over my work when Miss Mitchell arrives. Being away from the house a great deal of the day makes them necessary. These fellows are both married, are Christians, and live in the mission village. Elanga is a deacon in the church. They arrive at 5:30 a.m. and start breakfast, washing, ironing, cleaning, preparing milk for two babies, buying a market of wood, corn, eggs, rice, and vegetables; supervising my schoolboy gardeners, and caretaker of chickens, ducks, and rabbits. They plan well-balanced meals with what they can find at hand except when I have suggestions, or I am entertaining. They keep my bike in repair, care for the Frigilux except when it is balking; they feed the dogs and cats, keep flowers in the house; keep me in clean uniforms and other clean clothes; pack my bed and baggage when I must travel. So, this Sunday I have time for your letter because of them.

The other day I came home at noon to find a nice platter of delicious fudge with false almonds waiting for me; another day it is sup cakes, mushrooms on toast, breadfruit sticks like French-fried potatoes, or mulberry pie. They even can fruit and vegetables with the pressure cooker. I never get over the marvel of seeing a former rank heathen doing these arts in cooking.

These fellows are both quiet, steady workers but some of my former housekeepers were not so good and peaceful. One used to blow up every time I tried to have company or was rushed; another took my bike without asking and carried his friend around, running into a man; another was always fighting with his wife and took the attitude that, "You white folks are ruining our wives because you won't let us beat them." He has two extra now. The cobwebs and dirt are not always chased away, and the food is not always perfect; but I do not know how I could ever manage this busy year if I had a quarrelsome fellow, and I am usually not ashamed when white folks drop in, and how many details they take off my shoulders I could never name them all.

Buena Rose Stober to Friends, August 22, 1945—Mondombe, Congo Belge

A young male student nurse and I mixed fourteen liters of carbolic acid lotion and five liters of 70 percent denatured alcohol like good pharmacists, not to mention the other work of five nurses; treatments of all kinds and five of my nurses are running fevers, three of the five are working.

Last week a strangulated hernia came in after two weeks' attempt by the native doctors to reduce it. We tried, too, but failed, because when we opened it, the intestine was in bad shape, and he was an old man. A teacher's wife was brought in dying with meningitis and she left a two-and-a-half-month-old baby and three other children. The heathen relatives are accusing the poor husband of killing her, and they kidnapped the oldest girl as punishment and are trying to make him stand a native trial. I sent him to our white administrator. We are feeding the other children. A man who had a very pernicious anemia, hookworm, malaria, and what not, was told by a witch doctor that his wife was trying to kill him, so he proceeds to try to beat her to it. The territorial agent sent them both in for repairs and asks if he is strong enough for imprisonment or is he crazy. He is neither, but he is desperately ill, and his wife's wounds are healing, thanks to sulfa drugs. The deepest was in the abdomen and bad enough to kill her, but he missed vital organs. Pour misguided souls. They are dying for want of a little enlightenment. They need Christianity so much. We Christians mustn't fight over our doctrine but must go forward.

I will be home sometime in 1946 after Dr. Baker gets back to take over. It is so fine to have Miss Mitchell back and hear all of the latest news from our good old USA. We were glad that it is school vacation and the Hurt family was able to rent a truck and go to Stanleyville for medical check-ups and an oculist's art. Then to Mondombe on the former jungle paths is almost as wonderful as Moses and his Red Sea crossing. They will be back next week, it is only a two-day trip.

Buena Rose Stober to Friends, January 10, 1946—Mondombe, Congo Belge

The mail boat hasn't yet come downriver so I have this time to write, provided someone doesn't disturb me. (They did. Two of my dormitory girls got into a fight and the caretaker couldn't settle it, so I sent the night sentry to lock the girls in their rooms until they quieted down and then we could talk it over after 8:00 a.m. tomorrow when I hope to have your letters off and a good hundred patients treated, and my breakfast eaten). I owe so many of you letters this is the only way I can manage this month. Thank you each and all.

Since the first of December, I have been rushing around like mad, trying to keep up with abscesses, thorns in fingers, broken bones, bashed-in heads from fights, a baby fell into the fire and was burned terribly but is getting better now, along with all the rest of the miseries; in my spare moments I finally managed my eight yearly reports to the state, union work, provincial doctor, UCMS, and some of these had to be in both French and English. Then the Hurts had to leave because his heart condition is getting so serious. Then Christmas and New Year (we had a little tree all to ourselves, Hattie and I). We made Christmas for the natives a time of praise and devotion and gifts to the offering. Exchanging of gifts and greetings is done here as in Belgium on New Year's Day. Then our 100 rural evangelist-teachers and their families came in. We examined them all and signed their medical passports and the sick ones are being treated. Then came a group of little boys for checkups before they entered school, 15 or so. Clerks of the companies in the territory came for their yearly medical passport and now I suppose 50 or so police will be dragging in for their passports. Then all make another trip to each of the plantation dispensaries to examine two or three thousand workmen and their families (my last trip, I hope, before I turn over the work to its rightful director, Dr. Baker, but we have had no word of their sailing).

Miss Mitchell in the meantime has run the school for 450 boys and men, cared for 48 dormitory boys, arranged things for the church with a native pastor, Ntange Timoteo, received the offerings of the backcountry evangelist-teachers' villages, and paid them for six months. Their palavers are many and varied and a man-sized chore to settle, but their offerings were a little higher, so they had a raise.

I started this bright epistle about four months ago but never seem to find time to type it, now I have lost my scribbled notes I made in bed with malaria and my head buzzing with quinine. If you have never had the experience you would be surprised at the dizzy floating lightheaded feeling, not to mention the rocks-in-your-stomach indigestion, sometimes nausea and diarrhea, the splitting headaches, backaches, and sore spleen. I have just finished a cure of atabrine this week, too, but didn't feel so badly to begin with. Most of our thirty-three white folks in the territory had it last season and now we are all starting again. Hattie has just finished a cure, too, and all of this in spite of our faithfully taking prophylactic treatment. The only nice thing about it is when it is over. Poor natives, they are so full of it! That is, the ones who survived the toll of babies it takes.

Buena Rose Stober to Friends, July 9, 1946—Newkirk, Oklahoma

Here I have been in Oklahoma a whole month; in fact, I was in the States when you got my letter saying I was coming. I stayed with my brother in the East awhile.

I have surely been lazy and eaten my share of home green turnips, potatoes, eggs, and chicken, and real milk instead of powdered milk of Congo days. I have even had butter when I wanted it, but I had nearly gotten out of the habit of using it as what we received in Congo was such a poor excuse.

My Congo yellow atabrine tint is even replaced by common Oklahoma brown now.

You know my trip by Pan America Airways by the Constellation's first trip was really the way to come home.[3] I left Léopoldville, the capital of Belgian Congo, April 29, Monday at 9:10 a.m., and arrived in New York Wednesday afternoon at 2:30 p.m. May 1. We stopped only four times: at Robertsfield, Liberia, where the road signs over-rode pointing toward Moscow, Tokyo, Paris, Berlin, London, San Francisco, etc. Each pointed sign gave the number of miles from Robertsfield to the place. Cape Town was 3,395 miles and New York was 4,554 miles. We ate in the army officers' mess hall.

We were at Dakar before 10:00 p.m. and it was so chilly we had to wear our heavy coats, my first time since my South African vacation. During the night one of the propellers stopped but one could tell no difference in the plane's speed. At 4:30 a.m. we were in Lisbon, Portugal, and it was cold and rainy. They announced that we would be taken to a hotel and would have twelve hours to wait. We had been told at Léopoldville that we would have only forty-five-minute stops for refueling except for two or three hours in Lisbon. We were off again at 5:00 p.m. for Shannon, Ireland. From Shannon, Ireland, we were eight hours crossing the Atlantic to Gandor, Newfoundland. Long before we were near land, we could see miles and miles of icebergs and ice floats. At Newfoundland we had breakfast in another army mess hall. We were told it was 30° above zero but my tropically treated blood registered 30° below zero. Gangers pine forests were dotted with snow, but I was glad when we glided over Nova Scotia and then over Maine. I enjoyed the spring in the East.

Did you know that our good old white-haired Captain Inkema Jean of the SW *Oregon* has a nephew, Lonela Pierre, working for the Pan American Airways in Léopoldville? He was the last African to bid me *bon voyage*. He had been chosen out of a group of several Congo steamer captains, so I was quite proud of him frisking around refueling the big shiny Constellation. His one regret was that we hadn't taught him English since he needed it working with Americans who did not know his language. Not many of our natives need English so our short-staffed educational system on the mission stations included only French. How they crave knowledge, and how quickly

3. The Lockheed Constellation was a propeller-driven, four-engine airliner first used for commercial travel in February 1946, only months before Stober flew on one as she describes in this letter. It was the first cabin-pressurized airliner, making long trans-Atlantic flights much more comfortable than in unpressurized cabins. By the late 1960s, much faster jet airliners began to replace the Constellation and other propeller-driven airliners in commercial use.

they learn. When we fail we always feel so ashamed. He had learned the rest of his wisdom in our schools and his steamer knowledge under Captain Jean.

Buena Rose Stober to Friends, February 18, 1947—Unknown Location

Here I am making plans for my trip back to Congo. It doesn't seem like I've been in the USA nearly a year, but it will be a year the first of May.

My application for a Belgian visa for return to Congo has been sent along with a certificate of good conduct from the police station, its medical certificate, yellow fever, smallpox, and letters from the United Christian Missionary Society saying I am a *bona fide* missionary. Now I am having the pleasure of waiting until all the red tape in New York, Washington, DC, Belgium, Léopoldville, and Coquilhatville, Belgian Congo, is finished, and they send a permit and passport to enter and work in Congo.

I am writing as I am travelling around among the churches. This was started at Miss Hart's desk in Ft. Worth, Texas, while I was waiting for the pastor of the Brady, Texas, church to take me to Brady where we had a fine school of missions. On Sunday, they raised over $250.00 on an x-ray machine for Congo. Their fund is over $1,200.00 already. I am so pleased.

I had hoped to take back an x-ray, electric lights, and a new nurse for Congo. Did you know that not one of our Congo hospitals has an x-ray? So far, although both the x-ray and light plant funds are growing, there is no nurse ready to go back with me.

Jobs for doctors and nurses are too easy to find these days, I know. But I had hoped to find an army nurse rested and willing to spend her skill with our ailing Africans. Won't you help me find one or several nurses and doctors?

Buena Rose Stober to Friends, Undated—Mondombe, Congo Belge

I wanted you to know of my recent visit of observation to the National Leprosarium and to bid you goodbye, as I sail July 10 for Congo.

Through the kindness of the American Mission to Lepers, who asked permission of Washington, DC, for missionary nurses and doctors and others interested, our transportation is paid. There is a constant coming and going of missionary doctors and nurses who spend from a few days to two weeks observing the new method and drugs for treating leprosy.

I was met at the station of Carville by the Public Health Services car; even though it was raining, it didn't dampen my joy to see Goldie Alumbaugh, who had already been there a week. My permit came through too late for me to arrive her first week there. Another nurse from the Lutheran mission in Liberia was with Goldie.

We stopped at the little corner grocery and bought some Coca-Cola, as the girls said the water tasted pretty much of chlorine, etc. When the Mississippi River floods, it contaminates the hospital water supply as it is surrounded by the levy on all but one side. The river looks like our Congo, except that we do not have the levees to keep them in their banks.

What a lovely place was chosen for the leprosarium. In the staff quarters where the doctors, nurses, sisters, Catholic priests, Protestant chaplain, and other workers live, lovely big trees covered with Louisiana's famous moss, a tree parasite used for stuffing mattresses, etc. The secretary to the blind editor of *The Star*, the leper-owned magazine, lives there too. She came while we were there, and we think she is very nice.

The National Leprosarium covers some four hundred acres and the approach is lovely. We were given rooms in what is called the "big house," which is really the administration building with some rooms for nurses and the secretary upstairs. It was the old mansion of some estate, and is surrounded by tremendous trees with a greenish grey moss parasite festooning from all their branches. The room Goldie and I had was big enough for a banquet hall.

The patients' quarters were lovely, too, with single rooms in the dormitories furnished like hotel rooms, and the hospital proper is modern in every way. There were many types of amusement for the patients, including golf, a baseball park, recreation room, ice cream parlor, library, and theater.

Most of the doctors had their own homes and their families there. They were even provided with a theater for the staff and had good movies twice a week and then the next night the same picture would be shown in the patients' theater. One of the doctor's daughters was a champion at blowing bubble gum, much to the amusement of all of us moviegoers. Nearly all the staff went for the fellowship.

There is a nice Protestant church and one of our men, Chaplain Rash, is in charge. He is a fine man and both staff and patients love him. Mrs. Rash plays the piano for the services when there are no visiting musicians. He had to tell us of our work on Wednesday afternoon after Bible study period. Mr. Rash certainly is a master at making the Bible characters live for his audience.

The Catholics have a fine church and kind little old Father Paul looks after his people. The sisters do most of the nursing as they were in charge of the work long before it became the National Leprosarium in 1921. There are two public health nurses working for credit. The sisters have a special dining room, and the staff who haven't cooking arrangements at home eat in another dining room. Some of the Sisters of Charity have been nursing there for years, and giving their patients the very finest care so long that they can even brag that for thirty-five years not one of their sisters has contracted the disease, which is in itself a big score against our unreasonable horror of the disease and for their effective methods of protecting themselves.

The dairy was another place of special interest to me, as at Mondombe they have just recently acquired five cows. They have a head of some one hundred Holstein cows and furnish milk for the patients and staff. They have their own cooling, separating, and pasteurizing system and it is scrupulously kept.

The patients' dormitories were all connected with the hospital, the churches, their recreation center, their theater, ice cream parlor, model shop, printing press, etc., by long covered and screened walks of cement used by bicycles, wheelchairs, and pedestrian nurses, doctors, orderlies, and patients. There are about seventeen of these dormitories with some thirty to forty rooms each.

Outside the patients' rooms there were dozens of tiny gardens of flowers and vegetables. Off to the side was a group of the individual cottages where more prosperous patients own homes and live with their husbands or wives.

The spirit of optimism pervaded the place and although some were unhappy or disgruntled, many were now looking forward to discharge after [five years of successful treatment with the new drugs]. The patients were kind to help us learn all the virtues of the new treatments and we will carry back many useful suggestions to our Congo lepers. They prefer that the disease be called Hansen's Disease after the discoverer of the bacillus rather than leprosy with the obnoxious horror that has clung to it through the years. They appreciate a wholesome respect for the disease but wish it would not carry the old idea of "unclean" any more for Hansen's Disease than for other infectious diseases that we accept in public places.

The doctors and nurses and sisters of the staff did everything possible to furnish us the information we needed for our people of Africa. We were given bulletins, notes, lectures, and even offered cultures of useful drugs used in treatments. We were allowed hours in the laboratory.

The medical officer in charge, Dr. Johansen, was kindness itself.[4] There was a bone specialist; an ear, nose, and throat specialist; a skin specialist; a dentist; another doctor in charge of injections; and a bacteriologist, so every ailment even to the fitting of a shoe for a calloused foot was cared for carefully. So, we learned and learned and came away determined to use this new knowledge to relieve our distressed Congo people.

Now I am nearing sailing time. I have packed, crammed, unpacked and repacked, invoiced, and valued all the lovely things you sent me. I wish I could write to you each an individual thank you because I appreciate so much all the thousands of things you have done to equip me and make my trip back a pleasant one. The x-ray fund is growing, the car for Mondombe paid for and gone, the electric light fund growing, but the nurse not yet in sight. Thank you for everything, and please keep praying that the Lord of the harvest will send laborers into this field and all the needy ones.

Buena Rose Stober to Friends, September 4, 1947—Mondombe, Congo Belge

Here I am on the *Oregon* with the steady puff-puff of the engine and the buzz of the natives visiting below and above me. Captain Jean's quiet order above with his wheelman and his seven-year-old niece and her playmate above. I am in what we call the lounge in front and surrounded by boxes of sugar, sacks of flour, bales of blankets and mosquito nets (war surplus) for our dormitory boys and girls and the hospital, not to mention books of all descriptions from the press for our schools. We are going after everyone for a conference but since Agnes Rogers, Lotumbe's nurse, is sick, we are going past here to take her to Dr. Henderson at Monieka. She has had a heavy load since Goldie Alumbaugh left. The Tillerys and two children, the Hobgoods of Ifumo and one child, and Miss Musgrave are there, no MD in miles.

There is nothing like a trip on the *Oregon* to make you feel back at home on the Congo even though the tsetse flies, mosquitoes, and elephant flies do have good eatin' on me when I forget to apply freely my new insect repellent, "6–12."[5] It really seems to work and I wish I had a case of it to

4. Dr. Frederick Andrew Johansen (1889–1974) joined the medical staff at the National Leprosarium in 1924 and served as medical director from 1947 to his retirement in 1953.

5. The insect repellent marketed under the brand name 6–12 contained the active ingredient 2-ethyl hexanediol-1,3. Developed in the late 1930s, it was first approved for use by the US armed forces in 1942, and for civilian use in 1957. It was discontinued as a commercial insect repellent in 1991 after studies linked it to birth defects in laboratory animals.

make life more livable. I am anxious to see how it works on jiggers and Mondombe's sand flies.

Botuli Daniele, son of our Mondombe head nurse, about whom I raved so much in my talks at home, is doing splendidly in the Congo Christian Institute, also his wife is nearly ready for institute work. They are second-generation Christians, and worth all the effort put in training them. Another one of my pet subjects is Bohambu Pierre, son of the man who made it possible for our work in Mondombe years ago, he has just entered training in the English Baptist Hospital near Stanleyville. We are paying his tuition and we believe he will be worth every cent for our future work.

I had a very happy experience at Bolenge, as in all the years I have been proud of our Congo Christian Institute. I have never had the privilege of attending a commencement but just made it this time and now fourteen students from upriver are on board going home. Some stayed for the fourth year which has just been added and that included all three of our Mondombe graduates, two of them training as *moniteurs* (teachers) and one as a pastor, the latter a brother of Mondombe's pastor.

Mpoku Anoka of Bolenge preached the finest commencement address I have heard out here. The cutting of the fern chain after the graduates has sung, "Have Thine Own Way, Lord" took me back to my own College of Mission days: as the chain was cut, each group to each part of the field stood alone, then they cut the couples so that they two stood apart from other couples.[6] Those who were taking the fourth year were left in a group together and then the service was closed with a prayer for their success at their tasks on different stations and fields of service.

Buena Rose Stober to Friends, September 27, 1947—Mondombe, Congo Belge

Well, this is the end of a nearly perfect day; in other words, everything has gone very well. The two babies who have had high fevers are better; the fellow with a snake bite is better even if his leg is still swollen to nearly twice its size normally; my garden fence is finished; my rug cleaned and dyed a pretty wine color; a good roseapple pie made by a new hand at the job; a palm tree that was causing too much shade in my garden down, etc.

6. At the College of Missions in Indianapolis, one graduation tradition was the "Ivy Chain Ceremony." All students stood in a circle, holding a long chain of woven ivy. Officials cut the ivy chain held by those graduating, symbolizing their release into their assigned mission fields; only continuing students held the ivy chain, symbolizing their ongoing education. Then, officials gave a new ivy chain to missionaries assigned to the same field, symbolizing their new commitment to one another.

This afternoon I had a fine visit with the wife of a clerk who learned to knit while I was here before. She has done some nice work. I washed Cappy, and washed my hair, and the house has been scrubbed. Polly chewed his perch until it was so weak that when a chicken flew up there to see if he had left a tidbit to eat the whole thing came down and Polly almost got mashed under it. He is a bit quiet but not hurt seriously.

The cattle are getting so they know me and come to see if I have any rice for them, not too brave, but braver than at first.

Last Sunday one of the school teachers who had just returned from a long trip visiting our schools and churches in one or two districts talked about his trip. He told about how in some parts some of the Christians had fallen into the heathen practice of building little witch houses, supposedly to keep you well, etc. He reprimanded them and although they were not brave enough to tear them down themselves, they asked if the preacher Nkoi Paul the teacher, would do the job so they had themselves a swell job wrecking all the little "dog houses" in every backyard of these weaker Christians. Paul is one of the young men who has grown up since the mission started and was named after Boseke Paul the first evangelist who started the Mondombe work. You will probably remember my talking about Mondombe's Paul.

Buena Rose Stober to Friends, October 25, 1947—Mondombe, Congo Belge

Since everything is quiet I shall try to get your mimeograph letter typed, although October days do not give one much of the Christmas spirit. The other missionaries and the school folks will soon be back and the patients will come flocking in and I won't have time later. We are expecting the *Oregon* any day now but there seems to be plenty to do. We have six patients in quarantine for smallpox, a number of babies with fevers, an amoebic dysentery case, plenty of ulcers, anemias, etc.

I have been out to the leper village several times and we have done slides on all of them. Most of them are in fairly good shape, especially those taking Diasone, but all of them are anemic.[7] I hope enough Diasone will soon come for all of them. The wives of several of them have been to my young farm to get starts of bananas and sugar cane for their gardens. We

7. Developed first in 1937, Diasone contains the active ingredient sulfoxone sodium, and was widely used in the treatment of leprosy from the late 1940s to the early 1980s. When Stober used the antibiotic in Mondombe, it was still considered experimental.

prepared a plot for a palm tree nursery for them since they have no palm trees in the village.

I have been cleaning and repairing the teeth of the nurses who are working during vacation, and next week we hope to start with the dormitory boys who have already come back or did not go home during vacation. Unfortunately, my dental engine arm is not working too well and the new one I ordered hasn't arrived yet. We have cleaned the dental room, laboratory, maternity, and a little in the pharmacy.

I have twelve baby ducklings and am caring for three baby turkeys for the Bakers. The rabbits are having their cages and pen revamped. The garden is growing in spite of the lack of rain. Cappy, my dog, is still frisky, lovable, and is lots of company, even if she is old and deaf. The cattle take me for granted now but I still am not intending to make the bull mad or in any way annoy his gentle disposition.

My gardener mumbles and grumbles to himself and it was amusing to hear him wonder if this smart white woman would know how to mend his lantern that sputtered so much. As a matter of fact, there wasn't much to the matter except he was filling it too full of kerosene. A few days before, he had mended my two new lanterns by punching a few extra holes to let more in below the burner and it works so well I increased my tinkerer's reputation. I had paid $2.50 apiece for them and there wouldn't have been much loss even if I had ruined them as they spent most of the time sputtering and going out. Now they're good lanterns. During the war we had such a time to get lanterns that I took six or so old wrecks lying around on the station and made three good lanterns. While I was home it seemed Louisa, the maternity nurse, mended one for one of her patient's husband and caused quite a commotion. The natives all clapped their hands and called her Mama Mputu, my native name.

Buena Rose Stober to Friends, December 7, 1947—Mondombe, Congo Belge

It is a lovely bright afternoon and it will soon be vesper service time. It has been raining a lot and the sky is full of lovely, floating, pillowy-like clouds. In this morning's service, after a good sermon by Mr. Roberts, we had a very impressive service of ordination of Ntange Timoteo, our pastor here.

Louisa and I assisted at the arrival of a baby whose grandmother is one of the lepers in our camp. The mother so far it is not infected, and the father is only a kid and did not even show up. Our maternity room and ward leaks like a sieve and we almost had to cover the baby and mother to keep them dry. The pitiful grandmother took it for granted that they would have to go back to the leper camp as soon as the baby came and told me that she had no one to go with her in the rain; but of course, we fixed her up a bed in the maternity ward; fortunately, there were no other babies there and the room can be disinfected. As Louisa and I went home we were drenched and had to wade up to our ankles. Neither of us thought of raincoats.

The roofing question on the mission has become a real problem. We hope to get some tin or tile eventually, but it hasn't been available. The palm leaf type of roofing is fine if you can get enough of it and enough to reroof about every three to five years. The natives who make it live just across the river from us and have plenty of leaves, if they will make it. Dr. and Mrs. Roberts went up to have a chat with the state official about it, so maybe we can mend the maternity ward.

Buena Rose Stober to Friends, April 18, 1948—Mondombe, Congo Belge

Food! Food! Food! Evangelism with food seems to have taken up most of my week. I have purchased a ton or so of rice at the hospital for the patients, school folks, and their relatives, not to mention for the pig, cattle, rabbits, ducks, chickens, and turkeys. Next, I had to supervise the nurses heating it and storing it in a big steel drum to keep the weevils out. One tin they heated this way last year is still good, no weevils, even a year later after storage in this way.

We have such a mob of people on the station and although the school folks are required to have gardens, in spite of all our gardening efforts the food problem becomes very acute at times. There are no native food stores and when the villagers sell their own produce they ask such unreasonable prices our people are not able to get enough food. We buy food and sell it to our people for the government fixed prices, which pleases everyone even if it does make a lot of work. The villagers are pleased as they get rid of it sooner without trouble collecting, and we weigh and pay by weight.

I have purchased some hundred bundles of cooked manioc bread and had it sold to boys and folks who do not cook. Our mission orange trees were quite prolific this year and Mrs. Baker had the fruit sentry bring me several bushels of fruit for my girls, patients, and babies. Baby clinic has just finished with sixty-seven present, each baby and mother receiving oranges. The lepers came in for their share, too, and now I am waiting for them to come for their share of the bread. Several of them have been deserted by their wives.

My twenty-seven dormitory girls and some ninety of Hattie's boys have been busy most of the week planting sweet potatoes. Each of us white folks have a hunter, fisher, or more whose produce we divide among certain natives. We plant trees, and are trying to raise chickens, ducks, turkeys, pigs, and cattle and still the patients favorite greeting when I ask, "What news?" is "*Ngala*" (hunger), or worse yet, "*Jile*" (meat hunger).

Buena Rose Stober to Friends, May 28–June 10, 1948—Mondombe, Congo Belge

I am not sure how long this letter will be, but at least I will start it this week before I plunge back into the regular hospital routine. This afternoon I will go to the leper colony as I did last week with pay and rations.

I may even take a bunch of trousers for the men, but most likely that will have to be next Wednesday's chore as I still have some unpacking to do, although I have already taken the book box to the school book storeroom, unpacked what is left of my food, sent the three long boxes of church member records back to Mr. Roberts, the offering must still be counted with Mr. Roberts and Pastor Ntange. The offering for the eleven villages and evangelists was 1,666 francs and there were ninety-seven baptisms.

This will mainly be a story of backcountry evangelism, but I wanted to see the dispensary at Yayenga and give the nurse a few pills each day, and one day packed a badly injured nose that had been bleeding for an hour or so as the owner of the nose walked in from another village. She had been cutting wood for the evening cooking when a big branch of the tree gave a sudden lurch and drove a stick the size of your finger into her nose and tore its way through the tissues. I had sulfa powder and the nurse had plenty of cotton and bandage. We gave her sulfa by mouth also and she was in good shape two days later even though her nose was sore.

But I am getting ahead of my story. Friday a week ago Mr. Roberts drove the car to a village beyond Yayenga, where Doctor was doing a medical census and left it for Doctor to drive back while he and Pastor Ntange rode by bike deeper into the jungle to Ilonga and Tofoke *chefferie*, or counties, to meet another group of six evangelists and their Christians and inquirers. Then Saturday morning Doctor drove the car back with me to Yayenga, Mpango County, gathering of eleven evangelists, wives, children, Christians, and inquirers from their villages. It is one of our oldest and biggest fields.

June 1, 1948. It is a bright sunny morning, and the doctor has gone on a plantation dispensary inspection trip, we have treated a large group of patients, examined some fifteen new ones, prepared baby milk, started the planting of some twenty-five papaya trees, had breakfast, and it is now 8:30 a.m. I have several teeth to work on today.

After Doctor took me to Yayenga two weeks ago, he came right back to the station, leaving me with swarms of Christians, inquirers, and heathens. Many of the eleven evangelists and their families I had not seen since I had reached Mondombe last September. After dinner and a bit of rest, the evangelists and teacher who was to help me sat down and talked how we were going to present the crusade material and made our plans for the week's work. Two evangelists who haven't stuck to their villages very faithfully, and of course because of that had not made a success, wanted to be moved to other villages as they blamed the poor response on the villagers, but we vetoed their wishes at once and asked them to go back and stay on the job a lot better and they would find a better response.

Mr. Roberts had sent a whole packet of good reading material to help them in their work. Miss Mitchell had sent each an American magazine from which she carefully cut out the liquor and tobacco ads (they enjoy these not only for the pictures but also as a file for their papers). I had a pencil and some paper apiece from the folks in Oklahoma. Each child of the evangelists received a garment or two. And the wives of the evangelists received needles, pretty buttons which they could use for earrings, plain buttons, and a small packet of bath powder which they adore, but also they smear all over their faces and make themselves ridiculous. They have such lovely, soft, well-cared-for skin. I always try to instruct them that it is not face powder but body powder. That evening we were entertained by the young bucks and maidens game.

We started our first day with everyone happy and ready for a good week of instruction and inspiration.

June 10, 1948. To continue my story of the Yayenga trip. That first night a crazy man wandered into the drum shed just above my house on the anthill nearby and sang and shouted and beat the drum until no one slept much. Several attempts were made to chase him with only the result that he cursed the brave one until we finally got weary and let him alone. He also ruined my children's Sunday School class the next morning by climbing into an avocado tree close by and raving until all we could do was drown him out with our singing. He would have interrupted church, too, except two elders picked him up bodily and carried him home where he was carefully watched and kept away from our week's meeting.

Sunday morning really started with driver ants in the kitchen close to our house, where the four dormitory girls coming home to their evangelist fathers were cooking. They slept in the house with me and that morning had to cook outside. The evangelist's where we were staying is a lover of dogs, too, from a daughter of my Cappy she has made a lot of money selling puppies. She cares for them as if they were children (she has none). Unfortunately, the puppies were used to running back and forth from that particular kitchen and one little fellow plunged into the midst of the driver ants and out again yelping at the top of his voice. One of the dorm girls and I grabbed him and started removing vicious critters. They have terrible pinchers on them. Katalina came, too, and soon he was free, even if a bit sore here and there; but I couldn't stop with drivers, as I discovered he had fleas, so I mixed some kerosene and palm oil. We rubbed all five puppies, and everything was peaceful.

The teacher that was with me preached the morning sermon. It was really just to the point. He spoke on sharing their Christianity and gave an illustration: the open fire around which everyone likes to sit on a cool night. He said we must share this fire of God, the good news, with others so that they may be warmed as well as us.

I had an interesting discussion with two evangelists about their daughters who had been in the dormitory. Neither one had sent a responsible person to accompany the girls home when school closed. One sent his eleven-year-old daughter to accompany his twelve-year-old girl home about forty miles. Still another sent his ten-year-old girl into the mission to enter school chaperoned by a bunch of rather wild eleven- and twelve-year-old boys of his church. The same evangelist's wife insisted on him letting his fifteen-year-old girl come to live on the mission with her student lover. We thought the affair was officially finished and she was married to the fellow by native custom, but the evangelist told me that he almost fought with his wife trying to prevent it. One of the most difficult problems we have to help them solve is their irresponsibility. One excuses one's children's shortcomings by saying, "*Bomongo alanga*," (She or he himself wishes it).

We planned our five early before-breakfast meetings around the Crusade theme, "*Iso Ba- Masiya Toamna nd'olem'one te Ba- Bokiji bayaleme Ba- Masiya*," "We of Christ work together that those of the world become Christians," using the five subjects: (1) self-examination and correction; (2) prayer; (3) offering; (4) more evangelists and evangelism; (5) more courage, endurance, and perseverance. The school teacher from Mondombe explained the purpose of the Crusade and tried to make it personal and practical. They seemed to get something out of it but time will tell.

At 7:00 a.m. we had roll call for the inquirers and instruction, then they all worked a bit remudding and fixing up the principal evangelist's house, guest houses, and church as we were hard pressed for sleeping quarters. When they examined the inquirers, I didn't take part as most of them are simply scared speechless in the presence of a white person. I read church membership cards for as many villages as had representatives. It is a trying job to read and check two hundred or three hundred cards for names, parents, and check activity or inactivity, but the Yayenga Christians were a bit ashamed of themselves and came rushing in with more offering. Some had lost their baptismal certificates and wanted new ones, and their records had to be hunted out and copies made. Sometimes someone from a neighboring village would have been in marriage in this county and were baptized here, but the husband had died or for some other reason the marriage had broken up and everyone would have forgotten who she was. Some young buck had fallen heir to his father's name and property and his childhood name discarded and forgotten, but our church records had only the boyhood name, or nickname, whatever he had been given when baptized. A girl disliked the first Bible name Malia she had taken when baptized and was now known as Juliana. A child had been living with his divorced mother in another village and at baptism had given the stepfather's name as his father and later gone home to grow up in his own father's village. It is all quite confusing, but you should see the proud Christian's face when his card is read out that he was baptized in maybe 1921 or 1926. It is worth all the trouble for the rest.

We baptized 97 of the 107 applications. One man still had his harem, so he was told to arrange for just one and come back next time. Some children had not been very interested in church or school and were asked to show their interest a little more ardently. We baptized in the beautiful stream about a mile and a half out of Yayenga with an underfoot and a lovely backdrop of tree ferns, vines, shrubs, and rippling water. The teacher, Botemela, Principal Bosongelele, and I baptized three at a time between songs and prayers. Then there was the handshaking, happy calls, all ending in a mad rush back to the church for communion service. But before I reached the church it was pouring rain. The people were in the church waiting and the communion was ready, so we had the service even though we were like a bunch of soaked rats. It was a nice service.

This story ought to end beautifully but it didn't. Mr. Roberts got to Yayenga for breakfast expecting the car at noon before our baptizing service. He reported thirty-three baptisms and an offering over seven hundred francs. At noon a note came that Sunday as they had driven the car to another village they came back in a rain and broke a spring on the car so that meant both of us had to hunt carriers and go home the hard way. Mr. Roberts went that evening by bike and I followed the next day, after paying the evangelists, by a *teepoi*. At 10:00 a.m. my loads and Mr. Roberts had gone, and I followed with seven men for the *teepoi* singing at the top of their voices.

Buena Rose Stober to Friends, July 19, 1948—Mondombe, Congo Belge

I scribbled the notes for this letter while I was listening, with one ear, to Pastor Ntange explaining the purpose of the Crusade. We were in a little backcountry church with its whitewashed mud wall, only halfway toward its thatched roof, which gives you too good a chance to gaze upon the forest over the tops of some of the graceful pineapples, cannas, and papaya trees, and several huge wooden drums that had called us to begin our evangelistic in-gathering. The log benches were crowded and up in front with us sat the seven evangelists and some of their children. I was wondering how I could make the Crusade practical for them, these hard-headed Moma people, who had killed one of our earlier evangelists, later shot with a poisoned arrow a state police of their own tribe, and who are still so backward, shy, afraid, and burdened with witchcraft and witch doctors that many of our sick patients coming from their tribe arrive too late after all the treatment of the bleedings to be saved from the even less complicated maladies.

Yet from the same tribe have come some of our staunchest and finest Christians. The Moma principal evangelist, Botele Pierre and wife, Bocili Yoana; Pastor Ntange's wife, Bolei Mirium; Nkan'Itoke Timoteo, the head nurse; our head *monteur*, Bokako Pierre; and so on down a long list of fine Christian workers who have been with the mission for years.

Earlier going to church I had stopped to ask about a gnarled, hacked, and partially burned old Bokungu tree that had lived after being burned to clear a garden spot and from its bark had furnished hundreds of potions to discover thieves or liars or treat various ailments. It is a violent poison and if you live through it, it is a good drug, they say. If you put drops of this in your eye and it doesn't hurt, you are innocent of an accused crime. But in spite of all this foolish and rough treatment the tree was still spreading its branches of feathery leaves where the villagers could find kindly shade and a bench-like route to sit on while they visited. So, it was the example of what we hope Moma Christians will be through the years in my practical Crusade.

We have a new rural dispensary in Yampete Moma and a fine Christian nurse in charge. There were sixty-four converts baptized and the church offerings amounted to about $30.00 for the county Moma. Once again, we had presents of paper, pencils, buttons, pictures, embroidery thread, children's clothes, etc., from many of you at home to help along our evangelists, their wives, and children with their meager salary. One of them left us during the six-month period for a better paid job as a scribe or county clerk. So goes each six months of evangelistic in-gathering with its joys and heartaches.

Our task in Moma is still bigger than our staff and the time our missionaries have to spend with them, but what has been accomplished is encouraging.

Buena Rose Stober to Friends, September 29, 1948—Mondombe, Congo Belge

Last week and this week I spent most of my spare time caring for babies. The maternity nurse is on vacation, so I have been doing some of her work. Bathing the babies is always interesting anyway, but getting up at night and staying on waiting in maternity is not so interesting. I slept at the hospital a part of four nights lately and every time I get comfortable asleep, I'm awakened by a shrill little tune being played on a tiny flute by a patient who is receiving a long series of intravenous injections and must stay at the hospital. He is living in one of the twenty mud houses we have for patients and the relatives, as the ward is only eighteen-bed. His musical efforts are directed at the evil spirits but are not pleasant when they interrupt your sleep. He is very tall, wears a dirty blue shirt, and when I scold him, he just looks sheepish, grins, and keeps right on tooting away each night, so patients and nurses tell me.

Saturday morning, I was having breakfast before paying for the girls' caretakers, some gardeners, and wood carriers, and then going back to the hospital for the baby clinic. I could watch the mothers with their infants astraddle their hips going for the clinic from the village across river from the mission. We have over a hundred people coming to this clinic regularly on Saturday morning. There was a thin and pale ashy-brown colored mother carrying one child, and dragging another a little older, both thin and anemic like their mother from neglected and untreated malaria and perhaps too much witch doctor. Her hair was matted to her head with a greasy red powder and tied with a dirty rag. The baby was riding in another dirty rag sling. Three other regular clinic mothers past about that time with their confident, happy, clean faces and bodies, their husky infants, clean and growing. One little baby had pulled off his sun suit and was waving it in the air and the rest were laughing at it.

Buena Rose Stober to Friends, November 15, 1948—Mondombe, Congo Belge

This has been a very sad week for all of us who know the Forescom Plantation white folks, for whom our mission has done the medical work for years.[8] A twenty-seven-year-old young man just two years married and living just fifteen miles across the river at Ngombe with his happy bride was run over by the truck coming to take their trunks to the beach as they were flying home in about five weeks. He died before we could get to him after we had word, and poor little Madame had to make the fight for his life alone with a native nurse. We were at least an hour late as the messenger came to us on foot. Miss Shoemaker and I stayed with her all night while the doctor and Mr. Roberts drove to their main plantation for the director.

Poor little Madame has very few relatives left in Belgium and just last month had word of the death of an uncle who had been like a father to her, so even her pleasure of going to Belgium is broken. The natives loved and respected him so and the white folks all spoke so highly of him. I don't think I ever had a harder job than to make him presentable for a burial. We have to work quickly out here as there are no undertakers. I have their dog and, poor thing, he saw the accident as he was in the habit of following his master on the motorcycle. He jumps attention every time he hears a motor.

This morning as I came out after breakfast to see if some work in my flowers was finished, Cappy began frisking around under some vines and found the wounded animal that had been killing my young rabbits, a *boliya*, of the skunk family, I believe. He had eaten some fifteen rabbits and the natives had set a trap, but he had sprung it and went off with the steel wire around his leg, too badly injured to go far. Duchin, our guest dog, killed him for Cappy and then the both of them spent the rest of the morning rolling to get the blood off themselves.

Buena Rose Stober to Friends, December 20, 1948—Wema, Congo Belge

I am having a little vacation at Wema from my regular tasks and the Weeks have offered me the use of their Multigraph to write you a letter.

The year is drawn to a close and on each of our stations you will find missionaries adding up their successes and failures and wondering if their work has accomplished the purpose for which they aimed. I finished my reports before I left Mondombe last week: 46 lepers in our colony, 26 of them Christians, 19 of them baptized this year; 23–27 girls in the dormitory, 8 completing their three years and others taken in their places; 86 average attendance Saturday mornings at infant welfare clinic with an enrollment

8. The Forescom Plantation was a subsidiary of *Société internationale forestière et minière du Congo*, a lumber and mining company that operated in the Belgian Congo from 1906 to 1961.

of 198; 150 dental examinations and treatments for nurses, teachers, and school children; 5 infants fed; 7–8 patients a week received special nutrition. We planted some 100 trees of breadfruit, avocados, guavas, papaya, and rambutans, not to mention bananas, pineapples, and other garden products in order to feed ourselves, our school folks, and our patients.

Mr. Roberts has begun his visits to our 12 or so principal evangelists' fields checking on their work, baptizing inquirers, receiving offering, paying, and settling their problems. Miss Shoemaker's teaching force has just given term examinations. Wema schools are just beginning these examinations as they have had a quarantine, all school and church services banned, because of a meningitis epidemic. They lost two patients, but everything seems to be under control now. They have an even larger school than Mondombe although their boys' dormitory has 65 boys while ours has 82, and they have no girls' dormitory. Wema has the rawest of heathens, and girls' work is hard anywhere. Mrs. Boyer has, however, a nice women's and girls' school.

Here one sees all the fanciest tall headdresses. After saving all your old hair combings and other tidbits of this and that, the hair is pulled to a sharp ridge some six inches tall and deftly French braided across this ridge. Often this ridge is studded with brass tacks, shells, or buttons; instead of a hair net they cover the hair do with a piece of cloth well rubbed with palm oil and red wood powder. It is marvelous to see! This type of headdress usually indicates the secret society to which you belong. Around at Mondombe a we have one of the societies called *nkoi* or "leopard." It is a new fad and they have gone back to raffia skirts and are well rubbed with the red powder and oil.

Some years ago, the fad was *botamba*, or "tree," a medicine or charm which was supposed to make you live forever, or at least the witch doctor saw to it that no one saw you die. Little sticks of wooden bits of this and that were collected in a bottle according to the prescription for which she paid a fabulous sum and then certain secret ceremonies were carried on. Whole village churches would be ruined with the taking of *botamba*, and now although it still exists, *nkoi* has swept the country. There is little we can do about it except preach the truth and expose any atrocities we can prove to the government. Many of their bleedings and treatments cause a terrible anemia or other ailments that lead to death.

The younger educated Christians are our hope as a cure against these horrible customs and we pray constantly and hope you will join us in prayer that Christ's word may reach deep enough into their hearts to stamp out these curses.

Slowly but surely Christ will find the way into their hearts and bring the new day.

Buena Rose Stober to Her Diary, January 31, 1949—Mondombe, Congo Belge

I am a bit tired because all my siesta hour was taken up by a free-for-all fight at the hospital by the wife of a paralyzed patient who has leprosy also and is supposed to be a Christian. The other woman was the wife of a teacher, a graduate of Congo Christian Institute, and should have known better. This was her third major fight in six months. It is a good thing they are not all like that or we would go crazy. One is about all we can stand. Dr. Baker and Mr. Roberts came out at our SOS and brought quiet; whether it is peace or not we are not sure.

What is worse, I preached the sermon Sunday on trusting God instead of our old heathen ways and aimed at three other fights last week. Two of them had put poison in their eyes to prove that they had not killed a nurse's baby, who had died suddenly with malaria just before I got back from Wema. The nurse's wife had only asked where they had dug the manioc her baby had eaten the week before its death and they took it as a direct accusation.

Since I have been back from Wema I have mixed several varieties of potions and lotions we use, bought literally tons of manioc bread, meat, fish, etc., for our patients and schoolchildren, purchased a good two thousand leaf roofing mats ready for the hospital and other mission buildings. Doctor has made the rounds of his seven plantation dispensaries and Miss Shoemaker is now out on a two-week evangelistic tour while Mr. Roberts and the others care for her school. Mr. Roberts has just recently finished a month's evangelistic tour in other regions.

While I was gone, one of my favorite dormitory girls suddenly died in convulsions and Doctor never really found the cause; but her father, being a nurse, remembered that she had been bitten by a rabid dog earlier, so you can understand that this month has been a month of strain for everyone's nerves.

Buena Rose Stober to Her Diary, March, 1949—Mondombe, Congo Belge

My leprosarium patients are having another disagreeable spell of fights with each other. That takes the pep out of all of us concerned, but we probably will live through it. One fellow got his head gashed open because he tried to settle a quarrel between a man and woman resident at the leprosarium. Everyone concerned had to pay a fine as the chieftain settled the affair. He made each one pay a big fine, so perhaps they will behave themselves now.

The culprits have always been troublesome even to thieving. Once he put a Bible in the path where he was sure a woman he had wanted to punish for something was passing and did some very strong heathen cursing. So, when the woman had her next hysterical spell following a big malarial fever, she was so scared she almost died. He should be through with his leprosy treatments in a year and we will gladly be rid of him. We get many kinds of people in the leprosarium of many tribes and many kinds of witchcraft and many degrees of so-called Christians, so we never know what to expect.

Our Pastor Ntange Timoteo is away on a trip and one of the school teachers is in charge of the church services. He preached an excellent sermon Sunday that made us all proud of him. Before Sunday School I saw a young relative of his carrying a small potted palm tree and a small banana stalk into the church, and of course like everyone else I was curious. His sermon was built around the thought of constantly good services for others, not fitfully but consistently. Each banana stalk only puts out one bunch of bananas and then dies down; but the palm tree, although it grows much more slowly, bears one bunch after another of palm-oil nuts which the Africans use in all their greens and nearly every other dish they cook. Many of the palm trees planted a generation before this are still bearing. A Christian, according to Nkoi Paul, should be like the palm tree, serving as long as he lives instead of only thinking of himself.

Buena Rose Stober to Her Diary, August 4, 1949—Mondombe, Congo Belge

August 4 already. The Roberts are back from the conference, school has started. All my dormitory girls are back. A group of evangelists are in and Mr. Roberts and Pastor Ntange are busy counting their village offerings. There are still a lot of colds, pneumonia, and malaria, especially among those just returned from the villages.

We had a Belgian guest again over the weekend, a young man just starting his colonial carrier, a doctor's son and a soccer ball enthusiast. He played ball with the teachers and nurses and apparently had a fine time. He says they haven't much idea of teamwork but are good sportsmen otherwise. It would be good for our team if he could play with them a lot as they need an experienced white man's attention, but Ned hasn't the time.

I am shipping five sacks of Hydnocarpus tree nuts we have grown for the treatment of leprosy. The doctor's leprolog at Coquilhatville promised to put them through the oil press and prepare the oil for injections into the muscle.

We are out of all the drugs for leprosy except enough for twenty patients on the new drug, Diasone. We have thirty others who should be receiving it.

We have had two new babies at the hospital this week, healthy ones for a change. One last week was stillborn in a rather sad affair since the heathen relatives kept her under their care too long. She died, too, but should have been saved. Yesterday a fellow took his wife home to see the witch doctor and today relatives rushed her back with pneumonia. They come and go, have to pay for treatment after they run off like that. We are hard boiled.

We still have our epidemics: pneumonia, dysentery, influenza, and always mixed with them our constant enemy, malaria. Thank goodness we have plenty of Atabrine, sulfa pills, penicillin, and Sulfaguanidine for dysentery.

Mr. Roberts drove the car to our rural dispensary Yalofete, our first trip possible there on the new road by car. The nurse had everything in good shape. He had the ordinary run of patients, ninety-five to one hundred a day. A baby with pneumonia, a man who got mixed up with a leopard and won the battle but didn't look so good. On the way to Yalofete we took time out to visit the leprosarium where, in checking, I unearthed a hemp garden. It is against the law to grow hemp (marijuana), of course, but the patients think it relieves their ailments, so it brings in money there as well as in the USA. Since each case is being reported to the police and prison sentences are served it is not so prevalent as before. The fellow who had the garden was the one who gave me the nice piece of goat meat last week, and here I thought it was an appreciation gift. I am paying him for the goat today and giving a good lecture to all.

On Sunday they caught a crazy man who had been lost a week. He is raving mad but after morphine, food, kindness, and treatment, he is nearly normal again. One of our evangelists who is a poor fellow but has enough of the grace of God in his heart to help us got bread and other food for the frightened fellow. The evangelist has barely enough for his own family of children but he found enough to buy from his own pocket.

Buena Rose Stober to Friends and Family, September 2, 1949—Mondombe, Congo Belge

These are busy days what with three new babies arriving, three babies to feed, and three other very sick patients to have special foods, a leper who died, and a medical census in full swing with patients from 1948 all reporting back for their checkups on certain maladies, and Tuesday a car trip that included are threefold mission work: evangelistic, educational, and medical, with Mr. Roberts, Miss Shoemaker, and I all at work. Here is the sum up of the day.

5:30 a.m. Hurriedly eating papaya and drinking coffee, fixing milk and fruits where parents can get them for babies and patients.

6:00 a.m. Roll calls and packing into car of church roll cards, schoolbooks, Pastor Ntange, teacher Lotsuka, medicine kits, and us.

6:15 a.m. *Bon jour* at the administrator's office. He rushes out thinking we have brought back his crazy prisoner who escaped during the night. (He had been caught red-handed by our night sentry robbing us of educational supplies. Said he had to have four Bibles to preach with. I don't know what he was going to do with all the blankets, nets, and material for the girls' dresses. They caught him again before night.)

7:45 a.m. At Yalikungu, gave the dispensary nurse his basket of medicine and asked him to call patients for 2:30 and 3:00 p.m.

8:30 a.m. Regions school with little boys by the dozens. Leave the teacher and Pastor Ntange to arrange the school and baptisms ready when we get back. Breakfast on the side of a hill: coffee, bread and butter, and boiled eggs. We saw an evangelist that is being moved and gave the chieftain a piece of our mind. Bought an antelope for the Lofima schoolboys. Picked up a sick boy and took him and his relatives to the doctor at Bokungu.

9:00 a.m. Call at the territorial office to say *bon jour* to the official and sign out or in several evangelists changing villages. Call on a bankrupt colonial and wife for Miss Shoemaker to say her goodbyes before she goes on furlough and take them a basket of Mondombe's fruit.

10:30 a.m. Called on Dr. Clemmens (of Luxembourg) also a war bankrupt who had returned, then lost everything, so he is helping us a lot. He had borrowed my English books on leprosy and I needed them for a report. He was exceedingly kind and gave me some of the medicines I needed badly and fortunately I have some others he needed. He served us some delicious canned cherries as we waited. Leaving Bokungu we met another Bokungu government official who had been out laying a plot for an airplane landing field, believe it or not. He says he supposes it will just be for emergency landings but nevertheless we are going modern.

11:30 a.m. Lofima again. Miss Shoemaker inspects her school while I heat up the soup, baked beans, and roast the corn the teacher Lotuka and wife gave us. I attempt to give Lotuka's baby a dose of quinine and only succeed after a third trial. The baby didn't approve but the five-year-old child took its dose nicely.

We had lunch about 12:45 p.m. The pastor divided up the antelope which was needing to be done. The chicken that had been given to us by the chieftain of Bokungu was in turn given to Lotuka and wife as they had given away their only one to a begging relative.

2:00 p.m. Sixteen of Lotuka's school boys were baptized by Mr. Roberts and Pastor Ntange in a beautiful sandbox-*cum*-stream along the road while Lotuka, Miss Shoemaker, an elder, and I sang "There Is a Fountain," *Esolelo ea Bant'auma*. We bid them goodbye, leaving them with Lotuma and the elder and went on to Yalikungu dispensary. I tried resting on the ways and Miss Shoemaker slept while I worked at the dispensary.

2:30 to 3:30 p.m. Yalikungu (our only brick rural dispensary). I check patients' records, medicines, and other supplies. Left orange seeds for both the nurse Inonga and the teacher Lotuka. There were fifteen or so patients that needed prescriptions, etc. We put the dispensary sentry in the car with his basket of the empty bottles needing refills.

4:30 p.m. Stop to visit the Remont-Calonne plantation and ate some pie, drank coffee, and discussed flowers. She has many colors of cannas and other flowers.

Stober admired and respected Captain Inkema Jean, who piloted the SW *Oregon* for almost forty years. This photograph was taken in 1947, just before his "gospel boat" was retired. Photo courtesy of DCHS.

Pictured here with Stober in 1941, Lewis and Ambra Hurt and their daughter, Virginia Ann, were fellow missionaries and friends of Stober for more than thirty years. They are showing off the new motorcycle for Mondombe station. Photo courtesy of CTS.

Stober's fellow missionary and friend, Hattie Mitchell, helps a woman in a handicraft class at Mondombe in 1949. Photo courtesy of DCHS.

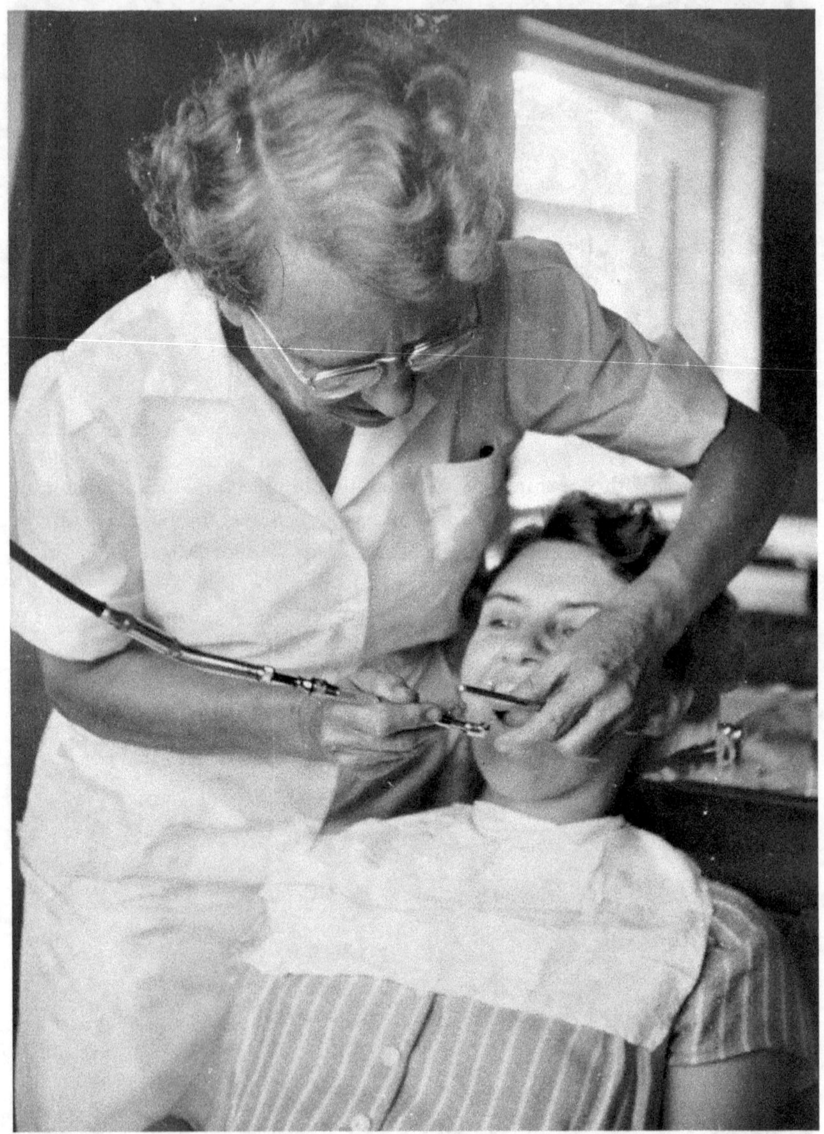

After an apprenticeship with an Oklahoma dentist, Stober used donated equipment to clean and repair teeth at Mondombe throughout the 1940s and 1950s. She was the only dentist in DCCM. Photo courtesy of DCHS.

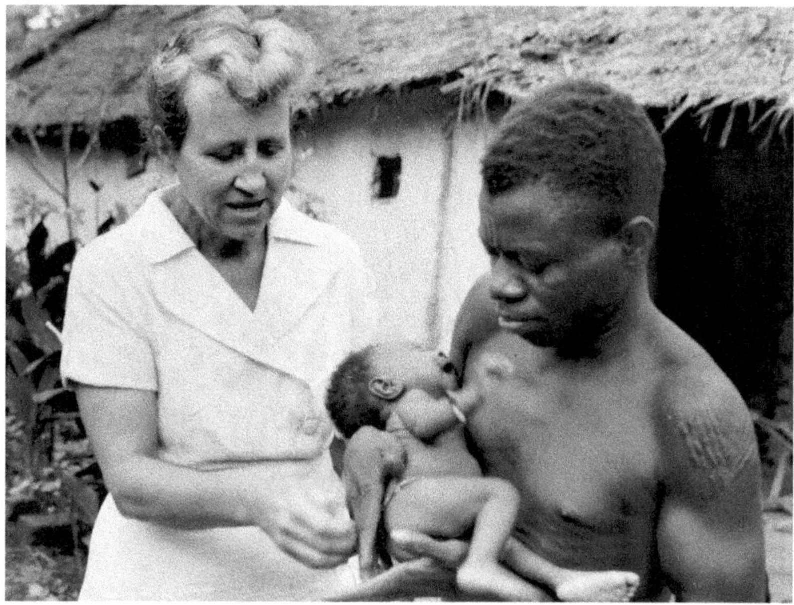

Congolese men often were reluctant to accept responsibility for caring for their infants. But Stober could be very insistent when the situation required her to be, as suggested in this 1948 photo. Photo courtesy of DCHS.

Stober says repeatedly in her letters that she and Dr. Donald Baker were made to work together in Congo. He is pictured here with his wife, Lelia, in 1949. Photo courtesy of DCHS.

4

1950 to 1959

Buena Rose Stober to Her Diary, January 18, 1950—Mondombe, Congo Belge

An African proverb says, "A rooster can't crow on two roofs at once." I sort of feel like I am trying to beat the rooster crowing on two roofs by doing several things at once. One of my new jobs is teaching the Heimers Lonkundo, our new couple who replaced the Roberts. They are working hard at Lonkundo and the Roberts are packing to leave. My trimester bills for the hospital must go out. Dr. Conwell made a control visit for the hospital and leprosarium.

Hattie Mitchell and I bumped all in our Mondombe truck to visit two Congolese churches and a rural dispensary. We soon discovered that it was safer to stay in the ruts than to risk slithering around on the slippery side, which might easily let us skid into the swamp, so we kept in them, reached our goals, and returned safely.

At one of the churches, nurse Bompoko Pierre preached the sermon: "We Christians have chosen the new road, the good way of life, and in the beginning it was very difficult for us to leave off our old ways, and sometimes it meant losing our friends and even our families. Although we used to think the ways of living by charms could be found and a horn stuffed with the witch doctor's concoction of a piece of monkey skin, a human bone, or in a secret society like the Leopard Society,[1] we know now that they are

1. The Leopard Society, also known as Anyoto Aniota, was a secret society for men

only skins, horns, bones, and man-made rituals, leading only into bad ways. Our paths in those days were very poor and led only into the jungle and the swamps, but now we have roads. Today as we drove through your village we heard the drums of the Leopard Society and some have fallen aside to follow this old bad path of life. Let us stay in the new good road where we find love, peace, and the powerful way of truth, even though the road is difficult."

Buena Rose Stober to Her Diary, February 12, 1950—Mondombe, Congo Belge

Last week I spent at the Ikombe dispensary and with the evangelists of that county as the inquirers were not able to come into the station for baptism with the others, as they are all hunting tax money with their own products for sale.

Women do not have to pay tax unless the husband has more than one wife; then he has to pay full tax for each extra wife, a luxury tax, you see. Unfortunately, he rarely pays it himself, but the extra women have to rustle their own tax money. This tax is collected by the chief of each county or group of counties with his scribes to keep the records for him. Most of them cannot read or write. They sell copal for our varnish, palm kernels and palm oil, rice, or manioc cooked or raw, to companies or missions for our school folks and sick folks. You are often offered some of their most valued knives, spears, ivory hunting horns, or ivory war clubs (head busters), especially by the improvident. This year taxes have interfered with church offerings in some places and we were only able to pay some evangelists half salary in spite of the money the mission added to help out.

At a village a few minutes from the dispensary, seven evangelists had gathered together with our twenty-four inquirers for baptism. In spite of the nearly all-day rain, we went the two miles across the dike through the swamp to a beautiful little spot where a sandy-bottomed stream rushed out of a lovely backdrop of vines and overhanging leaves and went under the bridge of the dike, which was once a much-used road to a coffee plantation, now abandoned. There at 5:00 p.m. with the Christians assembled on the dike and bridge they were baptized with everyone singing, "Whiter than

operating in the Congo during the late nineteenth and twentieth centuries. Its members dressed in leopard skin costumes and wore sharp weapons on their hands that resembled claws. In attacking unsuspecting people, the Leopard Men would cut off their flesh and feast on it as a group in a highly ritualized ceremony. Members apparently believed that this ritual cannibalism would strengthen both the group and the individual, possibly even securing their immortality. Interpretations of the Leopard Society vary, but the group may have been an early anti-colonial resistance movement.

Snow." The song is very appropriately translated, "Clean, Clean, Clean, Clean." They all went reverently back to the communion service before they dispersed.

Buena Rose Stober to Friends, March 16, 1950—Mondombe, Congo Belge

I ought to be freer for my medical work now as I have duly turned over all the girls' dormitory work to Ruth Heimer, and although they didn't take a lot of my time, I can't help being surprised every so often that I have a little extra time for something needing to be done.

Since January we have taken in three new girls, two of whom are very sweet and wholesome girls; the third is a daughter of one of our backcountry Christians, but she has not as yet shown many symptoms of having had any Christian training. She is a loud girl and seems always trying to tell the older girls how to do something or shushing the new ones. Besides, she has been caught in mischief several times. One other little girl that is starting her second year in the dorm is somewhat like her and forever into something. Saturday while the Heimers and Hattie were downriver doing the evangelistic in-gatherings on our side of the field halfway to Wema, I was walking toward the back path and noticed the new girl coming up from the river. They are not supposed to be at the beach unchaperoned anyway, let alone bathe, and here were both of our problem children. The older girl I spanked right there because she knows better, but let the new one go with only a lecture. When I got to the dorm, however, the caretaker was also ready to do some spanking as the new girl had been rather horrid to one of the other new girls while they were washing their clothes. So, Miss Smarty got a paddling, too, and both girls were put to bed at 5:00 p.m. When I asked the new girl what she came to school for, she answered, "To learn books," and I ask if that was all, and she said, "To get a husband." She is only about eleven years old. It is interesting to see what we can make of these wild little creatures. Even some of the worst ones turn out to be nice women.

Buena Rose Stober to Friends and Family, April 27, 1950—Mondombe, Congo Belge

While I am having four days' rest while I get cleaned up between trips, I will try to write some of you the highlights of my trip through the *chefferie* (county) of Liondo. It was a very pleasant trip and although the Christians had just paid their taxes and had not yet sold their rice, they gave 637.15 francs, which will apply to the pay of their evangelists. Of the seven villages we visited we have only four evangelists and a principal evangelist who travels from village to village to help them and serve communion, but he has about five other villages under his care. We will see one more of his next week that is across the river, and Pastor Ntange is with him now in two other villages.

Some of the villages have three or four big clans and several little ones so of course we could only stop in the main clans and called on the others, but we hope eventually to reach each clan. I travel by a *teepoi* as travel by bicycle is too hard for me these days and there are no roads for the car in that part of the *chefferie*. The *chefferie* I will visit the next week is in the same fix or even worse, as Dr. Conwell took me as far as our rural dispensary Yalofete to begin the trip but for the Bosondongo *chefferie* I start from here by *teepoi*. We have a nurse at the dispensary in that county, too, so I will check his work too.

As we were traveling through a deserted village, and with all eight *teepoieurs* singing at the top of their voices, we passed a house nicely white-washed with flowers in front of it and a sign painted in red clay in French, *Maison de David Livingston*. The natives like to attach names of someone they admire or a name that sounds pretty to them to their home names. So, we have Adolfs, Christines, Ballons, Deis, Ambulance, Hospital, besides all the Bible names.

As we traveled from village to village early in the morning, I was delighted with the rising sun coloring the sky and morning mists hanging all around the lacy leaves of the jungle trees. Before sunrise is the most delightful time to travel even on the forest road uphill and down dale. There is always a new flower, vine, or bird to marvel at and the carriers' songs are all the way from beautiful, interesting, to humorous. The downgrade hills were called "husbands" and the upgrades were the "wives." "Mercy! What a long husband!" was a frequent cry. "The wife is as big as the husband!" "This is hard work, but it is work we have learned. We carried for Mr. Hurt, for Dr. Baker, and the state official and now we carry for Mama Mputu" or when we got a bit hot the leader would cry out, "Carry, this meat is as heavy as an elephant." I had eight carriers and four took turns carrying. Once I was quite absorbed in the scenery when the leader cried out, "Mo! Mama doesn't talk anymore. We must have left her back at Yaleka."

Our churches are all little shed-like structures with halfway mud walls and benches made of light wood which often gave way when too many crowded in on one bench and the crack and break of these benches were a common part of each service.

The last group we visited was on the highway with a swish of one or two cars going by while we worked in a drum shed taking their offering of money, beads, onions, anklets, leopard's teeth, knives, glass cups, or whatever they head. The ones who had lost their baptismal record cards bought new ones for about a fifth of a cent as their offering record is recorded on the back of this card.

Buena Rose Stober to Friends and Family, May 8, 1950—Mondombe, Congo Belge

Our trip to Liondo *chefferie* (county) was very pleasant, in spite of their lack of money, as they had just paid their tax and had not yet sold their rice. Bosondono *chefferie* was no worse off but the response was poor, and the trip was really unpleasant.

One village in the county, Isoke, was full of pep, however. The evangelist there had just lost his wife in a childbirth last year and was struggling on by himself. Their offering was 184 francs and they had just finished a new church. They filled it to the limit that evening. When we first arrived, we found the men and boys tying the reed and pole benches, and the women and girls were smoothing the mud walls. One woman was industriously smoothing and pounding the mud platform for the pulpit into shape with an elephant rib, believe it or not; and I had discovered that elephants' ribs are very effective tools with which to shape the cooking pots before they are burned. These burned pots are very important in a Congo kitchen. Some of the pots are quite durable and also decorated beautifully. But when I asked for elephants' molar teeth for Dr. Conwell's bright idea for book ends, a cry of amazement went up. "There are plenty of them in the forest, but what can you do with them?" they wanted to know. They could understand the ivory tusks were valuable and ribs too. I even knew a white commercial fellow who cleaned out the bones and flesh from the big foot of an elephant and made a wastebasket. White folks are a bit crazy, anyway. This day was very fruitful but the next was a complete wash.

Our dates for the trip coincided perfectly with a big rice market, and at Yalingufa village the native clerks were there with all sorts of gaudy gadgets for sale. They had put up temporary stalls or booths with palm fronds and had their wares temptingly displayed to catch every last penny of the money received for the rice. All around were piles of reed sacks of unshelled dried rice. As we had come through the neighboring villages, we had found no one at home, so we couldn't do anything but make the best of it. We had chosen a bad day for spiritual uplift for Yalingufu and must make the best of it. It might prove that in selling their rice they would be more generous with offering. It was 8:30 a.m. and from the streets came the calls of greeting, "Loleko, are you there? Here is Mama Mputu for our market." I went directly to the chief to pay my respects, but he was an old man and was too fussed about the market to return the common courtesy due a visitor, besides a woman isn't very important. He gave us no place to stay but one of the Christians came to our rescue and fixed up his house for us, so we prepared to settle down and wait until the confusion was over.

Each healthy male had a pile of ten to twenty sacks of rice, about the size of a gunny sack. You can imagine what a crowd there was with two or three hundred men, each supervising the loads of rice their women were bringing in, and a swarm of children. Some mothers even carried tiny tots on their hips besides the bundle of rice.

I had not been there thirty minutes when the white folks who were to buy the rice arrived in their swanky cars, as this place is on a fine new road from our territorial capital, Ikela. The truck follows to load the price they would buy. Our friends, the Forsells, were among the buyers and Madame told me they didn't intend to buy unless the owners had removed the chaff of the stalks, as it clogged their sheller. The Forsell's sheller was nearly ruined last year by the chaff; however, the villagers had all been warned and when the men opened the sacks they found it had not been winnowed, so back to Ikela the buyers went, leaving the Africans to scramble around quickly to get their rice under roofs so that the oncoming storm would not ruin it. The next day as we traveled on, whole families were out winnowing their rice properly and getting ready for a few weeks later when the white folks had promised to come again.

The African is an artist at imitation and mimicry. The next day the carriers sang about the disrespectful chieftain and how we were rushing proudly passed his house and every other sentence they would let out a wailing chorus, "Mama Ai! Mama Ai!" until people all along were laughing and apologizing for the old man's ignorance of courtesy. I finally had to tell them it was enough, and they could change the tune without hurting my feelings.

I received another shock at Yalingufu that was new to me. We were having communion service when I heard a small child in back of me fussing and turned to see a young mother trying to force her two-year-old girl to take communion bread. She had taken an extra cup for the child too. After service the principal evangelist and I went to find out what it was all about, and the woman explained that she was pregnant when she was baptized, and so the child was already baptized. They explained that the Catholics did that, or at least she heard they did. Needless to say, she received some instruction.

At the next village everything went wrong, and we couldn't explain the indifference until we discovered that their evangelist had taken back the second wife he had supposedly disposed of when he accepted Christ fifteen years ago. He had also gone so far as to have all six of his children written into his own identification book as children of his Christian wife, but the last two belong to her younger sister, the second wife. The state official had found out. She was supposed to have had a dozen or so other husbands, but the marriage dot was not returned. What complicated affairs these African marriages can be. We have always considered his Christian wife the strongest character of the two, and we were disappointed to know she had let this happen. She broke down and cried when I asked her. They both promised to get this affair settled at once.

The next day was a trial, too, as it rained every time we tried to have a meeting and one of the carriers struck out for Mondombe and left us in the lurch. The next day I worked awhile at the dispensary at Ikombe. Then we spent the night at another evangelist's on the way toward home. But it had to rain the next morning and keep us from starting at the time planned, and the slippery path and dripping trees and underbrush made traveling hazardous even if it was cool.

We have a lot of work to be done, that will take years of patience before these people appreciate the abundant Christian life, even though we find many of them a long way from heathendom. We need your help more than ever for this big job.

Buena Rose Stober to Friends, Early 1951—Mondombe, Congo Belge

January 10, 1951. Just having returned from the hospital from sewing up an eleven-year-old boy's foot. He had been hunting with village men and boys across the river. They had killed three antelopes and were about to get the fourth when a lance poorly aimed went through this little fellow's foot, cutting the third toe off and clear through the ball of the foot. There is enough skin left to cover the amputation and exposed flesh, so he will probably be all right since the wound was clean and they brought him across river immediately. All this sewing when I was supposed to be typing a long-winded report, patient by patient, of all those under treatment for leprosy, 130 patients. Three different drugs were used, and since I only have four months left up to this term, I will need to leave all such chores in order.

Everyone is laughing at my worn-out shoes and clothing, a sure sign that a missionary is at the end of a term. When Dr. Conwell was nearly ready for furlough last year, I gave him a box of shoestrings to tide him over, and this Christmas I received a neat little package of strings from him. There were also some shoe tacks, which I didn't need as the pair I am wearing just back from an amateur Congolese cobbler had extra tacks sticking up in the heel I had to remove before I could wear them.

Sunday will be almost like women's day at church, as Mrs. Heimer will make her first public talk at the communion table and in Lonkundo. Mr. Heimer will have to take care of little Hal while mother passes one part of her language test. He has just finished trips paying the evangelists and baptizing in the backcountry villages. I am preacher tomorrow so . . .

Hattie now has some trips to make for inspection of her regional schools, and I have to change nurses at one of the rural dispensaries. We will take one nurse and his household affairs and wife out on one of Hattie's trips and I will inspect the nurse's work who is leaving and install the new one. There is another dispensary we cannot get to by car and the nurse there is changing, too, but we will have to hire carriers for his things and they will walk in. The nurse who has been caring for the leprosarium patients will relieve him. He has been so nice and kind to them all that they hate to see him leave, but it is an advance for him in responsibility and that dispensary has lots of work. One of the arrested cases of leprosy has been in the nurse's-aide class and now does a great deal of work at the leprosarium, but another nurse will still go with him every day and direct his work yet a while.

January 26, 1951. It takes about two hours to give out rations weekly at the leprosarium and we are hiring the healthier patients to build mud houses for invalid patients, white wash the new brick chapel built with a gift from the American Leprosy Mission. The building will be used as a school for patients' children as well as regular religious services. We also brought over enough leaf mats for roofing a mud house. The state official says he is nearly sure that we will receive another grant from the government of Congo for repairs and building at the leprosarium. The patients to do the building are also allowed to buy soap, salt, rice, peanuts, fruits, and sugar cane, and sometimes other foods if we have enough after we distribute food as necessary for the invalids. We took over tapioca root raw and cooked that we buy from villagers for them. We're trying to get certain fisher patients to sell fish to the invalids, but they get better prices elsewhere, so it is nearly impossible. Everyone at the leprosarium is supposed to have a garden in their back yard and one in the forest so that they provide a lot of food also.

Yesterday they brought in a little woman dying in childbirth, but they were too late for us to help. A second wife of the husband will care for the infant, although she is here in the hospital also with another sick child and is pregnant also. Now perhaps they have learned their lesson and will let them remain at the hospital.

Hal got back after the excitement was all over, reporting the principal evangelist doing a nice job, good offerings, 176 baptisms. He says the evangelist has a very fine school and told how one of his little ten-year-olds leads the church singing . . .

March 20, 1951. This letter should be named, "All in a Week." I lost out a week writing to you as everything seemed to be determined to be done at once.

A sister from the Catholic mission came for dental care on the first day, another white woman from a plantation another day; we had a very bad case in maternity, managed to save the mother but lost the infant; another arrived in a worse condition than the first, and died before we even got to work with her. As sorry as I am with them in a death, I am always a bit disgusted with their wailing, everyone rushing around frantically screaming and wailing at the top of their voices, rolling in the dirt, discarding all or nearly all of their clothes until the whole neighborhood comes to watch or wail. The dead person's relatives, friends, and all taking part in the horrible orgy, even in a hospital. I learned early in my Congo days not to try to stop them but get them and the corpse out of the hospital as fast as possible. In every crowd it is like this: there are always those who have refused to help carry the patient in time, or help with the wood, water, and food; but they are afraid of being accused of bewitching the dead one, so one hardly ever knows who are the hypocrites. Some even dance and sing, making it part of the orgy.

I didn't get very far as the sister got mixed up on the date to come back for more tooth pulling, today or tomorrow.

The schoolchildren from a regional school across the river came in today, this afternoon, and about eight of them had malaria and a few other ailments. They were also buying their schoolbooks for the year.

This week was especially important as Dr. Horner and Mr. Wickizer were with us from Friday afternoon to Monday morning, when they left for Stanleyville where Mr. Wickizer will get his plane for Cairo and another to Australia and New Zealand where he will visit churches.[2] We were very thankful that they sent him past our work. It is always inspiring to meet the

2. After serving for a decade in congregational ministry, Willard Wickizer (1899–1974) held several executive positions in the UCMS from 1936 to 1966, mostly in evangelism and church development. A committed ecumenist, he was the principal architect of Restructure, the process that would in 1968 create the Christian Church (Disciples of Christ) as a denomination.

home Society workers. He visited some of the backcountry work in Bolenge field and saw station work there.

Buena Rose Stober to Her Diary, Undated, 1951—Unknown Location

Our leper colony at Mondombe, called Lomina, was started in 1939 with about ten lepers, one of whom was a fellow who had worked in the copper mines of Congo, and since he was the first head man of the village, the natives began to call it Lomina. He has since gone home, and we have an ex-soldier as head man, Basele Joseph. It was very trying at first because our people at Mondombe have little fear of the disease, or rather just plain common-sense respect for its ability to be passed on to others; besides our people are very shy, afraid of many things, especially witchcraft, and we did not have the most effective drugs in those days and the natives knew it.

They can say *baketsi*, the local name for leprosy, with more real contempt than you can imagine. And the young men who are patients rarely have wives, and women patients often find themselves chased off by their husbands, sometimes even when they have little children to care for. But it is more fear of witchcraft than fear of contact with the disease. Since the disease is chronic and affects the nervous system, the patients are often irritable and disgruntled. And so they quarreled among themselves, even fought and beat each other, accusing each other of witchcraft and refusing to cooperate in making Lomina livable as a village. They also think smoking hemp relieves their symptoms, so we found patches of forbidden hemp growing in their backyards. When we warned about it, they only laughed at us and kept on planting it. It makes them more quarrelsome than ever, we were certain that half the trouble was hemp-smoking.

Two of the original ten are still at Lomina in spite of these discouragements, and back in 1944, Basele Joseph came hobbling into the hospital with his two lovely babies and his wife from far away Urundi, the cattle country.[3] When he was found to have leprosy he was dismissed from the army and sent home across a little tributary of the Tshuapa River near the mission, but his relatives began to accuse Ana of bewitching him and

3. First colonized by Europeans in 1885 as a part of German East Africa, Ruanda-Urundi came under Belgian control following World War I until 1922. At the time Stober is writing, the region was a "mandate" as defined by the League of Nations but remained essentially a Belgian colony similar to the Congo. By mid-century, the region was well known for exporting livestock (including cattle) to colonial African and European markets. Following independence in 1962, the region was divided arbitrarily into the modern nations of Rwanda and Burundi.

causing the disease, beating her, half starving the children, and neglecting him until the white state official sent them here. Ana is a faithful, good wife and mother and in spite of the fact that he was irritable and often beat her; at one time, when the state official's wife offered to pay her way back to Urundi, she thought she would go but could not quite bring herself to desert her little ones and Basele. Finally, the state official made Basele the headman, had a house built for him at Lomina, and gave him his soldiers costume, as he had just been demobilized from the North African Campaign.[4]

One year when we were examining Mondombe's workmen, one of our sawyers showed up with leper spots all over his body. He had been in our schools, played with some of the missionary children, and had an opportunity to see Christianity at work. When he entered Lomina with his young half-brother, who was also a leper, and his wife who decided she would stay with them, we immediately thought of him to teach the children of the lepers and preach. He proved himself a very valuable help. This is our Balilo Thomas. He first succeeded in making a Christian of his wife, Liyolo, then some of his schoolchildren, too, were baptized. He seemed to be able to quiet even the most heated quarrels, put confidence in place of fear, and helped them find in Christian living a refuge and comfort in their sufferings.

One of the most disgruntled, half-blind men who quarreled with everyone at Lomina finally began to listen to Balilo and believe, and soon was baptized along with his wife and two small children. He is the father of nine children and several of the older ones were already Christians. Then Basele became an inquirer and was baptized.

About this time, we began to receive a little Diasone and things began to look bright for the patients. The American Leprosy Mission asked how they could help, and finally sent us money to build the church, which also serves as a school building. Dr. Baker suggested that the stronger lepers start making bricks by hand, and although they worked at a snail's pace, the bricks were finally ready to burn by December 1948. The clay they used was not so good and the bricks were soft, and they were thoroughly discouraged.

The number of patients was increasing, and we suggested that each one try to learn or find a way to make a living. So one fellow and perhaps

4. The North African Campaign was a series of battles fought during World War II in Egypt, Libya, Morocco, Algeria, and Tunisia from early 1940 to early 1943. The battles pitted the Allies (especially Britain) against the Axis powers, all of which had economically significant colonial interests in Africa. Many Africans fought on both sides, depending on which European nation controlled their homeland. As a resident of the Belgian mandate Ruanda-Urundi, Basele Joseph would have fought on the side of the Allies.

others immediately started planting hemp and selling it unknown to us. We kept seeing strangers in the colony and were suspicious but all we could do was rave until one day Mrs. Roberts came over to see the flowers the patients were planting around their houses. [She] called me to see what a nice garden of greens a certain patient had, and after looking I began to wake up. It was a garden of hemp and I took some to the state official and asked him what to do. His police force was afraid of the "evil spirits of Lomina," so they said, but the white man sent one fellow to jail. But the culprit got free until he finally caused so much trouble I dismissed him from the colony. Still another father of a child in the school was found by the schoolchildren to be growing hemp too. The official couldn't put him in prison as he was a very crippled case, so he had to make a drama at which he is an expert. The schoolchildren and Balilo make a hunt every so often, but we haven't had any recent trouble with hemp.

How Basele and Balilo can bring peace out of some of their brawls is a marvel to me. But they seem always to calm them and find a solution along with the church elders now appointed among the Christians. Only a few more serious troubles have to be settled by outside law.

In 1950 the brick church was begun, and it was dedicated in March of 1951, as Mr. Wickizer and the Dr. Horner family visited Mondombe. The 156 patients now living in Lomina village are very proud of their church or *chapelle-école* as it is officially called. Even the Catholics among the group are proud of it, even though they have now a little mud chapel too. Mr. Heimer has almost finished Balilo Thomas's new brick house close by the chapel also, and the children and others have given a lot of their time carrying bricks and helping when they could.

Balilo still says that Christianity is the solution of their problems. Although he is nearly symptom-free of leprosy, he wants to see as many of the leprosarium people as possible become Christians. One of the finest attitudes that demonstrates the progress the Christian lepers are making is their willingness to help around the church without pay and a readiness to help unfortunate cripples. I hand out soap and sometimes a few pennies to the invalids for food when I can't get enough for them, and occasionally I forget and put it on the table instead of in a fingerless hand. But Balilo or Basele or some other thoughtful one is always there to pick them up for the patient, or when the rice or peanuts or palm oil is too heavy, someone rushes to help. A spirit of kindness and thoughtfulness has come with Christianity to replace the old fear of witchcraft in many instances.

Buena Rose Stober to Friends and Family, November 27, 1952—Mondombe, Congo Belge

I am packed and ready for the steamer to take us to Bolenge to conference. The Roberts, Mr. Sly, President Fiers, and the Davises went by car and will take the plane that is the Roberts family will. The Davises will get on board with us at Wema, but Mr. Sly and President Fiers will be taken to Monieka by car and then to the Lotumbe launch so that they will have a visit at each station. Mr. Fiers made a tremendous hit with the natives and us too. His sermon gets right down to basic Christian living.[5]

Yesterday while I was making a brave effort to pack my belongings, I thought I had better get out to the hospital and see if there was anything else I had forgotten to put out for the nurses left in charge, and here was Dr. Baker into a strangulated hernia that was in a bad fix. He saved the fellow, but I discovered that he had another surprise. The doctor of this province, inspector of all leprosy colonies, was watching the surgery and waiting for the doctor to show him our leprosarium. I was supposed to go out with him, so I hurried back to my home and put on a clean uniform and got my records of the leprosarium; before I could get out of the house, up rolled a swanky car with a young doctor from another territory who had a bad tooth or so. I hoped I would have time to pull one and fill another, so I didn't get to the leprosarium, but let the doctor do the honors while I struggled over the other doctor's teeth. The filling went all right, but the extraction was a bad one, roots like crochet hooks, and I had to have help from Dr. Baker after all.

The doctor visiting the leprosarium is just now leaving after dinner at Gertrude's. I sent him early coffee and we presented him with some gifts of work done by our patients. He seemed very nice and appreciated the attention, I guess.

5. Born in Illinois, A. Dale Fiers (1906–2003) was educated at Bethany College and Yale Divinity School. In the 1930s and 1940s, he was pastor of several large Disciples congregations in Ohio and served on many boards of the emerging denomination. In 1951, he was elected president of the UCMS and served in that role until 1968 when he was named the first general minister and president of the newly formed Christian Church (Disciples of Christ). Even after his retirement in 1973, for the next thirty years he served as pastor to several Florida congregations and advised many denominational and ecumenical bodies.

Buena Rose Stober to Friends, December 21, 1952—Mondombe, Congo Belge

We have just returned from a wonderful conference at Bolenge, November 27 to December 17. The Bakers and I returned by plane to Boende and from there on by car to Mondombe. We had the old Ford that is nearly worn out and now called the Reluctant Dragon by all, but it got us here. The Roberts, Doug Cardwell, and Miss Shoemaker will come next Tuesday and the rest of the way in our new Chevrolet delivery truck.

I already have my wonderful Servel kerosene refrigerator unpacked and going. It keeps me well cared for with a freezing compartment, ice cream, sometimes fresh meat, and always ice water. It uses about three gallons of kerosene a week. Kerosene is fairly expensive out here, but it is worth it. The next day after we got home, I had ice cream. Mmmmm.

At the conference everyone enjoyed Dr. Fiers and Mr. Sly so much. The business committee had quite a time to figure out assignments and funds for all the work, but through it all there was the realization of the growth, the bigness, the responsibility, and the joy of doing the work. Each station of course was clamoring for the builders on the mission staff. We wonder how we ever got along without them . . .

We were thrilled and inspired by Mr. Fiers's address. One sunny morning he surprised everyone, especially the Congolese, by giving his whole beginning paragraphs in Lonkundo which he had memorized after getting help to write out what he wanted to say. This really took work for him and for Mrs. Snipes who helped him, and then she translated for him as he gave the rest of it.

Buena Rose Stober to Her Diary, Undated, 1953—Mondombe, Congo Belge

Banza, the Little One, Goes to School.

Anna and Joseph had two husky children with no signs of leprosy. Bolumbu went into the girls' dormitory and Kayema walked back and forth from the mission school and after it was proven that they had no sign of leprosy, but Banza Malia was always so small for her age. When Banza was about two years old, tiny spots kept appearing on her otherwise perfect little brown body. Her father, Joseph, is head man at the leprosarium. He had been a patient there since 1945 and has had the sulfone drugs from time to time. Our first supply came from the American Mission to leprosy patients. But he didn't get the drug soon enough to protect her.

Soon she began to have fevers that didn't respond to antimalarials and one day when we examined a scraping from the skin, there we found the bacillus of Hansen, the man who discovered leprosy first and proved it to be the cause. One takes the scraping from the edge of the spots and stains them the regular way and sometimes one can prove the case is infected.

Malia's mother, Anna, is from the tribe that cares for the Watutsi's cattle, many miles from here, but Basele Joseph, her father, lives near Mondombe in a tribe that is badly infected with leprosy.[6] Anna was so distressed at the news that her baby had leprosy when her own people had never had it, that she threatened to drown herself; but after several Christians had talked to her, she realized that it would serve nothing, and her little ones would be left without a mother's love. She calmed down and continued to be as good a mother as ever.

Now she is old enough for school and has been without symptoms of the disease for two years, although she is taking DDS daily.[7] She was accepted with the permission of Dr. Baker for entrance into the girls' dormitory, and we are all thrilled to have her on the station as she is a very nice and industrious child, much like her mother; although she is a bit small for her age, she is at last growing.

Buena Rose Stober to Friends and Family, February 19, 1953—Mondombe, Congo Belge

Sunday in church I was struck by the number of elderly Christians in our congregation who are practically never absent from services. Most of these have been Christians for thirty years or more and had more sicknesses, sorrows, troubles, and trials.

6. Stober's passing comment here obscures a complicated situation. For centuries before European colonization, the social structure of Ruanda-Urundi was defined partly by an ethnic division of labor: the relatively wealthy Tutsi minority raised cattle while the poorer Hutu majority were agricultural farmers. German and Belgian colonialism exacerbated existing ethnic and economic tensions. Bolstered by racist colonial policies, Tutsi wealth and political power grew as exporting cattle to African and European markets became lucrative business by mid-century. Meanwhile, the Hutu remained impoverished farmers or worked for European and Tutsi cattlemen. Note that Stober says Anna is "from the tribe that cares for the Watutsi's cattle" (i.e., she is Hutu). The Tutsi-Hutu tensions continued to grow even after independence in 1962, finally erupting in the Rwandan Genocide of 1994. Hutu extremists slaughtered approximately eight hundred thousand Tutsi and their sympathizers in just under three months.

7. DDS is the common name for the antibiotic diaminodiphenyl sulfone. Discovered in 1937, it quickly proved to be an effective treatment for leprosy, often in combination with other antibiotics.

Bontole and his wife, Bolumbu Talesa, were each in the dormitories in the early days; later they married and have had eight nice, healthy children. She is an excellent mother and he is a good gardener. He learned carpentry and later passed the examinations to go to the Congo Christian Institute. They had come back with their three children before he finished his three years as he contracted sleeping sickness and was in a very bad condition. They struggled through the difficult years of treatment and then he went out to a group of backcountry villages to preach and supervise other evangelists' work, but soon the old ailment had him down again and they came into the mission to stay. He made a little money with this carpenter tools in a shed back of his house. This year they have taken charge of the girls' dormitory, but he is so nearly blind that the doctor thinks he will need surgery soon. Their oldest son has a good position as post office clerk in Gostermansville and has sent his folks help. Another son has just entered the Congo Christian Institute and the oldest girl is still in school here in the advanced classes. Their children have always led their classes.

Iyambe Thomas, still a nurse at the hospital, has had a bad time with wives, a son by a first woman isn't much account. The Christian wife he first had ran off with another man and the present one fights with all her neighbors so much no one wants to live near her. She actually fought with one woman last year and got her finger bitten off. But Iyambe works faithfully on and continues faithful to all the services.

Nkang'Itoke, the head nurse, and his wife, Ononga Yeana, have had seven children of which five are living. Yeana is hotheaded and he really had to take a lot off of her for years. She really used to tear up town when she was mad, but she has settled down a lot and is one of our leaders in the women's meetings. Their oldest son is one of the brightest and nicest characters we have on the mission, but unfortunately he worked so hard getting through his nurses' training and keeping at the head of the class he has tuberculosis now and is kept in bed. He has a nice wife and three children. The second son is a bit like his mother and although he is making good at the Congo Christian Institute, he is a hothead and keeps us wondering what will happen next. The oldest girl his married, too, and lives with her husband at a rubber plantation.

Old Besoke is partially paralyzed and drags one foot along but manages to get to church every service. He began work on the mission before I arrived here and was already sick when I came to Mondombe. He has no family or wife. Belombe, the church janitor, is alone too. He takes great pride in keeping the church and flowers around it in fine condition. He fell from a tree when he was a boy and has been a semi-invalid ever since. Liloka Joseph began work here early too. His first wife ran off from him and his second is a moron, but in his old age she has given him a healthy, nice son of whom he is very proud. Because Liloka loves flowers and planted many around his house, the heathens thought he was a witch doctor.

Evangelists Bowala Marc, wife Senga Yeana and Yoka Colonelie, wife Boonda Malia, too, are old timers, faithful to the task, but are out in the backcountry churches all the time. Pastor Ntange is out a good bit of the time, but Mirium Bolei, his wife, never misses a service.

Buena Rose Stober to Her Diary, March 4, 1953—Mondombe, Congo Belge

This week has been a mountaintop experience for all of Mondombe because Rosa Page Welch visited from Saturday at 5:00 p.m. until Monday at 3:00 p.m.[8] Crowds have thronged to every place she speaks or sings. They say in the stadium at Léopoldville there were thirty thousand people, including many Belgian dignitaries. At all the stations it was the same with crowds waiting all along the road. At first through curiosity, and then after they had heard her wonderful voice and message of goodwill through the wonder and love for such a fine Christian. At the leprosarium, the chapel was jammed and even the windows were filled. Sunday morning our church overflowed out into the yard under the lovely Bokungu tree and Mr. Roberts and I were kept busy seeing that benches were carried from a school building and the overflow directed to them. She sang many songs that captivated the Congolese even though they were in English. At vespers service she told them the story of Negro spirituals. She even taught them a song and then sang two for them in Lonkundo. They couldn't figure out how she could when we had been translating everything for her. Everywhere she told them that her visit to Africa was like coming home and some said it was just as if a child of ours had come home after many years. She brought us all closer to God and Christian fellowship.

She also visited our wild Nkole field, the latest to accept Christ.

8. Born into a family of Mississippi sharecroppers, Rosa Page Welch (1900–1994) received her education at Southern Christian Institute, a Disciples of Christ boarding school located not far from her home. Relocating to Chicago in 1926, she began pursuing a career as a singer, and soon she began receiving invitations to perform in many church-related events. For the next fifty years, she gave concerts and talked openly about race relations, urging her audiences toward reconciliation. Frequently hailed as the "ambassador of good will," she travelled on behalf of the Disciples of Christ all over the world. She retired to Mississippi in 1983 and spent the last decade of her life as a choir director in a predominately white congregation.

Buena Rose Stober to Her Diary, March 29, 1953—Mondombe, Congo Belge

I want to write this morning about Pastor Ntange's communion service talk before I forget as I have just come from the service.

Pastor Ntange said that the things of Christ last forever and grow stronger instead of dying out like many things of the Congo witch doctor. He said that when he was a young man there were three famous witch doctors in the region and the mission was just starting work here and the word of Christ is growing very fast and is much stronger now. But you do not even hear of those three witch doctors anymore. One was in a county north of here and was named Lofofe and people would not even approach his little hut; it was reported he kept a live leopard. The villagers would bring him nice presents of goats, chickens, and other delicacies so that he wouldn't send his leopard to eat them when they were in the forest. Another *nganga*, or witch doctor, was on the river Lofomi, a hundred miles further north east. He was said to be able to control the seasons so that when they wanted fish from the Lofomi they would pay him to "vomit up" all the water in his large stomach so that the Lofomi would dry up. The third was a fellow that lived across the river from the mission. They said that during the day he had the power to hide in one of their ordinary drums, although the opening in the drum is too small to get through, the drum may be big enough to hold a man, and also hollowed out enough for that. The people declared they saw him come out of the drum and they said when they called him he would often answer from the drum. He, too, was very much feared and received much attention from the people who feared him. Now you hear nothing of any of the three, but the name of Jesus is heard on every hand.

Pastor Ntange and Ned Roberts are downstairs counting the morning offering. My rooms are over the mission office and several storerooms. To safeguard the money, they have a trunk in the office. It is heavy and Pastor Ntange has the key to it, but Ned carries the key to the office door so there has to be two to get at the offering. It has been stolen when kept otherwise and elsewhere.

Buena Rose Stober to Friends and Family, April 21, 1953—Mondombe, Congo Belge

The last three mornings of my sleep have been interrupted by the arrival of new infants in maternity, so I am getting to be a real early bird. My dental assistant and I had just pulled a tooth apiece and prepared some cavities for fillings this afternoon, so the day is well started. We also worked a bit on a poster on proteins in different foods. Waiting on the infants helped me finish Mr. Moon's book, *I Saw Congo*. It is very good and anyone wanting a picture of early work here will certainly find it there.

He tells of how once when he had a big malaria fever and was home in bed, his masons pushed his plumb line out of the way when laying a foundation for his house, in which I am living now, and it reminds me that there are very few well-trained Congolese masons, even now. Mr. Roberts almost turned gray-haired trying to get the walls of Poly Ward so they didn't lean out or go in like a snake's trail.

Yesterday I was so disgusted with a premature infant mother. She wasn't coming regularly for milk, and then her conscience hurt her right in the middle of a terrible downpour, so out she came with that poor infant, drenching it on the way. I also found out that some heathens have taboos for animal milk by investigating why the infant wasn't gaining. I fixed that by spooning the milk into the infant's mouth and it began to gain. She missed again a few times and then brought it again in a bad condition, so it needed penicillin. It was a lot brighter, hungrier, and actually began gaining after my efforts.

Persistence is a wonderful thing. Along that line I felt really proud at the communion service this morning when two of my younger nurses were asked to serve communion. They had both been problem nurses. One nearly let his family starve while he bought and crashed up bicycles, and the other didn't like taking orders from a woman and wouldn't carry out orders very well. We had had to feed two of their children in the process, but they were settling down and respected enough by the elders to be chosen as deacons.

Buena Rose Stober to Friends and Family, August 18, 1953—Mondombe, Congo Belge

After our eleven-hundred-kilometer trip to Lubendai to leave Paul Roberts and the Presbyterian high school, I have so many interesting things to write about, one letter is not enough and I will never run down. I have seen mission work carried on by four other groups besides our own, and through them all educational, medical, industrial, agricultural, and all culminating in evangelistic work with the basic love of Christ standing out paramount and we were received as members of the same big inspiring Christian family. Our Mondombe Pastor Ntange who went with us can't stop marveling how he found *biote* ("relatives") in every place, and as he says in every place all a part of the wonderful Christian fellowship and evangelism. His talks have been filled with enthusiasm to teach Jesus's way to every heathen in the most unselfish way possible. We were surprised at his making the best of each situation as it came up, eating all kinds of foods never tried before, prepared in ways he had never heard of before, doing without water that surrounds as everywhere here at Mondombe, while at Luluabourg if you had a drink and a tiny bit to wash our hands and face you are doing well, the springs are so far from the village.

Pastor Ntange preached in several of the churches and once to a camp of soldiers in the trade language, Lingala. But in many places, we had no means of understanding except in French and he doesn't know much French.

We had some good laughs along the way too. When Pastor Ntange was visiting with some of the evangelists he ate whatever was offered to him whether he liked it or not, and when he wanted to or had no invitations, he ate with us. Of course, the food was usually strange to him, but he always said anything God had made for us to eat was good. One day Paul Roberts passed around his birthday gift of a jar of olives that were delicious and Pastor Ntange took one the first day. But the next day when it was passed again he said, "Thank you. I have already had one and that is enough."

Some days we were so tired of bumping down and around hills, swallowing so much dirt we could hardly talk as it was dry season and the road was full of sand pits and ruts. Jewell was watching some millions of black butterflies swarming on the beach of the Sankuru River as we were being ferried across and she said, instead of "It sort of makes me dizzy," "It mortar sakes me dibby." Later I explained my idea of a good supper after such a day. Instead of a "tin of soup," I said, "A sin of tupe." We would get hungry for green things, and Jewell and I went into ecstasy over collards, but the children decided we would eat our own collards. Then one day we were able to buy a whole basket of ripe tomatoes when we got back to our own evangelists, so they thought we exaggerated a bit when we nearly had tomatoes in everything we ate.

We learned that in one part of the Congo there is a secret society which has for its goal keeping peace, and although they say some of the practices are not too good most of the rituals are constructive, so that some of the missionaries have joined it when they were invited. That is a far cry from Mondombe's secret leopard society as it is a horrible mixture of cruelty, witchcraft, and fear. Bishop Booth himself joined this secret society of peace.[9] Their leaders carry a bell, or rather two bells on the same holder, and

9. Here Stober refers to Rev. Dr. Newell Snow Booth (1903–1968). Ordained in the

when there is a fight on, one of these fellows appears and raises his hand and says, "It is finished." It really is, or the culprits must pay a tremendous sum.

One patient we have at the leprosarium with nodules all over his face and the most infectious type of leprosy is from this peace secret society. He has been such a fine Christian example to others. When I got back I found his nodules diminishing and I asked Lempata to tell about this secret society and he smiled and said, "My father gave me this bell when he died but it was such a distance to come here to the leprosarium and I could scarcely walk so I left my bell." The natives of our part of the country stood around with their mouths open listing to him.

On our return from the long trip we spent two days on the lovely Lake Mukamba where several missions have land and have built cabins for rest houses for their missionaries. Pastor Ntange amused us by saying he at last found enough water to soak off the dust. It is lovely clear water and the beach is gradually sloping beach. It was a real change after our Tshuapa River's coffee-colored water with its deep banks here at the station.

Buena Rose Stober to Her Diary, August 27, 1953—Mondombe, Congo Belge

I have just returned from the leprosarium where they are doing fairly well except the poor old cripples, but even their ulcers are better since we started penicillin for some. An old fellow, totally blind, does not improve much and about all we can do to comfort him is to keep him fed and comfortable. Another old man died while we were gone, and another dirty old man with a dirty wife and six dirty children is still not cleaned up. Four of the children have so many jiggers in their poor little feet their toes are rotting off. Jiggers are tiny fleas that crawl under the skin and there develop their egg sacks, and after they hatch out their parent flea dies. Careful parents can avoid getting the feet in such a state by taking them out each day.

I have gone back to teaching new missionaries Lonkundo and so have some of the other older ones. It looks as if the Williams are going to be good as they are rapidly picking up the language in using it. They had two months in Bolenge and now must finish the job with our native teachers to help us.

Methodist Episcopal Church in 1926, he served briefly in congregational ministry in Massachusetts. In 1930 be began work as a missionary in the Congo, returning to the United States in 1943 to head the Africa department at Hartford Seminary Foundation. He returned to the Congo in 1944 as bishop, serving in that role for the next twenty years. As the Congo moved toward independence in the late 1950s and early 1960s, he was a vocal advocate for peaceful transfer of power in the deeply troubled Katanga Province, where the Methodist Episcopal mission was concentrated.

Pastor Ntange preached Sunday on John 12:20–30, *Tolanga Oene Yesu*, "We Want to See Jesus." He showed how he had seen Jesus in certain Christians along our trip. How that it was impossible to see Jesus in certain chiefs, soldiers, and villagers who work only for themselves. You will not see Jesus and unless you seek unselfishly you will not see Jesus.

Sometimes we get to looking at all the fine changes in the people here and think someone has done a good job, and then suddenly we are jerked up and realize some of it has not gone very deep. Two patients at the hospital started fighting during vesper service Sunday evening. After the service I thought it had blown over and went about distributing extra nice bananas to patients, when Mr. Roberts and Mr. Williams came in saying that it was not stopped, and one fellow had accidentally scraped Mr. Roberts's cheek while he was trying to stop them. One fellow was a cripple who uses crutches and had come to have them shortened a little and incidentally to settle an old feud in his family with a policeman in the hospital with an enlarged spleen. The cripple came into the ward. The witch doctor had been certain that this policeman was the cause of the death of his sister by bewitching her. The cripple proceeded to crack the policeman over the head with his crutch and of course the wife rushed in and made off with the little fellow's crutches. In the general scramble the cripple produced a knife, but the white man spoiled his fun. Then I came in and proceeded to order both patients out of the hospital. The cripple went first when they handed him his crutches. The policeman left a little later but was back the next day with a terrific jaw as a result of the first attack, so we had to put him back in the hospital. Ned's injury was slight. We probably have not heard half the story, either.

Our latest dealing with the results of witchcraft is a very sad story. An ex-student of one of our backcountry evangelists' schools came in Monday with a three-months-old daughter nearly starved. The infant weighed only six pounds and was a pretty miserable-looking sight. His wife had just died from taking one of witchcraft's most violent trials to prove innocence, *nsamba*, tea of poison root, the guilt trial. She had been accused of having an evil spirit because she could not nurse her infant properly, so her relatives insisted that she prove herself guilty or innocent in the old heathen way practiced before the law forbade the use of it. It is now a criminal offense. The husband even says he didn't want to do it, but he hunted the vine *nsamba*. She died the same day and now the whole thing is reported to the government and eventually he will have to go to prison. In the meantime, the father will have to care for the baby as all the female relatives are afraid of the child as it was born of a mother with an evil spirit. At least the father had enough courage to report the affair and bring the child for milk. It feels so much better; already it manages to give me a big smile for its bottle of milk. I am afraid there are many cases of this kind that are never reported to us, or to the government.

The night sentry's wife tells that when she was sent into a heathen marriage her mother-in-law doped the greens; she served Agata and served her *nsamba*. She said she had asked why the greens were so bitter, and she was told they were afraid she had an evil spirit. She says she was violently sick but finally got over it so that proved her innocent. She was just a young girl who had been away with her soldier father so of course did not know the danger she ran. She is now a Christian, married to a Christian, and has a lovely baby of two months old. Her baby was caesarean and so I suppose that if she had been in the backcountry she would have been accused of being a witch or at least bewitched. What a life the heathens live!

Buena Rose Stober to Friends and Family, July 5, 1954—Mondombe, Congo Belge

As I sat in church watching the Christian families march in front of the church and each one put in their offering, I couldn't help but think what a wholesome thing I was seeing. In three of those families there had been separated a while back for at least a year, and here they were back together, having worked out the Christian solution of their problems. A nurse, his wife, and three children had been able to conquer her gad-about ways, she had settled down to care for her little ones. Another nurse and his wife who used to scrap and fight furiously now have two sons, one a graduate of the Congo Christian Institute and another finishing his last six months of nurses' training and will be a graduate registered nurse. The school teacher, his sister, and five others sang a very lovely special this morning. What a wholesome thing to see.

Mrs. Baker has 155 boys in the dormitory and it keeps her busy settling their problems. We were discussing how we could get their dishes washed separately, as there is one boy known to be an active tuberculosis case at one time. She says some of the boys do not have plates and they do not keep what they have clean, but she is going to mark each plate with an adhesive and the name written on it as they have to turn in their plates ahead of time so that they can be served by the cooks, also boys, ahead of time. She was asking the ex-evangelist who is caretaker why they couldn't keep plates and pans clean and he answered, "Oh, well Mama you must remember most of these boys came from homes where they had no discipline, no wash pans, no plates, no knives, forks, or spoons, so they have to learn." She said they sometimes skipped out after roll call before church or work and that was another headache.

Yet a fellow who had only had a little while in the dormitory had sense enough after what he had learned at Mondombe to bring his ailing pregnant wife in for care, which included a caesarean. He saved his lovely baby and wife, too, by not letting her have her own heathen way.

The communion service was directed by Nkoi Paul. Nkoi means "leopard" in Lonkundo. He used the Scripture Luke 22:17–20, and says our pattern is Jesus. He said God made both the leopard and the *yo*, and they both have spots, but they are not alike at all. The *yo* is a civet cat. He said each must follow the pattern God had given him in life, and our model is Jesus, and we, too, must follow carefully the pattern of Jesus if we expect to be true Christians. In Jesus we have power and strength for our daily problems. Like the young elephant who heard that the antelope are going to make war on the elephants, he ran to his mother and knew there was strength. We, too, can find strength for our fears and troubles in Jesus.

Pastor Ntange preached on "Go and sin no more." We white folks felt lost with the Roberts gone. Mr. Cuppy is collecting their belongings left at Monieka before their furlough and Miss Shoemaker is to go downriver for a trustee meeting for the Congo Christian Institute, and so we are not many for the extra tasks, but we will soon have more white staff.

Buena Rose Stober to Her Diary, September 1954— Mondombe, Congo Belge

September 7, 1954. You should have seen the joy of the Africans and us, too, when Dr. Baker returned well and ready to serve anyone who needed his service. Now that he is here, I can go with the Williams as they take Miss Shoemaker to Stanleyville where she will get her plane to represent the mission at the convention there in Johannesburg.

September 22, 1954. We are back from Stanleyville and I enjoyed every minute of it with the Williams and their children. After getting Gertrude off we had the car repaired, absorbed a bit of civilization, did some shopping, and I had the special privilege of seeing the English nurses' school where two of our Mondombe boys are in school. The father of one is our head nurse and he came with us to see his son and wife at his school. His son, Botuli, is doing such fine work they would like to snitch him from us, but we need him very much. The other nurse is not doing so well and is not the character Botuli is.

We stayed at a hotel in Stanleyville and found a place for the head nurse at the Baptist mission house for passersby. Their rooms for missionaries were full, but I know they looked after the nurse very well. Speaking of being frightened of the heathens, I never saw anyone so frightened as that father nurse. He wouldn't cross the street he was so afraid of traffic, so he wouldn't have budged to go to his son if I hadn't hired a taxi and then a canoe that took us to the English Baptist beach at Yakusu. We arrived just at siesta time so had a time finding his son, but finally a nurse on duty at the hospital took time out to go after Botuli, who was off duty for the moment. Then Dad stayed with him and I called on the doctor. A nurse showed us around the hospital. She was an English nurse in charge of the midwife school for Congo girls.

Dr. Brown, the director of the school, is also head of their evangelism near Stanleyville, and has a leprosarium and sixteen rural dispensaries. Each rural dispensary and also the leprosarium have graduate registered nurses in charge, so that relieves him some. They have two nurses and two doctors, so they are a qualified school. We can have only nurse's-aide school since we haven't two MDs.

Stanleyville as a mixture of the best and worst in Congo. There is one tribe across the river from Yakusu where they have never accepted any missionaries, Protestant or Catholic, and very little of anything else of civilization. The people around Stanleyville have a very bad reputation for stealing, and they are very hateful about prices of their fish and other products. They say you can get all the fish if you have money enough to pay at their price. We saw hundreds of traps all up and down the river to Yakusu. This Wagenia tribe have a lattice work sort of trellis that holds their traps across the rapids. Stanleyville is at the end of navigation for the big river steamers on the Congo River.

September 28, 1954. We have a six-year-old child with his hip broken and he is getting along fine and suspended from the ceiling almost. He loves my sugar cane and I have sent him some. The patients have been checked, babies fed, and here I am typing at 8:00 a.m. I have had my breakfast too.

There are thirteen parents on the back porch shelling out peanuts by stomping them so that their little ones can have gruel with peanut meal in it. Each one must shell two gallons, so Bokonji says, and this will last each child about two weeks. Three of these are fathers whose wives are sick. There is one orphan boy in the babies but most of them are sick ones.

There were around seven hundred at our walk-in movie last night. These are sponsored government films and are very good. We get one a month. It is wonderful to have our electric lights working again and all the good things one can have with them.

Buena Rose Stober to Her Diary, October 12, 1954—Mondombe, Congo Belge

Two young men in the preparatory course were dismissed for disobedience and the students walked out the next day. These boys were from Monieka and they were from Monieka and many of the fellows are not very interested in their schoolwork and skip class too often and are quite sassy since they are only interested in getting a certificate that will get them better pay; but this is a preparatory school for higher training or so that they can go to high school. 9:00 a.m. the next day, they are all peacefully back and at school except for the departed ones.

Twenty-nine converts from the leprosarium were baptized Sunday. Our nice young Belgian doctor is home on furlough, reported to be married already, and making plans for studying surgery in the USA. We are expecting the new one to call on us. He has a wife and a baby. He wants to come and do some surgery with Dr. Baker.

The class of nurse's aides will be going to take their final examinations with the state doctor and are doing their last-minute cramming. I will be relieved to have that task over. They have been nice, and I have enjoyed them. Most of them will pass as they answer my questions very well and the doctor, too, thinks that they will make it. They have had to cover a lot of material in the year although they had passed their sixth year in school. They are a little older than the average fellows in that year of school and have wives and two have children. The girls are in school, too, and Mrs. Cuppy has four of them in her knitting class although one has to take out her work nearly every morning when she arrives at school. They are all rushing to finish their work before school is out.

The school folks are taking final exams right now and you can look around almost anywhere and see students hidden in corners cramming for exams. Quite often you pass a young fellow on the street mumbling in French to himself or some other subject, oblivious to anyone passing him. My nurses can come of evenings to my screened front porch where there is good light.

There are a number of backcountry evangelists in getting books and other materials or else being changed to a new place. They are to have refresher courses at the preacher's school this year for a certain number of picked men, and when we get back from conference a new group will be called on to the station for special courses. It is good to see some of them again. Their villages are so far away we rarely see them or their wives and children unless they are sick or expecting a new infant. There are two wives waiting now. It is nice to see how much cleaner and nicer they keep their children than the ordinary villagers. One of the wives who is in a village very far away has organized a bunch of girls in school and a number of them are already reading. She is especially interested in knitting and I wanted to get some thread off to her. They can make their own needles of hard wood. She is ambitious to teach them what she learned in school several years ago. They are working in the villages where they scarcely ever see a white person except state officials and our evangelistic trips. They are nice people but very backward . . .

When I first came to Mondombe there was a great deal of talk in hopes of opening a new station at Boende far on up the river from Mondombe and very difficult to reach. Through the years many attempts have failed to start work among these people, but only in the last few years work has been started with native evangelists and it gives fine promise. This last week Mr. Cuppy and Miss Mitchell actually made the first truck trip to their villages. The road was terrible, but they reached Mbandaka, the village where we have twenty Christians, a nice school by the evangelists, and his little wife has rallied the little girls together and had an unusually large group of them in school. Besides reading, writing, and arithmetic she has started sewing and knitting.

Buena Rose Stober to Her Diary, April 1955—Mondombe, Congo Belge

Two prayers heard recently at church:

"Father God, we thank you because you are worthy of praise. We ask you to be with us always. Let us stay close to you as the many tiny roots of the palm tree cling close to the trunk to nourish and strengthen the tree. May we strengthen your word. May all the people of the earth humble themselves and raise on high the name of your son Jesus Christ. We do not ask for riches or honor, but we ask for wisdom to help up your people on earth. Bless the master and those who care for the sick. We pray to you in the name of Jesus Christ. Thus be it! (Amen)." Ntange Timoteo.

"Oh! Christ Jesus you know what we like and the desires of our hearts. Take out the things that are not good and put there the things you wish to find there. Jesus our Savior, stay very near to us in our journeying that we may have strength. In the name of Jesus Christ we ask. Thus be it! (Amen)."

Three letters of greeting to the Christians in America.

"Greetings to all women in the church in America. May you remember the still sad lives of women in Congo. We are not able to stand firm as Christians as the men do. The hard thing is that the men always have the chance of education and a woman rarely does. We stay in the chains of our thoughts because we are not able to throw off the ties and customs of relatives. If a woman hasn't a husband and the mission is not able to give her a little work for a living, she will have a very difficult time. What can we do? When will we have enough teachers to help us?" Etoci Louise, the maternity nurse, a widow.

"Greetings from Mondombe to the Christian women of America. You women who have husbands what shall we do? You divorced women what shall we do? You women whose husbands are dead, what shall we do? You young educated single women what shall we do? The Congo women without husbands have no standing and are truly in distress in Congo. Most often we are accused of the bewitching our husbands. And when we have pretty skin the men like us and at that time we are trusted with anything our living husbands have in the house. Then as we reach the age of losing our nice looks and have no children to stand by us the troubles increase. If our husbands are dead or we are separated from them then we are in real trouble. We fall in temptation and then our power to learn is also falling away. This saying is common in Congo, 'Of what use is education for women?' What shall we do if your Christians do not carry the burden of teaching us after our husbands are gone, so that we do not lack wisdom to make a living? It is hard but if you will put aside certain women to teach us fitting work to save us from distress, it will become a very fine thing. Greetings in the name of the Lord Jesus Christ." Ekila Kala, a divorced woman who has learned in old age of more than fifty years to earn her living by mixing milk and preparing food for undernourished infants and adults.

"Greetings to all Christians, a message to you from one of Mama Mputu's nurses on her trip to America for furlough. I want to thank all of you who have sent clothes for our children and our sick folks. May your kindness increase with a love of the Lord of love, Jesus Christ. Remember the little children, the sick, and the needy in your prayers. Thanks to you also for the balls you sent the children. *Beseso Buke* (many greetings)." This letter unsigned is from a man nurse, father of several little children, and graduate of our Congo Christian Institute at Bolenge.

Buena Rose Stober to Friends and Family, November 1955—Nebraska

This is your Christmas letter, even if it is early as at the rate I am traveling around these days I will not have another chance with the typewriter at hand like this when I have the time. I am writing in Nebraska and no telling where I will be by the time you get it.

My ailment is just about a thing of the past and I am actually looking forward to a nice snowy winter. I don't seem to feel the cold yet as I did last furlough.

Bits of news from Congo brings the same old story of busy people trying to do twice as much as they are physically able. From Mondombe there is news of one of our good Belgian friend's death. He was a good friend of the mission and of the Congolese.

From Coquilhatville, Mrs. Elizabeth Lewis writes, "Coquilhatville is changing so fast you would hardly recognize it with the new government in Brussels. Public schools are springing up overnight and we have the privilege of starting primary schools anytime we are not satisfied with the results in public schools. Our natives are teaching Protestant religious courses in these public schools, each class has one hour a day, six days a week. These are under our mission supervision. In addition, the Coquilhatville mission staff is responsible for three hours a week in the state teacher's school, eight hours a week in the professional school, and four hours a week in the medical school. These are hours of Protestant religion courses. For the white children we teach two hours a week in the junior high and nine hours a week in the primary. In addition to the above we are starting kindergartens in four new areas of the native city. And we are now choosing a new chapel site in Coquilhatville and expect to begin construction in the next few weeks."

Coquilhatville is a city of twenty thousand Congolese and one thousand whites, and we have Mr. and Mrs. Lewis, Mr. and Mrs. Dodson, and Miss Peterson. They carry on the legal representatives, mission treasurers, school advisor for the mission, manage all our freight through customs for all upriver stations, the evangelistic work for those twenty thousand Congolese, and many other services for missionaries and natives.

Ekila Kaala, who prepares milk and food for undernourished children patients, writes from Mondombe, "To Mama Mputu. Are you there? Have you seen all your family? Are you still telling the news of Congo to the churches of America? What is the news there? Here I am doing the work you have left for me. I marvel at the number of people coming to the hospital. Some are even building little leaf shacks on the hospital lawn. Many women are coming to maternity for their babies; all the rooms are crowded. Some of the infants receiving milk when you left have now gone home. Those are Bombile Clement, Botondo Emile, and Elika Honorine. They were all well and went to their homes. We have twelve infants receiving milk and other foods. One from a Tofoke village was brought in three days after the death of its mother. Its name is Baila and it is very sad that it has no relatives.

There is a lot of work here. I fix the milk and clean all the windows of the hospital. It is harder because I have to carry the water from the spring (our hospital tanks of rain water run out during the dry season and we hope that over-and-above-budget gifts will provide us with enough money to put in an adequate water system for Mondombe). Mrs. Williams has a baby boy now. Receive my greetings in the name of our Lord Jesus. Ekila Kaala."

Nsambela ngola is a proverb about "catching *ngola*." *Ngola* is the oily red powder used to decorate the body. Unfortunately, it rubs off on the other fellow and so they "catch *ngola*." New mothers are honored by rubbing *ngola* from head to foot and the baby passes it on to you when you pick it up. Pastor Ntange as often uses this as an example of how you can spread good or bad as others take on our examples. He tells us how a little heathen lad had heard of Christ's kindness and one day as he was traveling a dusty path with the big bundle on his back, he slipped and spilled the contents of his bundle all over the path. A crowd passing up began to laugh at him and he was in tears, but a Christian helped him gather up his belongings and the little boy looked into the stranger's face and asked, "Are you Christ?" Our Christianity should be as easily seen and rubbed off as the *ngola* so that others can see Christ in us.

Buena Rose Stober to Friends and Family, April 13, 1956—Mondombe, Congo Belge

Come see what fun I am having: unpacking only packages sent before Christmas have come, no freight yet; greeting old friends, seeing new babies; a fellow is grinding coffee on the back porch; the sun is boiling down unmercifully making the aluminum roof crackle; I have cleaned the Servel and I am having a breather while Bokonji puts on some finishing touches, then I will light it. Polly died, cause not known. I am having corned beef, onions, and sweet manioc for dinner. Hattie loaned me some of her light bread.

Saturday a week tomorrow we left New York having a very nice trip, no hardships, annoyances, or casualties, except cramped muscles from sleeping in the plane seats. Arriving at Boende we were met by Bernard Davis of Wema, a Belgian friend, and the new pastor of Boende Christians, Ekofo Joseph.

Ekofo's story is an interesting one. He is a graduate of our Congo Christian Institute and was an instructor in the school for several years, then he finally accepted a very fine position with a big bank at Léopoldville. He has a very fine voice, sang in the choir at Bolenge, then in the quartet that made some lovely inspirational records in the native language. Recently he told his bank he was "leaving to do another work I must do." At that time, he was receiving $100.00 a month salary which is excellent pay here. The bank offered him a $40.00 raise if he would stay with them, but he answered, "No, I have another work I must do." He accepted the call to Boende, as pastor of this very strategic place. Believe it or not his present salary is only $40.00, and it is more than the Wema station can afford; but Mr. Davis says that he has crowds coming to him for counseling and they have even begged him to start an adult school at night. Hunger for a good leader, education, and spiritual guidance has brought numbers they have never had before at Boende. We have had an evangelist there for years, none of them has ever had the education, interest, and ability of this fellow. Besides, they were not ordained men. The native population of Boende is probably around ten thousand, and there are some one hundred white folks, government officials, soldiers, camp folks, plantation people, several commercial firms, etc. It is our district capital.

Clarence Williams came after us that first night at Wema. The Davises, Fran Jarman, Peggy Finney, and Goldie Alumbaugh, Weeks, Gertrude Shoemaker, Clarence, and I all ate together that evening of the tenth, then the next morning we started homeward. Wednesday the eleventh, just five minutes before midnight, we drove in and Hattie Mitchell had dinner waiting for us. It had rained so hard we traveled half the way at only twenty or twenty-five miles an hour. I wish we could share some of the rain . . .

What a terrible shock of the loss of Mr. Cobble![10] We need your prayers for the family and for the place left empty in the evangelistic work, and its many problems that we must solve now and properly.

Buena Rose Stober to Her Diary, August 15, 1956— Mondombe, Congo Belge

It is conference time again, but our Chevrolet delivery truck refused to take us to Boende where we get a plane to Bolenge, but a river steamer came along with enough space for us to Coquilhatville a little earlier, so that we got to Coquilhatville ahead of the plane we had scheduled to take.

10. First arriving in the Congo in 1931, DCCM missionary Robin Cobble (1903–1956) led the evangelistic work at Monieka. Travelling in the backcountry on March 28, 1956, he was thrown from his motorcycle and broke his collarbone and several ribs. At first his injuries did not seem serious, and diagnosis was difficult because the station lacked an x-ray machine. Mission personnel later realized that one of his broken ribs punctured a lung. He died from complications of the accident on March 31, 1956, and was buried in the Congo.

One of the highlights of the conference was a young man by the name of Yende leading the singing for the conference with his lovely voice. He is an old flame of mine as I had cared for him when he was very sick when he was only five. He is one of the happiest Congolese I have ever known, especially when he is singing. He also sang in a quartet with three white men who had fine voices and thrilled us with "The Old Rugged Cross," etc.

To put an extraordinary climax to an interesting conference and trip, Paul Snipes and the new builder family, the Bashores, and I started home in the repaired Chevrolet and saw eight or so hippopotamuses playing in the river as we crossed it by ferry. We were running out of gas and the only gas station near was at a lumber camp and mill. Unfortunately, we took the wrong road and landed up in the forest with mammoth trees towering over us and plenty of signs of big logs having been pulled out. We had to unhitch the trailer with all our baggage, and of course we had plenty since the Bashores have three little children. But they finally managed to turn the car around in a tight place and we headed back just before dark and this time we took the right road to get our gasoline. Unfortunately, after all this we were too late to find an empty rest house along the way. So, we decided to drive all night and go on to Mondombe. Then we took another wrong turn and found ourselves several miles on the way to an English mission far north of where we wanted to go, so we backtracked again. Finally, back on the right road, miles on a dike through the jungle, we almost ran into a lone elephant. Paul stopped the car, kept the lights on and kept honking for the right of way but the elephant didn't like our nerve and turned three times with those tremendous ears spread, tusks raised, ready to attack. We learned afterward that our lights and horn were the worst thing we could have done. Finally, however, he considered us not worth his trouble and went off the road. We sped out of there fast hoping he didn't have all the family along, that he was alone, and we had no other trouble. We arrived around 5:00 a.m. so tired we could hardly walk, but food and home fixed us up after our harrowing night.

We had ten women at the hospital care clinic Tuesday. Two will probably be caesarean and I am sending them to Wema for Dr. Bowers's care. They are both mission women. Two others lost their first infants and are in treatment. Two others are syphilitic patients who are following treatment. Fortunately, the others are normal, healthy women.

We have started white-washing the hospital with a white clay found in certain swamps. Today the fellow is working in the long hallway where patients wait for treatment in the various rooms, so everyone is milling around. How nice and clean it makes the walls look. We will do all the rooms and the dispensary, in the old ward, in the pharmacy, and in the new maternity ward. This young man doing the job is an arrested case of leprosy and needs a job to get started again in life.

Buena Rose Stober to Friends and Family, November 9, 1956—Mondombe, Congo Belge

As I came through Boende on my way to the plane for Coquilhatville and the government hospital for x-rays and observation, while we were waiting Mr. Smith and Dr. Bowers drove out to the plot where we are to have our new church. If we do not get the building started before Christmas, we will lose the plot, so of course they had already cleared the plot; next week, Wema's new builder, Mr. Bashore, is to start the foundation. It is a very nice location and we feel we must not lose it.

Boende is the capital of the Tshuapa District, and the nearest airport to Mondombe. Wema and it are growing by leaps and bounds, so this building will have priority over Wema's building projects.

If you remember my April letter, I told you about the Boende pastor, Ekofo Joseph, his very fine work, his zeal for the church, and his knack of reaching people in many stages of development. Wema has a very nice school of three years (primary) at Boende, with around fifty children; but the building is an old leaf-covered shed, and the houses where Ilofo and the school teachers live are ramshackle mud huts. Ekofo's children received some of your gifts of garments and he wishes to send you his thanks. He has two girls, seven and five years, and two boys, three and two years.

At Mondombe, Pastor Ntange, Paul Snipes, and Hattie Mitchell are covering all our backcountry work out of Mondombe, 150–200 miles each direction. The largest portion of these churches can be reached by car. They are out two weeks and then home two weeks, counseling, helping the Congolese evangelists, collecting their offering, paying these evangelists (of whom there are around a hundred), and then baptizing the new converts. In the meantime, Gertrude Shoemaker and Patty Snipes are carrying on school, etc., pretty much to themselves. The diplomaed nurse, Botshili Daniele, and the fifteen nurse's aides are running the hospital and dispensaries by themselves while I have been recuperating; and according to the last letter were getting along fine. The woman who prepares the milk for the infants reports that three new motherless infants have been brought in for milk. That makes eleven besides several patients and undernourished older children who are receiving multipurpose food, which is soybean meal with extra vitamins and minerals added.

The doctor has given me permission to start back by plane to Boende and I hope to get back to work next week, and plow through many tasks I left unfinished when Dr. Bowers of Wema sent me here for x-rays and treatment. So before I get too busy, I wanted to wish each of you a Merry Christmas and Happy New Year.

Besides the unpleasant experiences of sickness and treatments, I have had some very pleasant ones as well. Several nice MDs took care of me, and in this government hospital the Sisters of Charity are exceedingly kind and sweet. Then the chief doctor's office nurse was in the hospital for surgery and I had some nice visits with her. Also, an English missionary teacher had her appendix out and I was allowed nice visits with her. But the very nicest new friends I made were introduced to me by one of my very best first native nurses of Bolenge, Wanjola Jacques, who is working in the anti-leprosy clinic with two very devoted Belgian nurses. When he heard that I was in the hospital he asked Miss DeJonge if he could come in to see me, so she came over, introduced herself and asked if I could have company. Of course, I was delighted to know he had this nice position and is now an arrested case of leprosy, able to care for other unfortunates and make a living. She likes Jacques's work very much, and since we had many interests in common, she invited me to the clinic where I could get around. And then she and her assistant nurse invited me for dinner with them one night and we had a delightful evening. Her assistant is Miss DeWael. Together, with the help of three nurse's aides and one diplomaed nurse, they reach four or five leprosy clinics every two weeks in this district and treat fifteen hundred patients regularly. Miss DeJonge has wanted to be a leprosarium nurse since she was fifteen years old, but during the war she helped the underground. She was in a concentration camp for two years, and after the war finally made it here. Today I went to say goodbye and they loaded me down with medicines and supplies for my patients. They are given extra supplies so that they can help with the backcountry leprosariums. They even offered me a bicycle for our leprosarium nurses and instructed me how to get a subsidy for their use of personal bikes.

Buena Rose Stober to Friends and Family, March 1957—Mondombe, Congo Belge

March 18, 1957. This week I am finishing my trips to the five rural dispensaries and I am trying to get this letter sandwiched in before I go to bed. It is extra warm and not a good time to type, but I guess I will make it. Sometimes one almost wishes one could have a run to the Tshuapa River and jump into cool off before bedtime like the old hippo at our beach does. Sometimes he even snitches an extra bite of our sweet potato vines or delicious sweet corn.

This year the Congo government has started what amounts to Social Security for Congolese workers of all kinds, except ministers.[11] Most any native can get it if he wants it. It is such a new idea that some are not willing to enter it and pay their part, but all the nurses, including our three women, are starting. In fact, most mission employees are glad to have it. The evangelists are not yet allowed, but we are trying to work out a similar plan for them.

The dental motor is here but the rest of the supplies are still on the way. It will be much easier not having to run the drill by a pedal like an old-time sewing machine.

March 27, 1957. The other day while I was looking over some road cleaning work I kept hearing puppies crying in one of the huts where patients' relatives live at the back of the maternity in surgery wards. Since I hate to see cruelty to animals, I investigated and found three half-grown puppies with their little front legs tied up to their chests in such a painful way, and the reason given was that they snitched food. When I asked the owner why she didn't give them enough food, she said she didn't have it, but when I insisted, she produced some cooked rice. Later I found out the dogs belong to several people and since she has gone home, they are free and happy without beatings and tyings up.

The nurses were talking about what was new or better at the hospital this year at Mondombe. Our new nurse spoke up with, "We have lots of new things. Look at our new autoclave received from the Belgian Foundation for Well-Being of the Africans,"[12] and another nurse added, "Yes, and all those new steel beds for maternity ward for both babies and mothers, also all the nice tables and other needed equipment for the delivery room from the same fund."

11. At the urging of the newly crowned King Baudouin, in 1956 the Belgian Parliament enacted a law extending social security benefits to all eligible persons in its colonies. The law provided benefits to all eligible persons for what were considered immediate needs: workplace injury, permanent disability, and maternity. Retirement benefits were not included in the initial law, and independence came to the Congo before benefits could be expanded. Stober notes that ministers were excluded from this coverage, as was the case in both Belgium and the United States.

12. Stober is probably referring to the *Fond du Bien-Être des Indigènes*. Established in 1949 and headquartered in Brussels, the fund made grants totaling about 250 million francs per year throughout the 1950s to subsidize medical and educational work in the Belgian colonies of Congo and Ruanda-Urundi.

Another nurse added, "The twelve babies that are either orphans or their mothers haven't enough milk for them are being fed. The ones that started their milk last year are already walking and are looking so well. But we have been able to do more and better work this year." Another added, "Besides, look at all the tuberculosis cases that have received milk or soybean meal from the multipurpose food gifts and the many undernourished older children we have helped back to normal."

The diplomaed nurse who grew up on the mission and who took his nurses training at the English mission school in Stanleyville said, "For my children I have appreciated the cereal and milk that over one hundred infants receiving each Saturday morning and other foods teaching our wives better foods for babies, and the antimalarial suppressive given every Saturday morning to prevent those terrible convulsions from malarial attacks so common before have kept our children reasonably free from the death dealing attacks."

Another nurse spoke up, "We, too, have been given suppressive treatments for malaria and we have not had those weakening fevers that troubled us before. Two new dispensaries were added to our five rural dispensaries already serving our sick relatives and we are thankful for help for them, as medical help was so far away, excepting our old-time witchcraft that killed as often as it cured."

Buena Rose Stober to Her Diary, August 22, 1957—Mondombe, Congo Belge

Yesterday was a special day for one of our nurses, the head nurse. He is the father of our only diplomaed nurse and several other intelligent children in good positions. The Belgian Congo government presented him with a very special honor called *le Carte de Mérite Civique*. Now he has the right to buy a plantation of his own of coffee, rubber, palm-oil trees, etc. Pastor Ntange also has received one and has a nice plantation started at his home town. He is assistant president of the planter's organization. They asked him to be president, but the evangelistic work takes a lot of time, so he refused. Nkang'Itoko Timothy, the head nurse, has served sick folks for many years here under Dr. Pearson, Miss Williams, Dr. Baker, and I in recent years. He started his work in 1928. There was a government agriculturalist who also received the honor with Timothy. Our Belgian administrator gave out these awards at a special center at the government offices about five miles from here. He made a fine speech and we all attended.[13] Doctor took the nurse

13. The Belgian colonial government began granting the *le Carte de Mérite Civique*,

and his wife in the first car, and a bunch of us followed in the other station car. It was a gala time and the many friends who couldn't get in the cars were passed on the road with a great deal of waving and greetings.

This week I had a very special guest, an English missionary nurse with whom I spent my war vacation in South Africa. On Monday she went with me to see the leprosarium, and while we were working, up drives a jeep full of Catholic priests and she leaned over to me and whispered, "It's an invasion!" They were all young priests and full of enthusiasm and came out to greet us saying, "Miss Stober, this is an invasion." It was all we could do to keep our faces straight, but they had come for dental work and thought they would tell us and see the leprosarium while they were at it. We showed them around, including our coffee plantation where we hope we will eventually make some of our own expenses for the leprosarium. We also have several hundred palm-oil trees and many other fruit trees. They thought our trees all looked very healthy, but they were delighted when we showed them and gave them a lot of the wild edible mushroom that starts growing in a dead tree in the coffee plantation. Their teeth were not too difficult to mend.

The next visitor was that afternoon, the provincial doctor came to inspect the hospital and dispensary. He was very understanding that the doctor wasn't here and took notes about our nurses, equipment, and aspirations for the future. He was interested in the leprosarium work, but our rural dispensary visit was a flop, since we got there at 2:00 p.m. and the nurse was not there but had finished his work and was visiting a nearby village. We went over the drugs and equipment and the nurse who heard the drum calls was back before we left, out of breath and flustered, so he wasn't so bright. He visited another dispensary on his way back to the territorial capital, and I hope the nurse was there. It is much bigger, more patients of all kinds, and the nurse does not have much time to run around.

Buena Rose Stober to Friends and Family, December 15, 1957—Mondombe, Congo Belge

This week the school students in preparatory classes had a free-for-all. This school has a number of students from Monieka and they have always felt themselves superior to Mondombe. They are bigger in stature and have a

the "Certificate of Civil Merit" in 1948. Typically, applicants were emerging Congolese leaders who met certain requirements: completing sufficient education, maintaining a clear criminal record, and swearing off polygamy and witchcraft. Recipients of the certificate enjoyed considerable privileges, including an exemption from corporal punishment. Historians generally interpret the award as a strategy to assimilate a Congolese "petty bourgeoise" into the dominant colonial society.

little more money, so they are known to ridicule Mondombe students at times. They have even called Mondombe "pygmies," which is the next thing to a curse, and they said only pygmies use salt on their manioc greens. Bedlam turned loose and Mondombe students moved in cutting their suitcases, bedding, clothing, schoolbooks, and anything else they could get their knives on. Several elders heard the racket and rushed to stop it. A school and elder committee judged them, and no student could take his final exams unless each Monieka student brought a stare of firewood and each Mondombe student brought a two-hundred-liter drum of stones for building.

But the year ended peacefully with the trouble settled. A student in the evangelists' school preached a very fine sermon from Luke 2:11–13. He spoke of pre-Christian lives as dark like black paper, and said a man wasn't a man until he had partaken of human flesh. Basiomo's mother had deserted him and his mother's sister and evangelist husband raised him. He says we can be white as white paper if we follow Christ.

Buena Rose Stober to Friends and Family, July 3, 1958—Mondombe, Congo Belge

All our ten missionaries are on the station now: evangelists Snipes and Dawsons; Dr. Baker and Mrs. Baker; the Austin Smiths; Gertrude and I because it is in the school and time to finish evangelistic records, get medical reports off to the government, and get ready for conference at Bolenge. Gertrude and I will leave by boat on July 15 and the others will come by car and bring the native delegates, so there wasn't room for everyone. Snipes will take the dump truck to Boende where they will get their plane for the start of their trip for furlough.

Today was graduation for the fifth grade and all the 145 boys had had their hair cut and were wearing headbands to keep their hair straight at service last night. This morning for their big day they were dressed in white drill shorts and white shirts, and all were wearing shoes and socks, some even had to borrow them from their village brothers, but they all looked very nice. Wonder of wonders: there were five girls in the class. Mrs. Smith has spent weeks helping them get their pretty colorful yellow dresses made. They wore shoes and socks, too, and pretty head scarves. The service was between 9:00 a.m. and 10:00 a.m. and there must have been seven hundred to a thousand spectators including doting parents, friends, and probably some from curiosity. There were songs, recitations, and all the regular frills of graduation, but the sweetest thing was one of the little girls, [the twelve-year-old daughter of a nurse], leading the congregational singing. The other girls took part also, but not in such a spectacular way. One girl was wearing a sloppy dress instead of her graduation dress she had made.

The crowd was such a strange mixture of the most elite who speak French and have left most of their heathen shortcomings behind; there were dozens of folks from the leprosarium there as two of their boys were graduating; there were a lot of ordinary, average folks; other schoolchildren; and then some real old-time heathens. Two women were all but naked and were in mourning with the typical white clay rubbed all over their bodies, and one had black soot rubbed across her forehead. There were anklets and charms and tattooed faces here and there, and dozens of well-cared-for children playing near their mothers on the outskirts of the crowd. We have an open amphitheater at the side of the school building with a raised platform and a cement movie screen background which is very nice for such affairs.

The doctor did two surgical cases this morning, a hernia and a tumor that proved to be more complicated than we expected, so spinal anesthesia ran out and I had to give another anesthesia. During the woman's operation, we had visits of two state officials, one a sanitary agent hunting rabies vaccine for a six-year-old white child bitten by a cat. Ours hasn't come so we couldn't help him, but it should have been on this mail. The other official is on vacation from our Ifumo field, but he used to be here so stopped to say hello.

One of the amusing things [the doctor does during every operation] is to watch the natives outside covering their noses and mouths with their hands or a scarf or a hanky. They see all the nurses wearing masks, so they think they must protect themselves from the evil spirits, infections, odors, or whatever the case is, that might jump out and attack them.

I mixed up some drugs, mercurochrome, and potassium bromide solution this morning, too, and then came home to type and found this machine on strike. So I spent the rest of the morning changing the ribbon and turning screws, oiling, and punching here and there until it runs again as it should.

Buena Rose Stober to Friends and Family, January 15, 1959—Mondombe, Congo Belge

I am on my last two years before retirement. The Congo church of this region is trying to get legal rights from the government and of course need some sort of organization which they want to call *L'Église du Congo* (section Disciples). The first draft of their organization regulations is finished, but of course it will take several such attempts before everyone is satisfied. It is rather interesting how they differ from us and how they agree.

The weather this morning is rather cool, only 76°, but when the sun comes out we nearly roast as this is, believe it or not, dry season when it is cloudy a lot of the time but rarely rains. It stays cool because of the humidity stored up in rivers and swamps most of the dry season and though it often thunders and lightnings there still isn't much rain. January is the hottest part of the year.

Yesterday, besides having three fairly big surgical operations, there was a big fight between two of the nicest Christian women. One, the little wife of my chief cook and bottle washer, and the other, the wife of a clerk who runs a store across the swamp from us. The two husbands are very special friends, and everyone respects their wives who usually are quiet but industrious women. We have a station market of cooked foods every day for many hungry boys and girls of the school who have no one to cook special foods for them, and also for patients who have no one along with them. They bring cooked greens, dried or fresh fish dishes, roasted peanuts, a sort of peanut butter, bananas, and other fruits, along with their bundles of manioc bread. They sit by the side of the road in front of the hospital and the boys' dormitory and it is a very fine thing for anyone who has the money. Those who get their breakfasts there and those who cannot roam around hunting breadfruit, papaya, or oranges, and they nearly clean out our pineapple garden, but the thing that makes us really angry is to see the unripe fruit that has been picked and thrown aside to rot after all our teachings to let the food ripen first and not beat fruit off the trees and break the limbs.

Any woman is welcome to sell her cooking there so the clerks' wives as well as our mission women sell at breakfast time. We were right in the middle of a tough operation when the cry of the fight went up and when the doctor was near enough to finish off the case, I slipped away to see what I could do to stop it. There was little Talesa and the big woman from the company having a terrific brawl, and blood was running down the big woman's face. The woman had said some slighting remark about the new woman coming in to sell at the market or that her food was no good, and Talesa exploded into a demon. She is a mother of seven or so children and they appreciate her cooking, and her efforts to make a little extra money. The company woman has no children and doesn't need extra so badly, but I never would have thought of her starting a brawl like that. She is from Wema so all the Wema women joined her, and the other mission women cheered for Talesa. Wema people are famous for their fighting and seeing the blood I didn't expect it to end until the other side had some blood running, but when I steered the big woman into the dispensary and turned her over to a nurse for treatment of her scratches, I went back to send the others home. Some of the crowd of one hundred or more jeered at me, but with a little persuasion they went home.

The task of settling the dispute was left for Pastor Ntange and the elders. He called them all in the afternoon and talked pretty straight to them. When he had finished everyone admitted they had talked out of turn and fought out of turn and went away friendly and peaceably.

Pastor Ntange is an artist at calming down culprits. Long experience has taught him what to say and how to say it. They said when he was a young man, his father had wanted Pastor Ntange to take his chieftainship and provided him with four wives, but then Pastor Ntange met some of our early teacher-evangelists who had traveled from the new proposed station. On March 20, 1920, he was baptized by Mr. Moon.

This big son of the chief proved his ability to work with a very vicious tribe whose intentions were to kill this big foreigner. His success there helped mission folks to understand his ability and need for more schooling and training as an evangelist, so he was brought to the station and prepare [to be] one of our first students to the Congo Christian Institute which was only in its beginning and the standards were not nearly so high.

He never got the amount of French and Bible training they receive now. But his wisdom grew, and when I first came to Mondombe the old Monieka evangelist was getting up in years. Another fellow was chosen to take his place and he seemed all right for the job, but he got involved in some very crude heathen treatments for unruly wives, and so Ntange Timoteo was chosen instead, and how really glad we have been, for through the years he has been faithful with unlimited Christian spirit and wisdom for managing affairs of his fellow Congolese and also patiently training four or five young white missionaries into the intricate thinking patterns of his Congolese Christians and proven himself valuable to all of us with our problems.

Please remember Pastor Ntange in your prayers as he carries a very heavy load.

You have probably heard about the rioting in Léopoldville. The ones responsible seem to be like the little fish we had in Congo whose defense is to blow itself up like a balloon and make a funny noise that frightens folks away. The Belgians are very liberal with them that they are easily insulted. They are pushing the Congolese into higher paid, more responsible jobs all the time.[14]

14. Stober probably is referring to the Léopoldville Riots, the first significant

Buena Rose Stober to Friends and Family, July 23, 1959—Mondombe, Congo Belge

I went to the hospital before 6:00 a.m. and since the doctor is here and my expectant mother isn't hurrying too much I thought perhaps I could get your letter done at this time.

We have had quite a bit of American company this week and I have the Williams family at lunch, too, at my table. The lunch was all ready yesterday as we expected them yesterday, bringing Miss Grace McGavran, sister of Don McGavran. She writes children's literature and is here hoping to get out some stories for the African projects. I knew her, her parents, and family when we were in the College of Missions. She is so much like her sweet little mother as we knew her in those days. Margaret Baker, schoolteacher, second daughter of Bakers, saved her cash and made her summer vacation trip to see her mother and father. It is lovely to have her here again. Our other guests are Dr. and Mrs. Russel Putnam of Cleveland, old-time friends of all missionaries. She has been on the Church Women's Council and various international church affairs and he is an electrical businessman.

Yesterday I entertained the Putnams. The day before at noon both the Putnams and the Bakers, as the Bakers had just gotten back from the central committee meeting at Monieka. I must find a time when Grace and the Williams can dine with me again. Tomorrow I hope to go in the car to Ikela where Miss Shoemaker and the Putnams will take the plane to Stanleyville and the USA.

We are going to miss Miss Shoemaker terribly, but she must have a furlough and we must spread her jobs out between us somehow. She is such an efficient worker it will not be easy.

We had several blows from the decisions of the central committee: the Dawsons go to our secondary school at Bolenge, as he is the only one with proper credits to do it at present, and the Snipes will be here in September. She is credited to carry on our school and he does the evangelistic work. Unfortunately, they have three little girls, and when he is off on trips for the churches, she will have her hands full. Mrs. Baker is fully qualified for the

---

episodes of unrest that would lead quickly to Congolese independence. In early January 1959, Belgian colonial authorities refused to issue a permit allowing nationalist political party *Alliance des Bakongo* to hold a rally in Léopoldville. Urged by party leader Joseph Kasa-Vubu, thousands rioted in the streets of the capital city, clashing with police and the Belgian army. Estimates of Congolese casualties may have been as high as five hundred people and over three hundred arrests were made. Unrest like the Leopold Riots became increasingly common throughout 1959, leading eventually to independence on June 30, 1960. Significantly, Stober shows little sympathy for the growing independence movement here.

schoolwork from the US, but she hasn't the Belgian work, so Gertrude has been training a Congolese teacher to take the directorship with Patty Snipes and Lelia to direct him. He is slow and deliberate, and whether he will ever get it done we don't know, but at least he will be accepted by the government and has been chosen by the teacher here.

Dr. Baker was appointed as a mission secretary, which is a lot of work and will take a good typist, which Mondombe doesn't have. The best we have at present is trying to get in at the Baptist normal school as he is already one of our best teachers and hopes to learn more. I will probably have to take the girls' dorm whether I like it or not, but I hope Patty can manage the Girl Guides as I don't feel quite up to making it active and interesting for them. She was good at it before.

Mrs. Putnam talked to the CWF here on the lawn of one of the women's homes and we must have had a hundred women sitting around on the grass. The hospital women turned out in full force and there are plenty of patients and patients' wives. Being vacation time, most of the women are on vacation with their husbands but any here came. She brought them a message from Mrs. Green, the world CWF president, and gave them each a picture with one of Rosa Page Welch's songs on it in English, which Mrs. Dawson and I hope to translate and send out to all the women if we can get enough dittograph copies made.[15]

Buena Rose Stober to Friends and Family, September 17, 1959—Mondombe, Congo Belge

School has started and is whirling along in a terrific speed, a depleted staff, a new Congolese director, and first grade taught entirely in French. What a chore for Mr. Lotsuka and Mrs. Baker to have to step into. Fortunately, the Congo school authorities sent enough brochures for every primary school teacher to have a copy for his pupils. Of course, this teaching and French disqualifies some of our backcountry teachers and evangelists and a few on the station. They have had booster courses for all possible. My little girls think it is terrible but everyone will be thankful in the long run.[16]

15. The Christian Women's Fellowship of the Christian Churches (Disciples of Christ) was first established in January 1949. The CWF provided opportunities for spiritual growth, enrichment, education, and creative ministries for women. Like other women's ministries of the denomination, CWF focused on the common interests and concerns of women across the globe.

16. In 1949, the Belgian colonial government adopted the *Plan décennal pour le développement économique et social du Congo Belge*, commonly known as the "Ten-Year Plan." One provision of the plan required instruction in all schools, including

A Mr. and Mrs. Snipes and children have arrived September 24, so we are a little better off, but Dr. Baker has a deep abscess in his neck the needs a surgeon after he had tried to instruct we nurses what to do. Maybe we were too scared that he was going to Wema with Mr. Snipes to have Dr. Weare take over. And of course, freight arrived, six cases of school supplies and three cases of Quaker Oats and milk for the infant clinic. The Congolese and I were assigned to meeting the boats while just Lelia and I were carrying on, so we rushed down to get things going. Unfortunately, we have used the older schoolboys who were in class at the time to carry these loads to their destination, a hospital and school, but we finally found enough patients' strong relatives to do the job while the boys were in school.

Buena Rose Stober to Friends and Family, October 1959—Mondombe, Congo Belge

This is probably the last Christmas letter I will write you from Congo! I will go on furlough in July 1960 and will retire instead of coming back. At least those are the plans as of now. At any rate, Merry Christmas and Happy New Year throughout the whole year!

I have just had breakfast and a look at the hospital. Everybody seems to be happy with this lovely, comforting rain that seems determined to drip all morning.

I am to have six Belgian dental patients today if they can make it in the rain. We are about five hundred miles from a dentist, so they are glad to get whatever care we can give them. The man is a doctor serving some fifty miles from here. He has a wife and four sons under six years old. They are to have dinner at my house, too, in between settings. I have never met them, but the Bakers have. I can smell the dinner (rabbit) cooking, so if they don't come the Servel will have to take charge.

Last night the doctor had to do a caesarean, so we are a bit exhausted after working with the woman all day. She is okay this morning and the big boy is fine. She was lucky to be near a surgeon. They are people from a coffee plantation about thirty miles from here and she has been in the prenatal clinic, and sewing classes as well, for several weeks. She's been working on a little shirt that her infant is wearing this morning.

---

beginning elementary grades, to be conducted in French. Aiming to settle a long-standing debate in the colony's educational policy, schools were expected to comply by 1959.

Paul Snipes and Pastor Ntange got back Tuesday afternoon from their first trip since the Snipes arrival from furlough. They visited ten or so churches and baptized new converts. I haven't heard their report as yet . . .

You probably get tired of my continual harping on keeping the hospital grounds clean, but if you could have seen or smelled the dirt around the hospital, dispensary, and rest houses that the nurses and I had to wade through, you would understand that it is a real victory to be able to walk through the yards, and back of the buildings, and in the banana garden, without stumbling through all the patients' and relatives' trash. They are now required to clean these places for two hours every day as pay for room rent!

I was delighted over one of my girls in sewing class yesterday. Some of them pay very little attention to instructions and seams go wandering around like the snake's trail, but Eleka Malia—a tall, fine-featured girl—quieter than most—pleased me by following instructions and doing a beautiful job of putting on bias tape neatly.

The little first-grade girls have always learned the first stitches in these four weeks of school. Some of my girls are starting quilt block sewing bags, others have finished baby dresses by hand for the clinic, or knitted shirts for infants, some have done embroidery or crochet for themselves. The women, too, twenty of them, are learning to make undergarments for themselves, baby dresses for the clinic, and doilies crocheted for their own homes. Later we will do some cooking and knitting.

The only serious fighting we have had at school was over the jealousy of one group of girls over another group that sang a special in church on Sunday. They had to be separated twice, and that evening at the girls' dorm I asked three girls who had been in it what they had learned from their evangelist fathers, or nurse father, and from their teachers. When asked they quoted shamefacedly the golden rule, turning the other cheek, and loving one another. When we ask for a circle of prayers each of the guilty ones asked God to forgive her mistakes and to teach her to do better. Peace has reigned since.

The Bible institute has about thirty students this term from our field and Wema. The wives are all coming faithfully to their classes. There are some fine people in the group.

Several of our mission people have been called to deliberate at the chief's council to formulate procedure of local government, looking toward independence. The chief is a nice fellow, and progressive. My housekeeper is on this council and told me about some of their considerations. It sounds hopeful, but they need the prayers and guidance of all Christians to help them through this difficult time.

Buena Rose Stober to Her Diary, December 10, 1959—Boende, Congo Belge

Today found me at Boende for the arrival of the Williams' new baby at the government hospital. Boende's schools are still under Wema, as he is an engineer and builder and she is a religious education director, both of which Boende needs badly.

They also have to serve as entertaining committee for any missionaries coming through there by air. As did the Mills from Paraguay. We enjoyed their visit and they will be back here after their visit at Mondombe and take off for Europe on the way home to the USA. It was nice to have them.

We even had a Christmas tree up, a banana stalk in wet sand and branches of the Congo parasite that resembles cedar with his fine leaves stuck up and down the stalk until it is lovely with the ordinary tinsel, etc. The church is preparing pageants and other activities. The elder came and presented Susan with a pretty Congolese name, Elya Louisa, in memory of a very fine Christian woman . . .

Mrs. Williams looks after women's school here, but of course any medical is carried on in the government hospital. She has carried on this week and there is a lay school here at Boende for Congolese and white children, or any others. It is all in French, of course, and a priest comes for Bible training for Catholic children and Mrs. Williams has Bible training for Protestants. Sharon Williams goes to school and had the highest grades even before the French-speaking children. One of our Protestant nurses has two children in school and they're doing superior work too. The Africans can't get over how Kathryn kept of all this work until the night before Susan came.

Clarence and his workmen have put up a lovely church. We have had work in Boende for years but no missionary living there. It was all done through Wema and this being the district's capital and an airport, we needed to get busy. A residence for the pastor, a Mondombe man, brother of Pastor Ntange, is finished and a new social building and one teacher's cottage are finished, too, but now they have a new residence for missionary families nearly finished.

I will be back at Mondombe for the end of the month and new year and then it won't be long until my furlough and retirement come.

The people of Mondombe surround Rosa Page Welch (center) during her visit to Congo in 1953. Stober's missionary colleagues, Ned Roberts and Gertrude Shoemaker, are visible in the foreground. Photo courtesy of DCHS.

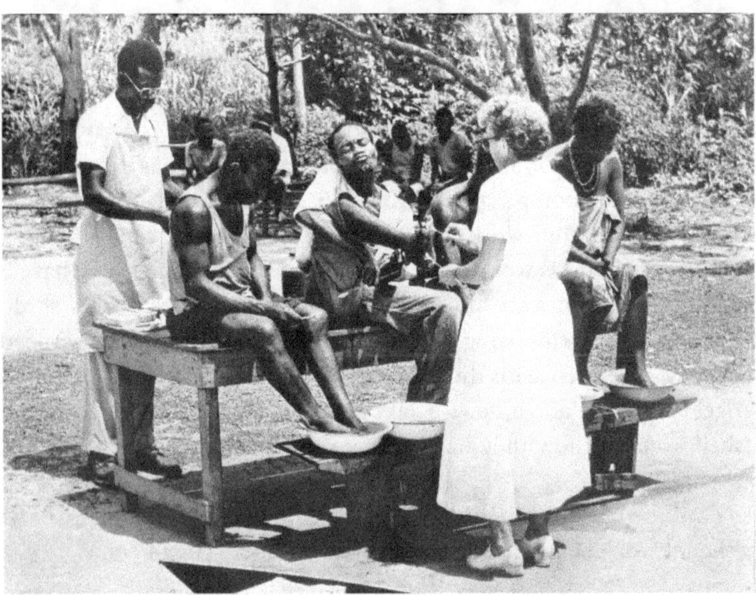

Initially, Stober was unable to offer much in the way of treatment for the lepers at Lomina. By 1953, when this photo was taken, she was able to cure most cases with the consistent use of sulfa antibiotics. Photo courtesy of CTS.

Each morning in the 1950s, Stober's back porch was a place where the children of Mondombe could get a healthy breakfast before school. Photo courtesy of DCHS.

A graduate of the Congo Christian Institute of DCCM, Ntange Timothy was the pastor of the church at Mondombe for many years. Stober developed a close, collegial relationship with him during the 1950s. Photo courtesy of DCHS.

Stober made countless trips into the backcountry to provide nutritional food and medical care at the many rural dispensaries around Mondombe such as this one in 1956. When she was unable to go personally, her Congolese nurses made the trip. Photo courtesy of DCHS.

Some of Stober's most astute observations about Congo and its people were made while riding in a *teepoi* through the dense rainforest. "Carriers" like these four young Congolese men were indispensable workers in DCCM. Photo courtesy of DCHS.

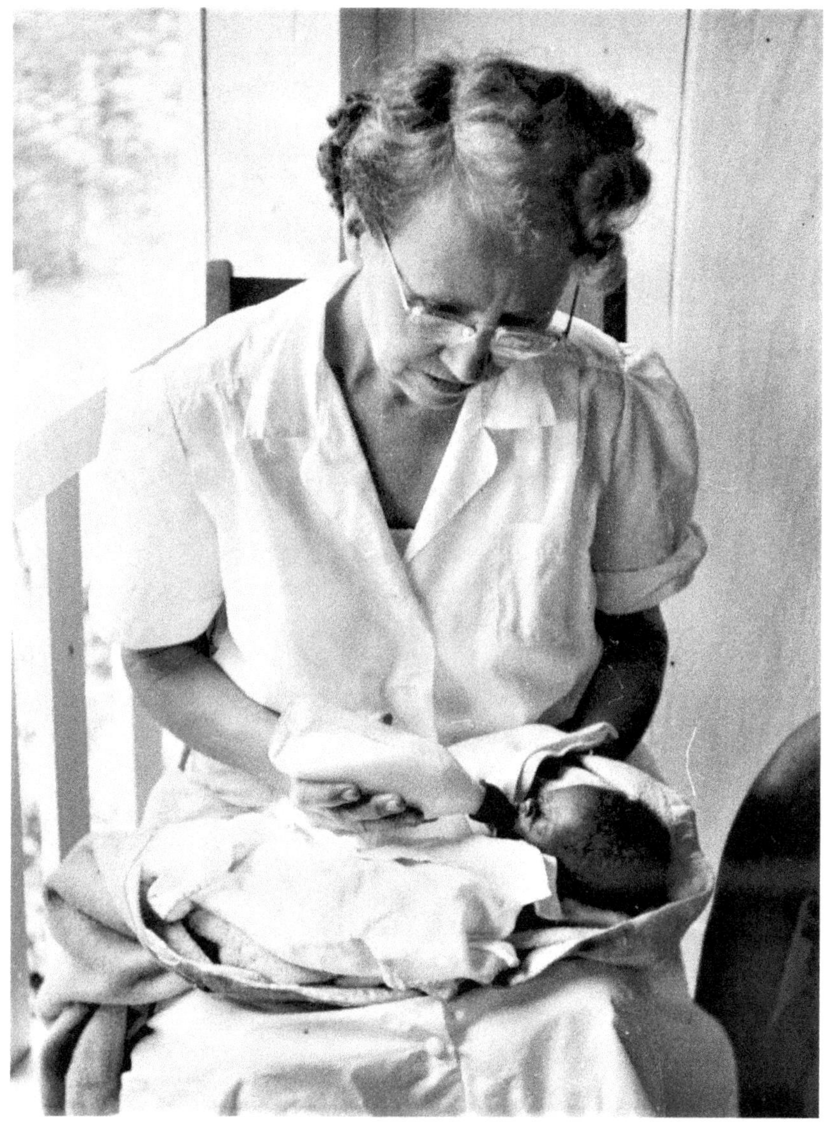

Even after almost forty years in Congo, Stober maintained her passion for the well-being of mothers and babies. Here she is feeding a premature newborn at Mondombe in 1958. Photo courtesy of DCHS.

Though she was evacuated from Congo in July 1960 amid the political unrest following independence, Stober officially retired from missionary service in 1961. Photo courtesy of DCHS.

5

1960 and Undated Anecdotes

Buena Rose Stober to Friends and Family, January 7, 1960—Mondombe, Congo Belge

Just six more months for me to write "Congo Belge" and perhaps one or two from the "Republic of Congo," and then I will be back in the US for furlough and retirement. In the first two hours after I arrived back at Mondombe, I found the doctor and the nurses preparing for a caesarean and was able to assist in that dilemma; Monday evening there was another of the same kind.

My house was full of dust and cobwebs. My dogs were delighted to see me, but they had been well cared for. The big fellow loves to hunt and Bokonji took him hunting several times. Bokonji Samuel has six children and has a time getting enough meat for them. He is on the station because he wants to keep his children in school and accepted an offer to cook for me and wash, etc., of mornings, and since he is a good tailor he works afternoons and makes extra money. He and his wife are also good gardeners, so in spite of the low pay I can give him, he makes out very well. The little dog is the Roberts' aging dog and the night sentry did a good job caring for him. He also cares for my cat, rabbits, and chickens.

About a month ago a cyclist who was in too much of a hurry ran into the sentry and broke his arm. He had to have some help for his job. He is older and doesn't hear too well. His wife is a young, pretty woman who has had three babies all by caesarean. The baby is still under a year old.

Our reports are not all off yet but nearly. A report for the World Church Service for milk supplied to us runs like this: in six months we used 240 pounds for sixty-nine schoolchildren; 365 pounds for sick children and adults, seventy-eight patients; for Congo orphans or infants who hadn't enough mother's milk we used Congo government milk provided for some and their mothers, 350 pounds.[1]

We had one hundred infants in the clinic this Saturday morning. There were only three cases of itch, which is a real improvement. One of them whose mother has been very faithful did not hesitate when I told her she would have to have the infant's hair cut before an infection starts. She went right to the nurse who was cutting another infant's hair and waited for him; they used to run off. Long hair harbors all kinds of dirt and infections.

I've gotten off with a lot of growling about girls observing dormitory rules and getting in at 6:00 p.m. Some stayed all night with relatives without permission, so I sent them home. I managed to focus the elders' attention on the girls' shortcomings and got permission to put some pretty heavy discipline on them if they disobeyed their caretaker. She doesn't seem to have any ability to control them. There are ten girls in the dormitory and two hundred boys about two blocks away, so you can imagine what a mess things can get in.

The doctor discovered another discouraging thing the other day. An ex-dorm boy fell from a tree and has been in the hospital for weeks without showing improvement. He had so many broken bones and other injuries that he didn't stand much of a chance in the first place, but when a nurse reported a broken leg swelling again after all that time, the doctor investigated and found an ape's bone under all the nice bandaging laying over the broken part. Right under our noses at the hospital. Ugh!

Our school teacher for the first grade at the leprosarium is an arrested case of leprosy. He has been preaching there for some time and teaching the beginners. Three of the children he has taught went on to school on the station and have since become evangelists.

1. Church World Service (CWS) was founded in 1946 as an ecumenical ministry aimed at alleviating poverty and hunger and working for justice and peace. The Christian Churches (Disciples of Christ) were founding members of CWS and worked cooperatively with the organization in almost all of its missions across the globe.

Buena Rose Stober to Friends and Family, January 28, 1960—Mondombe, Congo Belge

I have just returned from the hospital and checked up on a little patient that had an operation for a tumor that turned out to involve the whole kidney, which had to be removed with the tumor. We all felt so sorry for the parents of the three-year-old girl, but now there isn't much consoling one can say or do in a case like this one. The father is one of our school teachers and a Congo Christian Institute graduate. The doctor is sending a specimen to the laboratory in Léopoldville, hoping it isn't malignant, but it grew very fast and the child was losing ground.

Of all things I should find when I went out to see her, the room was full of anxious friends and relatives as if being there could help, except to use up a lot of oxygen the child needs. They were quiet enough, but they sure enough got out when I arrived. One was even one of the supposedly most intelligent teachers, also a CCI graduate. The child is in pretty good condition. She didn't seem very disturbed by all her ether. We gave it to her for nearly two hours at that.

We have another new infant getting milk at Kaala Ekila's milk supply room; that makes six for her care besides the older children, school children, and certain sick folks she tries to help along into a healthier life. She has been on the mission here at Mondombe a long time and was here in the early days of Mondombe, married to one of the evangelists, but is now a widow and makes her living helping feed our patients. She must be pretty close to sixty years old as she was a grown woman in 1921 when Mondombe got its start as a mission station. It has been a preaching place since about 1918.

One of the new students in the Bible class has a wife and three girls, two old enough to be in school so of course we said, "Well the father and mother with two heathen and dirty daughters wouldn't do so well as a preacher's family." Finally, they got up enough that they are fairly respectable looking girls and the baby has its charms off from around its neck. The girls are learning to make a sewing bag of quilts and things and do not look so terribly heathen now. I don't know the father very well, but he must make a pretty good impression or the church wouldn't have sent him for training.

We are again battling with teaching machine sewing, making uniforms for new girls, and putting on additions to dresses for girls who have grown so fast, letting down will do no good. If others are knitting, crocheting, and embroidering, the beginners are still on sewing bags and making quilt blocks. King's ex! while I kill a mosquito on my screen.[2] He or she has been chewing on me the last few nights and I couldn't get it until just now. He is dead now. Too bad for him!

My little dog, Tippy, died this last week and Cappy and I are lost without her, but she was over eleven years old and had asthma so badly she deserves to rest. Even the tomcat misses her.

The little boys are filing past my house with their fishing hooks, going to the river in hopes for a better supper, and it is about time I got out too. It has rained most of the afternoon and I have spent most of the time typing three orders for school supplies for sewing classes and this letter.

Buena Rose Stober to Jim Stober, May 3, 1960—Mondombe, Congo Belge

Bokonji Samuel and I enjoyed your letters. I translated the poem for him, too, and he thanks you especially for the good wishes for his growing little family. I enjoyed the part about the rosebud and the wonderland spring scents.

About the trailer for me to live in permanently: I'm afraid I wouldn't be too enthusiastic. I do need a place to live, it's true, and it need not be very big; but I think I have stashed away enough for the biggest part of a house building, and why should you go in debt again to buy a trailer for me when I still want a house? You probably will feel like, "You can't please a woman." I would be more pleased if you put that money, $20.00 a month or however much you will be paying, in something for your old age when you won't be enthusiastic about working, or in Social Security, or a savings account like they have at the post office. I dread thinking of your always having a debt to pay. It makes life too miserable. Sometimes it can't be avoided and maybe this is one of those times.

At any rate I would want plumbing, toilet, bath or shower, electric lights, butane or some kind of gas, and eventually I should still like to build a house where I can invite old missionary friends, church folks, or any relatives I can persuade to come and see us. There wouldn't be much room in any trailer I have seen for visiting, and I like visitors. To me the trailer would be only temporary; financially I doubt if I could afford the temporary trailer and the real house, and I don't believe in saddling someone else with my debts and problems at this time of life, although I realize one must be cooperative. Fixing a trailer for myself might be amusing for an adventure, but I

2. Likely this means King's X, a "cry in children's games . . . to call for a time out" (Merriam-Webster, s.v. "King's X").

am not so adventuresome now and I doubt if the money I have would hold out for both trailer and house.

You will have to use your own judgment and I thank you a lot for planning, but I would have a lot of thinking and planning before I would be entirely happy over it.

I would rather wait and see what I can do with the money I have put away. I am not young and gay enough to experiment, I'm afraid. However, I would appreciate the corner of your land and your cooperation in my decision to keep things on a cash basis as nearly as possible. I will have enough pension to live on with Social Security and my missionary pension. Neither will be big, but enough.

I have even wondered if it would not be wiser to build or buy in a town like Nicoma Park where we could be near, but my aches and pains could easily be pampered. Florence is too far out for having any friendships. Shady Nook is better, but we will see when I get a chance to look things over.

It has just now helped me finish this letter by raining, but it is cleared up, so I had better see what is going on in school and hospital.

Buena Rose Stober to Friends and Family, May 1960—Mondombe, Congo Belge

May 1, 1960. April swished by with my packing, selling out little by little, and preparation to turn over as many jobs to Africans as possible and hope that there will be a nurse to carry on until Mrs. Dugan can take over. There are the good old faithful Congolese who make you wish you could go on serving them forever. Then there are the ignorant you must fight against and which you could stay on and keep trying. There are others so brilliant they think they know everything, but because they do not know it all must sometimes be shushed down a bit to let the middle fellow have a chance. And then there are dozens of villages where the people have not been reached except in a very superficial way, who see only financial advancement from the mission and can't understand that they can have riches much more valuable through Christ. We wonder if our Congolese Christians are strong enough to hold out against these.

Jane Heaton and Edna Poole went back downriver together. Had a surprise perhaps but mostly discouraged that there is a spirit of insubordination in some school students.

May 13, 1960. I have finally received my reservations for flying home in July, although I had hoped it would be earlier. It is the best Miss Peterson could get. I will have a medical checkup in New York and then head for Oklahoma City.

The Bakers are taking their furlough at the same time as I am and hope to divide the little time they have left before retirement into smaller portions. Their trunks have left too.

The doctor has been operating in the new surgery and it is a wonderfully nice place, even though it isn't entirely finished. I have been in the dental room of the same building for some months, but we still lack some parts to our x-ray.

I am going to miss the lovely little gay-colored sunbirds that flit around my house and sing their trilling ecstasy when it is bright. I have had another charming little beauty around my bushes, it's called a black-bellied seed cracker and its head is a brilliant red which also covers its neck. Its song isn't quite so sweet as the sunbirds, which are a larger variety of hummingbird. They look like it at least.

There is another charming bird that is called the wag-tail because during its lovely solo and at most other times it wags its tail up and down. It is black and white and about the size of a mockingbird and one perches on the very highest part of my roof splitting its little throat with a song that when whistled sounds like "Wake up dearie! Wake up dearie!" and variations that would cheer anyone up for a happy morning start.

Buena Rose Stober to Her Diary, June 10, 1960—Mondombe, Congo Belge

I am whirling around in so many circles that it doesn't seem possible that one day it will all be done, and I will find myself learning how to live in the USA. But when getting my passport in order they wanted a statement of how many months I have served in each term of Congo actually on the field, and it added up to 291 months on Congo soil, after subtracting travel and furloughs.

We had a disagreeable church meeting called by villagers. Now the owners of the land on which the mission is located wanted to gripe because they had no key men in authority on the mission or in the evangelistic work. In fact, they haven't as a whole been very faithful Christians; so, of course, they were not put in these jobs. Pastor Ntange and the rest are from other tribes; and the tribe that actually invited the mission to live among them had been moved off to a place with others of their own tribe. The dental nurse that has helped me all along is the son of the man who opened his home to the first evangelists. They said some pretty unkind things about Pastor

Ntange and the church in general; and we all, including Pastor Ntange, were given no chance to answer but left the meeting with a very disagreeable taste. I noticed that Bokonji, a member of the tribe who invited us in and of the chieftain's family, wasn't there and wondered when I got home and asked him. His answer was, "You know, mama, our old men had a way when hotheaded young men were talking of going to war and making confusion; these old fellows would stay very discreetly away. But when it wasn't just griping but real war, they were in front; so, I stayed away purposely. What did they say?" and I repeated some of it and he said, "I'll fix them. That bunch never gave enough offering in the last six months to know they were Christians." He finished his work and left, but the next day after his visit to them they came and apologized to Pastor Ntange and Mr. Snipes . . .

At Bolenge I stayed with Edna and Georgia. Everything went quietly until Independence Day and a few days after. Then rioting began and Georgia had some wounded in Bolenge for care. Then Bolenge high-salary workmen were said to be in danger, and police hung around to keep rioting down. The army mutinied and locked up their officers, and all aircraft was grounded and suspense and anxiety increased as rumors of all sorts of horrible affairs. We four single ladies living at the end of this station near the highway were moved where there were others to help. Rumors flew wild. Soldiers from Coquilhatville did come in an armored car to Bolenge one night. Faith awakened me. "Stobie, there is an armored car in front of the house." Then they drove onto Tillerys and found a car loaded with baggage and were told it was baggage of missionaries going on furlough, so after investigating they drove on. Finally, the Belgian paratroopers came to Léopoldville and then to Coquilhatville and the airlift of women and children began. We left as refugees. What a way to leave a place I had loved so much for so many years, thirty-seven in fact.

Buena Rose Stober to Friends and Family, June 20, 1960—Bolenge, Congo Belge

I have neglected you for some weeks now but finally have found the time and the typewriter to write. This is a French-speaking machine so you will probably find things spelled every which way.

All of our travel plans were so uncertain that I was trying to finish my packing and be ready to go on a minute's notice. Car service to Boende was not available, so I had to leave on the eleventh with Mr. Coburn in order to get to my plane on the sixteenth.

Frank and I left Mondombe about 11:00 a.m. amid a shower of tears from my Congolese women friends and many thanks to Frank for putting in the big cistern to the hospital water system for which he had spent a good ten days at Mondombe. The truck was loaded with the queerest cargo you could dream up: a retiring missionary, a steer for Wema to butcher, nine rabbits (the Bakers selling them to Frank's masons), the five Wema masons, the Bakers' parrot going to live with the Weares at Wema, four chickens, my two that were left were supposed to be delivered alive, but the sentry misunderstood and dressed them so we froze them the night before. Our fried rabbit was almost too frozen to eat also and in putting up the lunch I just supposed Frank had a cup, but he didn't, and so when we started to drink our coffee I gave him the cup off the thermos and thought I would drink mine from the thermos. It wouldn't cool off and if you've ever tried drinking from a thermos you will know what a lively time I had, losing most of the coffee but managing to get my medicine down anyway.

The first part of the trip the steer was lying down and quiet; but after a while he decided to stand up and then he tried to figure out a way to get out of that moving horror. He was pretty well tied around the head and one front leg, but his back legs were free and so he experimented until he found he could get one front leg and one back leg over the side of the builders' truck. I screamed, Frank stopped the car and opened the car door in the steer's face. So, he decided to get back down in the car and try another method. Frank didn't approve so he tied the back legs and so we made it in to Wema about 4:00 p.m. amid shouts of the villagers who had never seen any cattle before. We were taking a shortcut road that isn't good in a rain. I paid for it with a terrific dust cold which I'm just now conquering, but we were glad to get in that much earlier, Frank to see his wife and four children and help them pack for furlough and I to see everyone at Wema. The Coburns are in Bolenge now and will leave Friday.

I was five days at Wema and went to Boende on the fifteenth with the Weeks family to get our yellow fever shots. I stayed all night with the Williams at Boende and flew here the next day. The Weeks will come later as their furlough is also due. The Bakers are coming down, too, for furlough. We will go together as far as Rome, but I go directly to Brussels and the USA. Margaret Shaw arrived in Mondombe to take over my job three days before I left, so I got her set up at Miss Mitchell's old house with the leavings of what I had not yet sold or given away to carry on her own household until her own things could be sent to her from Lotumbe. Our new Dr. Dugan will be out here in July, but they of course will need to learn the language before they take over.

Mr. Williams at Bolenge had been very sick with infectious jaundice or something of the kind and so the doctor at Boende was asking him to stay in bed for another three weeks. The Hendersons came over from Ifumo to get their students graduating from the seventh grade at Wema and incidentally to have their station pick-up repaired. Boende is a district capital and a place to get your provisions of some kinds and they say the Monieka Mr. Johnson was there the day after I left.

I had a very rough time on the plane, although the trip is only a little less than an hour; we went through clouds gathering for a storm and were tossed about too much for my comfort. The Coburns say their trip yesterday was lovely and smooth.

The Bakers and I will be leaving here July 15 and if our reservations hold, I will be in New York July 19 and in Oklahoma City on a TWA flight at the international airport on July 21 at 4:05 p.m. I plan to go in from there by the airport bus and then take the bus out to Florence's. I will have only two suitcases; I can manage well enough. I will let you know if there are changes.

Buena Rose Stober to Friends and Family, June 27, 1960—Bolenge, Congo Belge

I am actually on my way home, but by habit I wrote Mondombe for an address. This is Bolenge and in spite of all the unrest as we near Independence Day it is still very beautiful sandwiched between the six-mile-wide Congo and a main gravel road running from Coquilhatville right through the station and on to the other towns beyond, including a big Catholic leprosarium.

I just now had a walk toward the road to see what I could see past the old church and the new one, Dr. Dye Memorial. They use the old one for Sunday School. The houses of the missionaries mostly face the river and it is really like living on a big lake, but the road only produces dust and a constant line of traveling Africans, cars, trucks, bicycles, and pedestrians about their affairs. A truck stopped by the church to pick up a group of gayly dressed women and some children with their usual load of baskets of manioc bread, clothes, etc., on their backs. The truck had a big basket of wheat flour bread, a hundred or so long loaves, receiving its portion of the dust as it was uncovered.

I walked to a little store at the end of the mission station thinking I might buy a piece of the gay native-pattern cloth to use for curtains, but the store was closed, and the owner gone to Coquilhatville.

A woman standing there greeted me. *Oleko Mama Mputu?* "Are you there, Mama Mputu?"—my Congolese name given to me by the church elders at Lotumbe thirty-six and a half years ago. The woman I didn't recognize turned out to be the widow of a fine fellow that worked for years on the mission. But he got a very vicious tumor on his jaw and since it was incurable, he went back to his village to die after consulting all our best surgeons. The wife remained faithful and as he is gone now is faced with the usual tormenting from relatives who want her married again. She says she is going to stay a widow. She was waiting for another truck to take her to Coquilhatville. Apparently, a friend who wanted to help make life easier for her told her that a certain man at Coquilhatville had a debt with him and she was to collect twenty francs of it for herself.

My space is running out, but I just wanted to write to answer your letters and tell you I'll be in Oklahoma City about July 21 if reservations unfold as they are.

Buena Rose Stober to Unidentified, June 30, 1960—Mondombe, Congo Belge

"From this time united in carrying responsibilities and our loads will be light as Jesus has said in Matthew 11:25–30. Peace be in your spirits. Amen." Bongelemba Nathaniel, Pastor.

We had all faced this Day of Independence with fear because there were so many horrible rumors going around and our nationals were very much frightened. But to waken to a beautiful morning and the news that King Baudouin was in Congo for the day and there was only peace and quiet, the inspirational service above seemed fine to share with our US Christians, so we hope you can put it to use in some way, *World Call* or other places as you see best.[3]

Coming out of the church after this fine service, two of my old Bolenge women friends, Mputu Mata and Efoli Louise, came rushing around church and calling my name, "Mama Mputu!" and we exchanged happy greetings

3. A ceremony held at the *Palais de la Nation* in Léopoldville on June 30, 1960 marked the official end of Belgian colonial rule and political independence for the Republic of the Congo. Belgian King Baudouin delivered a patronizing speech in which he described independence as the culmination of the wise colonial policies of his infamous grandfather, King Leopold II. The newly elected prime minister, Patrice Lumumba (1925–1961) made an unscheduled response to the king's speech. He angrily denounced more than sixty years of Belgian colonialism and credited independence to a grassroots nationalist movement. Stober may not have known when she wrote this letter that this exchange nearly provoked an international diplomatic crisis.

and our delight over the service. I mentioned how lovely and peaceful it was when Efoli said, "Why of course Mama. Can't you see these are the fruits of the missions' many years of service? You first find your garden plot and examine it well; then cut the underbrush; then you burn it off; then you pile the underbrush, clearing, and plant a garden; then care for it, weed, and behold you have the heaven of your work. We have grown in the spirit and can now feed others."

Buena Rose Stober to Her Diary, Undated, Unknown Location

Flight from Congo.

This being my regular furlough due in April, but I had the hope not to leave Mondombe until after July 1, but all places on the planes were taken by the Belgian government in an attempt to get their women and children of officials out of the Congo, so I had to leave June 16 and wait at Bolenge until July 15 for a plane to get to Léopoldville. As it turned out there were no planes in Boende or Coquilhatville after Independence Day, July 1. By the time planes were in flight again July 14, we women and children were all refugees in danger of attack by Congolese soldiers who had mutinied and a government too weak to control them. The Belgian army had to come in to save their own women and children.[4]

Before then in Coquilhatville all workmen put on a strike for higher wages; like their new government officials, they were asking higher pay than some of the Belgians. A mob came in to Bolenge and informed Mr. Byerlee that if his mission printers didn't quit work they would break up the machinery of the mission press. Mr. Byerlee and his men agreed that they should go home. Then Mr. Byerlee rushed to the mission dispensary to help Miss Georgia Bateman in charge of the dispensary. "Send home your nurses," cried the mob, "or we will raid your hospital." Miss Bateman pleaded for her expectant mothers, new babies, and mothers and other sick folks among them, a puny infant struggling for life. "Let them die or care for them yourself."

4. In late June 1960, the newly elected government of the Republic of Congo entered into a treaty with Belgium whereby the commissioned officers of the Force publique would remain in their posts permanently, even after independence. By July 4, noncommissioned officers went on strike and mutinied the next day. Military order broke down across the Congo as rival factions vied for control, provoking the so-called Congo Crisis (1960–1965). Throughout mid-July 1960 Belgian paratroopers evacuated the remaining Belgian citizens in direct violation of the treaty.

The strike got worse and mobs raided and looted stores and destroyed several new officials' houses. There was bloodshed in Coquilhatville and three guilty ones ran as far as Bolenge for medical care.

Then it was rumored that all high-salary Congolese would be attacked—that might be at Bolenge—and that included our teachers and some nurses, so I stayed at the maternity with Miss Bateman that night and a new boy was born. Nothing happened to the teachers and nurses but as the days went on there were so many rumors one didn't know what to believe. Our missionary men had asked the army for protection. Then the army mutinied in Léopoldville and captured the Belgian officers they had asked to stay and help them. Then our mayor was reported missing. Several Congolese officials were not seen around.

But before this the mayor had told our mission it would be very dangerous to hold the mission conference we had planned for July, so our inter-station radios were busy trying to fix a smaller conference at Wema and the mayor said, "Don't do it."

Two or three times a day our Mr. Williams of Boende tried to contact each station to keep them informed of danger. We had a secret code because we were not licensed to give news. "Storm weather" meant trouble; "itchy feet" meant danger; "scratch 'em" meant leave the post; planes were "big birds," etc.

Ifumo's Andersons had to cross three ferries to get to Boende so they were told to take their vacations now.

We listened to the radio until our ears ached. "Stand by. . . . Clarence do you read me? Over." "John, do you read me? Over." "Does anyone hear Barbara? Over." Then finally one missionary was dreaming after a night of suspense and was praying, so in the middle of her prayer she woke up telling God, "Over."

Then we heard the soldiers had been to Wema, Monieka, Mondombe, and Bolenge was surrounded a good bit of the time. Finally, we couldn't get Clarence Williams of Boende anymore.

Then we heard Wema, Monieka, and Boende were taking a plane to Belgium the very next day. Then big DC-6 planes came to Coquilhatville, landed safely, no shooting at them as the word had come through that Belgian paratroopers had taken over the airport at Léopoldville after the Congolese had tried shooting other places. There were women and children trapped in the airport at Léopoldville when the Congolese tried to take over. They were hiding behind suitcases. Boats had tried to leave Coquilhatville, but the Congolese soldiers boarded the boats and took over, but by the time we landed in Léopoldville everything was under control. We only heard a few shots in the distance, but troopers were everywhere and we were treated with fresh European fruits, candy, milk, coffee; waitresses were everywhere on the second floor. A nursery was set up with a doctor and nurse in charge, blankets were handed out and everyone was looked after. I had come as a missionary with a sick baby but otherwise we had no real pressing needs, but many were wounded and some mothers with infants only a day or two old needed the beds. A Belgian doctor's wife had brought a couple of teen-aged English missionary's girls and was taking them to England. Many others had come, even without baggage. The plane of our upriver women came too; one had some fifty women on board, forty of whom had been attacked and abused. Most of them had very little baggage. Kathryn Williams had four children and a tiny suitcase. Her youngest was Susan, my Christmas gift. Clarence was taken to the prison and his radio was destroyed (he is in the US now). No one had expected that kind of violence to innocent people, so our Congolese Christians finally discovered they couldn't protect us without being abused or even killed.

Our Christians are doing their best to hold things together. Eleven missionary men are there now, and three older single women are going back soon. How much property has been destroyed we do not know and the expenses of getting folks back is going to be terrific. Pray for them to have strength and knowledge for the job.

Buena Rose Stober to Friends, September 6, 1960—Oklahoma City, Oklahoma

Yes, I am still in existence and having a very nice time getting my new home in order while I take pills for filaria and get my teeth repaired. They needed it because I lisp, murmur, and whistle when I talk, and my family says they can't understand it with all the vacancies.

Jim, my brother, and I are aiming at getting comfortably fixed for winter. Most of the work on the utilities is in. The plumbing isn't finished yet but soon will be. They put in the water heater today. The gas pipes are in, but the companies are slow in doing their part. I can't find half my belongings in my new quarters yet, but it is getting prettier each day and ditches in the yard are disappearing.

You would have enjoyed watching the "civilizing" of Stobie: a vacuum cleaner that all but runs itself, sliced bread, buying in a supermarket, chicken dressed, cut, and ready to fry, electricity at the tip of my fingers for all the little tasks I do. No night calls for infants' arrivals even when I am lying awake in the middle of the night and have no excuse to get up and prowl and really would like to.

I have very little news of Congo Christians although the Roberts said they had a letter from Pastor Ntange. He wrote of the tremendous burdens they are carrying in the church, but they are holding on. This week four of the older single ladies have been given permission to go back to Bolenge and keep the schools going as nearly as they can be kept open. Four doctors are on the field and seven other churchmen and school men.

The Congo must be a sad, sad place now and it looks worse as days go on! Poor people, they hadn't any idea what they were getting into nor for that matter could we anticipate the violence and disturbance they are having.

Please keep praying for them and our missionaries holding on there!

Mbile Theresa, Outcast Widows Welcome

When the women of certain villages contracted leprosy, they were abandoned and left to find their own solution for their ailments and livelihood. But many times, the uninfected women were faithful to their husbands to the very last. Relatives sometimes helped and sometimes when they had older children they would help. But when the news that outcast widows were welcome at Lomina, they began walking in many times from far away, several days' journey, and often on swollen, mutilated feet, carrying baskets on their backs containing their few possessions: a few old worn-out clothes, pieces of bread of manioc, more rarely a piece of meat, a cooking pot made of clay and burned in a crude kiln, and a woven sleeping mat so worn it had many holes, or sometimes an old blanket as weaving was too difficult for leprosy's related mutilated and nerve-anesthetized fingers. Most of them were lonely, pitiful sights to see. Once I welcomed an outcast mother who had been ordered to Lomina by the father of her three children, one pulling fruitlessly at her shriveled breasts and the older two tagging wearily behind her as they finished the last seventy-five miles of their journey to their new home. The children did not have leprosy, but all were anemic and undernourished. Their poor mother was in a very serious condition but tried to find help for herself and babies.

Many times, younger outcasts would soon find a happy, kind patient as miserable as she was, and make a good match. There was always a group of older women outcasts, some actual widows, who found friendship and comfort together at the leprosarium and welcomed and helped each new one to find a comfortable place to live and good food to eat. They were almost like a club.

Mbile Theresa was one of these women outcasts, but she was already a Christian, and prayers and messages had already preceded her to Lomina. She was a neat, trim little woman but her face was blotched with reddish and blanched spots until she was no longer welcome to her husband. When she appeared at the hospital for examination and permission to enter Lomina for treatment, we all felt pity for her tired body and drawn face, the news of her arrival went ahead to announce her arrival. After her examination we were going in the truck to visit the patients, so we could give her a lift and a whole group of clapping and singing women outcasts came to meet us and take her bundles. Others knew her and embraced her, some carried her bundles and took her off to their sun-dried brick cottages, making a comfortable place for her and providing a share of their food.

Her treatment proved successful and it wasn't long until she came in asking for a job to earn money for new clothes. Her face had filled, her spots had begun to dim, and she was so full of energy, making a backyard garden of bananas, papaya, sweet potatoes, etc., and a nice jungle garden of manioc. I knew she could earn the cash she needed now.

She worked on the Lomina roads and path two or three hours a day and was finally able to buy the pretty new print she wanted. Later she found a needy husband to make happy with her devotion and energy, until they were both dismissed as cured cases.

Mangaleta

I have been asked again and again to write the story of this little girl, Mangaleta, as I know it. I wrote about her in one of my letters: "You should have been with me yesterday morning and this morning when I caused a real show by washing and dressing the ulcers on the feet of a child whose father had deserted her and her only help was the Christians of the village who were taking full care of her." The first I saw of her was when Ruth Musgrave and I had moved into the village Wafania to spend a week and some days there paying evangelists, giving credit in our records of each group of Christians offerings, and trying to make ourselves generally useful to the churches represented at the gathering from all over that district, a routine that some white missionary does for the churches every six months or so.

When I went over to the head evangelist's house, I saw what looked like a very old lady crawling from her tumbled down house to her back yard. What a house it was! The poles that were supposed to support the house and thatched roof had leaned tiredly over and the roof was all but resting on the ground. I decided to cross the street and see what was wrong with the old lady. You can't imagine my surprise when the old, dried-up lady turned out to be only a girl of about fifteen years. She was all skin and bones, and dirt and itch because they forgot to bring her water to keep clean, her hair was a bushy brown woolly mess. But her feet were the most pitiful sight I ever saw. No medicines and no relative to care for her and her feet were so completely covered with gruesome, smelly sores so she had not been able to walk for years but had crawled upon her knees that were as calloused as the bottoms of bare-footed people. She crawled in and out of her tumbled down roof on these knees since it was not tall enough even if she could stand. The Christians brought her what little food and water she had. She was a good-sized job when I started in on her the next day, too, even though I had sent her a good-sized piece of soap the night before to clean as best she could.

I gathered soap, water, iodine, cotton, bandages, forceps, and scissors and a clean piece of cloth for her, what matter if it was only the heavy green piece that went over the head of my camp cot. It was at least cleaner than anything she had seen.

I had no more than started to wash her ulcers than the crowd began to gather and it would have taken a pretty strong police billy to keep them away. I finally gave up and let them gaze.

While her feet were soaking in hot water, I proceeded to remove the wool and its inhabitants. Of course, I had her outside in the yard. Before I had finished the bath, the crowd was ahhing and oohing until I couldn't think. They exclaimed that not even her own mother would do all that. I want you to know that they stayed there during the whole clean-up and every once in a while someone would get so excited to get nearer and see that he or she would knock the fellow in front of him over. The nurses of African persuasion gave her a dose of neodiarsenol and some of the Christian men raised the roof of her house and women brought her some water. I went through the same performance every day and toward the last the crowd got a little more polite. Anyway, after the roof was raised and things cleaned up a bit, we went inside for the bath. By the time the week was up she had begun to look like a girl again and the ulcers were making marvelous progress with cleanliness, disinfection, neodiarsenol, and plenty of food.

We took her to Lotumbe with us after a month. Her ulcers were actually healed and then we began the terribly painful process of teaching her to walk again. We began with massage and straightening her legs several times a day; then making her take a step or two. What a lot of tears and begging she went through every day before we got her to walk any distance at all. Finally, I made her walk from the hospital to my house where she had fruit to eat; but, poor child, she cried every step of the way for about a week then the tears began to cease, and it was a pleasure to see her enjoy the walk, with a stick as cane, of course.

From then on, she began to like getting around everywhere and would help another crippled with ulcers, this time it was an old lady. They live together in one room of the wards. After a while one of the hospital assistants who is from her part of the country invited her to live with them, so Mangaleta had a home at last. Miss Musgrave promised her that when she could walk without the stick she would give for a new dress, so one afternoon as we were walking home from vesper services Mangaleta was ahead of Ruth Musgrave and I and suddenly she placed the stick on her head and walked off as straight as anyone, and so proud she could hardly contain her joy. She was proud of the new dress too.

Now Mangaleta comes to school every day and is learning to sew. She sings in the choir and is an inquirer for baptism. She is a sweet, nice girl and the villagers respect her.

Longondo Samuel, the Happy One

At Lomina, Mondombe's leprosarium, most of the new patients on arriving were unhappy, embittered, resentful, and too frightened of modern medical practices that they didn't wish to enter the colony for treatment of leprosy. But Longondo was the happy one.

When Longondo was born, Congo boys were rarely sent to any school before they were ten and the mission schools were the only ones anywhere around at the time. So, he hadn't but a smattering of schooling from his parents, then living on the mission. The father was a sawyer, and both were Christians. Still, they didn't see any need of keeping him in school when he could learn to fish and hunt or other things that boys like to do.

The Congolese knew very little about childhood diseases and although he was sent to the dispensary for treatments popularly agreed to the diseases the mission doctor could cure, most parents trusted in witchcraft to save their children as their parents had for many generations. It was the only help they knew about. Cleanliness and hygiene were only talked about by the missionaries, especially the nurses and teachers who taught little children, "This is the way we wash our teeth," and the motions to go with it to the tune of "Here we go round the mulberry bush." Each health rule was sung out lustily by Longondo and his friends. Leprosy or tuberculosis were nothing to worry much about unless it took its most vicious form of nodules or mutilation of the members. What is a spot here or there? But fear of being bewitched was an awesome thing and most serious diseases were caused by some evil spirit which had bewitched one. So people with various diseases or infection or contagion were only avoided when they were disfigured or pocked with some disease. Then wives were literally thrown out, husbands abandoned, and children shunned by all but mothers. Sometimes the process of seeking out someone to blame for bewitching the victim had been going on long before this.

At about ten years of age, Longondo Samuel was sent to the hospital for treatment of nodules. His parents thought he had yaws, or syphilis, or something a few years back, and the doctor and nurse looked on in wishful thinking that it might be tuberculosis of the skin. But neither would admit what they really believed: that it looked more like leprosy. And when the laboratory tests proved it was leprosy they couldn't figure out how this happy little fellow could be isolated at the leprosarium with strangers and no relatives to help him, and at first they didn't know others of his family had it too. In spite of relatives' and others' fears, soon he went gladly among patients who smoked hemp—marijuana—wrangled, and came to blows over the slightest disagreement.

The best treatment for leprosy known at the time was chaulmoogra oil injections that were painful. Diasone was being tried in the big leprosariums, but it was only experimental and many were skeptical about long range results. Many drugs only masked the disease for a while and failed.

Soon after Longondo Samuel came to Lomina they received Diasone and he received it, but it was a long time before a real improvement could be seen. Somehow, he managed to remain happy and became a loved leader of the few children who had come with their sick parents. Then at the mission whispers went around that his older brother, Balilo Thomas, a sawyer, had spots all over his body, and at the hospital checkup of all mission workmen it proved to be true. So, he came to Lomina with his young wife. He had only got to about the fourth grade in school but even so Longondo gained a home and a schoolteacher, as there were about six or eight other children needing a teacher. Some of the thirty to forty other patients were glad to have their children in school. Longondo was the only child with symptoms of the disease at the time.

They had a tiny mud hut for a school building and tore windows out of some of its mud walls to give more light. Balilo Thomas was given a primary chart for a textbook and used a dirt plot in front of the house for paper with sticks for pencils until the mission school could furnish slates and other supplies. The other children already loved Longondo Samuel, so they soon loved his big brother Balilo Thomas also. Longondo was always the leader and also the comedian. They learned many songs; they usually sang a bit off key but enjoyed them lustily.

They were making bricks at the leprosarium to build a church with funds provided by the American Leprosy Mission, and so some patients earned a little money this way and Longondo scampered out to present himself as a free brick-carrier service, and the other children followed him. Then the truck began to bring other bricks from the mission and even the adults followed and offered free labor to unload the truck.

One day the mission nurse found hemp growing in a patient's yard. They had already informed the nurse that hemp was very good for leprosy, but she told them it was against Congo law to grow hemp, and they could be sent to prison and fined if they grew it, but they still thought it was all right if they didn't get caught. She sent the school children to inspect every yard and forest garden, and of course they found it growing in one of the children's father's garden. Longondo had scampered gayly ahead of the children's inspection group and would probably have reported his own brother if he had had it growing. But his singing gave the children courage and fun, so they went through with it. The father was taken in the mission truck with his hemp to the state official, who knew and sympathized with the patients, but figured he must punish him; so, since he was too crippled to serve a prison term, he fined him a good drum to be paid to the mission as soon as it was made. The father was an expert drum maker, in spite of his crippled hands.

Longondo began to look better and to grow, and then we received large quantities of sulfatron from the American Leprosy Mission and finally the Congo Medical Association sent it regularly. At last doctors proved that the sulfone DDS would do wonders for leprosy, and it did for Longondo Samuel; his nodules disappeared and the leonine face, typical lepromatous look, began to leave. Then Longondo grew up still happier than ever and learned to make sun-dried bricks for a living.

Romance came to him too, a daughter of another patient, but the parents fought the marriage because they were Catholics and pretty heathen besides, so he lost her.

In 1960, when examining the patients of Lomina Doctor found only one active case of the one hundred left, the leprosarium was closed. From nearly three hundred patients, DDS had already brought the number down to a hundred and that year any still needing treatment could receive treatment at their nearest dispensary. Some ten or so wanted to live permanently at Lomina and received permission to do this, but happy Longondo went to his home across the river to find a wife. He was still his happy self but free of leprosy's imprisonment of pain and misery.

Jungle Reverie

Congo! With its rounds of trivialities; Congo! With its momentous problems; its gorgeous silent forests; its weird grotesque customs; its gentleness and understanding; its secrets hidden deep in the hearts of men.

Congo! With its season of swarms of white butterflies; Congo! With its plants and flowers rare; its fierce crocodiles; its leopards preying on gentle life; its animals so beautiful, so ugly, so great, so deadly, so small. Its sunrays so healthy, so hot, sometimes so lovely to see.

Congo! With its songs, wailing, joys, and sorrows; Congo! Its widow mourning for the mate she hated; its parents grieving for the child they neglected and lost; its fear of spirits and evasion of truth; its toil of death from uncontrolled diseases.

Congo! With its intricate and beautiful languages; Congo! We loathe it, and love it, and return to it; its fascinated white folks: commercial, government, as well as missionary in Congo continually; spend and are spent for this is the way our Master went.

The Cross and the Likunda

Two Sundays ago, at our dispensary Yalikungu about forty miles from Mondombe, a young man came to church wearing white trousers and a nice clean shirt, but also a horn of spirit medicine hanging under his arm, suspended by a piece of animal skin from his shoulder. This was a *likunda*, an heirloom, and he was supposed to go up and down the paths at night playing his flute made of reed and making other fearful noises to scare away the evil spirits. Someone had given him a cross as a charm, too, so he was carrying it as well.

In the service he clutched his cross and was very interested, not only listening carefully but giving a big offering. After the service we found that he wanted to become a Christian but didn't know what to do. The Congolese evangelist took charge of him after that and he was taught what it means to follow the cross.

Rice for Congo

The government agricultural department has introduced several fine new products in Congo, among them cotton of a superior quality that has made a nice income for the people of the prairie lands; but for the rainforest region, it has been more difficult. Beans, soybeans, were all tried with not too much success but an improved variety of palm nut with lots of oil and a small seed has helped the sale of palm oil and the newest is rice, upland rice, that finds just what it needs to grow well in our Mondombe field. The Africans were at first furious when they were required to clear their forest plots several acres per man per year, but when the first rice came on and they began to learn that it was good and soon that it would bring them good profit, everyone buckled under and planted.

When the first markets were opened to buy this product, the Belgian officials notified us and we could buy in quantity for the school and sick folks. They are having the rice market now and all the commercial people are following the state markets, buying and bringing their cloth and many other products to sell to those selling the rice.

I ran into them in the backcountry soon after the war closed, and these were always gala occasions. Some of the baskets of unshelled rice would weigh fifty to a hundred pounds and it was always the women who did the carrying into market; but one state official figured he would require the men to bring it in, so he told them he would fine any man who made his wives do his heavy work, but they found a way to get around him. The women carried the rice into the market either at night when everyone was asleep or brought it near and the husbands had to make the last half mile without their help;, that is, until they were caught.

They are having a rice market now across the swamp from the mission, so I strolled over to see how it went. There had been a constant stream of Congolese passing with bundles of rice done up in Congo leaves, the big cooking leaf that is two feet or more broad and a little longer. They make a basket of palm fronds lined with these leaves and if the rice isn't kept dry they cannot sell it, so it is kept on the racks over slow fires.

Everybody helps carry from ten-year-olds to grandmothers, and poor men go groaning under their share of the load as if they were the only ones who carried. Some talk at the top of their voices and others sing in unison. In fact, no matter how tired they are everyone makes a big occasion of it and knows that he or she may go back home with gay bits of cloth, knives, beads, shirts, trousers, slabs of iron to have the blacksmith make knives, spears, arrowheads, or pieces of brass for anklets for favorite wives or new ones, and soap, and you never forget to get a sack of salt.

The companies buy the unshelled rice, shell it by machine, and make a nice profit. The Congolese shell it by pounding it in their wooden mortars. We are glad to buy whatever they bring us, but sometimes it is not enough, so we must buy from companies. They of course receive a better price for the shelled rice.

Once when the market was to be held across the swamp, I heard that an old commercial friend from Wema was to be there, so I wrote a note inviting him and his company men to dinner. I was expecting two or three of them, but I got nine men and had to stretch the menu quite a bit. Being a single woman, my dog wasn't used to having that many men call on me at once and nearly bit them until she understood that it wasn't an invasion of Belgians. They were good guests and we had a nice time.

The Africans of Mondombe are learning to laugh at themselves for their earlier fears of the rice market. They love it now and make many very nice dishes with it, one of which we did in school cooking class; it was fried sweet cakes of rice and ground peanuts. And it has been a good food for infants too.

Ekila's Tragedy

One day I was at Mondombe beach receiving and directing the storing of mission supplies that had just arrived on the river steamer at the beach. There was the usual crowd of onlookers as they unloaded huge cases of medicines, heavier cases of books, and one of the missionaries' groceries. Then I remembered this was the boat that was to take Botuli to his fine new job with a very big salary from a company toward Stanleyville. He bid me goodbye, and as he passed I saw her: not his wife, but a flamboyant creature. I had heard rumors of her but could hardly believe my eyes. A model husband, a model nurse, and formerly an exceptionally devoted Christian claimed completely in front of everyone. Ekila and their four children were nowhere in sight. He was truly deserting her and the children. Perhaps as an excuse he would say he was taking her to cook for him as in a new place Ekila would find it difficult with four children and so much work.

But when I met Ekila later on the road carrying the baby, another child dragging at her shirts, and a brave little six-year-old piloting another small one behind there were only tears, bewilderment, and discouragement in the faces. She was on her way to her mother's, about twelve miles away. When I wished her a safe trip and asked what she would do, tears started again in her eyes and she answered, "I don't know" and there was no hope in her voice.

Ekila had grown up on the mission receiving most of her schooling at the Congo Christian Institute where her father was in school. Both Ekila and her mother could read and write something, rarely known among African women. She had been put in the girls' dormitory at Mondombe as her father graduated from the school and then went out into Mondombe's teaching-preaching work in the villages. Later her father took a position in a company as a clerk, but they let Ekila finish her schooling. Ekila was a happy, conscientious school girl and a leader of the girls.

Before she finished her dormitory days, her father died and her mother lived on the mission with the other children as a widow. In the meantime, Ekila had this romance that delighted her mother and all the mission. He was such a fine lad and had been first in all his classes; besides, he had taken the nurse's-aide course and was doing fine, just as his father had. His father was now a head nurse and a fine assistant to the doctor in surgery. Botuli passed his examinations for entrance into the Congo Christian Institute and they were married and off for school at Bolenge.

Their love and devotion for each other was most beautiful and an inspiration to all. Ekila also entered school, but she hadn't enough schooling to enter the institute. In two years Botuli passed the entrance examination at Yakusu Nurses Training School; this is an English Baptist accredited training school. None of our hospitals have the required number of doctors to start a school of this kind, but we were able to finance his years there.

A New Canoe to the River, Heave Ho!

Yesterday we found a new job for the car. Getting a newly hewn canoe to the river has always fascinated, as the Africans make it a gala occasion with a lot of singing, chanting, laughing, and calling back and forth, and it was a new kind of evangelistic trip for the Chevrolet panel truck.

Two of my leprosarium patients had finished hewing a three-foot-by-eighteen-foot canoe from the trunk of a big jungle tree. It was about a mile into the jungle where they had chopped down the big tree, but what a mile!

Little by little hacking away the bark with a machete, then chip by chip hollowing the inside into a perfect canoe form with a little adze, a wry little axe-like instrument fixed firmly on a short handle to hack away the tough, hard, reddish-looking wood.

Mr. Roberts took me over to the leprosarium to see my patients and then went back to get another chore done. I wanted to see the canoe they said was to be moved out and see how they did it. It is clever the way they use leverage, such as tremendous logs, as they hack away at it. They shape it in the forest first, removing the bark, then shaping the ends and removing enough wood from the center to make it light and manageable enough to pull it out of the jungle in one piece.

Even though that took several months, finishing at the water's edge will take even longer days of hacking.

Iyambe Thomas, good old elder of the church and a nurse's-aide certificate, helped them select the tree and directed the fashioning. One hewer was a fairly husky patient making a living selling canoes. The other was a fellow who was an expert but had very few fingers on his hands with which to work, and his feet were only stubs with one or two toes left. But he managed to do his share and since he felt much stronger after the new drugs he went back to his old job along with several hewers in the leprosarium who found it a profitable business if the canoes were good. This one was for the mission and around $20.00. Now Iyambe was with us to supervise getting it out of the forest. We climbed under, over, and through vines and shrubs, walked through gardens of manioc, Congo's bread, over ant hills, sliding every which way until the swamp gave way to higher ground. We went through another garden and at last reached a place with mammoth trees towering over our heads and less green underbrush to ensnare us. How would they ever get an eighteen-foot canoe between those giants? But when we reached the log that was now a canoe we were in a clearing with stumps and branches everywhere.

I stood by watching this while the crowd of men, women, and children who had followed us tied a big strong vine to the end of the canoe, others hunted poles about the size of fence posts and laid them in the path in front of the canoe. The huskiest men got a firm hold of the canoe vine and experimented with its strength and theirs. There was a lot of shouting, chanting, and running about, and a pretense at moving the canoe, and before I knew it here it was bumping along over and around the stumps and branches, and we had left its old home behind and were threading through the big trees. Next came the swamp and all the time the canoe was rolling over those fence poles that never ran out as the young ones would grab up the old ones as soon as the canoe had rolled over them, then they would rush to the head of the line of shouting, singing, chanting people and put them down in a line for the canoe to roll over.

Thirty or so Africans were pulling at the vine at the signal from the leader of something like, "Heave Ho!" and believe it or not, that big log that was once a forest giant went rolling out of the jungle at an amazing pace. Then there would be a rest and much talking, then "Heave Ho!" and off it went again, the poles under it often as not turning over until the canoe past and someone grabbed them to rush them up in front again. Some places it looked impossible to me, but they managed it even through the swampy places and the edge of the gardens, or if an anthill couldn't be circled they went over it until at last we were in front of the leprosarium dispensary and here was Mr. Roberts ready to put his Chevrolet to work finishing the job, nearly three miles. Some children tried to climb it and to have a special kind of ride, but Mr. Roberts warned them that it wouldn't be so much fun if they got hurt as it was pretty dangerous, so they stayed off, but the troubles were not over. Then the canoe came untied and was left behind, so we had to go after it, but finally we reached the dike over the swamp near the mission where the canoe was to be tried on the water. We had passed a group of leprosarium women who watched the canoe untied and launched, dancing away on the river as if it was glad to be there. The hewers got in the canoe and paddled it out to the river to the mission beach where they were to finish their work of art.

Victory Following Death

The three- or four-year-old girl fell into an animal trap and was run through by one of the sharpened stakes, piercing her abdomen through the intestines. Careless people had set the trap in a concealed pit not far from the village, and two children of careless parents played too near to it. They carried her for the four days to the hospital and she made a brave fight for her life, but it was too much to ask.

Another heathen couple didn't bring their pregnant daughter until it was too late and then didn't tell the entire story, so we lost the infant before we found out.

Another young girl was brought to the hospital and a caesarean quickly performed by the doctor saved a nice big boy. We were all broken up about the mother, but the baby likes his bottles and his grandmother. What diplomats these Congolese are. The grandfather named the infant Victor after a very important Congolese official, Ilikya Victor. Ilikya's sister was in the hospital at the time so they knew Victor would receive nice presents as his namesake was wealthy. The sister really took tiny Victor under her wing and it wasn't long until grandmother sent for a granddaughter to help her carry the infant around and get his bottles of milk. She is a very sweet girl and did everything we told her conscientiously.

In later years this girl grew up and became the wife of our extra special student, Mbenga Paul, who has been to various schools, was director of the Congo Christian Institute, and is now studying in the USA.

An Evangelistic Student Lost

Tragedy stalked our station all day yesterday and all the night before; frantic drum messages boomed out from village to village. One of the student evangelists had gone with a group of others for Sunday afternoon preaching service at the leprosarium three miles from Mondombe, but he didn't return with the others and they thought he had gone to look at his traps in the jungle. But when it got dark he was still not home. Since he was a good hunter no one thought much about it. Some thought he might have fallen in an animal trap, others thought he had been caught by a leopard, still others thought he could have fallen into a little swift stream he had to cross and became ensnared in the branches under the stream and was sucked under. Half the students were out hunting him the next day and the drums continued to wail all day. Along about 5:00 p.m. the cry went up that he had come walking in, a little weary and hungry, but fine. It seems that he had seen wild pig tracks and tried to follow them, then a big rain came on and finally he found he was lost and it was getting too dark, so he slept in the forest and started to find his way back the next morning. You have no idea how tangled and how alike forests can be when you are on a much-used path, but the deep forest can really take you around in circles.

When he finally stumbled onto a path and followed it to a village he was some twenty miles from home. But at least he was able to come home.

Fights, Foods, and Wives

Miss Mitchell, Dr. Baker, and the elders of the church spent hours last night trying to quiet one of the angry nurses. He thought his wife had been eyeing another man, but he himself had not been blameless through the years. The only result they got from their long session with the screaming culprits, each telling their side and making it worse, was a final declaration from the nurse that if she came into his house again, he would kill her. They finally decided to take him to the state official at the prison and see what he would suggest. They decided to leave him in prison a day or so until he cooled off a bit. As the Congo proverb goes, "If a thing exceeds in heat, cool it off a bit."

On his way to the prison, the doctor left me off with my rations for the cripples and invalids of the leprosarium. There were about twenty of them and many other patients who liked to buy the products we brought for them. The twenty were paid for by the government medical, as most of them were pretty helpless. I had rice, at least half a sack; peanuts, some twenty-five pounds; a ten-pound drum of palm oil; a few bunches of palm nuts for their oil; salt; dried fish; and manioc bread in great lumps wrapped in large leaves.

There was a great deal of noise and I found a fight in full swing. A big woman was trying to beat the head man with a huge piece of wood. They were so mad I suspected hemp smoke at the bottom of the fight, and perhaps it was, as often it happens as the leprosy patients think that hemp is a good treatment for leprosy. It makes them forget their troubles and fears, but it makes them very quarrelsome. Add that to the fact that many of them are miserable and disgruntled with life, you can see why it leads to fighting. However, this fight seemed almost impossible to settle and after we got them calmed down a bit, we decided to ask all the culprits and witnesses to come into the station and seek Pastor Ntange's diplomatic help.

One patient, Nkoi Louis, was an epileptic and believed to have an evil spirit and the poor soul was nearly deserted at the leprosarium until an ex-wife, who also had a bad case of leprosy, came in for treatment. We all thought it was a wonderful solution to his problem, but his family thought differently and the kinder Christians wanted her to live with him. She went about his care happily, but her family were determined and this fight grew out of the mess they made. The big woman was her sister and just where the head man got in I am not sure, I couldn't tell, but he was one of the same tribe as the woman. At any rate he got a bloody crack on the head and was pretty mad about everything. At last, they agreed to leave hemp out of their gardens and listened to Pastor Ntange's advice to let the woman live as a widow and another Christian woman cooked for the poor old fellow.

Later as we drove back to the hospital that day there was a loud crowd milling around, state police on guard, and terrific wailing going on. A nearby villager had stolen the wife of another man and the culprit got stabbed; he died before they reached the hospital. Doctor signed the death certificate and got rid of them.

There was even another palaver of the same kind before evening, not so serious but shocking because it was a student evangelist. No one was hurt.

Two Flames Lighted

When I think of Inkema Jean, captain of the SW *Oregon*, and Njoji Mark, long-time pastor of Bolenge church, and their many flames lighted in the hearts of Congolese and whites I think of this poem:

And when my dying flame / flickers slowly or suddenly out, / Let there be no sadness / or mourning or wailing about. / And let there be no / afterglow the light to mar / but another flame lighted / sending its rays afar.

In 1923 Njoji Mark was doing a tremendous service for Christ and had a very great influence over many people. He was against the buying and selling of daughters and determined that whatever a man's family gave for his daughter, he would receive nothing but a sum of money to put in the bank for the young couple to use, but it was not to be so. When Sal Bombongo was ready to be married, Bofala Anoka, Mark's relative, broke his vows for him. What man is sole owner of his daughters in a big clan and big family like Mark's, the son of a famous medicine man! He had to accept the money exacted by the family and divided according to their dictates, even if he was an important man. By the time his second daughter was ready for marriage, he had fully submitted to the family's wishes.

1946. As he grew older he found it increasingly hard to submit to demands of younger, better educated men even though they had not spent the time studying in the United States. Like most of us, he couldn't help but be a bit jealous, disgruntled, and unhappy to learn he was no longer leading. Unfortunately, he tried solving it by taking an extra wife and leaving Amba as a cast-away widow. She has not wavered through the years but remained a faithful Christian.

1960. Mark was now an old man, returned to the church and still able to preach a powerful sermon and have a powerful influence in spite of his past. His weakened flame has lighted other lights along the way of life.

1923. When I first met Bofale Anoka, I was just a new missionary arriving on the big boat at the pier of Matadi. The Byerlees had brought him down with them as a treat to see the ocean and we five young green things were to take him back to Bolenge. We didn't know enough about Congo of course and didn't give him much money, and on his part, he was so green he probably was frightened and often spent more than was necessary. The Swedish missionaries were looking after him until we came as they knew a little of our upriver languages, but suggested we ask an American missionary going home about paying him for his services to our well-being. We did this but Bofale told us afterward that a Swedish mission Congolese told him he ought to steal our missionaries' nice shirts and sell them for the extra money he needed, but Anoka had been taught by Mark and would not do it.

We were taking a number of larger goats to Bolenge for the mission, so Anoka took the burden of their care on the train trip. We had chickens, too, and we were too green to realize what a burden they were. Then to clap the climax, Bofale received a telegram that his father had died and he must hurry home to inherit the twenty or so wives of his father. Poor boy was really in a jam as he was determined to marry Bombongo Sala. He didn't want the harem but only Sala and he had to dispose of the other women who of course had to have homes. He made it against all his heathen relatives wishes and married his Sala. He attended the Congo Christian Institute and was very proud when Sala was able to enter these more advanced classes.

1946. Now Bofale became director of the Bolenge school and helped in this position for many years, a fine influence for all the children who went through his school.

1960 found him resigning to retire after I am sure he had lighted many new flames for Christ, and he will probably continue to do just this.

1923. Inkema Jean, captain of the SW *Oregon*, was stolen as a little boy and taken to a faraway tribe, but when he was school age somehow he came to the Congo Balolo Mission working north of our Disciples field. They were a union English mission, and when Jean was a young man he came to Bolenge and received training as our steamer captain. He had married a Christian who had formerly owned slaves. When he took the steamer to Lotumbe he found his own mother and his old home as his mother recognized his tribal markings and began screaming, "That is my boy that was stolen!" while Jean quietly brought the boat into the beach.

He became one of the best captains on the river and many was the missionary that found a safe, quiet rest going to his station on the boat, and many are the Congolese that can say he heard Inkema Jean preach the gospel first at his night being beached at his home village. Many a missionary was wakened at 5:00 a.m. hearing the singing of Jean and his crewman and hearing the short, to-the-point talk and the prayer for the safe journey, and often remembered and repeated the talk in his own sermons.

Companies tried to entice him away from the mission by higher pay and bigger boats, but he had one answer to them all: "I want to preach the gospel of Jesus Christ and will serve where he sends me."

1960 found the *Oregon* rotted out and sunk in the bottom of the Congo and Jean, so dear to all of us, was an old man who had had a stroke and couldn't do much except sit on his porch and visit with his words of wisdom with whoever came to see him and retiring missionaries must see him before they leave. How many lights he has lighted we can never know, but Lomela his nephew was one of them; whatever fine he has in him he was guided to something better by his uncle.

1923. Lomela was a problem child in the Bolenge village and as he grew to manhood, Jean and Rose probably had many gray hairs because of him. He had so many difficulties, most of which were other men's wives, until at one time he was forbidden to come on Bolenge station. Jean and some of us kept on believing in this happy-go-lucky young man, but after a while when he had more than one wife, the latest victim nearly succeeded in killing him with a knife. He survived but Jean finally found him a nice, quiet, sweet girl and he was frightened enough I suppose to settle down. He went to Léopoldville to attend the school for steamer captains, taking his wife along, and they soon had a daughter. He received his captain's license and was given a steamer: at first small, then larger and larger, until he had a big freighter from Léopoldville to Stanleyville; through all that lovely expanse of islands and channels, big and little, he made his way from month to month. At Léopoldville he became interested in holding the Lonkundo-speaking Christians together who would meet him there.

Later he worked for Pan American Airlines and was our last sight of Congolese but went back to his captaincy and probably is still at it. But we know he used the light Jean gave for many people in his travels.

Star, Etoci Louisa

There was a new light, a star, in Mondombe as early as 1929. Miss Williams, Mondombe's missionary nurse, started training young African women as nurses. Her first two were Emili and Etoci Louisa. Emili was the young wife of a nurse and Etoci, or "Star," was the wife of a student evangelist. Etoci is still nursing in Mondombe's hospital maternity ward, giving light and encouragement and good advice besides good care to the young and old and often very frightened new mothers who have seen Congo mothers and babies weaken and die for no reason except their ancient belief that they had an evil spell cast over them. They even resorted to naming their little ones such names as "Runt" or Etuli to discourage the evil spirits so that they would ignore their babies. Others would tell no one but the helper that they were expecting their infants soon and when they came to call the nurse or doctor for help they would whisper the news so that no evil spirit could hear and destroy the infant or mother. Everyone loved babies, but tropical disease took an amazing toll on the newborn babies, from 50 to 75 percent in some areas, until no mother dared make preparation for her infant's arrival for fear an evil spirit would find out.

Early in 1931 when Etoci's husband finished his studies and was ready to go tell the "good news," as evangelism was called, they packed for a faraway village. Etoci had learned to give many kinds of treatments: hypodermic injections, among others, also injections into the muscle or into the vein. Emili had run off with another man and her training had stopped, so there was only Etoci, "Star," to take a light into those faraway villages. She was given a thermometer and two woolen squares for hot fomentation treatments. Each evangelist received sulfur for itch, a little boric acid, and ten or so quinine tablets, so that was all she had besides a store of practical knowledge.

Several months later there was a bad epidemic of influenza and people were dying all around, but a proud villager brought the report that the people were delighted over Etoci's wisdom as not one of her patients died. She later came to be known as one of the family although Longomo, her husband, was a good worker too. It was often, "Oh you mean Longomo the husband of Etoci, the little nurse."

Sometime in 1937 Longomo contracted tuberculosis and died at Mondombe early in 1939. A widow's life in Congo is very sad and usually very cruel and hard because the man's relatives always accuse the woman of killing or bewitching the husband. She is beaten by his relatives, all her clothes and property, such as the sewing machine Longomo had given her, even her pots and pans were taken by his relatives. A widow has to be good and pretend grief, so she throws off her clothes, wallows in the dirt and mud, cuts her hair, and wails and screams at the top of her voice and will neither eat nor drink for days. She does little or no bathing and often rubs herself with ashes or white clay. Her relatives are fined and must pay a large sum of money or goods to his family.

After much arguing, palavering, and many beatings when her family has satisfied the greed of his relatives, she is free to hunt another husband, but it is several months or many years even. In the meantime, she lives with his people and sometime a man of the family, young or old, may like her and take her as his wife, so of course that settles the debt, or there might at least be some money or things to be paid by the new husband. She takes off her morning clothes, bathes, lets her hair grow again, and her relatives or the new husband present her with a bright new piece of cloth.

Etoci went through all this patiently and courageously and everyone was happy when her time of mourning ended and her brother, the head of the family, had already secretly begun accepting advance payments from another young man. During the mourning, the missionaries tried to help save some of her property which was still locked up in the house, a little mud hut where Longomo and Etoci had left their things when they came in for his treatment. But native customs were stronger than all the persuasion, so she lost everything, even her fomentation blankets and thermometer.

She was given work helping prepare infants' milk and later with cooking for certain patients in need. Everyone loved Etoci. She even helped teach the dormitory girls how to prepare the babies milk, but her relatives were restless and impatient for money from her so eventually they made her unhappy and restless too. She finally became enamored with a young fellow who had a wife and two infants, but who had run off from him. How much Etoci's brother had to do with arranging their match before Etoci even knew or anyone else, no one knew. The young man was a Christian and they decided they could be happy together as he, too, wanted to be an evangelist.

His first wife was not a Christian and the relatives had refused to let her live with a Christian, so he turned to Etoci.

Again, she entered school for evangelists' wives. He was not very strong and it wasn't long until he was known to have epileptic seizures and probably some old chronic infection, insufficiently treated earlier. In 1944 Etoci came back to the hospital to receive further training in women's and children's care and maternity work. She was and is a big help in the work for mothers and babies.

Her second husband died in the fall of 1944 but we were determined that she should not go through the beatings and starvings she had endured before, so the first night she slept in my office and after that she lived in the girls' dormitory where she was loved and useful in serving as assistant matron in one of the buildings.

She has a sense of humor besides being kind and useful anywhere. She has gradually lost nearly all her teeth before dental work was begun at Mondombe, so when every one of the nurses came in for dental care, she came too, grinning and causing everyone to laugh at her nearly empty mouth. No two teeth left hit the others, so she chewed with her gums as big as if she really accomplished something.

One day when the missionary nurse recounted some slip of memory, she admitted she was getting old, too, and proceeded to tell how she was peeling her manioc just taken from the swamp where it had been soaking the required time to remove the poisonous acids in bitter manioc. She caught herself half-finished with the thick peelings carefully stored in her dish while the edible manioc had been tossed away in the swamp. This was a big, starchy tuber of forearm-sized chunks which she had intended to use in making her cakes of bread.

After Independence Day in Congo her assistant and she carried on the maternity work without missionary help and letters from her indicated she was enjoying it and other mission work, especially the woman's meeting which she reported to have been continually on the job. They reported thirty-five to fifty women each week at this meeting and almost three times as much offering as they had given before Independence, so Etoci and her friends are still being stars in the service of the church.

Bosenga Mark, We Are God's Seeds

Years ago in Africa, boys and girls, and especially girls, found it a chore to pray or sing or speak in public. Some adults, too, especially women, found it very difficult as many have no schooling, or very little, and reciting in class was hard too. So, they started on Friday night what was near to Christian Endeavor, and in the Congolese language was called *Eboko ea Mameka*, "The Church of Trying." Teenagers in their early years and younger boys and girls rarely got a chance, so a group was started for them. Many times, they were children who had only been in school a year or less. Very few village girls went to school, although a few Christian parents insisted and sometimes sent their daughters to the station's girls' dormitories.

Brave efforts to lead a song, pray, or speak their thoughts on the subject brought forth a series of wiggles and giggles, or once on her feet she would burst out with, "Now I don't laugh at me," and turn her back to the audience as she began. Separating this group from the older ones did help.

It was the same thing in the women's meeting, only a few brave souls would pray or lead the singing. Women had been shushed so long and beaten for nearly anything, the girls had rarely seen their mothers pray or sing and never speak in public, so many good thoughts of their mothers were missed. They were embarrassed just like the girls, and would more often than not pick their noses, scratch, and/or re-tie their wraparound skirt before they could get started.

In the meeting, if a boy dared giggle at the girl's embarrassment, that was the end of the effort. We met at the school and had a long table at which sixty or so boys and girls were seated, we had only kerosene lanterns, and the boys vied with each other to lead, read, pray, or sing. Many of them even made fine comments on the lesson, but the girls were brave only with the singing.

One of the boys made a fine talk that stayed with me all these years as I am sure it has for many of the boys and girls in the group that night. His name is Bosenga Mark, but his later years are forgotten to me. His topic was, "We Are the Seeds of God." And he read from 1 Corinthians 3:1–11.

Many of the boys and girls in that group were leaders, preachers, and teachers. Several girls are now leaders in Mondombe's women's meetings, mothers of large happy Christian families, not afraid to speak up and try to give their children a real Christian home. The CWF in 1961 at Mondombe sent me a report of their meetings during that year of rioting and independence. They averaged between thirty-five and fifty at each meeting and their offering had tripled even though many of their husbands hadn't been paid regularly.

Someone planted the seed long ago, others watered, and God has given the growth. The boys of that meeting are now the leaders in the church who have insisted on giving the girls a better education and starting the school for advanced girls at Bolenge. Some of the girls now in school are daughters of those girls and boys who were truly God's seed. They are ashamed the

Congo women are so backward and determined to correct it. God has given the growth.

"For we are fellow workmen for God. You are God's field, God's building. . . . Let each man take care of how he builds upon it. For no other foundation can anyone lay than that which is laid, which is Jesus Christ" (1 Corinthians 3:9–11).

Burns

When I went to Congo in 1923, I had no idea how many kinds of burns I would have to learn to treat or fail with many patients. There were epilepsy patients burned terribly because no one watched close enough and of course when a seizure came and the patient was near an open fire there were some terrible burns. A teenaged girl at Lotumbe was scarred from head to foot with burns. She had no near relative to look after her and in my first year at Lotumbe she was always at the dispensary with a burn just healing or newly burned.

There are the usual run of burns while cooking, blacksmithing burns, palm oil catching fire can cause some bad burns. Once I treated a wife that had been beaten by her husband with a fire brand. I was furious enough to beat him in my rage but was busy with her suffering.

Two men were left at Lotumbe as a small steamer went on its way. The letter said the boiler had exploded and would I kindly take care of these two workmen. They both died soon after they arrived.

There was always another type of burn at the hospital and they were usually deep and needing expert treatment and skin grafting which they couldn't get in many places in the Congo, let alone at a dispensary run by a nurse.

One horrid burn taught me a native proverb so that I will never think of it without seeing a month-old baby with its charred legs, swollen and helpless, whining its pitiful hopeless whines and a mother rocking back and forth wailing for her own negligence. "The first child is burned with fire, after that you learn wisdom." She had gone to sleep on the sleeping mat on a low bed near an open fire, her husband comfortably on the other side of her, and the infant rolled into the fire. We tried to help but the burns were too deep and covered too much skin.

Smoking native tobacco in bamboo water pipes is a continual source of burns that take time. It seems that they get so much nicotine that they faint and fall in the fire unconscious until someone pulls them out.

Many tribes thought that heat was a good treatment for broken bones, but at Mondombe they were specialists at it, burying the broken member in the ground and building a fire over the break. Nearly every time the tissue under the fire was burned and made a terrible condition. One of Mondombe's older nurses has a foot so crooked he can only walk on the toes. A broken back was treated this way and brought to me to heal, the back and the burn deep into the buttocks, so deep that great chunks of flesh fell out.

We had some modern burns that nearly turned my hair gray. To break Mondombe's habit of having such a terrific fire for a mother and newborn baby we used hot water bottles that Louisa or her helper were supposed to fill for the mother and infant in its little bed. Grandma thought they should be steaming hot and in spite of Louisa's instructions to call her when filling was needed, several babies received terrific burns until we threatened to take the bottles away entirely.

A white man leaned over a barrel of gas with a cigarette in his mouth, and he lived, but we could hardly believe it. A Congolese chauffeur for the government went to the garage at night to put gasoline in his truck as he had a long journey for the next morning but he was carrying a Coleman lamp and his bucket for the gasoline leaked. In spite of the flame around his legs he managed to roll the car out of the garage and saved it but spent months and months in our hospital and in the government hospital and even when he was well one leg never did straighten out. He used crutches for years but has finally gotten well enough to use just one.

The Rejoicing and Wailing Railing

My back porch along the railing is more or less bedlam from 5:45 a.m. until 9:00 a.m. or later when all the baby stomachs are comfortably full of powdered milk formula, egg, orange juice, papaya, gruel, greens and palm-oil gravy, bananas, avocados, soybeans, milk, peanut milk, or several of these foods. We have two little three-week-old babies whose mothers have been sick and do not have enough milk, so they wail a good bit until orange juice, egg, and milk are sufficient to satisfy them. Two of the older four lost their mothers and two other mothers lacked enough milk. If you can picture all these chocolate babies with their mothers sitting against the railing on the back porch being fed one of the various foods mentioned and wailing frantically when the food fails to come fast enough you will see me at home at breakfast time.

Three babies are about a year old and so are preparing to leave us. Each mother and foster mother has learned to care for their infant with Congo foods. Two are already taking unsteady steps; and two are trying to stand alone. Sound little teeth have been showing themselves to prove that these foods have been the right kinds to build sound bodies. It is all very gratifying to see them grow and the mothers make a regular picnic of it showing off their progress, but it isn't especially quiet and peaceful nor should we like it that way.

One of the dormitory girls comes every morning and evening to help wash their bottles and prepare the fruit and milk before she and I go to school or hospital at 6:00 a.m. and then she comes back after school at 8:30 a.m. again. Each girl takes a turn of a month learning and helping. They receive two francs extra a week so of course they like it. We prepare the peanut milk, Klim, gruel, or soybean milk for the day and the mothers take enough with them to last from 9:00 a.m. to 5:00 p.m. The rest we keep in the Frigilux and they come for it in the evening.

At present, after my breakfast the fifteen dormitory girls are coming also to my back porch to cut, fit, and sew their new print dresses. They are embroidering a chain stitch around the necks and their initials in a little square on the right side. Once a year they make their dresses entirely by hand and at other times by machine. We will soon have finished the dresses and the three older babies will have gone home but who knows but others may have come by that time.

Add to all the above confusion a tailor making me eight new white uniforms in my office, my cook getting breakfast, and a typist typing a revision of *Infant Care* in Lonkundo working on the front porch, a boy who cares for the rabbits coming after corn, etc., my dog Cappy and my yellow cat milling in and around the confusion and you have the picture, but we do get fed, taught, and our sewing and typing finished too.

Ekila and Botuli

Ekila was always happy and devoted to Botuli, but they had some difficult times at Yakusu. In the very first they were too trusting and left some of their baggage unguarded. The river people there are famous for fishing in the rapids. They have the largest canoes I ever saw, hewn from tremendous trees. They are also famous for one other thing: their thieving ability around unsuspecting whites or blacks, and they have been known to unlock a suitcase beside the bed where the owner was sleeping unsuspecting. You learn to lock things well when you visit there.

Botuli's father and I visited Stanleyville and took a special time out to visit the hospital at Yakusu and were delighted to find how all the staff praise

Botuli and Ekila for their dependability and fine reputation. His grades were the highest whatever subject he studied, but the English surgery nurse said he was the best they ever had and they would like to keep him.

When their first baby was born, Botuli wrote that he was not feeling well and it was all he could do to get through school. Then he began to show signs of tuberculosis and finally he had to be sent home for complete bed rest and treatment.

He kept studying flat on his back through Dr. Baker of Mondombe and the doctors of Yakusu's guidance and took their examinations regularly so that finally when he was negative and recovered long enough to have his strength back, they let him come back and finish the time he lacked to graduate. He managed again with honors and then came back to help us at Mondombe.

Doctor called him the Mondombe "one man hospital," he was so efficient. Other children came to Ekila and Botuli and they were so proud of them and together they became leaders of the young people.

Finally, rumors were floating around that he was courting another woman. We didn't believe it, but Ekila came one day to consult Doctor about what to do about the other woman and of course he counseled her to call Botuli in for a talk. It didn't work and Botuli began seeking a higher-paid position and permission to leave. When a summons came for a big company at Stanleyville, we were all broken-hearted but could do nothing. Poor Ekila and the babies wandered back and forth from her mother's to her in-laws and her old home like a lost soul.

Then after several months Botuli wrote and sent money for her to bring the children and join him and told her in glowing terms about his fine position and a lot of money. She went, but the other woman stayed on too; and finally, Ekila bowed to his wishes and became the wife in a harem in order to have a home and a father for her children.

Ntange Timoteo's Sermons

Pastor Ntange was an artist at weaving around some incident or Scripture and making a most efficient sermon such as "Not Putting Your Trust in Worldly Goods and Glory." He tells about the most beautiful forest tree that looked impossible to cut down and finally when it came crashing down it was found to be eaten out of the core by hundreds of termites.

He preached a splendid sermon about the example we set for others. He told about a very short, insignificant looking man of Yolombo who was a very brave Christian in that heathen country where Christianity had so very little encouragement. When this man's father died he was staunch enough not to accept the honor of his father's "chief of the hunt," as they call the one directing their hunts. Meat was so important and rather scarce that many African languages have a special name for meat hunger, *jilo*. In fact, it is so bad in some places that there is a protein deficiency disease that produces very serious complications, one less serious one is that the hair turns reddish, and the Africans do not like red hair; they look all washed out and of course they really are washed out, anemic and pretty listless.

The old village elders had spent days in the forest with their weird incantations, communing with the spirits of the hunt, only to come back with a decision that the spirits said they would accept no other chief of the hunt other than the son of their old chief. When he refused because it was so bound up with heathen practices, they trumped up a cause and sent him to prison. He served his sentence and much to their surprise when he came out still refused to accept the great honor of the chief of the hunt. But many villagers accepted Christ because of his bravery and now there is a flourishing church were once it had little chance because God gave this little man courage to stand by his convictions.

Pastor Ntange also told the story of the fish, Lokombe, which swims a very crooked course. The parents kept complaining because all their children were laughed at by the other fish. The parents taught them to no avail and the bewildered fish infants said to their parent, "We can't seem to go straight, you swim ahead of us and we will follow you." So, the parent fish led a course far from straight with many curves and turnings. Then Pastor Ntange mentioned how we, too, lead our children or new Christians exactly the same course that we follow. Our course should be set by Christ.

The he visited a big coffee plantation across from Mondombe once where they were dismissing workmen right and left during World War II. They had something over eight hundred African workmen, but later when their expenses exceeded their profits they had to cut down workmen. Even the lovely big director's house was standing idle and workmen's houses were falling down in disuse. Pastor Ntange said we must trust Christ and warm ourselves with his abundant living.

Another time Ned and Jewell Roberts translated this prayer of Pastor Ntange's about likening us to a palm tree: May thy faith grow strong as the trunk of a tree in hearts. / May thy grace sink deep in our hearts as the roots of a tree. / May thy love grow within our hearts as the branches, filling them completely.

Lofaka, the Big Chief's Son

One day a very big man came shuffling into the hospital, his feet swollen and ulcerated from his two-hundred-mile walk from his home in a village of Lomela. It was not difficult to diagnose his ailment as leprosy of the most vicious type, because of his leonine-looking face with lumpy cheeks, nodules on his earlobes, and on his nose. If you didn't know you might think he was a very tall, fat man; but experience had taught us that it was very sad in serious cases of leprosy, very hard to cure with causing a variety of miseries to the human body. Your heart gripped you with sympathy. All the laboratory tests proved positive for the bacillus of Hansen's Disease, or leprosy. He was sent to the headman of Lomina to arrange his new home.

Lofaka Antoine told us his story: he was the son of the chief of Lomela, a very rich and influential man who had been treated several years before at our hospital when he arrived in a big truck with baggage and servants and wives in such numbers we had trouble finding sleeping places for them all. His sickness was not leprosy but a chronic incurable disease that the doctor could only relieve a little. Later he went home to die. He had a tremendous reputation for leading in a famous fight when the Belgian government was trying to rid Congo of Arab slave traders. He won his part of the war and settled down afterward in his fame to build up a harem of some three hundred wives, one of whom was Lofaka's mother who seemed to be forgotten by the chief and probably the son also. But the son was a big fellow like his father and we realized afterward that he had inherited and improved on some of his father's talents.

Lofaka came with a card from the Wescot Mission of Sankaru stating that he was seeking Christianity, so our Lomina evangelist took charge of him, piloted him through to Christ and understanding more of his way of life. He was very much in earnest about seeking Christ and in fact about most things he did, so people began to respect him. New patients were told to seek a craft or some means of making a living: hewing canoes from trees; blacksmith work making knives, spears, arrowheads, hoes, axes; gardening and selling produce; weaving baskets, rugs, mats, etc., from reeds and other material from the forest. Some were carving statues from wood and some from ivory. He had seen some of the lovely work in ivory so that fascinated him, and he began to learn to carve with wood, then ivory: elephants, crocodiles, antelope, and finally people. If he had a model, he could copy almost any piece. The Mondombe people had done very little carving of ivory except war clubs and hunting horns, so there was a small market for his art, and he made a living.

He became a good Christian and finally even found a Christian widow of a fellow who had worked on the mission for years but had recently died; so it last this big husky man had a good wife; since he had plenty of relatives he had a family that he could remember and love. So, happiness and usefulness came to Lofaka and strength to follow his trade, but it was some time before we had the pleasure of seeing his nodules disappear and his face lose its leonine look. Finally, his feet cleared up and he walked down the road with all the confidence of the healthy man, having made a place for himself.

His confidence and sincerity and his Christian life had a fine influence at Lomina. When the leprosarium closed because only one positive case out of a hundred remained, any patient who wished to could make it his or her home; he and his wife stayed on and we hear of their faithfulness every so often.

Seven-Minute Speech

In Congo you have three doctors and two nurses working hard to lower the death rate. Fifty to 75 percent of the babies born die in their first year of life because of ignorance and disease. When any of our six stations are left without a doctor or nurse to check that death rate, you will hear some mothers and fathers wailing for their little ones. For the parents who live close to the mission station, we have baby clinics each week where these babies can be weighed, examined, and treated. How terrible is the despair of a mother who has carried her baby on her back a hundred miles only to find that she has arrived too late. Last year when I was returning to Lotumbe, where they had no doctor or nurse for months after Dr. Davis left, our steamer beached a short distance below Lotumbe as we are usually glad to have a walk in the village. We passed a dilapidated mud hut, a weak little voice called out, "Mama Mputu, have you forgotten me?" At first, I didn't recognize her and then she pushed the stump of her footless leg out from under her skirt. She was the frail little mother of Elimawela, the baby we had fed in 1930 and 31. The mother had lost her foot in the Rubber War, Africa's introduction to white man's greed. She had not been strong enough to feed any of her several babies, and they had each in their first year of life starved to death. She and her wrinkled old husband had brought Elimawela, the last child who was far on her way to starvation, because they had heard we cared for and saved such little ones. They were not quite brave enough to ask outright for help, so they carried Elimawela past our house until we saw her and begged them to bring her for milk and care. She is a pretty healthy child of nine years now, but her mother is again wailing because of the death of the baby boy. I scolded her, "Why didn't you take your baby to Lotumbe?" And she answered, "They told us that there was no doctor or nurse at Lotumbe." We had failed her again. I wonder how much of the 50 to 75 percent death rate we could check if we had at least a doctor and a nurse on each station. As it is, nurses seldom have the privilege of working with a doctor.

When I began work at Lotumbe, I found six children with yaws contracted from untreated cases in the backcountry. If a white doctor or nurse had been there, they would have been treated; but the native nurses are not authorized by the government to give such treatments.

The population of Congo is rapidly decreasing because of disease. The natives are really dependent on us. We need a real nurse training school but since the government requires two doctors and two nurses at any hospital training nurses, we do not qualify. We cannot have anything but aid nurses who have little standing in the eyes of the government. Dr. Baker has done an outstanding piece of medical work in Mondombe, besides the regular hospital work where over 150 patients are examined and treated by Dr. Baker and fifteen native nurses. He has five rural dispensaries that have to be visited once a month and that means at least one week of his month. He has four other dispensaries, a coffee plantation, and once a year he makes a medical census of at least ten thousand Africans. Goldie Alumbaugh treks through water over her waist once every three months to keep open another dispensary on a coffee plantation.

There is an African proverb which says, "Let us leave landmarks." All our mission work and missionaries need medical care. Shall we leave landmarks in graveyards or by healthy, wholesome Christian people?

Bibliography

American Leprosy Missions. *Ministry of the Disciples of Christ to the Victims of Leprosy*. New York: American Leprosy Missions, 1957.

Anet, Henri. "Protestant Missions in Belgian Congo." *International Review of Mission* 28, no. 3 (1939) 415–25.

Armstrong, W. D. *Sunrise on the Congo: A Record of the Early Years of the Congo-Balolo Mission*. Adam Matthews Publications Ltd., microfilm ed., reel 10. Special Collections, University of California, ca. 1934.

Au, Sokhieng. "Medical Orders: Catholic and Protestant Missionary Medicine in the Belgian Congo, 1880–1940." *Low Countries Historical Review* 132, no. 1 (2017) 62–82.

Baird, W. David, and Danney Goble. *Oklahoma: A History*. Norman: University of Oklahoma Press, 2011.

Baker, Donald. "Personnel Needs in Congo." *World Call* 28, no. 6 (1946) 26–27.

Barger, G. J. P. "Fighting Yaws, A Mission Service." *World Call* 7, no. 12 (1925) 31–34.

Bentley, William Holman. *Pioneering in the Congo*. London: Religious Tract Society, 1900.

Berman, Edward H. "American Influence on African Education: The Role of the Phelps-Stokes Fund's Education Commissions." *Comparative Education Review* 15 (1971) 132–45.

Bompela, Efoloka. "Enseignement protestant d'avant l'indépendance de la République du Zaïre: DCCM; Étude historique." Licence en pédagogie, Université libre de Bruxelles, 1974.

Brown, Arthur Judson. *The Foreign Missionary: An Incarnation of a World Movement*. New York: Revell, 1907.

Buckner, George Walker, Jr., ed. "Congolese Churches Set Up Central Fund." *World Call* 41, no. 1 (1959) 5.

———, ed."Health for Congo." *World Call* 35, no. 2 (1953) 34.

———, ed. "Station UCMS Broadcasting." *World Call* 21, no. 2 (1939) 34.

———, ed."Station UCMS Broadcasting." *World Call* 21, no. 4 (1939) 30.

———, ed."To a Changing Continent." *World Call* 41, no. 8 (1959) 9.

Buelens, Frans. *Congo, 1885–1960: Een financieel-economische geschiedenis*. Antwerp: EPO, 2007.

Burke, Donald, and N. R. Farbman. "Photographic Essay: Congo Mission." *Life* (June 2, 1947) 105–14.

Casement, Roger, et al. *The Eyes of Another Race*. Dublin: University College Press, 2003.

Chapman, Berlin B. *Federal Management and Disposition of the Lands of the Oklahoma Territory, 1866–1907*. New York: Arno, 1979.

Chesterman, C. C. "Medical Missions in Belgian Congo." *International Review of Mission* 26, no. 3 (1937) 378–85.

Christian Theological Seminary. Manuscript Collection 123, Buena Rose Stober. Indianapolis, IN.

———. Tabernacle Christian Church, Franklin, IN, Congregational Files. Indianapolis, IN.

Clarke, Virginia. *The Disciples of Christ in Africa*. Indianapolis: United Christian Missionary Society, 1945.

Corey, Stephen. *Among Asia's Needy Millions*. Cincinnati: Foreign Christian Missionary Society, 1915.

Cory, Abram. *The Trail to the Hearts of Men*. New York: Revell, 1916.

Crane, William H. "Congolese Leader Agrees That Partnership Is Needed." *World Call* 42, no. 2 (1960) .

Crowley, Daniel. "Politics and Tribalism in the Katanga." *Western Political Quarterly* 16, no. 1 (1963) 68–78.

Dade, Barbara Bates. "Capital for Congo." *World Call* 42, no. 3 (1960) 19–21.

Davis, Orval. "Educational Development in the Belgian Congo." *International Review of Mission* 43, no. 4 (1954) 421–28.

Dembour, Marie Bénédicte. *Recalling the Belgian Congo: Conversations and Introspections*. New York: Berghahn, 2000.

Disciples of Christ Congo Mission. *Manual of the Disciples of Christ Congo Mission: Adopted by the Biennial Convention, Bolenge, October 1926*. Bolenge: Disciples of Christ Congo Mission, 1926.

Disciples of Christ Historical Society. Buena Rose Stober Biography File. Bethany, WV.

———. Division of Overseas Ministries, Africa, boxes 7, 19, 20. Bethany, WV.

———. Donald Baker Biography File. Bethany, WV.

———. Gertrude Shoemaker Biography File. Bethany, WV.

———. Goldie Alumbaugh Biography File. Bethany, WV.

———. Manuscript Collection 80-61, Buena Stober. Bethany, WV.

———. Manuscript Collection 83-32, Buena Stober. Bethany, WV.

———. Manuscript Collection 94-077, Buena Stober. Bethany, WV.

———. Manuscript Collection 818, Hattie Mitchell Personal Papers. Bethany, WV.

———. Manuscript Collection 2001-068, Buena Rose Stober Papers. Bethany, WV.

———. Ruth Musgrave Biography File. Bethany, WV.

Dye, Eva Nichols. *Bolenge: A Story of Gospel Triumphs in the Congo*. Cincinnati: Foreign Christian Missionary Society, 1909.

———. "Bonkanda wa Nzakomba: Book of God." *World Call* 3, no. 2 (1921) 35–35.

Dye, Karen. *Newkirk: Carved in Stone*. Stillwater, OK: New Forums, 2023.

Dye, Polly. *In His Glad Service: The Story of Royal J. and Eva Nichols Dye*. Eugene, OR: Northwest Christian College, 1975.

Dye, Royal. "The Crescent Conquest or the Cross Triumphant?" *World Call* 8, no. 10 (1926) 8–10.

Efefe, Elonda. "La doctrine biblique du mariage et le problème de la polygamie au Zaïre." PhD diss., University of Strasbourg, 1976.

England, Stephen. *Oklahoma Christians: A History of Christian Churches and the Start of the Christian Church (Disciples of Christ) in Oklahoma*. Oklahoma City: Christian Church in Oklahoma, 1975.

Etherington, Norman. "Recent Trends in the Historiography of Christianity in Southern Africa." *Journal of Southern African Studies* 22, no. 2 (1996) 201–19.

Faris, Elsworth. "Native Education in the Belgian Congo." *Journal of Negro Education* 3, no. 1 (1934) 123–30.

Fey, Harold E., ed. "Through the Years." *World Call* 16, no. 1 (1934) 38–39.

50th Anniversary: University Place Christian Church. Enid, OK: Privately published, 1962.

First Christian Church, Newkirk, Oklahoma. Newkirk, OK: Privately published, 1949.

Gampiot, Aurelien Makoko. *Kimbanguism: An African Interpretation of the Bible*. University Park, PA: Pennsylvania State University Press, 2017.

Gates, Errett, et al. "Report of the Committee on Africa." *Missionary Intelligencer* 12, no. 11 (1899) 302.

Gerard, Emmanuel, and Bruce Kucklick. *Death in the Congo: Murdering Patrice Lumumba*. Cambridge: Harvard University Press, 2015.

Guinness, Fanny Grattan. *The First Christian Mission on the Congo: The Livingstone Inland Mission, Its Sphere, Nature, History, Present Position, and Prospects*. London: Hodder and Stoughton, 1882.

Guinness, Harry. *The First Thirty Years: The Story of RBMU*. London: Harley House, 1903.

Harris, J. S. "Education in the Belgian Congo." *Journal of Negro Education* 15, no. 3 (1946) 410–26.

Hastings, Adrian. *The Church in Africa 1450–1950*. Oxford: Clarendon Press, 1994.

Hawkins, Hunt. "Joseph Conrad, Roger Casement, and the Congo Reform Movement." *Journal of Modern Literature* 9, no. 1 (1981) 65–80.

———. "Mark Twain's Involvement with the Congo Reform Movement: 'A Fury of Generous Indignation.'" *New England Quarterly* 51, no. 2 (1978) 147–75.

Hensey, Andrew. *Master Builder on the Congo: A Memorial to the Service and Devotion of Robert Ray Eldridge and Lilian Byers Eldridge*. New York: Revell, 1916.

———. *My Children of the Forest*. New York: Doran, 1924.

———. *Opals from Africa: Short Stories of the Marvelous Transformation Wrought in the Lives of the Simple Folk of the Congo Region by the Story of Christ*. Cincinnati: Foreign Christian Missionary Society, 1910.

Heywood, Linda. "Slavery and Its Transformation in the Kingdom of Kongo, 1491–1800." *Journal of African History* 50, no. 1 (2009) 1–22.

Hightower, Michael. *1889: The Boomer Movement, the Land Run, and Early Oklahoma*. Norman: University of Oklahoma Press, 2018.

Hixson. "Newkirk Public Schools." 1908. Photography, 14 x 9 cm postcard. Oklahoma Digital Prairie, Oklahoma Department of Libraries. https://digitalprairie.ok.gov/digital/collection/okpostcards/id/810.

Hobgood, Betsy. "Returning Missionaries See Changes in Congo." *World Call* 41, no. 11 (1959) 36.

Hobgood, H. C. "The Emergence of a Congo Church." MA thesis, Christian Theological Seminary, 1926.

Hobgood, Tobitha. "The Lomongo-Lonkundo New Testaments." *World Call* 3, no. 7 (1921) 36–37.

Hochschild, Adam. *King Leopold's Ghost: A Story of Greed, Terror, and Heroism in Colonial Africa*. Boston: Mariner, 1998.

Hoig, Stan. "Boomer Movement." Oklahoma Historical Society. https://www.okhistory.org/publications/enc/entry.php?entry=BO011.

Holder, William. "The Church in Congo." *World Call* 8, no. 10 (1926) 15–17.

Hollinger, David A. *Christianity's American Fate: How Religion Became More Conservative and Society More Secular*. Princeton: Princeton University Press, 2022.

———. *Protestants Abroad: How Missionaries Tried to Change the World but Changed America*. Princeton: Princeton University Press, 2017.

Hope Rises International. "A History of Hope." https://www.hoperises.org/history.

Hutchison, William. *Errand to the World: American Protestant Thought and Foreign Missions*. Chicago: University of Chicago Press, 1987.

Institut médical evangélique. *Kimpese*. 1956. https://archive.org/details/kimpese00inst/mode/2up.

Irvine, Cecelia. *The Church of Christ in Zaire: A Handbook of Protestant Churches, Missions, and Communities, 1878–1978*. Indianapolis: Division of Overseas Ministries of the Christian Church (Disciples of Christ), 1978.

Isichei, Elizabeth. *A History of Christianity in Africa from Antiquity to the Present*. Grand Rapids: Eerdmans, 1995.

Jacobs, Sylvia. "Three African American Women Missionaries in the Congo, 1887–1899: The Confluence of Race, Culture, Identity, and Nationality." In *Competing Kingdoms: Women, Mission, Nation, and the American Protestant Empire, 1812–1960*, edited by Barbara Reeves-Ellington et al., 318–41. Durham: Duke University Press, 2010.

Johnson, Gene. *Congo Centennial: The Second Fifty Years*. Privately published, 1999.

Kanza, Thomas. *The Rise and Fall of Patrice Lumumba: Conflict in the Congo*. New York: Penguin, 1972.

Kenny, Gale, and Tisa Wenger. "Church, State, and 'Native Liberty' in the Belgian Congo." *Comparative Studies in Society and History* 62 no. 1 (2020) 156–85.

Lemarchand, René. "The Limits of Self-Determination: The Case of the Katanga Secession." *American Political Science Review* 56, no. 2 (1962) 404–16.

———. *Political Awakening in the Belgian Congo*. Oakland: University of California Press, 1964.

Loffman, Reuben, and Benoit Henriet. "'We Are Left with Barely Anything': Colonial Rule, Dependency, and the Lever Brothers in the Belgian Congo, 1911–1960." *Journal of Imperial and Commonwealth History* 48, no. 1 (2020) 71–100.

Lofos'ankoy, Eliki Bonanga. *La pénétration et l'oeuvre des missionaires Disciples du Christ a l'Équateur, 1897–1964*. Maîtrise ès arts, Faculté de théologie protestante au Zaïre, 1979.

MacGaffey, Wyatt. *Kimbanguism in the Independence Process*. Paris: Académie royale des sciences d'outre-mer, 1992.

Markowitz, Marvin. *Cross and Sword: The Political Role of Christian Missions in the Belgian Congo, 1908–1960*. Stanford: Stanford University Press, 1973.

———. "The Missions and Political Development in the Congo." *Africa: Journal of the International African Institute* 40, no. 3 (1970) 234–47.

Marshall, Frank H. *Phillips University's First Fifty Years*. 3 vols. Enid, OK: Phillips University, 1957.

McStallworth, Paul. "The Congolese and Self-Determination." *Journal of Negro History* 43, no. 2 (1958) 105–20.

Merriam, E. F. *The Congo Mission*. Boston: American Baptist Missionary Union, 1893.

Merriam-Webster. "King's X." Accessed March 30, 2026. https://www.merriam-webster.com/dictionary/King%27s%20X.

Merrill, James. "Bolenge—The Little Church That Wouldn't Stop Growing." *World Call* 35, no. 10 (1953), 22–23.

Mertens, Myriam, and Guillaume Lachenal. "The History of Belgian Medicine from a Cross-Border Perspective." *Revue Belge de Philologie et d'Histoire* 90, no. 4 (2012) 1249–71.

Moon, Everard R. "Breaking the Wilderness for Christ." *World Call* 8, no. 10 (1926) 11–14.

———. *I Saw Congo*. Indianapolis: United Christian Missionary Society, 1952.

Mpombo, Lokofe. "L'unité de l'église: Don et appel, un exemple, le cas de l'Église du Christ au Zaïre." PhD thesis, Faculté de théologie protestante de Bruxelles, 1986.

Murhula, Toussaint Kafarhire. "Jesuit-Protestant Encounters in Colonial Congo in the Late Nineteenth Century: Perceptions, Prejudices, and the Competition for African Souls." In *Encounters Between Jesuits and Protestants in Africa*, edited by Robert Marykys and Festo Mkenda, 194–214. Jesuit Studies 13. Leiden: Brill, 2018.

Myers, John Brown. *Congo for Christ: The Story of the Congo Mission*. New York: Revell, 1895.

Myers, Oma Lou. *This One Thing I Do: A Biography of Frank Hamilton Marshall, Pioneer Christian Educator*. Hillsboro: Binford and Mort, 1953.

Nzongola-Ntalaja, Georges. "The Bourgeoisie Revolution in the Congo." *Journal of Modern African Studies* 8, no. 4 (1970) 511–30.

———. *The Congo: From Leopold to Kabila; A People's History*. London: Zed, 2002.

Oklahoma Historical Society. "Photograph of the High School in Newkirk, OK." Accession no. 20939.9 of the photograph collection, added March 5, 2020. https://gateway.okhistory.org/ark:/67531/metadc1620119/.

Owen, George Earl. *A Century of Witness, 1875–1975: A History of Downey Avenue Christian Church*. Indianapolis: Christian Church Services, 1975.

Packenham, Thomas. *The Scramble for Africa: White Man's Conquest of the Dark Continent, 1876–1912*. San Francisco: Avon, 1992.

Parker, Michael. *The Kingdom of Character: The Student Volunteer Movement for Foreign Missions, 1886–1926*. Pasadena: Carey, 2008.

Pavlakis, Dean. *British Humanitarianism and the Congo Reform Movement, 1896–1913*. London: Routledge, 2016.

Pearson, Ernest B. "The Healing of Africa." *World Call* 2, no. 5 (1920) 22–24.

Pearson, Evelyn Utter. "The Mondombe Moons: Who Sent a Shaft of Light into Africa." *World Call* 9, no. 5 (May 1927) 36–37.

Pemot, Henri. *Kimpa Vita: Une résistante Kongo*. Paris: L'Harmattan, 2013.

Pereira, Jairzinho Lopes. "The Catholic Church and the Early Stages of King Leopold II's Colonial Projects in the Congo." *Social Sciences and Missions* 32 (2019) 82–104.

Phillips University. "Mission Studies." *Phillips University Bulletin* 11, no. 5 (1917) 142.

———. "University Hospital and Training School." *Phillips University Bulletin* 11, no. 5 (1917) 124–26.

Pittman, Don, and Paul Williams. "Mission and Evangelism: Continuing Debates and Contemporary Interpretations." In *Interpreting Disciples: Practical Theology in the Disciples of Christ*, edited by L. Dale Richeson and Larry D. Bouchard, 206–47. Fort Worth: Texas Christian University Press, 1987.

Poole, Edna. *The Time of Flying Butterflies*. Baltimore: Gateway, 1988.

Rains, Rose Stephens, ed. "Station UCMS Broadcasting." *World Call* 17, no. 3 (1935) 40.

Robert, Dana. *American Women in Mission: A Social History of Their Thought and Practice*. Macon: Mercer University Press, 1997.

———. "From Missions to Mission to Beyond Missions: The Historiography of American Protestant Foreign Missions Since World War II." *International Bulletin of Missionary Research* 18, no. 4 (1994) 149–62.

———. "The Influence of American Missionary Women on the World Back Home." *Religion and American Culture* 12, no. 1 (2002) 59–89.

Ross, Emory. "Phelps-Stokes Educational Commission in Congo." *World Call* 4, no. 1 (1922) 21–23.

Ross, Myrta Pearson. "The Ordination of Mark Njoji." *World Call* 3, no. 1 (1921) 30.

———. "The Union Mission House." *World Call* 6, no. 6 (1924) 29.

Russell, H. Gray. "A Christian School in the Belgian Congo." *World Call* 23, no. 1 (1941) 12–13, 16.

Shaw, Henry. *Hoosier Disciples: A Comprehensive History of the Christian Churches (Disciples of Christ) in Indiana*. St. Louis: Bethany, 1966.

Sly, Virgil. "Congo Golden Jubilee." *World Call* 31, no. 8 (1949) 12–13.

———. *The Congo Mission of the Disciples of Christ*. Indianapolis: United Christian Missionary Society, n.d.

———. "Farewell to the *Oregon*." *World Call* 32, no. 1 (1950) 22–23.

———. *Report on the Congo Mission*. Indianapolis: United Christian Missionary Society, 1946.

———. "Seven Missionaries Retire." *World Call* 43, no. 9 (1961) 29–30.

Smith, Herbert. *Fifty Years in the Congo: Disciples of Christ at the Equator*. Indianapolis: United Christian Missionary Society, 1949.

———. "How Shall the Congo Christian Institute Develop?" *World Call* 11, no. 10 (1929) 19–20.

———. "Training Leaders for Tomorrow's Africa." *World Call* 18, no. 3 (1936) 14–15.

Squires, Beulah. *Drum Beats in the Congo*. Indianapolis: United Christian Missionary Society, 1958.

Stanard, Matthew. *The Leopard, the Lion, and the Cock: Colonial Memoirs and Monuments in Belgium*. Leuven: University of Leuven Press, 2023.

Stober, Buena Rose. *Bonnes manières: Balako ba ndalongy lumba j'onto*. 3 vols. Bolenge: Disciples of Christ Congo Mission, 1956.

———. "Dental Problems in Congo." *World Call* 22, no. 2 (1940) 43.

———. *Mbatela bana ba tosisi: Hygiène de l'enfant*. Bolenge: Disciples of Christ Congo Mission, 1936.

———. "Mondombe in the Heart of Africa." *World Call* 22, no. 9 (1940) 26.

———. "New Missionaries Keep Busy." *World Call* 15, no. 4 (1933) 40.

———. "Report from Mondombe." *World Call* 22, no. 2 (1940) 39.

Thornton, John. "Afro-Christian Syncretism in the Kingdom of Kongo." *Journal of African History* 54 (2013) 53–77.

———. "The Development of an African Catholic Church in the Kingdom of Kongo, 1491–1750." *Journal of African History* 25, no. 2 (1984) 147–67.

———. *The Kongolese Saint Anthony: Dona Beatriz Kimpa Vita and the Antonian Movement, 1684–1706*. Cambridge: Cambridge University Press, 1998.

United Christian Missionary Society. *Njoji Mark*. Biography Set 1, leaflet 15. Indianapolis: United Christian Missionary Society, 1933.

———. *Our Workers in Africa*. Biography Set 4, leaflet 15. Indianapolis: United Christian Missionary Society, 1936.

———. *Strategy for World Mission: Basic Policy of the Division of World Mission of the United Christian Missionary Society*. Indianapolis: United Christian Missionary Society, 1959.

Van Bilsen, Antoine. *Congo 1945–1965: La fin d'une colonie*. Brussels: CRISP, 1994.

———. *Un plan de trente ans pour l'émancipation politique de l'Afrique Belge*. S.n., 1956.

———. "Some Aspects of the Congo Problem." *International Affairs* 38, no. 1 (1962) 41–51.

Vanderlinden, Jacques. *Pierre Ryckmans: Coloniser dans l'honneur*. Brussels: DeBoeck, 1994.

Van Lierde, Jean, ed. *La pensée politique de Patrice Lumumba*. Paris: Présence Africaine, 1972.

Van Reybrouck, David. *Congo: The Epic History of a People*. New York: Ecco, 2015.

Viaene, Vincent. "Internationalism, Religion, and the Congo Question: An Introduction, 1875–1905." In *Religion, Colonization, and Decolonization in Congo, 1885–1960*, edited by Vincente Viaene et al., 39–62. Leuven: University of Leuven Press, 2020.

Warren, W. R., ed. "Appointed to Serve." *World Call* 5, no. 6 (1923) 34.

———, ed."New Advance in Africa." *World Call* 2, no. 12 (1920) 50–51.

———, ed."The New Way on the Congo." *World Call* 11, no. 2 (1929) 42.

———, ed. *Survey of Service: Organizations Represented in International Convention of Disciples of Christ*. St. Louis: Christian Board of Publication, 1928.

W'ehusha, Lubunga. "Christianity in the Democratic Republic of the Congo." In *Anthology of African Christianity*, edited by Isabel Phiri, et al., 528–34. Oxford: Regnum, 2016.

Wells, Goldie Ruth. *Sila, Son of Congo*. St. Louis: Bethany, 1945.

Wente, Margaret Baker. *And We Ate the Leopard: Serving in the Belgian Congo*. Albuquerque: Privately published, 2007.

Wild-Wood, Emma. "The Interpretations, Problems, and Possibilities of Missionary Source in the History of Christianity in Africa." In *World Christianity: Methodological Considerations*, edited by Martha Frederiks and Dorottya Nagy, 92–112. Leiden: Brill, 2021.

Williams, D. Newell, et al., eds. *The Stone-Campbell Movement: A Global History*. St. Louis: Chaice, 2013.

Williams, Paul. "The College of Missions." In *The Encyclopedia of the Stone-Campbell Movement*, edited by D. Newell Williams et al., 226–27. Grand Rapids: Eerdmans, 2004.

———. "Disciples and Red Rubber: The Disciples of Christ Congo Mission, the Congo Free State, and the Congo Reform Campaign of 1907–1908." *Discipliana* 66, no. 1 (2006) 3–18.

———. "Disciples of Christ at the Equator, 1897–1903: An Essay on the History of Christianity in Congo." *Journal of Discipliana* 66, no. 2 (2006) 55–71.

———. "The Disciples of Christ Congo Mission (DCCM), 1897–1932: A Missionary Community in Colonial Central Africa." PhD diss, University of Chicago, 2000.

Wissing, Douglas. *Pioneer in Tibet: The Life and Perils of Dr. Albert Shelton*. New York: Palgrave Macmillan, 2004.

Yates, Barbara. "Shifting Goals of Industrial Education in the Congo, 1878–1908." *African Studies Review* 21, no. 1 (1978) 33–48.

———. "White Views of Black Minds: Schooling in King Leopold's Congo." *History of Education Quarterly* 20, no. 1 (1980) 27–50.

Year Book of Churches of Christ. Cincinnati: Standard Publishing, 1912.

Year Book of International Convention of Disciples of Christ. St. Louis: Christian Board of Publication, 1930–1962.

Yocum, Cyrus M. *The Disciples of Christ Congo Mission in Africa*. Indianapolis: United Christian Missionary Society, 1938.

———. "*Oregon*—A Gospel Boat." *World Call* 20, no. 5 (1938) 44.

Yocum, Edith Eberle. *They Went to Africa: Biographies of Missionaries of the Disciples of Christ*. Indianapolis: United Christian Missionary Society, 1945.

Young, Crawford. *Politics in Congo: Decolonization and Independence*. Princeton: Princeton University Press, 1965.

Index

C

D

E

F

G

H

I

J

K

L

M

N

T

U

V

W

Y

Z

www.ingramcontent.com/pod-product-compliance
Lightning Source LLC
LaVergne TN
LVHW020535100826
845148LV00010B/1473

* 9 7 8 1 5 3 2 6 9 2 5 9 8 *